Fodor's EXPLORING

ireland

FODOR'S TRAVEL PUBLICATIONS

NEW YORK • TORONTO • LONDON • SYDNEY • AUCKLAND

WWW.FODORS.COM

Copyright © Automobile Association Developments Limited 2001, 2003. Maps copyright © Automobile Association Developments Limited 2001, 2003

Published in the United States by Fodor's Travel Publications. Published in the United Kingdom by AA Publishing.

Fodor's and Fodor's Exploring are registered trademarks of Random House, Inc.

ISBN 1–4000–1218–X
ISSN 1524–6795
Fifth Edition

Fodor's Exploring Ireland

Author: **Lindsay Hunt, with additional "Hotels and Restaurants" material by Polly Phillimore**
Original Copy Editor: **Hugh Chevallier**
Cartography: **The Automobile Association**
Cover Design: **Tigist Getachew, Fabrizio La Rocca**
Front Cover Silhouette: **Blaine Harrington III**
Front Cover Top Inset: **The Automobile Association**

Printed and bound in Italy by Printer Trento Srl.
10 9 8 7 6 5 4 3 2 1

914.1504

How to use this book

ORGANIZATION

Ireland Is, Ireland Was
Discusses aspects of life and culture in contemporary Ireland and explores significant periods in its history.

A–Z
Breaks down the country into regional chapters, and covers places to visit, including walks and drives. In addition, Focus On articles consider a variety of topics in greater detail.

Travel Facts
Contains the strictly practical information vital for a successful trip.

Hotels and Restaurants
Lists recommended establishments throughout Ireland, giving a brief summary of their attractions.

ADMISSION CHARGES
An indication of an establishment's admission charge is given by categorizing the standard, adult rate as:

Expensive (over €6.50),
Moderate (€3.20–6.50), or
Inexpensive (up to €3.20).

ABOUT THE RATINGS
Most of the places described in this book have been given a separate rating:

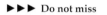 ▶▶▶ Do not miss

▶▶ Highly recommended

▶ Worth seeing

MAP REFERENCES
To help you locate a particular place, every main entry has a map reference. This is made up of a number, followed by another number, followed by a letter, such as 542A. The first number (54) refers to the page on which the map can be found. The second number (2) and the letter (A) pinpoint the square in which the main entry is located. The maps on the inside front cover and inside back cover are referred to as IFC and IBC respectively. A red square on the map denotes a place of interest.

Contents

5

Castletown House, County Kildare

My Ireland

Lindsay Hunt turned to travel journalism after a career in publishing. She has written, edited, and contributed to numerous hotel and travel guides, including books on Spain, France, Germany, Italy, Florida, and, of course, Ireland.

Some years ago, I stayed at a country-house hotel so welcoming and convivial that I forgot to pay my bill before leaving. This was embarrassing for several reasons, the main one being that I was inspecting it anonymously for a well-known hotel guide. The amazing thing was the fact that my hosts also forgot to remind me about this trivial matter as they said goodbye. As I galloped back apologetically across three counties to redress my oversight, I wondered whether this could happen anywhere but Ireland. I'd never met the hotel owners before, but after a single night's stay they felt like old friends. Since then, the experience has been repeated many times in Ireland—feeling like old friends, that is, not neglecting to pay hotel bills. There are, of course, exceptions to the rule, but I guarantee that those who prove it will outnumber those who fall short.

I find the extraordinary kindness shown to me by many Irish people (north and south of the border) particularly touching because I am English—unmistakably so. While I feel neither personal nor collective responsibility for Ireland's history, I was slightly apprehensive about the welcome I would receive on my first trip to the Emerald Isle. However, this was entirely unfounded; the "Hundred Thousand Welcomes" *(Cead Mile Failte)* slogan used by the Irish Tourist Board is more than mere blarney.

There is one memory from that first visit that is particularly vivid. It involves a party somewhere in Galway, full of Gaelic merriment and good *"craich,"* at which everyone joined in with a song, a story, and a dance. The star turns were an Orangeman (a northern Protestant in favour of maintaining the union with the UK) and a committed Nationalist, who regaled the assembled company with a string of good humoured and hilarious jokes. One day...perhaps the trend will catch on.

Lindsay Hunt

Ireland Is

Many of Ireland's charms are straightforward. Visitors head there for the spectacular scenery and the warmth of the people. Ireland's real fascination, though, is its ability to confound people's preconceptions. The Irish can be as unpredictable as their country's fickle weather, changing in a moment from gregarious to taciturn, or from solemn to profane.

ONE ISLAND Is it one place or two? The South evokes all things green and Gaelic; the North is an outpost of the UK. To enjoy Ireland, you need barely be aware of this division. On both sides of the border are glorious landscapes, friendly people, and plenty of good pubs. On one side the mailboxes are Irish green, on the other red, and for visitors (except in Belfast or at the border, perhaps) few other differences are apparent. There is certainly no need to feel anxious about visiting the North. Statistically, Northern Ireland is recognized as one of Europe's safest places.

On the edge of the island perches Dunluce Castle, in County Antrim

LANDSCAPES Ignoring the boundary, then, there are 32 counties of Ireland, each with its own distinctive character. Though at a glance Ireland may seem universally damp, mild, and green, with no very high mountains and little variation of climate or landscape, it has more variety in its small confines than many larger countries. The scenery varies from rural pasturelands cut by many rivers, through wild boglands and low-lying hills, to the most spectacular mountain scenery (mostly in the west and north) sweeping down to the sea in high cliffs and craggy promontories. Offshore lie many islands, some of which are inhabited or contain ancient forts and ruined

monastic settlements; several others are bird sanctuaries.

The commonest of Irish rocks, limestone, produces great systems of porous caves, some containing stalactites and stalagmites. Volcanic activity created the highlands of the North, and the extraordinary crystalline formations of the Giant's Causeway in County Antrim. The surface of the land was glaciated during the last Ice Age, leaving classic geological features such as U-shaped valleys, corries (circular hollows), tarns (small lakes), and eskers (long, winding ridges).

ECONOMY One of Ireland's continuing struggles since the 18th century has been against economic depression and unemployment, and the resulting exodus of many of its most energetic and talented citizens abroad. The North continues to receive large amounts of investment directly from the UK to alleviate its chronic problems. However, since joining the European Union (EU), the whole of Ireland has benefited from vast sums in Regional Development Fund grants that are aimed at helping poorer EU member countries. Great improvements have been made to its road system, while funds have also been

The pace of life is noticeably slower to the west of the Shannon

allocated to develop tourism and manufacturing industries. The tide has now turned, and from being one of the EU's poorest countries a few years ago, the Republic now enjoys a booming and rapidly growing economy, nicknamed "the Celtic Tiger." Many former emigrés are returning to seek work in their native island, particularly in the electronics and computer industries. Ireland now has about five million inhabitants, with a higher proportion of young people than virtually any other country in Europe.

PLANNING A TRIP For visitors, Ireland still seems pleasantly old-fashioned. The sociable, lively Irish are always ready to strike up a conversation, play some music, or buy the next round of drinks.

If you have little time to spare, the best bet for a trip to Ireland is a short break in Dublin, combined with excursions to the Wicklow Mountains, or perhaps the Boyne Valley and the antiquities of Newgrange. If you have more time, head west for Connemara, Cork, Kerry, or Donegal. Longer still, see the rest of the country, including its great monastic sites and grand houses. For extensive touring, you will definitely need a car, a bike, a horse-drawn caravan, or even a boat on its huge inland waterways.

"If you think you understand Ireland," some legendary wit once remarked, "you've been sadly misinformed." And, indeed, almost every aspect of Irish life is full of contradiction. That rule also applies to its politics, which are inextricably entwined with religion.

PARADOXES Certain elements of Irish political history may strike an outsider as somewhat contradictory:
• Anti-English feelings have long been associated with Ireland's Catholic majority, but some of Ireland's greatest nationalists (or at any rate critics of the English as Irish overlords) have been Protestants, some from English backgrounds. Examples of such men include Jonathan Swift, Henry Grattan, Wolfe Tone, Robert Emmet, Charles Stewart Parnell, W. B. Yeats, and even William Gladstone. Two of the Republic's presidents have been Protestants.
• Both the Pope and the King of Spain supported Protestant William III's cause at the Battle of the Boyne, not the Catholic Jacobites (see page 36 for more details).
• Only about 2 percent of the Republic's population are Protestants, yet many of its most

important churches are actually Church of Ireland (Protestant), including both of Dublin's cathedrals.
• Northern Irish Unionists, far from being in line with the UK, are often in bitter opposition to London. While British politicians have met, talked, and reached amicable agreements with the Republic's leaders, the Unionists, until the 1998 Good Friday Agreement, had adamantly rejected all compromise.

IRELAND'S CONSTITUTION The Republic of Ireland's constitution operates under a prime minister (*Taoiseach*), two chambers (senate and assembly), and a president (who is largely a ceremonial figurehead). Its main political parties sprang up during or soon after the struggle for independence in the early 20th century. Since then, parliamentary power has been dominated by Fianna Fáil (Soldiers of Destiny), the party set up by Éamon de Valera in 1926. In 1933 its equally conservative rival,

Ministerial buildings next to Leinster House, seat of the Irish Parliament

Mary Robinson, Ireland's first woman president (1991–1997)

Fine Gael (Tribes of Gaels), appeared. Roughly speaking, these parties mirror the positions taken by pro- and anti-treatyites during the Civil War; in other words, they either accepted (Fine Gael) or rejected (Fianna Fáil) Ireland's partition in 1921. Both parties have found it difficult to achieve majority rule, and elections (based on proportional represent-ation) often result in an uneasy stale-mate followed by behind-the-scenes horse trading with minority parties to form a workable coalition.

The wild card is Sinn Fein, the political wing of the IRA. Originally founded in 1908 (making it older than any other party), it has achieved massive popular support at certain stages in its history, but now commands only a fraction of Southern Irish votes. In 1990, Sinn Fein and the IRA began the slow move from the bullet to the ballot box, which culminated in an IRA cease-fire and the 1998 Good Friday Agreement on power sharing between Nationalist (including Republican) and Unionist parties.

A CONSERVATIVE MENTALITY The winds of change are blowing through Irish politics, a notable event being the election in 1991 of a woman president (a possibility absolutely discounted by social historians only a few years before). Mary Robinson was a liberal attorney with known sympathies for certain issues (such as the liberalization of divorce laws) that currently perplex Ireland. The position of women in the Republic is much affected by the power of the Catholic Church, and Pope John Paul II's reaffirmation of its doctrines on contraception, abortion, and divorce. Ireland ranks last among the world's developed countries in access to birth control (though the impact of AIDS has had a sharper effect than decades of religious dogma), and until 1996 was alone in Europe in having no civil divorce. In 1992, the case of a 14-year-old girl made pregnant by rape and refused an abortion, or even permission to travel abroad to obtain one, hit world headlines and caused yet another complex referendum. Again, Ireland voted against liberal-ization of these laws.

Catholics complain justifiably of their lack of civil rights in Northern Ireland, yet the Republic's Protestants would also have an interesting case in any international court of human rights. But on both sides of the border compromise seems a real possibility, with liberalization in the south and a tentative move towards power-sharing in the north.

13

Ireland's musical traditions date back over many centuries, but the current scene is exceptionally lively, with interest in popular folk music encouraged by tourism. Irish musicians are prominent in rock and country-and-western groups, and some virtuoso performers, such as James Galway, have become world famous.

A CELTIC TRADITION The poems and stories related by Gaelic bards at court were often accompanied by music, most typically played on the harp, Ireland's national emblem. The 12th-century historian, Gerald of Wales, praised the deftness of Irish fingerwork, and the expertise of Irish harpists was recognized as far afield as Renaissance Italy. After the Battle of Kinsale (1601), the great Gaelic clan houses declined, along with their patronage of the arts. Music was perceived by the ruling English as potentially dangerous, arousing nationalist sentiments, and it was suppressed along with other aspects of Irish culture. Musicians became itinerant, travelling from house to house to seek their fortunes at the hands of the new aristocrats; the

The tradition of live folk music lives on in countless Irish pubs

blind harpist, Turlough O'Carolan (1670–1738), was the most celebrated exponent of this tradition. The 18th century witnessed a new flourishing of musical talent in Dublin's Anglo-Irish circles, mostly influenced by European developments; Handel's *Messiah* was performed for the first time in the capital in 1742, conducted by the composer.

Meanwhile, traditional music continued to be played in Gaelic households. The ancient styles were either plaintive melodies with no distinct rhythms (possibly inherited from Spanish or North African cultures), or brisk, lively dance tunes. In 1792, a great harp festival held in Belfast aroused interest in more traditional Irish forms, and folk tunes increased in popularity. The lyric ballad, with words by such poets as Thomas Moore set to music, was sung in elegant drawing rooms

throughout Ireland. Many budding musicians left their native land, as did many writers, to seek fame in England. John McCormack, the famous lyric tenor, spent most of his life in the United States (see page 240).

IRISH INSTRUMENTS Most distinctive of the instruments used in Irish music, besides the harp, are the *uilleann* (elbow) pipes, a relative of the Scottish bagpipes but with a more elegiac tone particularly suited to reflective Irish tunes. The violin (simply called the fiddle in Ireland) is held casually on the shoulder and played with only a small section of the bow. Expert Irish fiddlers are technically highly skilled, however; Fritz Kreisler is said to have declared that if he practised for a thousand years he would never be able to play as well as the Sligo fiddler, Michael Coleman. The *bodhrán* is one of the most ancient Irish instruments, a goatskin drum played with a small stick. Wind instruments include the tin whistle (no mere toy to a skilled player) and the flute, whose capacities have astounded worldwide audiences in the hands of James Galway.

THE MODERN SCENE In the 20th century Irish music played an important role in the revival of nationalist sentiment, and has subsequently achieved enormous popularity. The most usual venues to hear it are *ceilis*, where whole communities gather to dance and make music, or pubs, where *seisuns* (sessions) are held all over Ireland. The popularity of Irish music is unquestionably affected by tourism, sometimes losing both its dignity and its authenticity in the process. In the summer, when an audience is guaranteed, every pub seems to offer musical happenings. Out of season, however, they may be quite difficult to find. Doolin in County Clare is a particularly well-known mecca for groups of musicians. Other forms of music are encouraged at major festivals—opera

15

In Ireland, as in the Celtic areas of Britain, dance continues to be an important facet of life

at Wexford (see panel page 144), light opera at Waterford, and jazz at Cork.

One of the most influential figures in Irish music in modern times was Seán O'Riada. Though classically trained, his main interest was folk music, which he greatly popularized. His group, Celtóiri Chualann, was a forerunner of the world-renowned Chieftains. The tradition continued through groups such as the Clancy Brothers and the Dubliners. The stage spectacular Riverdance has ignited a global interest in traditional Irish music and dance. Other groups have taken a different line, notably U2, The Corrs, Westlife, and The Pogues, while individual performers include Van Morrison, Enya, Sinéad O'Connor, and Ronan Keating.

The Irish are famously articulate. From the loquacious Celts, alleged by the Greek traveller Strabo (writing around the time of the birth of Christ) to be fond of "wordy disputes" and "bombastic self-dramatization," through the Earl of Blarney, to today's stage Irishman, words have been a constant source of delight—sometimes at the expense of action. Oscar Wilde said, "We are the greatest talkers since the Greeks—but we have done nothing."

A PROLIFIC STREAK The Irish have written much; Ireland's contribution to English literature in all its forms—poetry, drama, novels, essays—is colossal, considering the size of its population. It seems as strong today as ever, with new talents bursting onto the stage and filling bookshops with new novels and poems.

Four writers have won Nobel prizes (W. B. Yeats, George Bernard Shaw, Samuel Beckett, and Seamus Heaney). Both speech and writings take innumerable forms, but are characterized by a natural flamboyance, passion, and wit, coupled with idiosyncrasy. Much of the inspiration

Jonathan Swift, satirist and cleric

❑ Ogham script was used in Ireland from the 4th century and, though eventually superseded by the Roman alphabet (introduced by Christian missionaries), continued to be used into the 8th century. It was written as a series of scratched lines, and usually appears on commemorative standing stones or monuments. Its uses for practical purposes were very limited. The key to interpreting the characters is the *Book of Ballymote*, written in 1391 in Sligo. Examples of ogham stones can be found in several places; there is a good one in the church at Killaloe (Clare) and another two in the abbey ruins of Ardmore (Waterford). ❑

comes from the tensions generated by persecution and oppression.

THE GAELIC HERITAGE Besides Ireland's outpourings in English, it has a rich Gaelic tradition. At various periods during the imposition of English rule, the Gaelic language (now mainly referred to as "Irish") was suppressed. After independence, strenuous attempts were made to revive it; indeed, it was declared—and remains—an official language. Éamon de Valera wanted to use it for political reasons, to assert Ireland's separate identity from Britain. Ireland's first president, Douglas Hyde, was a distinguished Gaelic scholar who loved the native language for its own sake. Despite compulsory schooling in Gaelic, and

Samuel Beckett

THE TRADITION LIVES ON In the 20th century, Irish writing reflected the turmoil of independence, and a long twilight of censorship. Modern Ireland out-pruded the English Victorians, sending many great writers into self-imposed exile (James Joyce and Beckett are the two outstanding examples); J. M. Synge's and Seán O'Casey's plays caused riots in Dublin. Novelists and poets have proliferated within and without Ireland, however. Patrick Kavanagh, Louis Macneice (now deceased), and Seamus Heaney are among its best-known modern poets; Maeve Binchy, Molly Keane, Edna O'Brien, and Roddy Doyle are popular novelists, along with Brian O'Nolan (Flann O'Brien) and Christy Brown. Frank O'Connor, Seán O'Faoláin, Mary Lavin, and Liam O'Flaherty perfected the art of the short story, and talented dramatists include Brian Friel, Hugh Leonard, Billy Roche, and Frank McGuinness. The writer Christopher Nolan won great acclaim for his poems, *Damburst of Dreams*, and his novel, *Under the Eye of the Clock*, while author Frank McCourt won a Pulitzer Prize for his best-selling novel, *Angela's Ashes*.

regular radio and television broadcasts, the use of Gaelic as a first language has dwindled to a few areas largely in the West, and there is now little writing in Gaelic.

ANGLO-IRISH WRITERS The first flowering of Anglo-Irish literature occurred during the late 17th and early 18th centuries. Jonathan Swift (see page 62) was the giant of the age, publishing savage satires to expose the hypocrisy and injustice of life under English rule. In a lighter vein, Oliver Goldsmith, R. B. Sheridan, William Congreve, and George Farquhar entertained English upper classes with their lively comedies of manners. Edmund Burke wrote philosophical and political essays in elegant prose, complex enough to win present-day admirers from the whole political spectrum. Irish writing in the 19th century came thick and fast, from George Moore and Maria Edgeworth's sharply observed novels about the Irish "Big House," such as *Castle Rackrent*, to Shaw, Oscar Wilde, and Yeats towards the end of the century, and even Bram Stoker, who introduced the world to Dracula. Anthony Trollope, though born in England, wrote many of his novels while working in Ireland; some, such as *Phineas Finn*, have Irish characters.

The formidable George Bernard Shaw

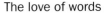

In today's Ireland, it seems almost impossible to imagine the grim days of the 19th century when many poor people did not have any food to eat besides potatoes, and even those were frequently scarce. Nowadays, it is possible to eat both well and heartily all over the island.

CHANGING TASTES Tourism has made a vast difference to the standards of cuisine in Ireland. Until recently, there was hardly any tradition of eating out in many districts, except perhaps on very rare occasions at a local hotel. Patterns of diet were conservative, based firmly on "meat and two veg" (somewhat overcooked), potatoes (of course), and large quantities of dairy fat. Now things are very different. Tourist demands for predictable, inexpensive fast food are met, as everywhere, with hamburgers and pizzas—a better bet being fish and chips. But more sophisticated tastes have introduced organic foods and vegetarian restaurants (almost unheard of before), and a vast number of new eateries, often French in style, have

A traditional—and substantial— Irish breakfast

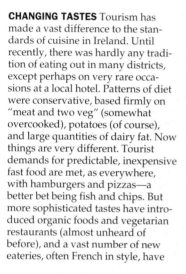

opened in the main visitor centres. Food "events" such as Kinsale's Gourmet Festival or Galway's Oyster Festival arouse great interest. With VAT (sales tax) at its present high rate, eating out in the Republic of Ireland is expensive, particularly if you like a drink with a meal. Casual (but respectable) dress is the norm just about anywhere.

One of the best meals in Ireland (as in Britain) is breakfast. A "traditional Irish breakfast" (or the "Ulster fry" north of the border) is a brimming plateful of bacon and eggs with soda and potato breads. Accommodation rates are nearly always quoted with a full breakfast included, so you might as well fill up for the day and get your money's worth!

IRISH CUISINE Whatever Irish cuisine lacks in finesse, it nearly always makes up for in copiousness, and ingredients are of a high quality. Home-grown produce includes rich dairy foods, beef, lamb, and pork, a fascinating range of Irish cheeses, and a great variety of seafood. One of its great favourites is bread. Traditional Irish soda bread made with buttermilk, eaten fresh and warm, is a banquet in itself. At midday, a basket of Irish bread, a bowl of seafood chowder, and a glass of Guinness makes a cheap and completely satisfying lunch.

There has been a welcome return to simple, hearty Irish food, and Irish stew and potato dishes feature on many menus. Try colcannon (potatoes with onions and white cabbage), champ (potatoes mashed with butter and chopped chives), or coddle (potatoes with boiled bacon and onions). Black puddings use up those

bits of pig not usually found on the dinner table, including its blood. At teatime, try barm brack, a delicious sweet tea bread made with dried fruit and spices.

Fish can easily be found in most of Ireland, and you don't have to be rich or posh to enjoy oysters here. If you're adventurous, try dulse or carrageen (types of seaweed), used to make various desserts—a change from apple pie and ice cream.

WHISKEY AND STOUT All alcohol (especially in the South) is highly taxed and expensive, although measures of spirits are generously-sized. Take advantage of your duty-free allowance if you like a

If you wish to order half a pint, ask for a "glass"

drink. Pubs, though, are more than mere boozing sheds; they are the social heart of many communities and often full of life and atmosphere, especially if there is some music. Pub food is rarely very imaginative, but you can usually get snacks at lunchtime, and coffee all day. At some stage every visitor should try Ireland's "nectar," Guinness (see panel on page 56). Some consider it tactless to request Scotch in an Irish pub—try the local Bushmills, Powers, or other Irish brands, either straight or with a splash of plain Irish water. It is also delicious in Irish coffee, or in one of those creamy liqueur concoctions. The local lager is Harp (brewed by Guinness). If you prefer something akin to English bitter or US dark beer, ask for Smithwicks ale.

19

Not for nothing is Ireland called the Emerald Isle. Its greenness is legendary, the stuff of postcards and purple prose—and the national colour. As you travel through the island, landscape after landscape seems to scorch the retina with shades of that vivid Kelly green.

❑ "Wearing of the green" takes place on St. Patrick's Day (17 March), when Irish people all over the world join in national celebrations to commemorate their country and their patron saint. The largest festivities and grand parades are held in Dublin. Traditionally, everyone on that day wears a shamrock, Ireland's national emblem. This cloverlike plant is alleged to have been used by St. Patrick to illustrate the nature of the Trinity to King Cormac at Cashel. ❑

In a few remote areas old farming methods are still employed

THE COLOUR OF IRELAND In places Ireland is chocolate brown or almost black, the colour of stripped bogland, glinting with clear pools that mirror the sky. It is grey with mist or cloud, with the wan limestone of the Burren, and the lace of stone walls. It is splashed with yellow furze, scarlet fuchsia, or purple heather. Most of all, though, it is green, a verdancy induced by frequent rain and the tempering effects of the Gulf Stream.

Ireland is still a predominantly rural country, with few mineral resources and little heavy industry. For centuries, the main changes to its landscapes were brought about by farmers who cleared the primeval oak woods and drained the peat bogs to make pastureland. Sheep, cattle, oats, and barley have been raised on its fertile soils since neolithic times. Later, crops such as potatoes and flax have waxed and waned according to the vagaries of economics, and recently the rate of change has accelerated, particularly since Ireland's membership of the European Union (EU). Agricultural grants flood into Irish farmers' pockets, enabling them to introduce more intensive methods of production. The use of artificial herbicides and fertilizers is growing, causing pollution to seep into waterways, threatening wildlife. Compared with some other EU countries, however, the problems are minor. Ireland has successfully attracted "clean" industries, such as electronics and financial services, rather than the mills of more industrialized nations.

GREEN CONCERNS Nearly all of Ireland's original oak forests have long since been felled for fuel and building materials. New forestry is replacing some of these trees, but mainly (until recently) with non-native conifers. Many old Anglo-Irish estates are now in state hands and forest parks, and broad-leaved woodlands are being planted, sometimes on stripped peatlands. The exploitation of the bogs continued unchecked for many years, and large areas are virtually denuded. Boglands, however, are now recognized as a unique and irreplaceable habitat for many rare species.

Other threats to Ireland's wildlife are significant. Increased tourism means more disturbance of Ireland's wild places. The Office of Public Works has angered conservationists by proposing construction of visitor centres in sensitive areas such as the Burren, Boyne Valley, and Wicklow Mountains (court cases have forestalled two of these so far). Unfortunately, more places for people mean fewer places for wildlife.

A GOLD PROBLEM Another threat to the environment is the discovery of gold in Mayo, Galway, and the Sperrin Mountains of Northern Ireland. Gold has always been known in Ireland, of course—prehistoric peoples used it for their ornaments—but until recently it was thought to be uneconomic to extract it. The Croagh Patrick site in County Mayo is particularly sensitive, for it is both an area of scenic beauty and a site of great religious importance, where St. Patrick is said to have banished the snakes from Ireland and where thousands of pilgrims gather annually. Prospecting for minerals disturbs the landscape and can threaten the surrounding area with serious pollution by heavy metals and cyanide.

PINK TROUT In certain coastal areas, puzzling signs have sprung up by the roadsides, depicting a fish, with the legend "Save the Sea Trout" emblazoned on it. This reflects a growing local concern about the effects of one of Ireland's fastest-burgeoning industries—fish-farming. The farming of salmon and trout in huge hatcheries in Galway and Donegal has affected wild populations in ways not yet fully understood. One theory is that vast numbers of parasitic sea lice among farmed fish are debilitating wild species. The fish on your plate is just as likely to have been reared artificially and fed pink-tinted hormones as to have swum the ocean and leapt waterfalls.

The greenness of Ireland, here seen on Mizen Head, County Cork

21

The passion for competitive sports of many kinds reaches unprecedented heights all over the Republic. Its specialist games such as hurling and Gaelic football draw capacity crowds and cause vast excitement. Soccer is also popular, and Irish hopes were raised by the national team's qualification for the 2002 World Cup in Japan and Korea.

THE BIG MATCH When there's a big match on, even the least enthusiastic sportsman or woman is condemned to know about it. Flags and banners of the colours of the competing county teams sprout all over the land, on telegraph poles and gateposts, from car windows and rooftops. Switch on the radio for the news, and you will find nothing of importance has happened in the world, except the match. Needless to say, huge crowds cause boisterous disruption to everyday life (especially on the roads), and plenty of noise in the pub afterwards, but they are rarely the occasions of hooliganism once seen at British soccer matches. Highlights of the year are the All-Ireland hurling and football finals, held at Croke Park, Dublin, in September, where

tickets are prized. In the past, however, Gaelic games were regarded as a focal point for nationalist sentiment, and were alternately discouraged or banned by English authorities, and fostered by Republicans. In 1884, the Gaelic Athletics Association (GAA) was formed in Tipperary to halt the spread of anglicized games and promote Irish ones. The organization, like the Gaelic League, was a fertile recruiting ground for political activists.

Rugby enjoys limited popularity, but is remarkable in that the national team represents *all* of Ireland, with southern nationalists playing alongside northern Unionists.

HURLING This fast and furious game has an ancient pedigree, dating back to before the Christian era. The Ulster champion Cuchulainn was

The distinctly Irish sport of hurling

renowned for his prowess at hurling, and teams of warriors are supposed to have played it for days on end. It is something like no-holds-barred lacrosse, played with an ash stick or "hurley" and a small leather ball—"sliotar." Players (15 a side) may strike the ball any distance and at any height, or carry it on the hurley. It's most popular in Cork and the southeast and west of Ireland, but also played in Antrim, almost exclusively by Catholics.

GAELIC FOOTBALL

There are two types of football in Ireland (Gaelic and soccer), with

minimal support for the Gaelic game among Protestants. The ball is smaller than a soccer ball, and teams score one point by hitching the ball over the crossbar, or three by putting it into the goal below the crossbar. The game requires great strength and stamina.

VISITOR ACTIVITIES As a visitor, you are unlikely to do more than watch these exciting pastimes, but there are splendid opportunities for exercise in many forms, especially golf, equestrian sports, cycling, and fishing. There are more than 300 golf courses throughout Ireland (this number continues to rise), some of international class or in wildly beautiful settings, especially in the North. Green fees vary considerably. Many claim Ireland is an unparalleled fishing destination, both for the quality of the sport and its low costs. Sea fishing for shark is popular in some areas (such as Achill Island). Permits are necessary on privately owned waters (and on public waters in the

North), and you need a national licence for rod fishing for salmon or sea trout.

That other Irish passion shared by the British is racing (horses and greyhounds), and many towns have dogtracks or racecourses. Sailing centres are mostly in the southwest, between Youghal and Dingle, with lake and river or canal cruising focused on Lough Derg, the Shannon River, the two Loughs Erne, and the Grand Canal. In May 1994 the restored Shannon–Erne waterway opened, enabling boaters to cruise all the way from Upper

23

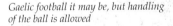

Gaelic football it may be, but handling of the ball is allowed

Lough Erne to the mouth of the Shannon. Hiking is increasingly popular in Ireland. Many long-distance footpaths are now in place, and more accessible open spaces are planned. In the meantime, take sensible precautions before setting out. Prepare for bad weather, take the best map you can find, and let someone know where you are heading.

Both Bord Fáilte and the Northern Ireland Tourist Board produce plenty of literature on specialist sports.

The bogs of Ireland once covered immense tracts of the central lowlands. To former generations, it would have been inconceivable that they could ever disappear, or perhaps that it would matter much if they did. However, conservationists now recognize them as unique ecosystems, and are racing to ensure that what little is left is preserved before they all vanish.

THE FORMATION OF THE BOGS After the Ice Age, the saucerlike bowl that forms the centre of Ireland lay awash with lakes. These gradually filled up with compost from lakeside vegetation and, eventually, peat accumulated because the micro-organisms that cause decay cannot survive in these wet conditions. There are two main types of bog in Ireland. Blanket bog, composed of dead sedge and grass, develops to a depth of 6m (20ft) in the wettest areas and is found mostly in mountainous parts of the west, or in the Slieve Bloom Mountains. Raised bog, consisting mostly of sphagnum moss, covers wider areas of the central plain, where rainfall is lower. This gradually builds up into a dome above the ground water and can reach depths of 12m (40ft).

Roundstone Bog, Galway, one of the last untouched bogs in Ireland

A VANISHING LANDSCAPE As a result of massive exploitation, the boglands have shrunk to a fraction of their original size. Ireland has almost no coal or oil reserves, so peat has always been used as fuel. In the past, turf (the Irish term for peat) was cut by hand, using a spade or *sleán*, and many people still have "turbary rights" to cut turf on local bogs. The top layers of living plants are removed and replaced on the cut surface to encourage regeneration; as a result, the effects of cutting peat by hand were minimal.

In 1946, Bord na Móna (the Peat Development Authority) began mechanical digging, and now great tracts can be seen laid waste in black, sodden wildernesses, later replanted with coniferous timber. Peat moss from the surface layers is bagged up and distributed to garden centres, while peat from the lower levels is used for fuel—about a quarter of Ireland's electricity comes from peat. It has become obvious that if the present rate of extraction continues there will soon be none left, so some of the best bogs are now protected as nature reserves. About 10 percent of Ireland's land surface is peat bog, but bogland is still disappearing at an alarming rate.

A UNIQUE ECOSYSTEM Bogland flora is fascinating and very varied indeed. The only plants that can survive are highly specialized—some have roots reaching deep down through water-retentive mosses into a compost of half-rotted vegetation; other, fly-trapping plants supplement their diet with animal protein. Few mammals can survive true boglands, but rare

insects, flowers, and birds can be seen. The bogs are also of great interest to archaeologists. Their virtually sterile environment preserves animal and vegetable matter—tree stumps, bog butter (see panel on page 239), even corpses have been pulled from the bog, virtually intact, after centuries.

SAFETY ON BOGS Walking on peat bogs can be dangerous. Some deep pools may be disguised by soft mats of vegetation. It is easy to get lost as there are few paths or visible landmarks. An insect repellent is useful at some times of year, and rubber boots are essential.

BEST BOGLAND ATTRACTIONS:
- **Peatland World** Lullymore, County Kildare (tel: 045 860133).
- **Peatlands Park** near Dungannon, Lough Neagh, County Armagh (tel: 028 3885 1102).

Re-creation of a bog village at Glenbeigh, County Kerry

- **Céide Fields** Ballycastle, County Mayo (tel: 096 43325)—neolithic settlements preserved in bog.
- **Corlea Trackway Exhibition Centre** Kenagh, County Longford (tel: 043 22386)—pre-Christian timber track found beneath bog.
- **Clonmacnoise and West Offaly Railway** Shannonbridge, County Offaly (tel: 0905 74114)—9km (5.5mi) tour over bog.
- **Raised bogs:** Mongan and Clara (both County Offaly).
- **Blanket bogs:** Roundstone (County Galway), Owenduff (County Mayo), Slieve Bloom Mountains (County Laois).

For more information, contact the Irish Peatland Conservation Council, Capel Chambers, 119 Capel Street, Dublin 1 (tel: 01 872 2397 or 872 2384); the National Parks and Wildlife Service, Office of Public Works, 51 St. Stephen's Green, Dublin 2 (tel: 01 661 3111), or in Northern Ireland, Peatlands Park (see above).

The tradition of Irish storytelling can be traced back to the Celts, whose sagas of epic battles and great champions, gods, and supernatural events were passed down orally at firelit feasts, then transcribed by early monks in manuscripts such as The Book of Leinster.

INTERWOVEN TRADITIONS Irish mythology is incredibly complex; different accounts of similar stories are often interwoven with other traditions, and echoes of other Indo-European legends can often be found—epic tales of Greeks and Romans, for instance, or biblical stories. At first the stories were not written down, but related orally as evening entertainment, which meant embroiderings in every telling. A trained *file* (bard) was expected to be able to relate about 350 full-length

The Children of Lir

tales in poetry by heart, and would spend years learning his art. The early Christian fathers were the first to record these legends, sometimes interspersing them with their own material and turning Celtic gods into Christian saints (such as St. Brigid).

THE CELTIC REVIVAL Although bardic traditions declined under English rule, interest in Celtic legends revived sharply towards the end of the 19th century under the influence of writers such as W. B. Yeats and the rise of Irish nationalism. The leaders of the Easter Rising of 1916 were imbued with ancient myths, seeing themselves as heroes battling against dark forces of evil. Even today, paramilitary groups sometimes use mythological rhetoric to justify their violence.

Celtic mythology remained alive in rural Ireland until the age of television, with a storyteller in every parish; superstitions and tales of fairy folk and monsters still abound. Ireland's leprechaun is the best-known figure of popular lore—the little man in green who mends shoes and guards his crock of gold—while the banshee is a more sinister creature, a female spirit whose wailings are believed to portend a death. Places associated with ancient magic are often treated with great respect by country people, for fear of disturbing whatever spirits or fairies inhabit them.

GROUPS OF SAGAS Irish sagas are classified in four main groups. The Mythological Cycle deals with pre-Celtic gods and heroes and their long-running and complicated struggles for supremacy; the Children of

A romanticized depiction of Cuchulainn by E. Wallcousins

Lir is one of the best-known stories. The Ulster Cycle contains the epic adventures of the Red Branch Knights of Navan Fort and their champion Cuchulainn, one of the most famous being the Cattle Raid of Cooley. The later Ossianic (or Fenian) Cycle revolves around another hero, Finn MacCool (Fionn mac Cumhaill), builder of the Giant's Causeway and Gráinne's betrothed (see page 28). The Historical Cycle (or Cycle of Kings) recounts tales from various early Irish

kings, and is similar to Malory's tales of Arthur. The Celtic "otherworld," *Tír na n'Og* (the Land of Eternal Youth, believed to lie somewhere on an island in the far west), figures in these sagas—the paradise every culture dreams of for its afterlife, where pain and suffering are no more.

THE CATTLE RAID OF COOLEY This was one of the first stories to be written down. Queen Maeve of Connaught became jealous of her husband's possessions, in particular his magnificent white bull. She tried to obtain the mighty brown bull of

The Flemish cartographer Ortelius chose an east–west orientation for his 16th-century map of Ireland

Cooley to match it, at first peacefully, then by force. The hero of Ulster, Cuchulainn, defended the province alone, and defeated Maeve's army. But he was mortally wounded, and died strapped to a stone pillar, facing his enemies.

GRÁINNE AND DIARMUID The very beautiful Gráinne was betrothed to the ageing hero, Finn MacCool, but fell in love instead with the handsome Diarmuid. They eloped, taking refuge under dolmens. Eventually, Diarmuid was killed by a boar on the slopes of Benbulbin Mountain in Sligo. The story has clear parallels with Tristan and Isolde.

CUCHULAINN, HOUND OF ULSTER
At the age of five, Setanta, nephew of King Conor, set out to join his uncle's court, taking his hurling stick and ball with him to play on the way. At a banquet held in the house of Culainn, he was attacked by a great mastiff guard dog. Setanta hurled the ball down the beast's throat and killed it. Culainn was glad he was safe, but distressed at the death of his dog, asking "Who will guard my house now?" Setanta promised that he would take over the role of protector, and so found his new name—Cuchulainn, the Hound of Culainn, and champion of Ulster.

See panel on page 238.

Biblical stories are carved onto 10th-century Muireadach's Cross at Monasterboice, County Louth

Ireland Was

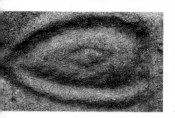

Remnants of Ireland's prehistoric and early Christian past lie scattered throughout the island, although many are shrouded in mystery and still a puzzle to archaeologists. The megalithic tombs of the Boyne Valley or the ornamental jewellery of early populations are evidence of highly sophisticated peoples.

30

PREHISTORIC IRELAND The earliest inhabitants to have left traces of their existence probably arrived from Scotland in about 6000 BC or 7000 BC. These were hunter-gatherer peoples who slowly adopted more settled lifestyles and advanced methods of farming as the Stone Age progressed. They wove cloth, made pottery, fished from coracles (simple boats), raised stock, and cleared trees to plant a few grains. One of the earliest settlements is Glenaan, in the Glens of Antrim, where flint axe heads have been found.

The clearest legacy of the Neolithic Age is burial places. Between 4000 BC and 2000 BC, many megalithic tombs (using large blocks of stone) were built. Most impressive are the passage tombs at Newgrange, but important sites can be found in Sligo and eastern Ireland (the court tombs of Creevykeel; dolmens, like those at Proleek; and wedge tombs, as at Labbacallee in County Cork). From the Bronze Age (1750 BC onwards) came stone circles or mysterious single standing stones, such as those at Drombeg in Cork or Lough Gur in Limerick. Little is known of the people, but ancient lore terms them the *Fir Bolg* (Bag Men, because they carried fertile soil to rocky fields in large leather bags), a short, dark race who lived to no more than 30 or so.

THE CELTS In about 700 BC a new wave of invaders began to arrive on Irish shores: the Celts, a disparate group of tribes whose cousins can be found all over Europe. Driven west by the Romans, who called them *Galli*, they were known as *keltoi* by the Greeks, and became Gaels in Ireland. Their loose clan structures revolved around a leader or chieftain (*Taoiseach*—the word still used for Ireland's prime minister) who was elected rather than dynastic. As time progressed, leadership became more centralized under a single high king, though the idea of "nationhood" never developed fully in Celtic times; clans continued to live in isolated settlements of round huts, protected by sturdy defences or by lake moats.

CELTIC LEGACIES Some aspects of Celtic culture seem to have filtered into the Irish character. The Celts were hospitable folk who enjoyed feasting, music, and storytelling. Their love of adornment is evident in the gorgeous jewellery they made— bands of decorated gold and other metals, of great artistry. Most of all they loved fighting—no mere internecine squabbles, but epic battles between warrior champions epito- mized by the legendary heroes, Cuchulainn and Finn MacCool. Elevated into semi-divinities, the myths (perhaps the Celts' greatest legacy) tell of their great deeds, ringing with the clash of sword on

Drombeg Stone Circle, County Cork

shield, dripping with gore. They worshipped many gods, often adopting the sacred sites of past inhabitants for their rituals and royal residences (Tara is one of the most celebrated). Efforts to propitiate these gods were unsparing—vast quantities of treasure were heaped on the altars of the dead, and grisly sacrifices took place. One of the most chilling rituals was the "wicker man," a huge effigy of straw and wood filled with living creatures—men, women, children, animals—and set alight.

BEYOND ROMAN RULE Ireland is unusual in western Europe in having no significant Roman history. The Romans gazed across at the Emerald Isle, and Tacitus wrote, somewhat airily, "I have often heard Agricola declare that a single legion, with a moderate band of auxiliaries, would be enough to finish the conquest of Ireland," but they never colonized it. (Cynics say that, if they had, the roads might have been better!) As it was, the Celts held sway in their piecemeal fashion through several Christian centuries. Some recolonized west Britain in the first centuries AD, joining with the native Picts to plague the Romans along Hadrian's Wall. These Irish Celts were known as Scots, some of whose descendants are the Protestant occupants of Ulster, now regarded by some extreme Nationalists as aliens.

PREHISTORIC AND CELTIC SITES

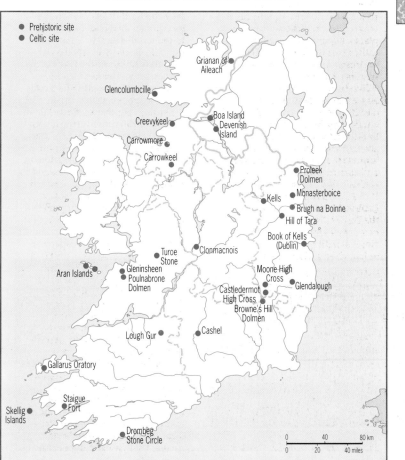

- ● Prehistoric site
- ● Celtic site

Grianan of Aileach
Glencolumbcille
Creevykeel
Boa Island
Devenish Island
Carrowmore
Carrowkeel
Proleek Dolmen
Monasterboice
Kells
Brugh na Boinne
Hill of Tara
Book of Kells (Dublin)
Turoe Stone
Clonmacnois
Aran Islands
Gleninsheen
Poulnabrone Dolmen
Moone High Cross
Castledermot High Cross
Glendalough
Browne's Hill Dolmen
Lough Gur
Cashel
Gallarus Oratory
Staigue Fort
Skellig Islands
Dromberg Stone Circle

0   40   80 km
0   20   40 miles

After the arrival of Christianity in the 4th century, Ireland enjoyed a golden age while the rest of Europe languished in the dark aftermath of the fall of the Roman Empire. Monasteries flourished as great cultural centres, and Irish missionaries travelled back to mainland Europe to spread the Good Word.

32

VIKING INVADERS The good times were not to last. From AD 795, pirate raiding parties began to attack Ireland's shores, envious of the riches of the Celtic monasteries. By AD 837 a wholesale Norse invasion was taking place, and this time the interlopers stayed. The native Gaels and monks built Round Towers as lookouts and refuges, and reinforced their simple wood or wattle dwellings and churches with hard stone. The Vikings caused immeasurable destruction and bloodshed as they arrived, but later settled into more peaceable habits, often intermarrying and becoming assimilated with the local population. Though illiterate, they had many skills, and founded sophisticated walled cities to defend the estuaries by which they had entered Ireland (Waterford, Wexford, Cork, Dublin, Limerick). They passed on their great knowledge of seafaring and boat building, established

important foreign trade links, and introduced coinage. Some converted to Christianity. The Vikings were eventually routed at the Battle of Clontarf (near Dublin) in 1014 by the famous High King, Brian Ború. Unfortunately, a retreating Viking treacherously dispatched Ború after the battle, and Ireland's chances of becoming united under a strong leader receded again.

MACMURROUGH AND STRONGBOW
In one of the subsequent feuds, Dermot MacMurrough abducted the wife of a rival chieftain, Tiernan O'Rourke. The other clans turned on him. In retreat, with many of his lands and his Leinster throne lost, MacMurrough sought help from abroad. Henry II of England, already considering the conquest of Ireland, and with the support of the Pope (himself an Englishman), allowed MacMurrough to recruit from among his barons. Richard FitzGilbert de Clare, Earl of Pembroke, better known as Strongbow, was rewarded for his

Fearsome Strongbow now lies peacefully in Dublin's Christ Church Cathedral

The Anglo-Norman keep of Carrick-fergus Castle has walls 2.5m (8ft) thick

timely aid with the hand of MacMurrough's daughter and great parcels of land. The Normans had arrived, and they stayed. In England, Henry II looked anxiously over his shoulder at these powerful adventurers and decided to assert his authority. He came to Ireland with his army and demanded allegiance from Irish leaders who, also fearful of MacMurrough and Strongbow, gave it. From then on, England was Ireland's overlord. Henry granted the province of Meath to his follower, Hugh de Lacy, and empowered him to act as deputy governor. English control radiated from the Dublin area, which later contracted to a small region about 48km (30mi) north, south, and west of the capital, defended by an earth rampart, known as the Pale.

NORMAN RULE Irish subkingdoms were established farther afield ("beyond the Pale"), enabling Gaelic rulers to hold sway as long as appropriate tributes were paid to England and loyal support given in times of war. Needless to say, not all Ireland's inhabitants were content with such meek subjection, and many rebelled. Land was confiscated as punishment, leaving an enduring

legacy of resentment among the Gaelic chieftains, and great English estates began to develop, based on the feudal manorial system. All the colonizers remained free; the Irish peasantry were serfs, tied to the land. Nonetheless, their lot in a productive estate under strong leadership may well have been happier than before. In 1177, John de Courcy invaded Ulster and conquered it swiftly. On Strongbow's death without heirs, Henry's son, Prince (later King) John, took over as Lord of Ireland. Anglo-Norman administrative structures of government and law were set up within Ireland, great castles were built, and city walls strengthened. Outside the towns, clan chiefs and Norman lords protected themselves with tower houses, sometimes enclosed by a "bawn," a high wall with turreted corners.

Henry and his heirs consolidated their claim on Ireland by invoking heavenly allies and strengthening the position of the Church. The monasteries flourished anew, and many great churches and abbeys were built, emerging gradually from modest Romanesque to lofty Gothic as architecture progressed. The Irish Church was reorganized along Roman lines and Continental monastic orders appeared—Augustinians, Cistercians, and Franciscans.

The Normans, like the Vikings, invaded with ferocity, but integrated surprisingly quickly. English rulers perceived a dilution of their influence as the distinctions between Anglo-Norman and native Gael blurred.

CATHOLIC REPRESSION In 1366, one of the most repressive of attempts to subdue Ireland took place. The Statutes of Kilkenny aimed to quell the Anglo-Norman tendency to "go native." Irish citizens were prohibited from intermarrying with Normans, forbidden to enter walled cities, and their dress, language, names, and customs were outlawed. Like all such measures, they were doomed to fail, and Gaelic influence continued to grow until the Pale had dwindled to a small area immediately around Dublin, despite the construction of many more castles across Ireland.

While England was enmeshed in the Wars of the Roses (1455–1485), a powerful Anglo-Norman family, the Fitzgeralds, extended their influence over much of east and southeast Ireland. The Tudor kings, who gained the English throne after the war, saw the Fitzgeralds (warily) as allies. But when Henry VIII renounced the Catholic Church, handing out its land to his Protestant supporters, Lord Offaly of the Fitzgerald house of Kildare (Silken Thomas) staged an insurrection. Thomas was defeated and executed (see panel on page 70), but the precedent was set for future stands against the English Crown. Henry tried to assert his overlordship, demanding that the mutinous lords surrender their property and assume vassal status. When they refused, he took their lands and gave them to the first Protestant "planters" from England and Scotland.

THE FLIGHT OF THE EARLS In the latter half of the 16th century, the

Fourteenth-century English settlers are brought provisions

THE Right Honorable and vndaunted Warrior OLIVER CROMWELL Lo. Governour of IRELAND

Cromwell in Ireland

process of plantation continued under Mary I, a Catholic, and then Elizabeth I, who fought four wars in Ireland in defence of the Reformation. Her aims were to assert the Protestant religion and to prevent any intrigues against England hatched by Ireland and Spain. The first plantation attempts were failures—more rebellions took place, led by the Desmonds of Munster, and more seriously, by Hugh O'Neill, Earl of Tyrone, a formerly compliant court protégé who had hoped to become Lord of Ulster.

When he realized how little autonomy he would have under Elizabeth he joined forces with Red Hugh O'Donnell, Earl of Tyrconnell, and resisted. The final showdown came at the Battle of Kinsale (1601). Spanish reinforcements caved in under siege, O'Donnell fled to Spain where he met his death, and O'Neill was forced to sign the Treaty of Mellifont, unaware that Elizabeth I had died six days earlier. All the lands of the defeated chieftains were handed to planters from Scotland, encouraged to emigrate by James I. The proud O'Neill and Red Hugh's brother and successor left Donegal forever in 1607, in the sad exile known as the Flight of the Earls.

PLANTATION This cleared the way for further plantation, this time more successful. Ulster's new settlers were hard-working Calvinists, chalk to the Catholic cheese, and they have never integrated. They quickly made great improvements to the land they acquired, introducing advanced methods of agriculture. Many of the settlers were skilled craftsmen, bringing new talents to its workforce.

In 1641 at Portadown, the dispossessed Irish made another attempt to regain their lands, violently and killing many Protestants. Gaelic leaders allied with the "Old English" Catholics to defend their faith, property, and political rights in the Confederation of Kilkenny. Meanwhile, in England, the Civil War began. Rumours of atrocities towards Ulster planters circulated, so Cromwell brought over 20,000 Ironsides, storming Drogheda and Wexford, slaughtering thousands, and sending many into slavery. Most Catholic landowners were dispossessed and banished west of the Shannon River ("to Hell or to Connaught," in Cromwell's phrase). When he had finished, much of Ireland was devastated and its Catholic population had dwindled to half a million, bitter beyond belief at English injustice.

35

The agony of Cromwellian times was briefly dispelled by the restoration of Charles II in 1660, although he was never in a strong enough position to help Irish Catholics significantly. The dangerously pro-Catholic leanings of his successor, James II, precipitated the Glorious Revolution and William of Orange's accession. James II fled to France, from where he invaded Ireland for a last stand.

36

THE BATTLE OF THE BOYNE James II was initially successful at drumming up support in Ireland, but his ambitions were thwarted when he reached Derry. There the young trade apprentices slammed the gates of the city, and (London) Derry endured the longest siege in British history. The Protestant cause prevailed, but only after much suffering, which further polarized Anglo-Irish attitudes. In 1690, William III won his decisive victory over Jacobite (Catholic) forces at the Battle of the Boyne. Further conflicts took place at Athlone, Aughrim, and finally Limerick, where the Jacobite army eventually surrendered with honour. The Treaty of Limerick granted civil rights to Catholics, but the English reneged on it, to Ireland's everlasting disgust. Measures were taken to consolidate Protestant ownership of land and Catholic subservience.

William III senses victory at the Battle of the Boyne…

PENAL LAWS A series of repressive laws were passed, collectively known as the Penal Code. This forbade Catholics to practice their religion publicly, or educate their children in the Catholic faith. They could not enlist for military service, buy land, or inherit it other than by equal division among all sons. Viable estates became useless divided parcels of land. If one child converted to Protestantism, he (or she, as daughters were allowed to inherit in this case) would get everything! Land ownership by Catholics tumbled to about 14 percent by 1700, and Irish language, music, and literature were suppressed. Once again, opposition fanned the flames. "Hedge schools" (where teachers and pupils could hide) were run for Catholic children, and Mass was said in secret, with members of the congregation acting as lookouts for English spies.

GEORGIAN IRELAND The 18th century in Ireland was peaceful and full of achievements—literary, artistic, and economic. Many of the great country houses of Ireland date from this time (naturally, these were for the Protestant settlers, not the native Irish). Greatest of all the architects of this period was Richard Cassels (anglicized as Castle, or Cassel), from a Protestant family who had settled in Germany (see panel on page 250).

Whole villages and towns were planned, with wide streets, tree-lined malls, and grand civic buildings. Domestic architecture excelled in Dublin, with dignified terraces and squares satisfying the new aspirations of the city-dwelling middle

classes. Comparatively few churches survive from Georgian times (in particular Catholic ones), but they generally followed neoclassical patterns inspired by Greek temples. Michael Stapleton and the Swiss-Italian Francini brothers were masters of stucco work, a popular medium in Ireland in the mid-18th century. Literature and music flourished (see pages 58–59 and 62–63), as did many applied arts, such as silverware and furniture-making.

AN ATTEMPT AT REFORM The surface prosperity and success of the Anglo-Irish Protestant Ascendancy hid tensions seething among the underprivileged peasantry, many of whom lived in appalling conditions. The Catholics were not the only ones to suffer; Presbyterians were also disadvantaged, and during the 18th century many Ulster settlers

…while the vanquished James II flees from Irish shores

emigrated to seek their fortunes across the Atlantic. Protestants were irked by Westminster rule, and gradually a spirit arose in favour of more autonomy. The American Revolutionary War appealed to both Catholic and Protestant sentiment, and prosperous merchants ceased to equate their interests with those of England.

Henry Grattan, a Protestant lawyer, was at the forefront of this movement. He entered Parliament in the same year as the American Revolution began, declaring "the Irish Protestant could never be free until the Irish Catholic had ceased to be a slave." Westminster sat up and listened. In 1782, Grattan's Parliament was formed, an assertion of Irish constitutional independence. Some minor measures to alleviate the lot of Catholics were passed. Before any major achievements could be seen, the spectre of the French Revolution intervened in 1789, and once again, England battened down the hatches of reform.

37

Ireland caught the prevailing revolutionary mood from France and, for a while, Dublin's inhabitants went around calling each other "citizen." In the countryside, violence grew as secret societies dedicated to overthrowing their oppressive landlords maimed horses, burned barns, and drove cattle over cliffs.

38

RELIGIOUS TENSIONS During the days of the Penal Code, Irish Catholics had learned that dissimulation and evasion were necessities for survival. To follow their faith, they had to attend secret meetings and, as they had no redress in law, they took the law into their own hands. As Cecil Woodham-Smith says in *The Great Hunger*, "These were dangerous lessons for any government to compel its subjects to learn, and a dangerous habit of mind for any nation to acquire." After relaxation of the laws that had prevented them from owning land, many Catholics moved to Ulster, forcing up prices. The Ulster planters began to feel threatened and formed their own ruthless organizations. A vigilante group called the Peep o' Day Boys attacked Catholics, burning them out in dawn raids and, in 1795, the Orange Order was formed to defend Protestant interests.

Emmet prepares for the insurrection that was to cost him his life...

WOLFE TONE AND ROBERT EMMET
In 1796, the radical Protestant attorney Wolfe Tone (see page 42) set up the Society of United Irishmen in Belfast. Initially it existed as a middle-class debating society, but after its suppression by Prime Minister William Pitt, it became seditious. Tone rallied support from France and attempted a naval attack on Bantry Bay (see page 151). After its failure, Pitt imposed martial law. United Irishmen were rounded up and publicly tortured to inform on their comrades, but fury at this led to open revolt, and in 1798 thousands took up pikes and rusty swords against the English soldiers. Over 30,000 died and Tone was captured, later committing suicide in his cell.

All concessions to Catholics were withdrawn, and, on 1 January, 1801, the Act of Union was passed, centralizing government in London. Initially the mood was buoyant; triumphant proclamations of equality were made for England, Ireland,

...and the life of the unfortunate Lord Kilwarden, caught up in the chaos caused by Emmet's uprising

Scotland, and Wales within the new legislative structure, but the high hopes were unfounded. English imports swamped the Irish economy and its industries collapsed. Ireland was now hopelessly divided between the impoverished Protestant ruling class and the dispossessed and powerless Catholics. Robert Emmet, a middle-class Protestant, staged yet another abortive uprising of United Irishmen, and was hanged. His speech from the dock inspired future generations of freedom fighters.

DANIEL O'CONNELL Twenty years later, a new inspirational force arose in the form of Daniel O'Connell (see page 42), known as the Liberator, who championed the cause of Catholic emancipation and the repeal of the Act of Union. Voting rights were granted to Catholics in 1829, but O'Connell's attempts to change Ireland's fate peacefully failed.

In the mid-century Ireland was struck down by the complete failure of the potato crop in 1845, 1846, and 1848. Terrible famine ensued, but the British did little to help; while Ireland starved for lack of potatoes,

vast quantities of beef and grain were being exported to Britain. A million died, and a million emigrated.

CHARLES STEWART PARNELL The next great figure on the political stage was Parnell (see pages 42–43), who campaigned for Home Rule and reform of the oppressive land tenancy laws. The English Prime Minister Gladstone's attempts to introduce a Home Rule Bill were rejected by the House of Lords, despite a groundswell of support for it. More violence took place, and in 1882 the British chief secretary and the undersecretary for Ireland were stabbed to death. British opinion turned against Home Rule and, by the turn of the 20th century, the scene was set for the breakup of Ireland. The Sinn Fein party (meaning roughly "Ourselves Alone") was formed by Arthur Griffith in 1908, advocating secession from Britain. On the brink of war, Britain finally acceded to demands for Home Rule in 1914, but postponed it until hostilities had ceased. The Irish Republican Brotherhood (precursors of the IRA and with financial support from emigrants in the US) staged the Easter Rising in Dublin (see pages 54–55) in 1916; meanwhile in Ulster, the Orangemen prepared for battle.

Ireland's history since partition has been tragic, at least in the North. The IRA's ceasefire in 1994, followed by a wary resumption of negotiations, gave the war-weary province a fragile respite from its exhausting Troubles. Although the peace process has been agonizingly slow, the 1998 Good Friday Agreement and a holding cease-fire has given the people of Ireland, and Britain, new hope that it will return permanently on both sides of the Irish Sea.

40

THE CIVIL WAR In 1918, Sinn Fein, led by the Easter Rising veteran Éamon de Valera, won a massive 73 seats at the general election, and independence was declared at a meeting of the first Dáil Éireann (Irish Parliament). The Irish Republicans (now the IRA) attempted to undermine British control using guerrilla tactics, and British soldiers (the Black and Tans) were brought over to maintain order. Under the 1920 Government of

British Prime Minister Lloyd George, left, meets de Valera in 1921

Ireland Act, separate parliaments were created for Northern Ireland (the Six Counties, which remained within the UK), and Southern Ireland, which was granted dominion status under Crown authority. The Anglo-Irish Treaty was signed in December 1921 by Michael Collins and Arthur Griffith. De Valera refused to accept its terms, and Ireland was plunged into a disastrous and bloody civil war. Many politicians, British and Irish, hoped that partition would be temporary, and that eventually the two sectors would unite peacefully when emotions ran less high. They failed to take account of Loyalist feelings in the North. Under Sir Edward Carson (see page 43), Protestant Unionists resolved to fight to the death to prevent being absorbed into the new Irish Free State.

EIRE IS BORN A victory by the pro-treaty forces in the south was followed by 15 years of inward looking, parochial government. In 1932 de Valera's new party, Finna Fáil, took over power and held it for 16 years.

The new Ireland suffered badly in interwar depression, made worse by de Valera's poor relations with Britain. In 1937, political links with Britain were reduced, and the name of Eire was introduced. During World War II Ireland remained officially neutral. Over 50,000 citizens of the Republic enlisted voluntarily in the British armed services, but anti-British feelings were sufficiently strong to encourage some collaboration with Germany, too. De Valera was the only world leader to offer condolences to the Reichstag on the death of Hitler.

After the war, many people emigrated from Ireland; ironically many chose Britain for their new home. Many also headed to the US where Irish/Americans were rapidly becoming a political force with an interest in the Troubles. The election of the forward-looking Sean Lemass in 1959 signalled a welcome break from the politics of Kilmainham Gaol, which de Valera had symbolized. Gradually, economic prosperity increased and Ireland's stifling doldrum of artistic censorship and priest-ridden Victorian morality began to lift. Ireland joined the European Community (EC) in 1972. Soon after this, immediate benefits were felt in agriculture, tourism, and the construction industry.

THE TROUBLES CONTINUE The upswing did not improve the situation in the North. In 1968, the civil rights movement began, demanding equality for Catholics. Demonstrations and marches provoked rioting on both sides; Derry was a particular flashpoint. In 1969, British troops were sent to protect the Catholics, who were now barricaded in ghettos, but soon their protective role was perceived as an aggressive one. Just eight days after Ireland joined the

The Irish delegation to the Anglo-Irish Treaty of 1921

EC, 13 unarmed civil rights demonstrators were shot by British paratroopers (the event became known as "Bloody Sunday"). An angry crowd burned down the British embassy in Dublin, Stormont (the Northern Irish parliament) was suspended, and the province came under direct rule from Westminster. The IRA made a resurgence in a new "Provisional" guise.

Since 1972, persistent attempts have been made to bring the two sides together. "Power-sharing executives" came and went, at Sunningdale in 1973, and at Hillsborough (the Anglo-Irish Agreement) in 1985. The latest initiatives, begun in 1994, offer renewed hope. A series of meetings between constitutional nationalists and Sinn Fein led to an IRA cease-fire and direct talks with the British government. The election of a Labour government in 1997 reignited the movement for peace, and on Good Friday 1998 all the major parties in the North signed an agreement that would see an end to violence, the establishment of a power-sharing executive and direct rule, plus guarantees of civil rights for the Catholic minority. Large majorities of voters on both sides of the border approved the agreement. Disagreements over disarmament, the role of the Protestant police force, and the British Army have stalled progress, however, and the search for a lasting peace in Northern Ireland remains elusive.

41

It is impossible to ignore Irish history as you tour the country. Its central figures (heroes or villains, depending on your point of view) keep cropping up. What follows puts just a few of them in context, and pin-points one or two places closely associated with them.

PATRICK SARSFIELD, 1st Earl of Lucan (died 1693). Hero of the 1691 Siege of Limerick, with 500 troops, he made a daring raid on William III's supply train at Ballyneety, destroying all his munitions. After the Treaty of Limerick was signed, he sailed to France (Flight of the Wild Geese) and died, fighting again, in Belgium. He was married in Portumna Castle (Galway).

WOLFE TONE (1763–1798) The father of Irish republicanism, this middle-class Protestant lawyer founded the United Irishmen in

Sir Edward Carson, as depicted in 1912

Belfast in 1791. After a period in America, he instigated two unsuccessful attacks using French naval support, at Bantry Bay in 1796 (see the Armada Exhibition at Bantry House, page 151), and in Donegal during the Great Rebellion of 1798. After capture at Letterkenny he was sentenced in Dublin to be hanged, drawn, and quartered, but cut his throat before it could be carried out, lingering in agony for seven days.

ROBERT EMMET (1778–1803) A disciple of Tone, Emmet staged an abortive revolt in 1803, planning to seize Dublin Castle. Emmet was sentenced to the same grisly death as Tone, whereupon he said, "When my country takes her place among the nations of the earth, then and not till then let my epitaph be written." Padraic Pearse, leader of the Easter Rising of 1916, paid tribute to his sacrifice.

DANIEL O'CONNELL (1775–1847) Known as the Liberator, O'Connell was a witty, eloquent, and brilliant lawyer who gave up his career at the bar to fight for Catholic emancipation and the repeal of the Act of Union. Elected MP for Clare (1828), he won popular support, greatly alarming British authorities, although he always renounced violence. His house at Derrynane (Kerry) is a museum to his memory.

CHARLES STEWART PARNELL (1846–1891) A political giant, Parnell (a Protestant) was born at Avondale House in Wicklow (see page 92). Elected MP for Meath in 1875, he campaigned tirelessly for Home Rule and agrarian reform. In 1877, he founded the Irish Land League with

Charles Stewart Parnell

MICHAEL COLLINS (1890–1922) Born near Clonakilty in County Cork, Collins was an imposing Republican hero who took part in the Easter Rising. His tactics were ruthless and he was responsible for some brutal killings. He signed the Anglo-Irish Treaty, intended to partition Ireland peacefully. A British signatory, F. E. Smith, said, "I may have signed my political death warrant." Collins replied, "I have signed my death warrant." Anti-treatyites ambushed and killed him near Macroom (Cork) a few months later.

ROGER CASEMENT (1864–1916) Born at Ballymena, County Antrim, this career diplomat was knighted by the British in 1911. He was arrested as he landed at Banna Strand near Tralee in 1916 in a German submarine containing arms for the Easter Rising. His case was not helped in those days by the knowledge that he was a practising homosexual, and he was hanged for treason. His grave is in Glasnevin Cemetery, Dublin.

Michael Davitt. He used peaceful tactics, favouring "filibustering" (disruption of parliamentary debates by long speeches) and "boycotting" (ostracizing oppressive landlords). His career ended in a scandal involving the wife of a fellow MP.

SIR EDWARD CARSON (1854–1935) Champion of the Ulster Unionists and the architect of partition in 1921, Carson was a Dubliner, knowing little of Ulster or its people. A brilliant lawyer (defending Lord Queensbury at Oscar Wilde's trial), he organized resistance to Home Rule and Irish independence, founding the Ulster Volunteers, an armed band of Loyalists. He is buried at St. Anne's Cathedral, Belfast.

Dublin celebrates the release of Daniel O'Connell, September 1844

ÉAMON DE VALERA (1882–1975) "Dev," the "Long Fellow," was born in New York, but grew up at Bruree, Limerick (where there is a small museum). A veteran of the Easter Rising (pardoned because of his dual nationality), he, more than any politician, determined Ireland's course after the formation of the Free State, and was the founder of Fianna Fáil (Soldiers of Destiny). Three times premier, he was president from 1959 to 1973, but did little to heal the divisions between North and South.

Above: Ha'penny Bridge over the Liffey
Right: looking north up O'Connell Street, named after Daniel O'Connell, "the Liberator"

DUBLIN The capital's very size and city-like qualities in what is still a largely rural country make it atypical, yet it encapsulates so much that is endearing and exasperating about Ireland that it represents the Emerald Isle better than any other town. Not that the rest of Ireland necessarily thinks so: Dublin is regarded with the same mix of wistful envy and resentment by its provinces as most capital cities, and its inhabitants as a race apart. Some locals feel the recent tide of economic prosperity has washed away some of the grimy character that lent the city its charm. But the old Dublin lives on behind the facades of new apartment complexes and the faces of bustling professional types. It's a city of pubs, churches, grand buildings, and fine museums, boozers and talkers, down-to-earth commerce and airy pipe dreams—above all, an intimate place whose pulse must be taken over some time, possibly through a glass of Guinness.

THE FAIR CITY? It is indeed a beautiful place, set on a broad river basin fringed by the majestic sweep of Dublin Bay and the tantalizingly close Wicklow Mountains. Yet the "fair city" of song was better described by James Joyce, one of its most famous citizens, as "dear, dirty Dublin." The best of its Georgian architecture rivals anything that can be seen in Bath or Edinburgh, but much has been destroyed by development or sheer neglect. Some of the demolition is forgivable; those pretty Georgian facades often disguise impossibly friable brickwork and tottering

Dublin

St. Patrick's Cathedral, Dublin

Right: a beautiful stained-glass window greets visitors to the Writers Museum in Dublin

DUBH LINN

The *dubh linn* (dark pool) that gave its name to the city was the confluence of the Poddle and the peat-coloured waters of the Liffey. From the 9th century it was the harbour, where the original Norse settlers moored their long-ships on the low-lying banks below their fortress. A grilled opening in the south wall of the quay by Grattan (or Capel Street) Bridge shows the last remains of the Poddle River, which now runs underground for the final 5km (3mi) of its course. This site was the port of Dublin until the 18th century, when a new one was built to the east by the Custom House. The original Gaelic name for Dublin (still its official name in Gaelic) was Baile Átha Cliath (town of the hurdles). This name is visible on the front of some buses, on road signs, and on postmarks.

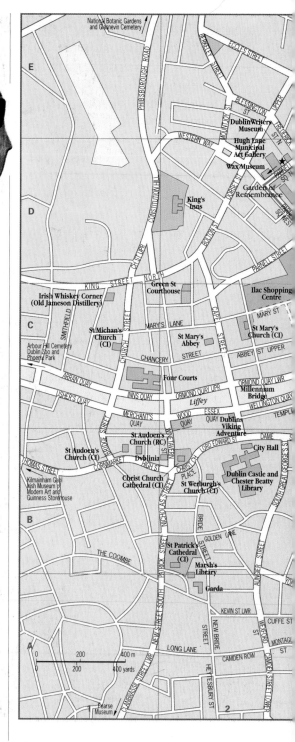

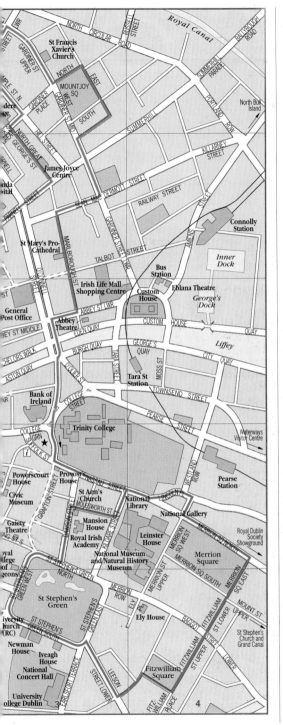

Dublin

The motto means "happy the city whose citizens are obedient"

foundations that only total reconstruction would cure. What has replaced those seemly proportions sometimes defies belief, however, especially around gap-toothed St. Stephen's Green or mutilated Fitzwilliam Street. The main thoroughfare on the north bank, O'Connell Street, is disappointing, its monumental dimensions and few remaining dignified buildings interspersed with seedy fast-food outlets and dull office buildings. Fortunately, though, Dublin has avoided the high-rises that have ruined the skylines of other cities, and north of the river, the unsightliness is really due to dereliction. Now, thankfully, the process is being reversed, and Dublin's fanlit doorways glow amid newly restored surroundings.

THE SOCIAL DIVIDE To some extent, as in London, the great divide is the river. The Liffey neatly bisects Dublin from east to west, meeting the Poddle near the Grattan Bridge and forming the *dubh linn*, or dark pool, that gives the city its name (see panel on page 46). The respectable classes enjoy elegant architecture, chic restaurants, and fashionable shops now based mostly in the south around St. Stephen's Green and Trinity College. In a few other areas the city's poor inhabit twilight zones of bricked-up windows and dubious back streets where visitors are recommended not to stray. Street crime, some drug-related, some intensified by stubborn inner-city unemployment, is more of a problem here than in Belfast, though less than in many other capital cities. But in its salubrious quarters Dublin is a distinctly enjoyable and friendly place. A conversation struck up with strangers is not regarded as a sign of impertinence or lunacy, but a simple acknowledgment of fellow humanity. There is a natural and wholesome friendliness about both its citizens and the very atmosphere of the city.

Laid out by Sir Arthur Guinness in 1880, St. Stephen's Green is one of the city's most popular meeting places

THE CAPITAL Although the central areas feel compact and can be explored on foot, the capital is by far the largest city in Ireland. Currently the Greater Dublin area contains about a million people, almost a third of the Republic's population, many of whom have drifted in from country

The magnificent coffered dome of the City Hall; this building, on Lord Edward Street near Dublin Castle, was designed between 1769 and 1779 by Thomas Cooley

BILLY-IN-THE-BOWL

This extraordinary character terrorized the neighbourhood of Stoneybatter, near Arbour Hill in northwest Dublin, in the mid-18th century. Billy was born without legs, but learned to get about by propelling himself in an iron bowl with his arms. Naturally his upper limbs developed great strength, which he turned to criminal use. He lured passersby to his side by appealing to their sympathy, then seized them and strangled them for their purses. When he was eventually convicted for his multiple felonies, he was sentenced to "as much hard labour as his condition would allow" for the rest of his days.

areas in search of work. A large proportion of Dublin's inhabitants are under 25. It is a cosmopolitan city with many nationalities and social groupings drawn by the booming economy, but there is by no means the same racial mix as in, say, London or Paris. Dublin has declined somewhat since its 18th-century heyday, when great architecture sprang up all over the city, when the first performance of Handel's *Messiah* was held here, and when it was considered one of the foremost cities of Europe. Things have improved in recent years, however, with Ireland's entry into the EU and a vast influx of funds for redevelopment making great changes to the city.

A newfound prosperity and confidence inspires the Dublin scene: Georgian buildings and their contents are cherished and conserved, restaurants buzz with patrons, and many fashionable celebrities have made the city their second home.

Traditional music in Dublin's Brazen Head pub

CHIEF O'NEILL

The new Chief O'Neill complex in the Smithfield market area of Dublin contains a snazzy hotel and restaurant, Ceol museum, and numerous designer shops. The eponymous Chief wasn't the head of any ancient clan, but rather of Chicago's police force at the beginning of the 19th century. Francis O'Neill left Bantry, Co. Cork, for America in 1865 when he was just 17 years old. After adventures in the New World as a sailor, school teacher, and shepherd, he joined Chicago's police force and rose to power. However, O'Neill is remembered and loved in Ireland not because of his career, but because of his hobby. He was one of the most important collectors and publishers of traditional music, his books preserving hundreds of tunes and melodies that would otherwise have been lost forever.

From the oriental collection at the Chester Beatty Library

►►► Bank of Ireland   463C

College Green, tel: 01 677 6801
Open: Mon–Wed and Fri 10–4, Thu 10–5
Admission: moderate

Straight across from Trinity College, this striking neoclassical building was created in 1729 to seat the Irish Parliament. After the shameful self-dissolution of that body in 1801, the building was sold to the Bank with instructions that its interior be changed so that it might never again be used as a debating chamber. Much of the original structure was maintained, including the pedimented portico fronted by six great Corinthian columns. Inside the main banking hall has a coffered ceiling adorned with delicate stucco rosettes. Just down the hall, in the original House of Lords, tapestries still hang celebrating the Battle of the Boyne under the 1,240-piece Waterford crystal chandelier. Guided tours are given every Thursday at 10.30, 11.30, and 1.45.

►►► Chester Beatty Library   462B

Castle Street, tel: 01 407 0750, www.cbl.ie
Open: May–Oct, Mon–Fri 10–5, Sat 11–5, Sun 1–5;
Nov–Apr, Tue–Fri 10–5, Sat 11–5, Sun 1–5. Admission free

Sir Alfred Chester Beatty (1875–1968) was an American mining engineer of Irish ancestry. By the age of 40 he had acquired a vast fortune, but had also developed incipient silicosis, so turned his prodigious energies to the more sedentary occupation of collecting exotic fine art. He made many trips to the Middle and Far East to add to his hoard and improve his health. He settled in Dublin in 1950, and gave his astonishing collection to the nation in 1956, living on to attain the grand age of 93. Occupying Dublin Castle's elegant clock tower, the collection contains outstanding examples of mostly oriental and Middle Eastern art, including gorgeously decorated Chinese silk robes, Japanese *netsuki* and lacquer boxes, illuminated manuscripts and scrolled Korans, books of jade or ancient papyrus, snuff bottles and rhinoceros-horn cups, woodblock prints, and miniature paintings. Apart from its academic importance, the collection is simply beautiful to look at and should not be missed.

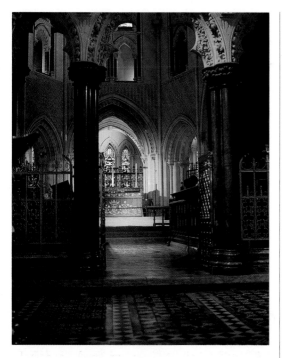

Christ Church Cathedral, known officially as the Cathedral of the Holy Trinity

DVBLINIA
This entertaining, multi-media presentation of life in medieval Dublin can be seen in the old Synod Hall over the bridge from Christ Church. It features a model of Dublin ca 1500, a display of items unearthed from Wood Quay, and a medieval maze, along with an exciting audio-visual show.

51

▶▶▶ Christ Church Cathedral   *462B*
Christ Church Place, tel: 01 677 8099, www.cccdub.ie
Open: daily 9.30–5. Admission: inexpensive

Oddly for a staunchly Catholic city, both of Dublin's cathedrals are Protestant. Christ Church is the seat of the Anglican Bishop of Dublin and Glendalough. It has been a Protestant church since 1551 and is inevitably closely linked with English rule of the city, though it has some rebellious streaks in its history: In 1487, the Yorkist Pretender, Lambert Simnel, was crowned here by his supporters in a counterclaim to Henry VII's throne. The cathedral stands within the original city walls, and until 1871 it was the official state church. Its long history stretches back before the Anglo-Norman invasion to 1038, when Sitric Silkenbeard, the first Christian Viking King of Dublin, founded a wooden church on this site. This was replaced by a stone edifice in Norman times. Part of this, the south wall, collapsed in 1562, and the north wall is still about 45cm (18ins) out of line. Today, the buttressed, grey, early Gothic buildings show evidence of a ruthless 19th-century restoration that time has not yet softened. Inside, are the tomb of "Strongbow" (Richard de Clare, Earl of Pembroke, who commanded the Anglo-Norman invasion in 1169) and the heart of St. Laurence O'Toole, arch-bishop and patron saint of Dublin, in the chapel of St. Laud. Some of the original 13th-century tiles are incorporated into the floor, and the eagle lectern is also medieval. The crypt contains an odd jumble of quaint broken statues and the city stocks. Other curiosities include the bodies of a cat and a mouse, which apparently died in full flight when they both got stuck in an organ pipe, and the 1689 tabernacle and candlesticks of James II.

THE FENIAN SOCIETY
This secret, militant group was formed in a Dublin timberyard on St. Patrick's Day 1858, financed by $400 donated by expatriate Irish who had emigrated to the United States during the Famine years. Its members were bound by oath to loyalty to the aim of establishing an Irish Republic. From it the Irish Republican Brotherhood, and later the IRA, developed, and it was suspected of many terrorist activities in its efforts to get the British out of Ireland. Parnell's Land League had links with the Fenians, which damaged an otherwise sympathetic hearing in Britain. Its anticlerical, Republican stance put it at odds with the Catholic Church, and known members faced excommunication. Today, Republican paramilitary groups are allegedly still partially financed by expatriate funds.

The Throne Room of Dublin Castle also contains a brass chandelier weighing more than a ton

▶▶ Dublin Castle 462B

Dame Street, tel: 01 677 7129, www.dublincastle.ie
Open: Mon–Fri 10–5, Sat–Sun 2–5. Admission: moderate

This is no longer so much a castle as an assembly of courts, offices, and ceremonial accommodation dating from many different periods. Although it stands on high ground that was originally a strategic site at the junction of the Liffey and the Poddle, it is now hemmed in by the surrounding buildings and offers little in the way of a city landmark. Nor does it command significant views; in fact, Queen Victoria is said to have been so disappointed by the rear outlook onto slum tenement buildings that she insisted a wall be built so that she shouldn't be reminded of such indigent neighbours next time she visited. The castle has been a fortress, prison, viceregent's residence, and function rooms for important state occasions. It also serves as a useful hotel for high-risk VIPs whenever they visit to discuss Ireland's tangled affairs. Dublin Castle has also been a venue for peace talks, and a headquarters during Ireland's 1996 presidency of the EU.

The most castlelike part of the building still standing is the round Record Tower, dating from the 13th century. It stood on the site of an earlier Viking fortress, sections of which have been excavated and can be seen in the undercroft (vault), along with the old moat and bits of city wall. After 1684, a lot of the structure had to be replaced because of fire, and much of what you see now dates from the 18th century. The church next to the Powder Tower is the Church of the Most Holy Trinity, modelled in neo-Gothic and consecrated in 1814 on the site of the earlier Chapel Royal. The arms of all the viceroys from 1172 to 1922 can be seen inside. Modern buildings around the courtyard house the tax office and conference facilities. One of the most charming parts of the older buildings is the inner courtyard with its clocktower.

Visits are by guided tour only, which, though informative, are somewhat impersonal. If you have time to wait, it is a good idea to see the photographic exhibition in the reception building (where they serve good refreshments) to get a clear idea of the layout of the complex. Inside, you see the main state apartments (provided no functions are going on there), which are sumptuously furnished to provide a suitably opulent setting for the many dignitaries who have made use of the castle. Vast Waterford chandeliers, tapestries, hand-tufted Donegal carpets mirroring the ceiling plasterwork, and Adam fireplaces abound, revealing the palatial lifestyle led by the viceroys acting on behalf of the Crown. St. Patrick's Hall is one of the most impressive rooms, all cluttered with banners and coats of arms, beneath an ornately painted ceiling. It is now used for the inauguration of Ireland's presidents. The throne room contains a massive throne believed to have been brought to Dublin by William of Orange after his victory at the Boyne. During the Easter Rising the castle was briefly threatened by an assault from the roof of the nearby City Hall. After the suppression of the rebellion, the captured rebel, James Connolly, was held (wounded) in one of the state rooms before being taken to Kilmainham to face execution.

▶ Dublin Civic Museum   473B

58 South William Street, tel: 01 679 4260
Open: Tue–Sat 10–6, Sun 11–2
Admission free

Housed in what was once the City Assembly House, the Dublin Civic Museum traces the history of the city from Viking times with items from excavation sites, old maps, photographs, and prints. The city's mercantile past is portrayed in sections devoted to various aspects of Dublin's trade and industry, and there is an interesting section on transportation, including a model of the Howth tram. One curiosity is a sculpted head of Lord Nelson, placed here after his column in O'Connell Street was blown up in 1966, on the 50th anniversary of the Easter Rising.

LIMITED RESOURCES
As the centre of English power in Ireland, Dublin Castle was for centuries probably the most heavily guarded fortress in the country. Yet, during the Easter Rising in 1916, insurgents abandoned a scheme to take the castle —without knowing that, at the time, it was manned only by a corporal's guard.

53

Dublin Civic Museum has a section devoted to fire-fighting. In this is a collection of fire-insurance plaques, such as the one below. They were once placed on houses to guide the insurance companies' own firemen to houses insured by them

The Easter Rising was a curious event, tiny in comparison with the rebellion of 1798, for instance, with only about 2,000 people actively taking part in it. It was disastrously badly organized and commanded very little public support, but its martyred heroes still glow in the imagination of Republican Ireland as icons in the struggle against British rule.

PEARSE MUSEUM
This little museum can be found in the house once run by Padraic Pearse and his brother William as a boys' school. Their curriculum placed a strong emphasis on Gaelic studies and Irish culture. The United Irishman Robert Emmet courted his bride in the grounds. The house is devoted to memorabilia connected with Pearse's life and the events that led to his death. It stands in St. Enda's Park in Rathfarnham, a southern Dublin suburb.

The General Post Office soon after the Easter Rising

Irish heroes The leaders were Padraic Pearse and James Connolly. Pearse, a shy schoolmaster, was an unlikely commander, but he was inspired by a kind of mystical belief that bloodshed was necessary to cleanse Ireland. He was an Irish Volunteer, a group pledged to establish Home Rule at all costs. James Connolly was a more practical man, a socialist, born into a poor Irish family in Scotland, and in the British army at 14. He founded the Irish Citizens Army, closely allied to the Irish Volunteers.

The Rising On Easter Monday, 24 April, 1916, Pearse, at the head of 150 men armed with ancient rifles and farm tools, took over the General Post Office, where he solemnly read out a stirring document proclaiming the new Irish Republic. Meanwhile, volunteers took over other buildings—a brewery, lunatic asylum, factory, and bakery. Many Dubliners were as bemused as the British forces by the collapse of the city into chaos and, instead of joining the rebels, they made tea for the British. The fighting lasted for six days, and on the Saturday Pearse surrendered, by which time over 400 people had died. Twice as many police were killed as rebels, and four times as many civilians. Much of central Dublin lay in ruins, and the leaders of the Rising were even less popular than they had been at the start.

54

The tragic aftermath Then the tide turned. Instead of listening to the advice of moderate Home Rule supporter John Redmond not to execute any of the rebels, the British shot 14 of them, including Pearse and Connolly. From then on, they were heroes in the classic Republican tradition. The release of hundreds of Irish internees later that year (among them Arthur Griffith, founder of Sinn Fein, Éamon de Valera, and Michael Collins) did nothing to assuage the bitterness that surrounded the aftermath of the Easter Rising. The fact that thousands of Irishmen died just a few months later on the battlefields of the Somme, fighting in the British Army, was all but eclipsed. A bronze statue in the rebuilt General Post Office, depicting the mythical hero, Cuchulainn, at the moment of death, symbolizes the glorified leaders.

Kilmainham Gaol This prison (*Inchicore Road, Kilmainham, tel: 01 453 5984, www.heritageireland.ie. Open Mon–Sat 9.30–5, Sun 10–5. Admission: inexpensive*), last used as such in 1924, is an excellent museum documenting the Irish struggle for independence. Many political prisoners were held here—United Irishmen, Fenians, Land Leaguers. It is a gripping and memorable place, and a fascinating, if partisan, insight into political and prison history. The main body of the prison, a classic barnlike shell of metal stairways and chicken-wired galleries, contains numerous display cases of items and documents. The guided tour begins at the scaffold where just one prisoner was hanged, and continues to the west wing where political internees were held in tiny, separate, dark cells. Passing the much more comfortable room where Parnell was imprisoned for seven months, it leads, finally, to the stonebreakers' yard where 14 leaders of the Easter Rising were executed by firing squad. James Connolly had a gangrenous leg and was shot strapped to a chair. Another prisoner, Joseph Plunkett, was married to Grace Gifford by candlelight in the prison chapel, two hours before he was shot. They were allowed ten minutes together.

Fighting lasted for six days, after which much of central Dublin lay in ruins

The monument in the General Post Office

The children's corner at Dublin Zoo…

GUINNESS

Arthur Guinness established his brewery in Dublin in 1759 and soon began experimenting with a London-brewed beverage made with roasted barley, known as "porter" (after its popularity with the porters of Covent Garden). By 1799, he concentrated all his production efforts on this distinctive drink, a rich black liquid topped with that "foamous" creamy head (as James Joyce called it). After the Napoleonic Wars of the early 19th century, an even stronger ("extra stout") beer was produced, and it rapidly reached most parts of the globe, even the South Pole (freezing is not generally recommended!). Though technology is now greatly advanced, the basic recipe of Guinness remains the same—Irish-grown barley, soft water, hops, and the strain of yeast Arthur Guinness used in 1759. A highly successful marketing policy has employed many talented artists in poster campaigns. The profits from Guinness have funded worthy enterprises such as the Wexford Opera Festival and the Georgian Society.

▶ Dublin Zoo   461C
Phoenix Park, tel: 01 677 1425, www.dublinzoo.ie
Open: Mar–Oct, Mon–Sat 9.30–6, Sun 10.30–6; Nov–Feb,
Mon–Fri 9.30–4, Sat 9.30–5, Sun 10.30–5
Admission: expensive
Established in 1830, Dublin's zoo is the third oldest in the world. It is attractive, set in 11.7ha (29 acres) of gardens with fauna roaming in pleasant surroundings. Its most celebrated inhabitants are the lions, one of whom achieved undying fame as the beast roaring above the MGM film studios' logo before every cinematic presentation.

▶▶ Guinness Brewery and Storehouse   461B
St. James's Gate, tel: 01 408 4800, www.guinness.com
Open: daily 9.30–5. Admission: expensive
Way upstream of most central sights is a Lowryesque skyline of smoking factory chimneys and giant metallic storage vats. This is the largest brewery in Europe, producing what can only be described as Ireland's *vin du pays*, though in fact it was first invented in London. Arthur Guinness's famous "porter" is shrouded in a sort of misty-eyed Celtic mythology that declares it can never be the same drunk outside Dublin, or from a can, or that the art of pulling a pint takes years to learn. This may be nonsense, but the production process is certainly a complex one and conditions of storage are important. You can't visit the brewery itself, but Guinness have converted the nearby 1904, six-floor, brick warehouse into "The Storehouse," a high-tech museum that borders on a temple dedicated to "the black stuff." Every floor has exhibits taking you through the brewing process, from grist and malt to a hundred years of Guinness advertising. Highlights include the top-floor, circular Gravity Bar with 360-degree glass walls and an unrivalled view of Dublin.

▶▶ Hugh Lane Municipal Art Gallery   462D
Parnell Square, tel: 01 874 1903, www.hughlane.ie
Open: Tue–Thu 9.30–6, Fri–Sat 9.30–5, Sun 11–5
Admission free (Bacon Studio: expensive)
The pictures are displayed in an elegant house designed by Sir William Chambers for the Earl of Charlemont in 1762. This north Dublin area is no longer very fashionable, but the house is a fine example of early Georgian architecture and its contents are even more splendid, and in some ways it is more enjoyable and intimate than the National Gallery. Corots, Courbets, and Monets glow on the plain walls, along with some good Jack Yeats. Francis Bacon, arguably Britain's premier 20th-century artist, bequeathed his studio to the gallery, where it has been reconstructed.

▶▶ Irish Museum of Modern Art   461B
Royal Hospital, Military Road, Kilmainham, tel: 01 612 9900
Open: Tue–Sat 10–5.30, Sun noon–5.30. (Royal Hospital tour
every 30 minutes; Museum of Modern Art tours Wed and Fri
2.30, Sat 11.30). Admission free
This museum deserves a visit, more for its glorious setting than its contents. Based on the style of Les Invalides in Paris, the Royal Hospital is one of the finest 17th-century buildings in Ireland, constructed in 1684 as a home for retired soldiers. Restored in 1986, it now houses ultra-modern works of variable quality. There are lively

temporary exhibitions, as well as educational and community theatre, and visual arts events. Seek out the chapel with its riot of papier-mâché decoration on the ceiling.

▶ Old Jameson Distillery 461C

Bow Street, tel: 01 807 2355, www.irish-whiskey-trail.com
Open: daily 9.30–5.30; tours every 30 minutes
Admission: expensive

The original Dublin distillery of Jameson Whiskey has been converted by Irish Distillers into a museum showing the production process of the "water of life." An audiovisual show and a model of an old distillery illuminate visitors, who are treated to a tasting to establish the difference between Scotch, Irish, and bourbon. If you are touring, there are larger and better whiskey distilling attractions in Northern Ireland (Bushmills) or County Cork (Midleton).

▶▶▶ Kilmainham Gaol 461B

See Focus On the Easter Rising, page 55.

...and the children's corner at the Municipal Gallery

HUGH LANE
When Hugh Lane went down with the *Lusitania* in 1915, he bequeathed a problem as well as a magnificent art collection. He had left his estate "to the nation." The difficulty was (in the light of contemporary political events) to decide which nation he meant. Britain naturally claimed he intended the collection to be British, whereas Dublin said it should stay in his native land. Eventually the dispute was settled with a classic British compromise. The collection was simply split in two parts. Half the pictures stayed in Dublin, half in the National Gallery in London, and every five years they changed over. Would that all Anglo-Irish problems could be solved so amicably! (Under a new agreement, most of the bequest is now actually on view in Dublin.)

A re-creation of a cooper's workshop at the Guinness Brewery

57

The period from about 1714 to 1830 was Dublin's apogee, a great flowering of architecture, literature, philosophy, and art. The quality of Irish craftsmanship in silverwork, glassware, and furniture, and in Dublin's superb Georgian buildings, epitomizes the "age of elegance."

Dublin's heyday After the depredations of Cromwell's visits and the turmoil of Williamite battles, the 18th century was a time of comparative peace and prosperity in the English Pale. For the upper classes, life was highly civilized. Aesthetes and businessmen, wealthy gentry and talented artists merged resources to make Dublin one of the foremost cities of Europe. Terraces, parks, squares, imposing monuments, and dignified town houses burgeoned throughout the central parts of the city, bounded by the Grand and Royal canals. In 1757, the Wide Streets Commission, Europe's first planning authority, established new guidelines for building development, and in 1773, the Paving Board set up sensible regulations on lighting, cleaning, and drainage, making densely populated residential areas much more

The figure of Hope rests upon her anchor atop the magnificent Custom House

salubrious. This confident assertion of the good life for the Anglo-Irish Ascendancy disguised the wretched lot of the poor; in 1770, even the English viceroy was forced to admit that the Irish peasantry were "amongst the most wretched people on earth."

North of the Liffey In the earlier years of the 18th century, Dublin's fashionable centre of gravity lay north of the river, and the first typically Georgian housing appeared around Mountjoy and Parnell (formerly Rutland) squares and Henrietta Street. These did not fare well after conversion to tenement buildings when the Act of Union caused a dramatic fall in property values, and the buildings long presented a sad picture of neglect and decay. But a sharp rise in the housing market has led to a spate of restoration and development in areas such as **North Great George's Street**. Other quality examples can be found in **Parnell Square▶▶**. The **Hugh Lane Municipal Art Gallery▶▶** (see page 56), is in a splendid town house of the period; **Belvedere House▶** on Great Denmark Street, now a Jesuit college, is another. Two grand set pieces north of the river, monumental buildings designed by James Gandon, can be seen to advantage from the opposite bank of the Liffey. The weighty **Custom House▶▶** of 1791 (tel: 01 679 3377, see panel) floats on a fragile platform of pine planks on swampy riverside land. Farther west is the **Four Courts▶** of 1785 (tel: 01 872 5555), the seat of the High Court of Justice for Ireland. The Courts of King's Bench, Exchequer, Common Pleas, and Chancery radiate from a circular central hall, liveliest at lunchtimes when bewigged lawyers hob-nob with their clients. Another Gandon building stands away from the river, in Henrietta Street: The **King's Inns▶** (1795–1827) were Dublin's Inns of Court (tel: 01 874 4840). The **Rotunda Maternity Hospital▶▶**, the first specially built maternity hospital in Europe, has superb stucco work in its chapel (tel: 01 873 0700).

South of the Liffey The best preserved and the most enjoyable examples of Dublin's Georgian heritage can be seen south of the river. The shift in popularity occurred around the year 1750, after the construction of the opulent **Leinster House▶▶** (now Ireland's parliament building, tel: 01 618 3000) for the Duke of Leinster in 1745. At the time, he was ridiculed for his choice of a green-field site away from the hub of fashionable Dublin, but as he rightly predicted, "Wherever I go, they will follow."

Dublin's Georgian heritage was largely spared aerial bombing during the World Wars, but it has fared ill at the hands of 20th-century developers and politicians. After the creation of the Free State in 1922, renovation of buildings reminiscent of English rule was not exactly a high priority. Much thoughtless and irreparable destruction took place. But there is still much to enjoy among the fanlit doorways of its 18th-century squares. A new generation of conservation-minded citizens who do not blame bricks and mortar for Ireland's disastrous history now seem bent on preserving what is left.

See the following two pages for a walk around Dublin's finest Georgian buildings.

59

North Great George's Street: The lantern above the door was lit when the mistress of the house was "at home to visitors"

Walk

A walk around Georgian Dublin

See map on pages 46–47.

Within the bounds of 18th-century taste, Irish craftsmen found great scope for personal expression, and the details of buildings are hugely varied and imaginative. Little touches, such as door-knockers, coal-hole covers, and boot-scrapers, are the rewards of a wander around Georgian Dublin.

College Green is a good starting point for exploring Dublin. This was the centre of power during the 18th century until the Act of Union central-ized government in Westminster. What is now the **Bank of Ireland**►► (see page 50) was built by Edward

60

Lovett Pearce between 1729 and 1739 to house the Irish Parliament. During banking hours, visitors may see the former House of Lords, sump-tuously furnished with a Waterford chandelier, 18th-century tapestries, and coffered ceiling. **Trinity College**►►, on the other side of the Green (see page 72), dates mainly from the 18th century. Its 90m (300ft) facade, attributed to Theodore Jacobsen, was built between 1752 and 1759, and the **Provost's House**►► on the corner of Grafton Street is one of Dublin's grandest Georgian mansions.

Turning down Kildare Street, you find Georgian **Leinster House**►►►, the most imposing of several monumental public buildings (see pages 58–59), while nearby Molesworth Street contains three early Georgian houses built for Huguenot families between 1736 and 1755. Known as **Dutch Billies**►, they are a revival of a style popular after William of Orange's conquest, featuring curvy gables and huge chimneys. On Dawson Street, 18th-century buildings include: **St. Ann's**►► of 1720 (see page 70); the **Royal Irish Academy**► (tel: 01 676 2570) of 1785, housing a splendid library of Irish manuscripts; and the balustraded facade of the Lord Mayor's residence, **The Mansion House**► (tel: 01 676 1845), a Queen Anne building that dates from 1705, is sometimes open for exhibitions. **St. Stephen's Green** is one of the land-marks of the Georgian city, although its buildings date from many periods and its park was not laid out until Victorian times (see page 68). The best of the Georgian buildings are: the 1806 **Royal College of Surgeons**►► (tel: 01 402 2100), scarred by the Easter Rising; **Newman House**► (tel: 01 475 7255), Nos. 85 and 86 on the south side, original home of the Catholic university (one of these houses, ironically, was built for a vehement anti-Catholic, Thomas "Burnchapel" Whaley, by the great 18th-century architect Richard Castle); and **Iveagh House**►► (1736), now the Department of Foreign Affairs (not open). Off St. Stephen's Green are **Harcourt Street**, **Ely Place**, and **Leeson Street**, with many attractive and well-preserved domestic town houses.

St. Stephen's Green

Leinster House, designed by Castle

Fitzwilliam Street► contained the longest stretch of Georgian buildings in Europe until an astonishing piece of civic vandalism in the 1960s permitted a hideous office building to tear a hole in it. The Electricity Supply Board (whose administrative headquarters it is) has now sheepishly rebuilt one of the houses it tore down. **Number 29►** (tel: 01 702 6165. *Admission free*) is open as a little museum, and its elegant rooms re-create something of the atmosphere of late Georgian times. **Fitzwilliam Square►►**, although not the largest or most famous Georgian example, is actually one of the best preserved. Many fanlit doorways retain original features such as glass recesses for lamps, and antiburglar spikes set in the walls. A glance down Mount Street reveals the attractive late-Georgian church of **St. Stephen's►►**, known as the Pepperpot from its unusual dome. In the mid-18th century, the **Grand Canal** beside the church would have been a bustling highway of commerce and passenger traffic.

Merrion Square►►► is the final great "set piece" on this walking tour. The blue plaques on many houses commemorate famous former occupants, suggesting how fashionable it once was. Planned in 1762 for Lord Fitzwilliam, it is one of the finest of all Dublin's squares. Oscar Wilde's parents lived here, as well as statesman Daniel O'Connell, W. B. Yeats, and many other respected figures.

Georgian elegance in every detail

Dublin is an emphatically literary city. Most great Irish writers gravitated there at some stage so, to some extent, the literary history of Dublin is the literary history of Ireland. The ghosts of Yeats, Shaw, Synge, Beckett, O'Casey, Wilde, Swift, and others haunt its streets and bookshops. The National Library, near Leinster House, contains a splendid collection of first editions and works of 17th-century Irish authors, as well as later writers, including Swift, Goldsmith, Yeats, Shaw, and Joyce.

Top: Oscar Wilde

62

JAMES JOYCE TOWER
The 22-year-old Joyce spent only a week or so there in the August of 1904, though he later immortalized it in the first chapter of his masterpiece *Ulysses*. The Martello Tower belonged to Oliver St. John Gogarty, an ebullient surgeon and poet, who invited Joyce to stay with him there. For more details of his eventful stay in the tower, see page 97.

STELLA AND VANESSA
Jonathan Swift's women friends are immortalized in his letters and other writings under pseudonyms. "Vanessa" was Esther Vanhomrigh, who lived in Celbridge, County Kildare (at Barberstown Castle, see Hotels and Restaurants, page 280). Swift met her in London in 1708 and may even have fathered her child. She followed Swift to Ireland but broke off her friendship with him when he became involved with "Stella." The second great attachment of his life was another Esther (Johnson), with whom he had a deep but apparently platonic relationship. Memorials to Swift and Stella can be seen in St. Patrick's Cathedral (see page 71).

Georgian flowering Along with its architecture, Dublin's literary scene blossomed during the 18th century, a time of great intellectual ferment and scientific discovery. One of the giants of the era was the Dean of St. Patrick's Cathedral, Jonathan Swift. Probably the greatest satirist in the English language, he is most famous for *Gulliver's Travels*. He was a Protestant and obviously part of the Anglo-Irish Ascendancy, but some of his bitterest invective was directed against the cruel and unequal conditions of the Irish poor. In *A Modest Proposal* he attempted to stir up the complacent attitudes of the time by suggesting, deliberately outrageously, that Irish children should be fattened up for English tables.

Swift's contemporaries included William Congreve and George Farquhar, both of whom were educated at Trinity College, Dublin. Like many other Irish writers, however, they soon left for London, as did the later authors, Oliver Goldsmith and Richard Brinsley Sheridan. During the 19th century, dramatists who achieved greatest fame were Oscar Wilde and George Bernard Shaw (who lived on until 1950), both of whom, following the usual pattern, left their native land to dazzle London society.

The Gaelic Revival Meanwhile, however, another strand of writers began to receive attention in Dublin. At the end of the 19th century a renewed interest in all things Irish (the Gaelic Revival) was inspiring artists such as W. B. Yeats and his friend George Russell; Celtic myths interweave their work. The turn of the 20th century saw a great flourishing of theatrical talent, this time a home-grown version using Irish, specifically Gaelic, themes. John Millington Synge's works for the Abbey Theatre were among these, followed by the pacifist works of Sean O'Casey. Both these writers were controversial and aroused much furore when they broke away from the norms of light social comedy.

James Joyce The literary giant most closely associated with Dublin, James Joyce (1882–1941), is surprisingly not among Ireland's four Nobel Prize-winners (Beckett, Shaw, Yeats, and Heaney), three of whom have strong links with the capital, too. Joyce, however, lived and breathed the place, although he always had a love–hate relationship with it and spent most of his adult life abroad. He referred to his native city as the "centre of paralysis": "How sick, sick, sick I am of Dublin. It is a city of failure, of rancour and unhappiness. I long to be out of it," he wrote. The works in which Dublin appears, almost as the central character, are *A Portrait of the Artist as a Young Man*, *Ulysses*, *Dubliners*, and *Finnegan's Wake*. Ironically, Joyce, spurned and hounded into exile while he lived, is now fêted by the tourist authorities as one of the city's greatest ambassadors—every step of his Dublin-set masterpiece *Ulysses* is carefully documented in self-guided walks and wall plaques. Keen followers of his work can buy a map and follow the route taken by Leopold Bloom on that famous 16th of June. The trail leads well out of the city centre to the southeast suburbs of Dalkey and Sandycove, with its James Joyce Tower that features in the opening chapter of *Ulysses*. Inside is a museum set up in 1962 by Sylvia Beach, original publisher of his great novel, containing Joycean memorabilia and some letters. Next to the tower is the Forty Foot Pool, where Buck Mulligan (based on Gogarty, see panel) swims at the start of *Ulysses*. Nearby Dalkey was the setting for Flann O'Brien's novel, *The Dalkey Archive*.

The prolific George Bernard Shaw

63

BRENDAN BEHAN
Of all the characters who trod Dublin's literary stage during the course of this century, few were more rambunctious than Brendan Behan—variously remembered as a lovable rogue or an arrogant sot—whose over-indulgence of Guinness contributed to his untimely death in 1964 at the ripe young age of 41. During his creative years, the pubs in Dublin were officially closed on St. Patrick's Day, and one of the few places where one could openly get a drink was at the annual dog show in the Royal Dublin Society's premises in Ballsbridge. On repairing there one St. Patrick's Day, Behan is said to have howled "Who the hell brought a ****ing dog into a place like this, anyway?"—or words to that effect.

William Butler Yeats (1865–1939)

Walk

A walk around literary Dublin

See map on pages 46–47.

Most of Ireland's great writers spent time in Dublin, and this walk explores some of their haunts.

Start off in Parnell Square, at the **Dublin Writers Museum**. Housed in a restored 18th-century mansion, this contains a fascinating collection of first editions, portraits, manuscripts, and memorabilia. A couple of doors away is the **Hugh Lane Municipal Gallery**►► (see pages 56–57), where you can see works by Jack Yeats and a portrait of Maud Gonne, who drove his brother, W. B. Yeats, to heights of romantic distraction. On the corner of Granby Row, the **National Wax Museum** displays effigies of the writers Joyce, Yeats,

It's worth looking up when visiting the Dublin Writers Museum

Shaw, and O'Casey in a suitably bookish setting. In the centre of the square lies the Garden of Remembrance, a park commemorating all who have fallen for Irish freedom. Plans for the Easter Rising were made in a house nearby, and the captured rebels were held prisoner in this square overnight. The fountain pool and its swan sculptures by Oisín Kelly evoke the myth of the Children of Lir, turned into birds for 900 years (see page 236). The rest of Parnell Square is taken up by the **Rotunda Maternity Hospital**►► (see page 59). Founded in 1745, it has excellent plasterwork and woodcarving. Part of it is now the Gate Theatre, where many Irish and foreign playwrights staged productions from 1929 onwards.

  Leaving Parnell Square at the southeast corner, head for North Great George's Street, where heartening restoration work of the fine Georgian houses has taken place. One of them (No. 35) contains the **James Joyce Centre**: library, bookshop, Joycean walks, lectures, and more (tel: 01 873 1984). Belvedere House in Great Denmark Street is another well-preserved Georgian mansion, now a

On the Ulysses *trail along the streets of Dublin*

Jesuit college (Joyce was a former student). A detour up Temple Street North leads to Eccles Street, site of Leopold Bloom's fictional home in *Ulysses* (No. 7 no longer exists, though you can see the front door in the Bailey pub on Duke Street). Heading northeast, you reach St. Francis Xavier's Church, an ornate Jesuit building. Mountjoy Square was once home to several writers, this side of town having cheaper rents for impecunious writers than the classier, and more expensive, south bank. Sean O'Casey lived at No. 35 and later at 422 North Circular Road, using the area as the setting for *Shadow of a Gunman* and his other plays for the Abbey Theatre. Brendan Behan grew up in 14 Russell Street.

Continuing down Gardiner Street, you follow the same route as Leopold Bloom on that famous day in June 1904. Up Railway Street stood Bella Cohen's Brothel, immortalized in *Ulysses*, typical of many houses of ill repute in this area. Cutting down Waterford Street and Marlborough Street, note the Pro-Cathedral, Dublin's most important Catholic church. On Abbey Street is the **Abbey Theatre**, where many significant dramatic productions are staged. The theatre was first opened in 1904 under the auspices of Lady Gregory and W. B. Yeats. One of its most memorable productions was the first staging of John Millington Synge's *Playboy of the Western World*, which caused riots among the Dublin audience because of its depiction of a parricide and its mention of an item of female underwear ("shift"). Sean O'Casey's play, *The Plough and the Stars*, also caused a furore because it bravely refused to idolize the leaders of the Easter Rising. The Abbey was burned down in 1951, and rebuilt in a modern, blockish style. Once back on O'Connell Street there are more Joycean sites—Prince's Street, by the General Post Office, where Leopold Bloom worked at the *Freeman's Journal*, and Graham Lemon's sweetshop.

Finish the walk over the bridge at Trinity College, in the Long Room, where the ghosts of many graduate *literati* stalk, from Swift and Goldsmith to Shaw and Wilde, connecting Ireland's current lively writing scene with those unknown monks who illuminated the Gospels of the *Book of Kells* in the 8th century.

One of many memorials to Joyce

The intricate beauty of the Tara Brooch, housed in the Treasury of the National Museum. Despite its name, it has no known connection with Tara in County Meath

▶▶ **National Gallery**   474B

Merrion Square West, tel: 01 661 5133
Open: Mon–Wed and Fri–Sat
10–5.30, Thu 10–8.30, Sun 2–5
Admission free

The National Gallery is a very interesting collection, though not in the first rank of European art galleries. About 2,000 works are on show at any one time, representing Irish, US, and all other major European schools of art up to the 19th century. More recent works are on display at the Irish Museum of Modern Art, housed in the Royal Hospital, Kilmainham, and the Hugh Lane Municipal Art Gallery (see page 56).

The National Gallery first opened in 1864, with only a tiny fraction of the paintings it now possesses. Much of it's growth was due to the energies of William Dargan, a railway magnate largely responsible for building Ireland's rail network. He was the moving spirit behind the Dublin Exhibition of 1853, using the profits to found the gallery, and his statue stands on the lawns near the entrance gate. The building was designed by Francis Fowke, who also designed the Victoria and Albert Museum in London.

The collection contains a number of works by Jack B. Yeats, brother of the poet, W. B. Yeats, which make a gritty contrast to the sentimental productions of other members of the Irish School. Other highlights include Degas's *Ballet Girls* and Caravaggio's *The Taking of Christ*. The Impressionists are well represented, as are Italian and Dutch schools and earlier French artists from the 17th century onwards. A fascinating collection of Irish portraits lines the grand staircase, culminating in the fiery Countess Markiewicz, who was furious at being pardoned for her part in the Easter Rising (see pages 54–55). There is also a coffee shop and restaurant.

▶▶▶ **National Museum**   473B

Kildare Street, tel: 01 677 7444, www.museum.ie
Open: Tue–Sat 10–5, Sun 2–5. Admission free

This museum houses many of the finest masterpieces of Irish Celtic art from the Bronze Age to the Middle Ages. Its greatest treasures (appropriately housed in the Treasury) include the Tara Brooch, the Ardagh Chalice, the Cross of Cong, the Shrine of St. Patrick's Bell, and many other exquisite pieces of gold jewellery and croziers. The Tara Brooch is perhaps the most important, and most copied, of all Celtic jewels. It dates from the 8th century AD and is made of white bronze, silver gilt, amber, and glass, and although it measures only about 5cm (2in)

VIKING FOUNDATIONS
One of the first additions to the National Museum's collections was a Viking sword that came to light when the builders were digging the foundations for the museum just over a century ago.

across, it is intricately decorated with scrolls, spirals, and strange beasts on both sides. The Ardagh Chalice, from about the same period, is inspired by Byzantine art—a shapely wide goblet of gilded bronze, chased with gold filigree and studded with coloured glass.

A department called *Ar Thoir na Saoirse* (The Road to Independence) has mementoes of the Easter Rising and the Civil War, including a fragment of the flag flown over the General Post Office in 1916. Other sections contain superb porcelain of Irish, English, European, and Asian origins, many items from Japan, rare textiles, glass, ceramics, silver, and old musical instruments such as Irish harps and uilleann pipes. A particularly interesting section called "Viking Age Ireland" shows what life was like for those fierce Norsemen, using exhibits from settlements in and around Dublin. Temporary exhibitions are regularly mounted. Collins Barracks (*Open* as National Museum) in Phoenix Park has been taken over by the museum and now houses a growing collection of glass, silver, furniture, and other decorative arts.

▶▶ Natural History Museum   473B

Merrion Street, tel: 01 677 7444, www.museum.ie
Open: Tue–Sat 10–5, Sun 2–5. Admission free

This is part of the National Museum (and has the same opening hours), but is housed in a separate building. In a large hall, a crowded display of taxidermy can be seen, including a comprehensive collection of Irish mammals, birds, fish, and insects, together with various mineral exhibits. Upstairs are animals from other parts of the world, while whales once stranded on the Irish coast now hang from the roof.

The gallery of Dublin's Natural History Museum

Weather permitting, it is never difficult to find a place to get away from the traffic noise in Dublin. The Georgian layout of the city naturally produced a system of spacious squares and landscaped gardens around its principal monuments, and Dublin is full of green open spaces, neat and municipal, or wilder and more natural.

Town squares The most famous of the Georgian squares is **St. Stephen's Green**, which was formerly common land. In 1880, Lord Ardilaun (heir to the Guinness fortunes) paid for the present gardens to be laid out, and they now encompass 8.5ha (21 acres) of lawns, flower beds, paved walks, shrubberies, and an ornamental lake with wildfowl. Bandstands, statues, and pergolas dot it at intervals; its various monuments include Henry Moore's memorial to Yeats and a statue of Wolfe Tone amid stone slabs ("Tonehenge"). The gardens are open during daylight hours, when they become one of Dublin's most popular spots for strolling or having a lunchtime sandwich.

Merrion Square is another attractive open space dating from Georgian times. The restored Rutland Fountain is inset in its railings. During the Famine years (1845–1848) a soup kitchen was set up in this well-heeled residential square to feed starving refugees who poured in from the devastated country areas. Today you are more likely to find artists selling their wares on weekends.

Phoenix Park At the west end of the city lies the huge open space called **Phoenix Park**. It stretches along the Liffey for about 5km (3mi) and covers 688ha (1,700 acres), about five times the size of London's Hyde Park. The park's name comes from the Gaelic *fionn uisce*, meaning "clear water," referring to the spring in the Furry Glen. In it are lakes, woods, fields, a racecourse, and sports grounds. It also contains Dublin Zoo (see page 56) and the headquarters of the *Garda Siochána*, or Irish police force. Its most striking monuments are the 60m (200ft) obelisk to Wellington and the Phoenix Column, erected in 1747 by Lord Chesterfield, a former lord lieutenant. The parklands once belonged to Kilmainham Priory, until they were seized during the Reformation, and later became a deer park owned by the Duke of Ormonde (deer still roam the park, descended from the original herd). During the 18th and 19th centuries, it was a fashionable place with desirable residences, one of which now houses the Irish president. The so-called 15 acres (now playing fields) were well known as a duelling place in the 18th century. Violence of a different type erupted in 1882 when Lord Cavendish, the chief secretary, and Burke, the undersecretary, were stabbed here by obscure malcontents called the Invincibles. The assassination caused a great furore at Westminster, where the question of Home Rule for Ireland was at last being seriously debated. The park's main entrance is at the southeast corner, off Parkgate Street.

The Three Fates quietly watch life pass by from their vantage point in St. Stephen's Green

Other green spaces A little way east lies **Arbour Hill Cemetery**, a quiet memorial garden where the leaders of the Easter Rising are buried, their names carved in stone beside a copy of the stirring proclamation of independence. Dublin's other interesting cemetery is in **Glasnevin**, in the north of the city, where lie the graves of Éamon de Valera, Gerard Manley Hopkins, and Roger Casement (see page 43). Close by are Dublin's **National Botanic Gardens►►**, set up in 1795, and containing about 20,000 species of plants and trees, including specialist rose and vegetable gardens. The ornate glasshouses known as the Curvilinear Range were constructed by Richard Turner, a famous 19th-century iron founder also responsible for producing the Palm House in Belfast. Riverside walks lead through bog and peat gardens and the arboretum (tel: 01 837 4388).

One of Dublin's wilder spaces is **North Bull Island**, a strip of dunes and beaches off the coast, reached from the road to Howth. It is now a nature conservancy area, but visitors can walk out along the causeway to the lighthouse. You can see many species of birds there, and further information can be gleaned either from the guided tours or at the interpretative centre.

The Curvilinear Range of greenhouses at the Botanical Gardens

Poet James Mangan, St. Stephen's Green

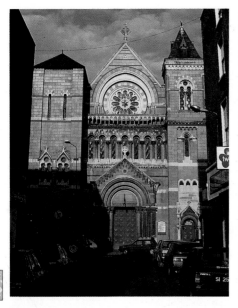

▶▶ St. Ann's Church   473B

Dawson Street
Open: Mon–Fri 10–4 and Sun for services

This church's Italianate facade of 1868 in neo-Romanesque granite disguises an 18th-century interior including polished wood balconies and ornate plasterwork. Wooden shelves beside the altar were constructed to hold loaves of bread for the poor, a bequest left by Lord Theophilus Newtown.

▶ St. Mary's Abbey   462C

Meetinghouse Lane, tel: 01 872 1490
Open: Jun–Sep, Wed 10–5
Admission: inexpensive

Remnants of the Pale's most prominent Cistercian monastery, founded by the Benedictines in 1139, lie here. Much of the stone was removed to build Essex Bridge nearby, and only the chapter house still stands.

St. Ann's is built from pale granite interspersed with single courses of red brick

▶▶ St. Michan's Church   461C

Lower Church Street, tel: 01 872 4154
Open: Apr–Oct, Mon–Fri 10–12.45 and 2–4.45, Sat 10–12.45, Sun service at 10AM; Nov–Mar, Mon–Fri 12.30–3.30, Sat 10–12.45, Sun service at 10AM. Admission: inexpensive

In a run-down area at the back of the Four Courts, this church (begun in 1095) arouses a certain ghoulish excitement for the mummified corpses in its vaults. Visitors can only see them as part of a guided tour as access is via locked hatches outside the church walls. Their preservation is due to the hygroscopic action of the surrounding magnesian limestone, plus a few whiffs of methane gas

SILKEN THOMAS
In 1534, the 10th Earl of Kildare, known as Silken Thomas for his love of fine clothing, mutinied against Henry VIII. He declared vengeance on the Henry at St. Mary's Abbey for his apostasy against the Catholic Church and the supposed beheading of his father (a false rumour). Thomas was captured and executed in 1537.

Some believe that one of the mummified bodies in St. Michan's Church is that of a medieval Crusader

from some subterranean disposal site. Handel is supposed to have played the organ here, and at the "penitent's pew" malefactors knelt to make their offenses public.

▶▶ St. Patrick's Cathedral 462B
Patrick's Close, tel: 01 475 4817, www.stpatrickscathedral.ie Open: May and Sep–Oct, Mon–Fri 9–6, Sat 9–5, Sun 10–11 and 12.45–3; Jun–Aug, Mon–Fri 9–6, Sat 9–4, Sun 9.30–3 and 4.15–5.15; Nov–Apr, Mon–Fri 9–6, Sat 9–4, Sun 10–11 and 12.45–3. Admission: moderate

The precise status of this cathedral is a puzzle. Just a short distance down the road stands another Church of Ireland cathedral, Christ Church. The two have always been great rivals. St. Patrick's is the national cathedral, the home of the first university in Ireland (1320–1520), and is Ireland's largest church. It is legendarily associated with St. Patrick because of a neighbouring well, where the saint was believed to have baptized many converts. From 1191 onwards, the original church was replaced by the present building, much restored in the 1860s on the proceeds of Guinness. The cathedral stands in a desolate wasteland of tenement housing, outside the city walls. By far its most celebrated incumbent was Jonathan Swift, author of *Gulliver's Travels*, who was Dean here from 1713 to 1745 and is buried in the cathedral beside his beloved "Stella," Esther Johnson. A plaque is inscribed with Swift's self-penned epitaph which, translated from the Latin, reads: "Where fierce indignation can no longer rend the heart,/ Go traveller, and imitate, if you can, this earnest and dedicated champion of liberty." Nearby is a memorial verse from Alexander Pope dedicated to Swift, and Swift's death mask, chair, and writing table can be seen in the north pulpit. At the west end of the church is a 17th-century monument to the Boyle family. The young Robert (the scientist who was later to formulate Boyle's Law) is on the lowest tier. Mattins (9.45AM) and evensong (5.35PM) are sung on most days.

Next to St. Patrick's is **Archbishop Marsh's Library▶▶** (tel: 01 454 3511), similar to (but smaller than) the Old Library of Trinity College. The barrel-vaulted upper room houses a wonderful collection of ancient leather-bound tomes in dark floor-to-ceiling cases. Several fascinating manuscripts, such as old herbals with beautiful plant illustrations, are separately displayed. Swift's annotated copy of Clarendon's *History of the Great Rebellion* is here, among 25,000 other volumes. Cages where readers could be locked in to consult valuable books can also be seen.

▶▶ Temple Bar 462C
The epicentre of Dublin's revival in the last decade has to be ultra-trendy Temple Bar. Renowned for its restaurants and nightlife, the narrow-streeted, cobblestoned area south of the Ha'penny Bridge also has some notable sights. **Meeting House Square▶▶**, named for a nearby Quaker house, is definitely *the* gathering place for young Dubliners; in summer, a stage is erected in the open area for free performances. **Arthouse** (tel: 01 605 6800; *open* Mon–Fri 9.30–6. *Admission free*) boasts of being one of the first multimedia art galleries in the world, and **The Ark** (tel: 01 670 7788; *open* Mon–Sat 9.30–4. *Admission free*), is a children's cultural centre including an outdoor theatre.

CHANCING YOUR ARM
A curious feature in the nave of St. Patrick's Cathedral is a freestanding wooden door with a hole in it. This was formerly the chapter door of the south transept and is the subject of an intriguing tale. The warring earls of Kildare and Ormonde confronted each other at the cathedral in 1492, where Ormonde had barricaded himself inside the church for protection. The Earl of Kildare offered to make peace, and cut a hole in the door through which he thrust his arm to shake hands with Ormonde. The phrase "chancing your arm" was born.

71

St. Patrick's has no crypt because the Poddle River flows directly beneath the cathedral

AN ANCIENT THEFT
The *Book of Kells* was stolen one night from the western sacristy of the great stone church of Kells (Meath) in 1007. The *Annals of Ulster* tell that it was recovered after two months and twenty nights, "its gold having been taken off it and with a sod over it."

Above: the Old Library of Trinity College
Below: TCD's frontage extends for over 90m (300ft)

▶▶▶ Trinity College 473C

College Green, tel: 01 608 2308, www.tcd.ie
Open: daily 7AM–10PM. Admission free

This single-college university was founded by Elizabeth I in 1592 on confiscated monastery land, ostensibly "to civilize Ireland with both learning and the Protestant religion." Small wonder, then, that it became a source of division in the city. Catholics were always allowed entry to the college, and free education—provided, of course, they converted; up until 1966, Catholics had to obtain a special dispensation to attend on pain of excommunication. Now, however, the proportion of Catholic students at TCD, as it is known, is about 70 percent. The "honour roll" is impressive: Edmund Burke, Jonathan Swift, Oliver Goldsmith, Bram Stoker, Wolfe Tone, William Congreve, Oscar Wilde, J. M. Synge, and Samuel Beckett have all passed through these hallowed portals.

Today TCD occupies a prime location at the heart of Dublin, in an oasis of gardens and parks. Little remains of the original buildings; the imposing, classical facade and Corinthian columns give it an unmistakably 18th-century feel. Inside, like ancient English universities, its buildings are arranged around quadrangles of lawns and cobbles. The theatre, examination hall, chapel, dining hall, and the old brick student accommodation known as the Rubrics can be seen as you pass from the Front Court to the Library Court. The campanile, by Charles Lanyon, marks the site of the original priory. To the right is the Old Library, where the *Book of Kells* is housed.

Since 1801, Trinity College has had the right under copyright law to claim a free copy of all British and Irish publications, and it now houses nearly 3 million volumes in eight buildings. About a kilometre (half a mile) of new shelving is needed every year to keep up with all the new publications.

Bus tours roll up to visit Trinity's concession to the tourist industry, a 40-minute video called *The Dublin Experience* that gives a brief history of the city in the Arts Building behind the library, from late May to October.

The intricate decoration and bright colours of this Latin text of the Gospels gives clear proof of the inventive skill and dedication shown by early Irish scholars. The glowing patterns illuminated not merely the pages of the text, but the whole of the Christian world.

The **Old Library of Trinity College**▶▶▶ houses about 2 million volumes, stacked in a double-decker layer of huge floor-to-ceiling shelving in 20 bays of a splendid cathedral-like hall accurately called the Long Room, measuring 64m by 12m (210ft by 39ft). The building was designed by Thomas Burgh in 1712; its barrel-vaulted ceiling was added in the 19th century in order to provide more much-needed shelf space. At the far end of the library are two harps, one of them tradition-ally associated with the great Irish king Brian Ború (926–1014), though actually from the 15th century. By far the most famous and precious of all the treasures in the Old Library of Trinity College is the 8th-century illuminated manuscript of the four Gospels, known as the *Book of Kells*. Inscribed in Latin on vellum parchment, its pages are magnificently ornamented with patterns and fantastic animals. The designs closely resemble the interlacing patterns found on Celtic metal-work and are obviously influenced by those traditions. Although the manuscript was certainly kept at the monastery of Kells in County Meath, there exists some doubt whether it was actually produced there, some authorities believing it may have been copied in Iona or Lindisfarne. The book's 680 pages were re-bound during the 1950s into four separate volumes. Two of these are generally on display in the Old Library, with the pages being turned every so often to give a different view. Conservation of such a priceless document is of the utmost importance and a constant battle; you may have to be content with a facsimile version. The Colonnades is an exhibition area featuring annually changing displays and a well-stocked shop. Besides the *Book of Kells*, there are several similar manuscripts kept at Trinity—the *Book of Durrow*, the *Book of Dimma*, and the less colourful *Book of Armagh*.

The startlingly beautiful and complex Book of Kells

73

THE OLD LIBRARY OF TRINITY COLLEGE
Tel: 01 608 2308. *Open:* Jun–Sep, Mon–Sat 9.30–5, Sun 9.30–4.30; Oct–May, Mon–Sat 9.30–5, Sun noon–4.30. *Admission: moderate.*

Genealogy is now big business in Ireland, and hundreds of visitors annually attempt to find their roots. Around 60 million people, mostly in North America and the Antipodes, are estimated to be of Irish descent. Of these, by far the largest number live in the US (40 million), 5 million live in Canada, and another 5 million in Australia and New Zealand. The rest are somewhere in Britain or scattered around the globe.

Before it became the Heraldic Museum, No. 2 Kildare Street was the home of a gentlemen's club. On one of its columns (and visible from the road) are two monkeys playing the gentlemanly sport of billiards

74

Finding your roots Ancestor-tracing is particularly popular in Dublin, where most of the records are held, and in the west of Ireland, which saw vast emigration during the Famine years. Ulster also has strong links with the New World; many "Scotch-Irish" Protestant settlers have made their homes in Canada or the United States. In September 1992, Ireland staged a large cross-border Homecoming Festival. Along with the *ceilis* (evenings of folk music and dancing) and the *craich* (fun) went many more earnest events such as clan rallies and history seminars, and lots of hints on the tracing of forebears.

The great interest in origins is fostered by recent research overseas. Canada, for example, has carried out a detailed survey on Irish settlement of its Atlantic seaboard. For many people, a visit to Ireland is a chance to see the Old Country, to track down the family town or homestead, and perhaps look up a few living relatives.

An exhibit at Dublin's Heraldic Museum, showing the Irish harp

Irish archives A burgeoning number of organizations and centres throughout Ireland will now help you draw your family tree. Increasingly, family records and databases are being computerized and interlinked, making it much quicker and easier to track down records that would have taken hours of patient poring over documents in the past. Inevitably, there's a cost involved, but unless your roots are particularly elusive, the charges are generally quite modest. You could just pay a small fee for a five-year search through the births, marriages, and deaths certificates, or considerably more for a detailed survey of several generations, neatly documented. Research concentrates mainly on civil and parish records, census forms, wills, papers dealing with land or property transactions, etc.

Emigration records Irish data is somewhat patchy. In 1922, at the start of the Civil War, the Public Record Office, then housed at the Four Courts in Dublin, was shelled and many documents were lost (fortunately some copies were kept elsewhere). During the Famine years, scant records were kept of those who emigrated or died on the way—such was the despair and chaos of those times. The best bet is to start at the other end, where detailed immigration papers were completed in most American and Australian ports of entry. Seven volumes of immigrant records list every arrival into New York from 1846 to 1851 (*The Famine Immigrants*, published by the Baltimore Genealogical Publishing Company). Australia's records are also good, particularly of those who left Ireland on "assisted passage" schemes, or who were deported for a criminal offence (often a trivial misdemeanour or political involvement—the chances of unearthing some serial killer in the family archives are small). Contact the National Library in Canberra, or the Mitchell Library in Sydney.

If you want to track down your Irish roots, try to do as much research as you can before you arrive. Living relatives, family papers, and records in your own country are the first sources to tackle. Build up as complete a picture as you can of the ancestors who emigrated—full name, trade, religion, and which town or county they came from. (Many emigrants named their new homes after their former parish or town, which can be a clue). When you arrive, visit one of the organizations or genealogy centres in the county of origin. It is wise to make an appointment in advance, especially during the summer. The Republic's tourist office, Bord Fáilte, produces an information sheet on tracing your ancestors, which contains useful advice, lists of publications, and addresses. (Please enclose international reply coupons or a self-addressed stamped envelope if you write for advice.)

NORTHERN IRELAND ADDRESSES
Public Record Office of Northern Ireland, 66 Balmoral Avenue, Belfast BT9 6NY (tel: 028 9025 1318).
Ulster Historical Foundation, 12 College Square East, Belfast BT1 6DD (tel: 028 9033 2288).
Association of Ulster Genealogists and Record Agents, Glen Cottage, Glenamehan Road, Belfast BT4 2NP.

PROVINCIAL ADDRESSES
Clare Heritage Centre, Corofin, County Clare (tel: 065 6837955).
Mayo North Research and Heritage Centre, Enniscoe, Castlehill, Ballina (tel: 096 31809).
Roscommon Heritage and Genealogy Centre, Strokestown (*Open* May–Sep; tel: 078 33380).
Irish Family History Foundation, 1 Clarinda Park North, Dun Laoghaire, County Dublin.
Irish Family History Society, P.O. Box 36, Naas, County Kildare.

DUBLIN ADDRESSES
Genealogical Office, 2 Kildare Street, Dublin 2 (tel: 01 661 8811).
The Heraldic Museum—full of arms, banners, crests, and such like—is at the same address.
National Library, Kildare Street, Dublin 2 (tel: 01 661 8811).
National Archives, Bishop Street, Dublin 8 (tel: 01 478 3711).
Births, Deaths and Marriages, Joyce House, 8–11 Lombard Street East, Dublin 2 (tel: 01 671 1000).
Registry of Deeds, Henrietta Street, Dublin 1 (tel: 01 670 7500).
Genealogy Bookshop, 3 Nassau Street, Dublin 2.

75

Banners in the Heraldic Museum add a colourful touch to ancestral history

Hotels

THE SHELBOURNE Dublin's grandest hotel is no less than an institution. The 19th-century Shelbourne, on the most fashionable "Beaux Walk" stretch of St. Stephen's Green, is part of the nation's heritage; in the movie of Brian Moore's novel, *The Lonely Passion of Judith Hearne*, it is the ultimate proof of wealth and status. The Irish Free State's constitution was drafted here in an upper room. Despite its lofty pedigree, the Shelbourne is pleasantly unstuffy. Everybody is welcome, at least for a coffee or a drink in the Horseshoe Bar. For the restaurant, you are advised to dress up a little and remember your wallet.

CHEAPER ALTERNATIVES If you find the Shelbourne's tariffs are a bit steep, there are plenty of other options, though nothing is inexpensive in Dublin anymore. The best bet if you want somewhere within reach of most of the sights and stores is to stay south of the river, somewhere around the St. Stephen's Green area, or farther out in the pleasant residential suburb of Ballsbridge. Many attractive Georgian town houses have been stylishly converted into guesthouses and small hotels, where you can glimpse something of Dublin's former glory in an appropriate setting. The Georgian House is probably one of the best, and also best-located, of these, with a lively seafood restaurant. An excellent and refreshingly different style is provided at No. 31 Leeson Close, in an architect's former home (see panel).

Farther south, the tariffs will be lower and the buildings more recent, probably Victorian or Edwardian. Be prepared for a bus or taxi ride to the city centre. Some of the best are Butlers Town House, Raglan Lodge, Ariel House, and Merrion Hall. Elsewhere in the city, pick your location with care: Some areas are not particularly pleasant for walking after dark. The seedier dives around Connolly Station and off upper O'Connell Street are best avoided, and are not even particularly cheap. The Gresham Hotel, one of Dublin's best and longest-established, once in a

NUMBER 31

One of Dublin's most surprising guesthouses lies hidden behind a high stone wall in a quiet cul-de-sac off Leeson Street. The former home of a leading architect, Sam Stephenson, it is now a coveted, small B&B. The centre of these double town houses has been gutted to create a large, sunken sitting room with a small bar. Huge breakfasts are served in an upper dining room overlooking a roof garden billowing with exotic vegetation, while intriguing objects bestrew the house. The rooms are simple, but all have good bathrooms. The atmosphere is civilized, but relaxed.

The Shelbourne faces St. Stephen's Green

*The Gresham Hotel,
O'Connell Street*

prime location on O'Connell Street, now suffers from run-down surroundings.

If you want a hotel with all the trimmings, try one of the modern business hotels such as the Conrad or the Westbury. Buswell's, a favourite haunt of politicians and journalists, has more character and a certain 18th-century cachet. Jury's, the Dublin flagship of a well-known Irish hotel chain, or the Burlington can provide all possible facilities, including lively nightlife, in modern boxlike premises south of the river.

FARTHER OUT If you have a car, consider staying even farther out in the more peaceful suburbs, or on the coast, say in Dalkey or Blackrock. Parking in the city centre is always difficult, and a car is a constant security risk. Avondale House in Scribblestown is a good out-of-town choice, a former hunting lodge dating from the 1720s with a country-house atmosphere. There are many cheaper B&Bs in the coastal areas. It will be difficult to enjoy Dublin's night scene (or pubs) staying this far out, however.

HOSTELS AND SELF-CATERING If you are on a tight budget and want to stay centrally, consider a hostel. You may have to share a room, but an increasing number of decent, privately run hostel-style rooms are now available. Isaac's (see panel) is a good bet for young travellers. For slightly more comfort, Avalon House in Aungier Street (near the Carmelite Church) offers simple but stylish accommodation and a pleasant coffee shop.

Apartments and houses can be rented at all price levels, and some even have maid service. A number are listed in Bord Fáilte's self-catering (rentals) guide. There are no central campsites in Dublin: The nearest you'll get is somewhere south of Dun Laoghaire or in Donabate to the north of the city. Unofficial camping is not recommended and may be risky.

BOOK AHEAD Accommodation in Dublin is plentiful, but the best is not inexpensive and can fill up rapidly during special events or conferences. Book ahead if you can. The tourist office provides a booking service and will telephone around (for a fee) if you turn up on the spot. (See also Hotels and Restaurants, pages 269–283.)

ISAAC'S
This popular hostel, also known as the Dublin Tourist Hostel, can be found a block or two behind the Custom House on the north bank of the Liffey. It is an agreeable conversion of a wine warehouse dating back to the early 1700s, and as far as possible its architectural features have been kept intact. For simple accommodation at a low price it is hard to beat. The self-service restaurant (*Open* daily from 7.30AM, and to nonresidents) serves cheap, filling fare with an emphasis on organic and vegetarian dishes. There is music laid on in summer. A similar hostel (with the same name) exists in Cork.

*Outside the
Shelbourne Hotel*

DUBLIN CODDLE

4 slices of bacon
4 large sliced potatoes
4 large sausages
black pepper
2 onions, sliced
cornflour
Place the bacon, sausages, potatoes, and onion in a pot and cover with cold water. Bring to a boil and simmer gently for 1–2 hours until the meat is cooked. Thicken with cornflour, season with black pepper, and serve immediately with fresh soda bread.

Food and drink

A WIDER CHOICE Although Ireland cannot claim to be the gastronomic capital of the universe, the eating scene in Dublin is immeasurably better now than it used to be, with a far wider choice of cuisine, and more emphasis on healthy, high-quality ingredients rather than filling, high-fat dishes. Needless to say, there is plenty of fast food available, especially in areas north of the river. Most outlets are predictably indifferent, with the exception of a couple of good fish and chip shops (such as Burdock's) and pizza joints (like the Bad Ass Café). For gourmets, the city has plenty of choices in the classy town-house restaurants around St. Stephen's Green, most of which produce classic French *cuisine moderne* dishes, but you can expect to pay handsomely for the privilege there. The best of these (Patrick Guilbaud, The Commons, Thornton's) have earned their high reputation; others verge on pretension.

For several years now Dublin has been home to a number of very good ethnic restaurants—the Rajdoot and Shalimar produce interesting Indian food, the Imperial and the China-Sichuan are the best of the Chinese restaurants, while, for Italian food, Il Primo and Nico's are recommended. Besides foreign cuisine, though, Irish cooking is making a healthy comeback, so you may try a Dublin coddle (boiled sausages, bacon, onions, and potatoes in a thickened sauce; see panel) or oysters and Guinness. One of the most unusual restaurants serving Irish food is Gallagher's Boxty House, in the lively Temple Bar quarter. (A "boxty" is a sort of Irish potato pancake with all kinds of savoury fillings.) The ambience and decor are agreeable and the prices not at all expensive, hence its popularity, although the food could be more reliable.

PUBS Dublin pubs concentrate on drinking rather than food, but the demands of tourism have meant that more and more serve snacks at lunchtime, though the selection is rarely particularly imaginative. A civilized touch, however, is that most will serve coffee at any time of day, including, of course, an Irish coffee. The mystique surrounding the serving of Guinness is less overt here than you might

Stop for refreshment in a Dublin café, like this one in O'Connell Street

Two Irish favourites, oysters and Guinness

BROWN SODA BREAD
*550g (4.5 cups)
wholewheat flour
125g (1 cup) white flour
1 teaspoon salt
1 teaspoon bread soda
50g (0.3 cup) oatmeal
600ml (2.5 cups)
buttermilk*
Sieve all the dry
ingredients together. Make
a well in the centre, pour
in the buttermilk, and stir
until the mixture forms a
soft dough. Turn on a
floured surface and knead
lightly to form a round disk
roughly 35cm (15in) in
diameter. Cut a deep
cross into the dough with
a sharp knife. Place on a
buttered baking dish and
bake in the middle of the
oven, 220°C (425°F), for
15 minutes, then reduce
the temperature to 180°C
(350°F) for a further 25
minutes until rich and
crusty. Cool on a wire rack.

79

expect, but if you look as though you would appreciate it, a shamrock might be etched deftly into the creamy head.

CAFÉS For lunchtime snacks some of the most attractive restaurants are in museums or shopping centres, such as the National Gallery, Hugh Lane Municipal Gallery, Kilmainham Hospital, Dublin Castle, Kilkenny Shop, and the Powerscourt Townhouse. One place that cannot be ignored is that great institution known as Bewley's Café. There are four of them in Dublin altogether, set up by a Quaker family of tea and coffee importers over a century ago to enable customers to sample their products. The most famous, Bewley's Oriental Café, is on Grafton Street, a wonderful dark, mysterious emporium of stained glass and mahogany serving traditional food and staying open late. Upstairs is a quieter café area.

OTHER OPTIONS If you don't want to spend too much in the evenings, head for Temple Bar, which is young and upbeat. Restaurants here come and go with the wind, but some of the more long-lasting ones include the Elephant and Castle, and the Bad Ass Café.

If you want an excursion, there are several excellent restaurants in some of the coastal resorts: Morel's in Dun Laoghaire, Ayumi-Ya in Blackrock, or King Sitric in Howth are perhaps some of the best. Seafood is usually excellent. Check what days they close before you plan your excursion.

On Sundays, Dublin can be a desert as far as eating goes. Many of the good places are closed, and those that stay open are likely to be fully booked. If you are in the city on a weekend, plan your eating well ahead of time and make sure you have a table.

Cuisine more Italian than Irish is advertised on this wall in Cecilia Street

Shopping

MARKETS At the north end of Grafton Street is an eye-catching statue in bronze, affectionately known to Dubliners as "the tart with the cart." The subject, of course, is the famous Molly Malone (see panel), wheeling her wheelbarrow. To find today's Molly Malones, you will need to head for the old-fashioned street markets held in Moore Street (mostly selling fruit and vegetables, off Henry Street near the General Post Office), or alternatively the Liberties in Meath Street beyond Christ Church Cathedral, where dozens of stalls of inexpensive clothing and household goods are on sale.

SHOPS FOR VISITORS Most visitor shopping is done in rather different surroundings, either in the safe, if highly priced, confines of a modern hotel, or in one of the city's specialist shops. The main shopping area in the centre of town lies between Grafton Street and O'Connell Street. The big department stores are there—Clery's and Eason's north of the river (along with Marks and Spencer and bargain basement shops such as Dunne's in the Ilac Centre, or Arnotts), and more exclusive Brown Thomas in Grafton Street. Many international chain stores such as Benetton, Next, and Principles can also be found around pedestrianized Grafton Street. Smaller side streets contain most specialist craft and fashion shops. Nassau Street is a particularly good area to head for if you are looking for typical Irish craft products such as ceramics, knitwear, tweed, linen, crystal, or Celtic jewellery. The outlets vary considerably in quality, one of the more classy being the excellent Kilkenny Shop, which has a fine stock of traditional Irish crafts. Others worth checking out (also situated in Nassau Street) are the exclusive tweed and clothing store, Kevin and Howlin, the Sweater Shop for Aran knitwear, Blarney Woollen Mills, and the House of Ireland. For traditional Irish music, Claddagh Records (2 Cecilia Street) and Celtic Note (Nassau Street) are among the best shops.

MOLLY MALONE
In Dublin's fair city where the girls are so pretty I first set my eyes on sweet Molly Malone. She wheeled a wheelbarrow through streets broad and narrow Crying "Cockles and mussels, alive, alive-O!"

80

Nassau Street has a fine range of shops, from second-hand bookshops to retail outlets more geared to visitors

Dublin boasts a number of shopping malls. One of the best is in the imaginatively reconstructed shell of an 18th-century building, called the Powerscourt Townhouse, with splendid plasterwork ceilings and exterior facade (just off Grafton Street). Another central shopping mall is on St. Stephen's Green, an unmissable, modern, greenhouse-like structure with yet more shops and cafés. Tierney's has one of the better craft displays here.

Bookshops are legion in this literary city, most of them around St. Stephen's or College Greens or the quaysides. Several of these sell collectable second-hand volumes. Fred Hanna's (27/29 Nassau Street), Greene's (Clare Street), Hodges Figgis (54 Dawson Street), and the Winding Stair (40 Lower Ormonde Quay) are some of the best known, besides the larger and more general retailers, Waterstone's and Eason's. For antiques, head for Francis Street in the Liberties (beyond Christ Church Cathedral).

BEYOND THE CENTRE Out of the city centre, the suburbs of Blackrock and Dalkey have their own shopping complexes and markets, not necessarily worth a special trip. The malls at Tallaght and Blanchardstown, however, merit a visit. Closer into town on Pearse Street (take a bus two or three stops from Pearse Station) is the Tower Design Centre, a 19th-century sugar-refining tower now run by the Irish Development Authority and housing about 35 separate craft enterprises producing souvenirs in fashions, stained glass, painted silk, knitwear, and jewellery.

PRACTICALITIES Shopping hours in Dublin are generally Monday to Saturday, 9AM–6PM, with some of the smaller shops geared to visitors (as well as Marks and Spencer and Brown Thomas) also opening on Sundays. For non-EU residents, the VAT waiver scheme called Cashback makes high-taxed Irish goods more attractive, although there is a fair bit of red tape involved in claiming this back at Dublin or Shannon Airport. Collect a form as you shop, and have it stamped when you leave the country.

Shopping is an enduring pastime for these two Dubliners

A crowd-pulling display in Brown Thomas, Grafton Street, one of Dublin's most famous shops

Dublin

82

JOYCEAN PUBS

In The Bailey (Duke Street) Joyce fans can find the door of No. 7 Eccles Street, the fictional home of Leopold Bloom in *Ulysses*, rescued by the pub's proprietor, John Ryan, from a builder's skip. At Davy Byrne's, you can be served a faithful version of the lunch Bloom enjoyed there on 16 June, 1904 (Bloomsday)—a glass of burgundy and a Gorgonzola sandwich.

The capital has a thriving youth culture

Nightlife

DECISIONS, DECISIONS Dublin is famous for its pubs—over 900 of them if you care to count—and for its theatre. These form the core of the city's evening entertainments. Like most capital cities, however, it can offer much more—many kinds of music, from rock to classical, around two dozen cinema screens, and a whole host of nightclubs and wine bars. Some larger hotels offer well-advertised cabaret shows, Jury's being the most widely publicized.

Over the last few years a host of new clubs has sprung up around the city centre, especially in the Temple Bar area. The Kitchen, owned by U2, and the dance hothouse known as PoD are two of the most popular. They are at their liveliest on weekends (Thursday to Sunday) and get going after 10PM. Check out also Lillie's Bordello, off Grafton Street, and Rí-Rá off South Great George's Street.

PUBS Pubs and bars are scattered all over the city and take innumerable forms, some modern and plastic, others ancient and Victorian, most of them somewhere in between, suitably "modernized" for visitors. The "pub of the moment" is difficult to pin down, with fashions changing, although regulars may stick to one or two favourites all the time. Most of the well-known places are very busy at night despite the high cost of alcohol in Ireland. They seem generally good-tempered, but they can be very noisy and boisterous. Some have notable gay scenes; others may be popular with drug users, of which Dublin has many.

Some of the best-known and most "characterful" bars on the south side are Doheny and Nesbitt (5 Lower Baggot Street), O'Donoghue's (Merrion Row), Toner's (139 Lower Baggot Street), Neary's (1 Chatham Street); farther west are the Stag's Head (1 Dame Court, off Dame Street) and Mother Redcap's (Back Lane, off High Street). Near the Liffey, upriver from O'Connell Street, the Brazen

In 1897, the Star of Ł. music hall changed its name to the Empire Palace. A few years later it became the Olympia Theatre, as it remains to this day.

THE ABBEY THEATRE
The Abbey is one of Dublin's most classic traditions, yet it has staged some controversial productions. The first performance of J. M. Synge's *The Playboy of the Western World* in 1907 caused riots because an Irishman used the word "shift" (meaning petticoat) on stage. Police had to be called to protect Synge from the outraged audience for over a week. In 1926, O'Casey's play *The Plough and the Stars* caused a similar uproar when the national flag was shown in the presence of a prostitute. After a later production of this play in 1951, the theatre burned down (accidentally).

Head (20 Lower Bridge Street) and Ryan's (28 Parkgate Street) still have old-fashioned interiors. Ryan's is a confection of mahogany and brass unchanged since 1896. The Brazen Head claims to be Ireland's oldest, where Wolfe Tone and Robert Emmet dreamed of Irish independence. Davy Byrne's and the Bailey (both in Duke Street) have Joycean associations that keep them eternally popular.

MUSIC AND THEATRE Many of the pubs offer evening music sessions, Irish traditional, jazz, etc. Whelan's on Wexford Street is a top live-music venue for local and UK bands. Dublin, of course, has launched many a rock or pop star on the way to fame and fortune: U2, the Chieftains, the Dubliners, Sinéad O'Connor, and Chris de Burgh have all performed in Dublin's nightspots on many occasions. For more classical music, head for the National Concert Hall in St. Stephen's Green; the Royal Hospital at Kilmainham also stages a number of concerts and evening events. One of the theatres offers music on weekends—Midnight at the Olympia on Fridays and Saturdays involves dancing between aisles of plush red seating. Earlier in the evening (and during the week) it usually offers an assorted range of light entertainment. The Gaiety is similarly popular. For more heavyweight theatre, head for the Gate or the Abbey, where Dublin's great theatrical tradition started. The annex to the Abbey, called the Peacock, and the Project in Temple Bar, specialize in avant-garde or experimental work.

FILM There isn't much of an art film scene in Dublin, although some films may be released three to four months later in Dublin, than in New York. Most of the two dozen screens on or near O'Connell Street are fairly run-of-the-mill or downright seedy. For an alternative, head for the Irish Film Centre in Temple Bar. There are some cinemas in the suburbs (such as in Blanchardstown and Tallaght). To find out what's going on in Dublin, get the *Irish Times*, which has daily listings, or the magazine *Big Issue*, sold by street vendors all over the city.

The Brazen Head

Ireland's Oldest Pub

ESTD. 1198

...ns sightsee-
...g bus tours of Dublin
using open-top vehicles
(covered in wet weather).
The heritage tour visits 10
locations near city sights,
and with an all-day ticket
you can hop on or off at
any point. Buses run
hourly between 10AM and
4PM in high season.

84

Practical points

WHAT'S HAPPENING Dublin is an exceptionally friendly city and most people will be only too happy to help you out. Dublin Tourism Centre (tel: 01 605 7799; www.visitdublin.com; *open* Mon–Fri 9–5.30; later in high season) is in Suffolk Street. It is usually crowded, but there are many leaflets to pick up, not all of which are free. Walking tours around the city are also advertised here, and can be fun and informative. Another useful start to city orientation is the Dublin Experience show at Trinity College, on view during the summer months.

If you are short of time, plan carefully and cut out extraneous attractions. Some of the big sights close for part of the weekend or on Monday, and Dublin Castle is occasionally shut altogether. Ask before you set off. Things not to miss are the Castle, Trinity College, and the National Museum and Gallery. Try to catch some of the Georgian architecture around Merrion Square and St. Stephen's Green, and the two cathedrals to the west of the city. If you can, visit Kilmainham Gaol and Hospital, and walk in Phoenix Park. Art lovers will want to find Hugh Lane's Gallery, and, if the lighter side of culture appeals, head for the Guinness Brewery and Storehouse. Choose a promising-looking day for excursions to Howth or Dalkey; the best beaches lie around Killiney Bay or Sandymount (some dangerous currents). There is also a magnificent stretch of sand on North Bull Island.

If you happen to be in Dublin during a big match, you'll certainly be aware of it. Gaelic games are played at Croke Park, north of the city centre. The All-Ireland Hurling and Football Finals take place in September. St. Patrick's Day (17 March) is a fine time to be here, with parades and other happenings, although celebrations are smaller than in New York and Boston, for example. To find out what's going on, get a listings magazine (the best is *In Dublin*).

*Dublin's coat of arms
embellishes this
street sign*

CITY TRANSPORTATION A bus map is worth getting. Although the central areas are reasonably compact, Dublin can make you footsore, and hopping on a bus occasionally may be welcome. The routes, if not always the schedules, are more or less adhered to. Most of them start from Busáras, the main station, just north of the river near the Custom House, or from the streets near College Green. If you plan to do much exploring, it is worth getting a pass lasting one or several days. The words *An Lár* on the front of a bus indicate it is going to the city centre. For longer trips, contact Bus Eireann's offices at the central bus station in Store Street. A branch of Thomas Cook (118 Grafton Street, tel: 01 677 1721) can answer general travel inquiries. For youth travel and student discounts, contact the USIT office on Aston Quay.

For travel to the nearest coast, the DART (Dublin Area Rapid Transit) route, a single rail line between Bray and Howth, is an entertaining excursion with fine coastal views. You can catch the DART trains at Connolly, Tara Street, or Pearse stations. For train services farther afield (between Dundalk and Arklow), you should head for the main station, Connolly. Heuston Station serves the western and southern regions.

Taxis can be hailed in transit, but they also queue on some of the main streets, and are fairly expensive. Parking is always difficult and costly in the city centre. Never leave anything remotely valuable in your car.

CRIME The problems of urban life have caused a sharp rise in street crime generally, exacerbated by drug and alcohol abuse. Conspicuous visitors are easy prey. Don't carry too much money, and don't stray into unknown areas off the main tourist trail. The streets west of St. Patrick's Cathedral, or many north of the river, are not advisable for unscheduled sauntering.

ROCK 'N' STROLL
Self-guided walks around Dublin inevitably focus on its Georgian architecture or literary associations, or perhaps pub crawls for the thirsty. An alternative themed walk is the Rock 'n' Stroll Guide, which leads its followers to the principal places in Dublin associated with the contemporary music scene. Revisit The Chieftains' first gig at the Gresham Hotel, Mary Black's stamping ground at the Olympia, or U2's launch pad in Mount Temple Comprehensive School! Pick up the tour guide in any tourist office.

O'Connell Bridge, at the heart of the city

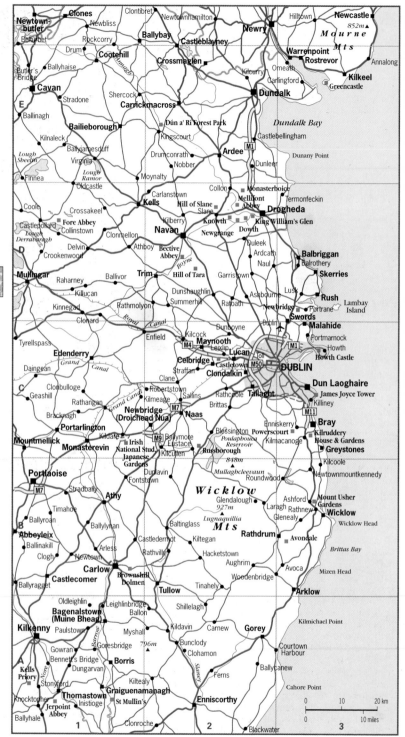

EASTERN COUNTIES The counties immediately around Dublin constitute the Pale, the area most strongly influenced by English rule from Norman times onwards. What lay beyond the Pale was less easily subjugated and often perceived (accurately) as a threat to English interests. The pull of the capital ensures these eastern counties still receive a steady flow of visitors, though scenically (with the exception of Wicklow) they are not Ireland's most exciting regions. There are, though, a good many reasons to spend time here. They are enormously rich in history, layer upon layer of it from prehistoric to recent times. The famous passage graves at Newgrange are Ireland's best-known neolithic site. Then there are Celtic High Crosses, the evocative monastic settlement of Glendalough, many later abbeys and churches, castles, and several of Ireland's grandest houses and gardens. Horse lovers will want to visit the Curragh at Kildare and the nearby National Stud. For walkers, the heather moors and wooded glens of the Wicklow Mountains bristle with opportunities. If you are thinking of a beach holiday in Ireland, the drier, sunnier climate of the southeast makes a seaside stay a reasonable gamble instead of a long shot. The best beaches in this region are in County Wicklow.

County Louth is the smallest of the 32 counties of Ireland. Inland, it echoes the drumlin country of those other border counties, Cavan and Monaghan, a gentle, placid landscape of little hills and lakes. Its easterly section is more dramatic, a precursor of the Mountains of Mourne that loom enticingly across Carlingford Lough. The Cooley Peninsula, setting for one of Ireland's greatest epics (*Táin Bo Cuailgne*—the Cattle Raid of Cooley), makes a fine excursion, where the lakeshore village of Carlingford is one of the most delightful low-key holiday bases, managing to avoid (for the most part) the strains of other border towns such as Dundalk or Monaghan. Drogheda, Louth's other main town, seems to have weathered its Cromwellian torments more resiliently than most and amply repays a stop, or even a stay. All around it, stretching into County Meath, is a rich cluster of prehistoric and Celtic sites, great abbeys and castles,

The gentle aspect of the Wicklow Mountains

THE LITTLE GENTLEMAN IN BLACK VELVET

This favourite Jacobite (supporter of the deposed King James II of England) toast during the reign of Queen Anne is still drunk in certain nationalist and Catholic circles. The "little gentleman" is the mole that is alleged to have killed William III. When, while out riding in England on 21 February, 1702, his horse, Sorrel, stumbled on a mole-hill and threw him, badly fracturing his collarbone. The king died in London two weeks later. If this sounds a heartless tradition, the anti-Catholic toasts of the Orange Order are much more savage. The 19th-century British prime minister, Sir Robert Peel, apparently drank to these in his early life, and became nicknamed "Orange Peel" by the Irish.

The lonely Vale of Glenmacnass in the Wicklow Mountains just south of Dublin. Glenmacnass means "the valley of the sons of Neasa"

the Hills of Slane and Tara suffused with legends and national symbolism. The Boyne River is a place of pilgrimage for many tracing the progress of that famous battle of 1690 along alternate banks, although this was only one of numerous skirmishes between Jacobite and Williamite troops in those troubled years.

DUBLIN'S HINTERLANDS Closer to Dublin, the coast is studded with small fishing ports, most fairly dull. Howth and Malahide are the ones to visit—the first for its breezy headland views and castle gardens, the second for an interestingly furnished castle and art collection. The capital's immediate hinterland is County Kildare, where the rolling, springy grassland provides pasture and an exercise track for dozens of fine-boned thoroughbreds. This is the heart of Ireland's bloodstock industry, one of the more solid mainstays of Ireland's economy. Keen followers of horse-racing may want to time their arrival carefully to coincide with one of the big annual races. Naas (the county seat) holds its big race meeting in April, at Punchestown Racecourse. The Curragh, famed for horse-racing since time immemorial, hosts all of Ireland's classic events—the Oaks, the Derby, and the St. Leger.

Naas, Kildare's county town, is near enough to all this to benefit from horse-borne prosperity and far enough from Dublin's suburban tentacles to have a spirit of its own. It makes one of the best places to pause and plan a route. If horses aren't your scene, you can search for Round Towers and Celtic High Crosses, follow the great canal routes that crisscross the county, or investigate the mournful Bog of Allen, where there is an interesting interpretative centre explaining the significance of bogland ecology: Peatland World, Lullymore, near Rathangan (tel: 045 60133). Kildare's most important stately home is Castletown; one of Ireland's largest houses, Castletown is built in the Palladian style.

South of Dublin lies County Wicklow, one of the capital's favourite "lungs." A glance at its topography soon indicates why—the Wicklow Mountains reach a significant altitude by Irish standards (Lugnaquillia is Ireland's third-highest peak at nearly 1,000m/3,039ft) and contain

The tower of Trim Abbey, as seen from the town's castle

some very beautiful and unpopulated scenery. The coastline, too, has attractions—breezy headlands and great sweeps of sand stretching from Bray southward, the best being Brittas Bay south of Wicklow Head. A journey over the central heights is most rewarding; choose one of the routes around the Sally Gap and take in the awe-inspiring views around Glencree and Glenmacnass, or seek out the hidden lakes of Tay and Dan. Powerscourt Gardens and Russborough House shouldn't be missed; ensure you time your visit to find them open. The other "unmissable" is Glendalough, a collection of ancient monastic buildings in a gorgeous setting. Wicklow's impressive range of sights also includes the great gardens of Kilruddery and Mount Usher, and Charles Stewart Parnell's house at Avondale, now a forest park and museum to his memory. There is no shortage of excellent accommodation or restaurants in County Wicklow; its nearness to Dublin ensures a steady year-round trade and the county exudes a quietly prosperous air.

The most famous parts of the Boyne Valley and the holiday resorts of the east coast are also pretty well equipped, and County Kildare has a number of good places to stay or eat. The less popular regions of Louth and Meath, however, offer rather patchy choices and a fair amount of forward planning is necessary to stay anywhere pleasant. If you have time to spare, it's worth reaching Carlingford.

LEINSTER TABOOS

In ancient Ireland, the lives of kings and other notabilities were hedged in by taboos, doubtless going back into the mists of prehistory. Death was the inexorable outcome of these being violated one by one, a subject beloved of the dramatic storytellers of medieval Ireland. Five taboos recorded for the king of the Leinstermen included those forbidding him from:

• travelling widdershins (counterclockwise) around the Wicklow Hills on a Wednesday;
• sleeping between Dublin and the Dodder River with his head facing to one side;
• setting up camp for nine days on the plains of Cualu (Bray);
• travelling alone on the road to Dublin on a Monday;
• riding on a dirty, black-hooved horse over the plain of Mullaghmast (County Kildare).

The meaning of the interwoven spirals, found on several stones at Newgrange, remains unclear

THE BOYNE VALLEY

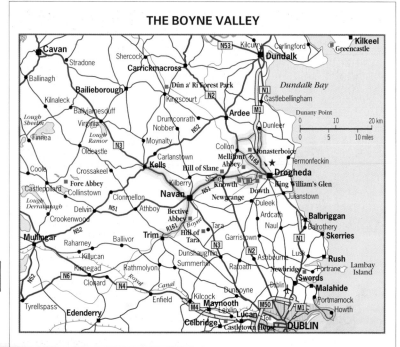

From prehistory to 1690 along the Boyne Valley

A drive through the past from prehistoric times to Ireland's most significant battle site, whose divisive echoes reverberate more than 300 years later in the streets of Belfast and London. (It is recommended that you follow the precise route of this drive on a detailed, large-scale map.)

Head north from Drogheda on the N1. Clearly signed to the west are the High Crosses and Round Tower of **Monasterboice** (see page 106). Looping back south again by the Mattock Valley, watch for signs to the remains of **Mellifont Abbey**, in a maze of quiet lanes (see page 105). About 6.5km (4mi) west of **Drogheda** (well signed off the N51 from the town) is the historic **King William's Glen**, site of the famous Battle of the Boyne in

1690. An orange and green sign by the river marks the main site of conflict. A marked trail from the Townley Hall Estate (the extensive grounds of a Georgian mansion) leads to a viewing place above the battleground showing where the opposing armies camped, and where William's army crossed the river from the north at two separate points, taking the forces of James II on the southern banks by surprise. An explanatory diagram and display board outlines the battle manoeuvres. It is worth getting a leaflet or map (available from local tourist offices) showing the battle sites if you want to explore in detail, since dodging back and forth across the river can be disorientating. The battle route passes the Boyne Navigation Canal, part of a grand scheme to connect Ireland's major waterways.

The battle was a historical landmark for many reasons, a minor point of interest being that it was the last conflict in Europe in which opposing monarchs played an active military role; William III himself narrowly escaped death from a sniper's bullet on the morning of the battle. His soldiers used sprigs of leaves to

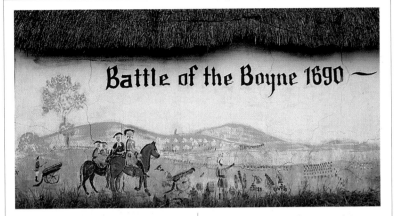

A mural on a cottage near Drogheda celebrates the famous battle

distinguish themselves from the Jacobite forces, since they wore no clearly recognizable uniforms. As they crossed the river they played the Orange marching tune *Lillebulero*. Gradually, James's forces were pushed back south towards **Duleek**, where one of Ireland's oldest stone churches once stood. St. Ciarán's was built in the 5th century soon after Christianity first reached Ireland. The remains now visible date from later centuries. The final skirmish of the Battle of the Boyne took place at Duleek, and William is thought to have spent the night after the battle near there. Buried in the churchyard is Lord John Bellew, a Catholic who died at the subsequent Battle of Aughrim. He was shot in the stomach and is said to have died bravely, facing his enemies.

Farther west lie some of Ireland's most important neolithic remains, including the passage graves of Dowth, Knowth, and Newgrange, collectively known as **Brugh na Boinne** (see pages 108–109). Besides the main tombs, at least 40 other burial places are believed to lie in and around this fertile farmland within a strategic bend of the Boyne River. Some of these sites have not yet been excavated, although from the Newgrange tomb several strange humps and mounds are clearly visible in the surrounding landscape.

Kells (formerly known as **Ceanannus Mór**), up the Blackwater Valley, is best known for the *Book of Kells*, a splendid illuminated manuscript now housed in Trinity College Dublin (see page 73). Many other antiquities and sacred sites are clustered along the Boyne Valley around **Slane**, **Navan**, **Tara**, seat of the High Kings of Ireland, and **Trim** (see their respective entries throughout this chapter; the Hill of Tara is on page 107). Castles dating from more recent times are scattered throughout the region. Trim itself has an enormous fortress, the largest dating from Norman times. The evocative ruins of **Bective Abbey** are also worth looking for on the peaceful meadows by the river between Trim and Navan.

This simple church at Kells dates from the first millennium

▶▶ Avoca
863B

Avoca, a pretty hamlet of neat white cottages in a wooded setting by the meeting of the Avonbeg and Avonmore rivers, is the home of Avoca Handweavers. They produce some of Ireland's most energetically marketed craft products from a group of whitewashed buildings containing the oldest surviving handweaving mill in Ireland, dating from 1723. The business was built up over 40 years by the Wynne sisters, who claim to have invented the car blanket! Bright tweeds of natural fibres are manufactured (mostly on modern machinery) and made into hats, suits, and voluminous cloaks. High-quality Avoca products can be found all over the country. Bus tours converge to watch weaving demonstrations, enjoy good lunches or teas in the café, and (perhaps) take something home with them.

Avoca Handweavers give daily demonstrations of their craft

▶▶ Avondale
863B

Deep in one of County Wicklow's most beautifully wooded areas is the Georgian birthplace and home of the 19th-century politician Charles Stewart Parnell, now a museum dedicated to his memory. Parnell was one of Ireland's greatest campaigners for democracy and land reform. Though at first regarded by the English as a dangerous revolutionary because of his association with the Irish Land League, he eventually won Gladstone's abiding respect and persuaded many people that Home Rule was a viable option for Ireland. His career foundered abruptly after his long-standing liaison with the wife of a fellow Member of Parliament became public knowledge (see panel). Soon after divorce proceedings were instituted, Parnell was ousted from his political position and died of strain and ill-health. A film relates the background to Parnell's life story and the history of the house, which is interestingly furnished and contains many touching mementoes and political cartoons. Some of his eloquent love letters to Kitty O'Shea are framed on the walls, as is the extensive Parnell family tree, many of whose members died tragically of madness, vaccination, fevers, or grief.

The grounds were taken over by the state in 1904 as a forestry school. Much research on arboriculture is conducted there and the forest park is full of fine and flourishing trees of many different species. Walks lead through the 200ha (500-acre) park by the riverside.

PARNELL AND KITTY O'SHEA
Parnell fell in love with Kitty, wife of Captain Willy O'Shea, by whom she had three children. It was not a successful marriage, however, and the two spent long periods apart, constantly impecunious. She first met Parnell outside the House of Commons in London, and the attraction was instant. Within a short time the two were secretly living together, and Parnell fathered her remaining children. O'Shea put up with the situation at first, hoping for the inheritance from Kitty's wealthy aunt. When his chances were dashed, he sued for divorce. (See also pages 42–43.)

▶ Bray 863C

Bray is a convenient place for Dublin's citizens to get a breath of sea air, though it cannot be described as the most exciting piece of Ireland's coastline. It is the southerly terminus of the DART suburban railroad line from Dublin, so is easily reached without a car. The best views are from Bray Head, the final projection of the Wicklow range, from where the Great and Little Sugar Loaf mountains can be seen. North of Bray is the long sandy beach of Killiney Bay.

Bray has literary associations with James Joyce, who lived briefly at 1 Martello Terrace, which featured in *A Portrait of the Artist as a Young Man*. It is now privately owned and not generally open to the public. A more accessible place of interest is **Kilruddery House and Gardens▶** (tel: 01 286 2777; *open* May, Jun, and Sep, afternoons only. *Admission: inexpensive*) to the south of the resort, a rare example of 17th-century landscaping. Ponds, avenues, parterres, and hedges are laid out with mathematical precision. The house dates from the 1650s (extensively remodelled in the 1820s) and contains many interesting features—Grinling Gibbons carving, Chippendale furniture, and a water-powered stable clock.

93

▶▶ Carlingford 863E

The most enjoyable place on the Cooley peninsula (see page 96) is Carlingford, between the green slopes of Slieve Foye and the blue waters of the lake, with the Mourne Mountains beyond. This delightful village is by far the best base in the area, with several excellent, inexpensive pubs and guesthouses. For its modest size, it has some imposing monuments, indicating that it was a place of some significance during the Middle Ages. King John's Castle stands on the north side of the harbour, a massive D-shaped fortress dating from the 13th century. Its opposite number is Greencastle, on the Northern Irish side of the lake. In the village itself are Taafe's Castle and the Mint, both fortified houses, and the old town hall, or Tholsel, an arched gateway.

Avondale House is famous as the birthplace of Charles Stewart Parnell. In the surrounding Forest Park you may be fortunate enough to catch sight of an otter

DROGHEDA ALE

"Of one part of its manufactures, every traveller must speak with gratitude—of the ale namely, which is as good as the best brewed in the sister kingdom…And while satisfying himself of this fact, the philosophic observer cannot but ask, why ale should not be as good elsewhere as at Drogheda: is the water of the Boyne the only water in Ireland whereof ale can be made?"

William Makepeace Thackeray (1842)

The banner of a local fishermen's guild now in the Millmount Museum, Drogheda

▶▶▶ Castletown House 862C

*Celbridge, Co. Kildare, tel: 01 628 8252, www.heritageireland.ie
Open: Apr–Sep, Mon–Fri 10–6, Sat 11–6, Sun 2–6; Oct,
Mon–Sat 10–5, Sun 2–5; Nov–Mar, Sun 2–5. Admission:
inexpensive*

This huge stately home is rated as one of the finest examples of Palladian (classical) architecture in the Republic. It has many intriguing features, and has been extensively restored by the Irish Georgian Society. It was built in 1722 for William Connolly, Speaker of the Irish House of Commons, who made a fortune from forfeited estates after the Battle of the Boyne—it is hardly surprising that local attitudes to the house have been somewhat ambivalent. Designed by Alessandro Galilei in the style of an Italian villa, it contains wonderful plasterwork by the Francini brothers, and a sumptuous Pompeiian Long Gallery with splendidly hideous Murano chandeliers. The extensive grounds feature clipped yew trees and a folly obelisk. Though no longer lived in, its contents clearly reveal the character and tastes of its former owners. Lady Louisa Connolly, who married in 1758 at the age of 15, was one of its most influential collectors and decorators. An extravagant woman in some ways, she appears more compassionate and socially aware than many of her class, declaring when faced with the gargantuan banquet menus of the time, "It can never be right or useful that one set of people should be gorged with food and the other part in want."

▶▶ Drogheda 862D

This was originally a Viking town, later expanded into one of Hugh de Lacy's principal Norman strongholds, although little remains of the old town walls. In 1412, the two parts of the town on either side of the Boyne were united by charter to become the largest English town in Ireland; something of this ancient medieval pattern can still be seen in the hilly streets. The Millmount to the south side is topped by an 18th-century military barracks and fort, with a view of the northern part of the town and the viaduct.

Drogheda stands at the lowest bridging point of the Boyne River, just a short distance from the site of the famous battle of 1690. Wartime violence was nothing new; in 1649 Drogheda saw one of Cromwell's bloodiest assaults. Women and children who took refuge in one of its churches were burned alive and the defending garrison, driven south of the river to the

hilltop Millmount Fort, were massacred after their surrender. The garrison commander, an English royalist, was battered to death with his own wooden leg. "I think that we put to the sword altogether about 2,000 men," Cromwell wrote smugly. "It is right that God alone should have all the glory." Today the Millmount Fort houses a strangely peaceful collection of items in the excellent, privately run **Millmount Museum▶▶** (tel: 041 983 3097; *open* Mon–Sat 10–5.30, Sun 2.30–5. *Admission: inexpensive*)—medieval guild banners, old trade machinery and tools, and a coracle made of willow and leather. Other sections of this garrison have been converted into craft studios and a restaurant.

Over the river again, several buildings in the densely packed main town catch the eye: the 1224 Magdalene Tower, last remnants of a Dominican friary; the fine 13th-century St. Laurence Gate, surmounted by two drum towers; the little chapel of the Siena Convent; and the Tholsel, an 18th-century town hall now used as a bank. The two churches of St. Peter's are also worth a look, the Protestant one for its grim "cadaver" gravestone, the Catholic one for the famous shrine of St. Oliver Plunkett (see panel on page 114), primate of all Ireland, whose blackened head was rescued from the flames after his execution at Tyburn (London) for high treason (his crime was simply unrepentant Catholicism).

Despite these somewhat grisly memories, Drogheda is an attractive place, with some good music pubs (notably Carberry's on North Strand and McHugh's on Lawrence Street) and it makes a convenient base for exploring the rich heritage of the Boyne Valley.

DROGHEDA AND CROMWELL

The atrocities committed by Cromwell's troops are well documented in many sources, although the precise number of casualties is hard to establish. Yet the municipal records of Drogheda on both the day before *and the day after* the alleged massacre in 1649 deal with the vexatious topic of street lighting, and make no mention of Cromwell's frightful conduct, even in cowed acquiescence. It is indeed an odd omission. There is no doubt that some of Cromwell's actions have been exaggerated for propaganda purposes, though he amply earned his hated reputation in Ireland.

95

Castletown House, considered by some to be the finest 18th-century mansion in the Republic

THE LONG WOMAN'S GRAVE

Near the Windy Gap on the Cooley Peninsula a plaque relates the strange tale of the Long Woman's Grave. A man courted a tall Spanish beauty, telling her he owned all the lands that could be seen from a high place. She married him and came to Ireland, then asked him to show her his inheritance. He brought her to the Windy Gap, where the views are closely obstructed by cliffs. She died of shock and is buried in the Long Woman's Grave.

Colimore Harbour in Dalkey, not far south of Dun Laoghaire

▶ Dundalk
862E

Dundalk is a border town, uncomfortably close to the most sensitive section of the Northern Ireland frontier. However, it is able to boast a few features of interest, the most noteworthy building being its **Cathedral of St. Patrick▶** (*Open* daily, 8–6), a pastiche of King's College Chapel, Cambridge, that has rich mosaics inside. A museum and interpretative centre, which are housed in an old 18th-century distillery, relate the history of County Louth.

Just outside of the town, there is a huge bird reserve at **Dundalk Bay▶**, where thousands of wading birds can be found searching for food and shelter among the mudflats. North of the town, a few minutes' drive takes you into the lovely scenery of the hilly, granite **Cooley Peninsula▶ ▶**, attractive in its own right, but also overlooking tempting views of the Mountains of Mourne across the lough that divides the Republic from Northern Ireland. Cooley is associated with one of Ireland's best-known myths, the Cattle Raid of Cooley, in which Queen Maeve, who is jealous of her husband's prize white bull, attempts to take the brown bull of Cooley by force. Cuchulainn, the Hound of Ulster, becomes the hero of the hour, but is mortally wounded during the battle (see pages 27–28). Curiosities on the Cooley Peninsula include the giant Proleek Dolmen, accessible via a footpath from the Ballymascanlon House Hotel, and the Windy Gap, a mountain pass closely hemmed in by cliffs and crags, and scene of an incident in the Cattle Raid epic.

Dun Laoghaire's coat of arms clearly shows the town's seafaring connections

▶ Dun Laoghaire   863C

Visitors from abroad have difficulty either spelling or pronouncing the name ("Dun Leary") of this major entry port into the Republic. Its former name (Kingstown) commemorated the English George IV, who visited in 1821. Its Irish name refers to an earlier monarch, the 5th-century High King of Tara, Laoghaire, who allowed St. Patrick to set up his mission in Ireland. When the harbour was constructed by the Scot, John Rennie, in the early 19th century, its vast granite piers were the largest in the world. Besides its commercial traffic, Dun Laoghaire is a prestigious yachting centre. Apart from catching ferries, visitors stray to this Victorian town of brightly painted houses to look at the **National Maritime Museum**▶ (tel: 01 280 0969; *open* May–Sep, Tue–Sun 1–5. *Admission: inexpensive*), in the former Mariners Church on Haigh Terrace, which houses a French longboat captured at Bantry, County Cork, in 1796, and the old optic from the Baily Lighthouse on Howth Head.

The **James Joyce Martello Tower**▶▶ (tel: 01 280 9265; *open* Apr–Oct, Mon–Sat 10–1 and 2–5, Sun 2–6; Nov–Mar by appointment. *Admission: moderate*) at Sandycove is another place of interest. Joyce spent a brief and disturbing time here with the poet-surgeon, Oliver St. John Gogarty, who later appeared as Buck Mulligan in *Ulysses*. Apparently, one of the guests had a nightmare and fired several shots into the fireplace of the room where they were sleeping. Gogarty then shot at a row of saucepans above Joyce's head, shouting "Leave him to me!" Joyce left the next morning. The Martello Tower houses a small museum of Joycean memorabilia. The gunpowder magazine (*Open* Apr–Oct) now houses the Joyce Library and Joyce's death mask, made on 13 January, 1941. Close by is the Forty Foot Pool mentioned in *Ulysses*, a natural seawater swimming hole where nude bathing was once permitted, for men only. Nearby **Dalkey**▶ (pronounced Dawkey) is an attractive resort with ancient fortified mansions and summer boat trips to Dalkey Island, a bird sanctuary and home to a herd of wild goats.

A detail from the Christ in Majesty *sculpture, in Dun Laoghaire*

97

THE VANISHING STONE

The antiquarian, W. F. Wakeman, noted in 1893 that a "celebrated inscribed stone, which was supposed to mark the grave of an Irish monarch, gradually disappeared from the *Rightfert*, or 'King's Cemetery,' at Glendalough. Bit by bit it was sold to tourists by the lying 'guides' (so called) who infest that time-hallowed spot."

TRADITIONAL FARE

An unsubstantiated story tells how Grace O'Malley, the famous 16th-century pirate queen from the west of Ireland, came on a visit to Howth and found the gates of the castle barred against her. She then abducted the young heir, and promised to return him only on condition that a place should always be laid at the family table for any unexpected guests—a practice still scrupulously followed to this day.

▶▶▶ Glendalough   862B

Glendalough, tel: 0404 45325, www.heritageireland.com
Open: mid-Mar–mid-Oct, daily 9.30–6; mid-Oct–mid-Mar,
daily 9.30–5; last admission 45 minutes before closing
Admission: inexpensive

This collection of monastic remains is one of the most important in Ireland. Bus tours visit it from Dublin, and the crowds have brought about a tawdry rash of souvenir shops, pubs, and cafés in the local villages, along with plenty of guesthouses and hotels. Once away from this, however, the utter peace and beauty of the location are captivating, perhaps more than the ruins themselves. It is easy to see why St. Kevin (see page 115) sought solitude here in the 6th century, but his plans were somewhat thwarted. Beset by acolytes and lovelorn women, he eventually set up a large religious settlement here, which was attacked by Vikings in later centuries and overrun by English forces in 1398, after which its influence declined.

The ruins stand around two lakes in a beautiful wooded valley sheltered by great spurs of the Wicklow Mountains. The main concentration can be seen near the Lower Lake, by the visitor centre, where traffic converges. This modern building contains an exhibition of religious antiquities and an audio-visual presentation of monastic life in Ireland. From there you can take a guided tour or make your own way around the remains. The famous sites are the well-preserved 30m (100ft) Round Tower and the intact church often called St. Kevin's Kitchen because of its chimneylike bell tower. Against the backdrop of the wooded slopes, this assembly of quaint stone rooflines and pencil spires is unforgettable. Also visible are the

One of the most famous, and most visited, of Ireland's Round Towers can be found in the beautiful wooded setting of Glendalough

shells of the roofless cathedral and the Priests' House, and many crosses and gravestones. Farther up the valley (a pleasant walk or short drive) near the more spectacular and peaceful Upper Lake are various minor sights—a beehive cell, an early fort, and another ruined church. St. Kevin's Bed is a suitably masochistic rocky ledge high on a cliff face (safely accessible only by boat) where the saint used to sleep. Keen walkers have an excellent choice of routes in this area (a national park information point is open in summer, and there are several local hostels).

▶▶ Howth   863C
This is now little more than a suburb of Dublin, but its attractions are still easily appreciated, particularly at the coast. Howth (it rhymes with "both") Head gives fine views of Dublin Bay, the Wicklow Mountains and Boyne Valley beyond. In the bay is the rocky bird sanctuary and monastic island of Ireland's Eye, to which you can take a boat trip in summer. Cliff paths lead around the coastline, through Howth village and its ruined abbey, and past Baily Lighthouse. The partly ruinous, 15th-century Howth Castle is inland, near the Deer Park Hotel, and has fine rhododendron gardens. A small transport museum can be visited near the DART railway station, featuring Howth's famous open-topped tram. Howth's pubs, hotels, and fish restaurants make it a pleasant outing from Dublin.

Howth remains a working fishing port, and has a good range of fish restaurants

Both this High Cross and the Round Tower have lost their summits, but Kells small oratory remains intact

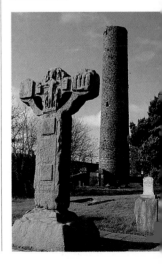

▶▶ Kells   861D
North of the Boyne lie several fine monastic buildings. Kells (formerly known as Ceanannus Mór), up the Blackwater Valley, is best known for the *Book of Kells* (see page 73). A facsimile copy is in the modern Church of Ireland occupying the site of St. Columba's 6th-century monastery. A Round Tower, five High Crosses (the best is the South Cross, carved with biblical scenes), and a simple two-storey church all date from the first millennium.

Kildare, popular with canal enthusiasts

HIGH CROSSES
South Kildare contains several well-preserved High Crosses. The best are at Moone and Castledermot. The Moone example stands over 5m (16ft) and depicts biblical scenes (lane signposted near post office). There are two crosses at Castledermot, again carved with scriptural themes. Both sites stand in the ruins of ancient monasteries.

CANAL TRIPS
County Kildare is traversed by two great canal systems, the Royal and Grand canals, which connect Dublin with the interior lakelands and the Shannon and Barrow rivers. They were major arteries of trade during the Industrial Revolution until the 1801 Act of Union stifled Ireland's economic development. The place to find out more about the canals is Robertstown. There, trips run from the restored Old Canal Hotel (exhibition), which was built in 1803 to serve canal-borne passengers; candlelit dinners with music are sometimes held in summer.

A range of shoes is on offer to Kildare's four-footed residents

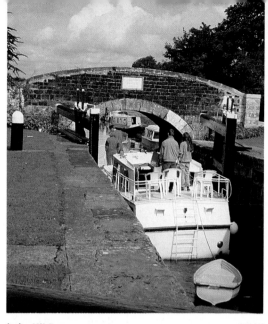

▶▶ **Kildare**   *861C*

The county town, Naas, has a villagelike air: gaily painted shopfronts, old pubs, and, of course, a betting shop cluster around its market square by the sturdy tower of **St. Brigid's Cathedral▶** (*Open* daily 10–6. *Admission: inexpensive*), dating from the 13th century, but much altered since. Stained-glass windows depict Ireland's great saints—Brigid, Patrick, and Columba. During the 5th century, Kildare was one of the few religious houses in Ireland exclusively for women. The cathedral is flanked by a tall **Round Tower▶▶**, which you can climb in summer for extensive views of this rolling horse country (tel: 045 521 229; *open* May–Sep, daily 10–1 and 2–5. *Admission: inexpensive*). Immediately outside town is the wide, springy, gorse-speckled plain called the Curragh, which will stir the heart of any racing *aficionado*. The Curragh is Ireland's largest military camp, where the armoured vehicle that carried Michael Collins to his fatal ambush in 1922 is on display.

If you are at all interested in horses, visit the **Irish National Stud▶▶**, based at Tully just outside the town (tel: 045 521 617; *open* mid-Feb–mid-Nov, daily 9.30–6. *Admission: expensive:* includes Japanese Gardens). Visitors can tour the buildings and see the horses being exercised and groomed, or at ease in fenced paddocks. These animals enjoy a standard of living many humans would envy. The stallions work from January to July; the rest of the year is their "holiday." They have to perform as stalwartly in the covering sheds as they ever did on the racecourse.

The stud was set up in 1902 by the British, and transferred to the Irish state in 1943. Its eccentric founder was Colonel William Hall Walker, who believed that the stars influenced the horses' form. The stallion boxes are built with lantern roofs to allow heavenly bodies their full effect on the horses. Every time a mare foaled, Colonel Walker would cast its horoscope, and race or sell the progeny accordingly. The system, it is said, was uncannily successful.

Spring and early summer are the most interesting times to visit, when you will see new foals with the mares. The foaling area contains a special unit in which orphan foals can be safely fostered. Later in the year the Sun Chariot Yard holds promising yearlings whose paces are just about to be tested. Veterinary research is carried out at the stud, along with all aspects of the complex and rarified science of horse breeding. The animals are not pets and should not be approached; apart from their extreme value, they can be fierce and may bite or kick, and mares with foals can be particularly savage.

The ornamental lake near the stable units provides mineral-rich drinking water for the horses, said to encourage good bone structure. Also in the grounds are the ruins of the Black Abbey, dating from the 12th century, along with the **Irish National Stud Horse Museum►**, dedicated to all aspects of the equine species, and with plenty of racing memorabilia.

Next to the Stud are the **Japanese Gardens►►** (same hours as National Stud), considered by many to be Europe's most beautiful. The gardens symbolically depict man's progress from birth to eternity via a series of landmarks representing disappointments and failures on the road to enlightenment and final happiness. On the way, visitors pass such features as the Marriage Bridge, the Hill of Ambition, and the Tunnel of Ignorance. The intricate landscaping makes the gardens seem much bigger than they really are. They were created by the Japanese gardener Eida and his son between 1906 and 1910. A garden centre sells bonsai trees, and there are tearooms.

TWO BODIES
A saint's relics were of huge importance to the economy of a monastery because of the pilgrims who came to venerate them, and strife between monasteries for the possession of such relics was by no means uncommon. One recorded instance concerned the relics of St. Abban, a south Leinster saint. His medieval *Life* tells of a struggle between the monks of Killabban (his County Kildare birthplace) and those of his monastery at Maganey for the possession of his body. The former claimed it because they were his first followers, while the latter based their claim to it on the fact that the saint had lived and died among them. Divine Providence, however, stepped in and settled the matter satisfactorily by bestowing an identical body of the saint on each of the communities!

The elegant Japanese Gardens next to the National Stud

The English and the Irish probably come closer to understanding each other through their mutual love of horses than in any other way. Ireland is currently estimated to have about 55,000 horses, including 15,000 racehorses.

LAYTOWN RACES

The much loved and highly unusual Laytown Races are held just once a year in either July or August. The course is a gently shelving beach of soft sand in a little coastal resort in County Meath, near Drogheda. As soon as the tide goes out, the six-furlong track is quickly marked and the horses thunder across the strand amid a lively seaside atmosphere of candy-floss stalls and paddling children. The competitors race not only each other, but the advancing tide! Sadly, a serious accident in 1994 cast a shadow over Laytown's future. Races are still held, however, but with more safety measures.

A focal point of Ireland's racing country is Punchestown racecourse, County Kildare

A land of horses Ireland is the heart of the racehorse industry, where many of the world's best thoroughbreds are reared and trained. It also has facilities for every type of equestrian sport: flat-racing, steeple-chasing, show-jumping, eventing, or trekking. Equestrian centres abound, and fox hunting is alive and well. For other aspects of the horse world, turn up at the jolly Connemara Pony Show (Clifden, August), the fashionable Dublin Horse Show (August), or the horse fairs in Buttevant (County Cork, 12 July) and Ballinasloe (County Galway, October), where all classes of horseflesh change hands amid an arcane code of palm-slapping and luck money (a small amount that the seller gives so the horse's new owner will have "good luck" betting on his purchase).

Irish breeding Horses thrive in Ireland's mild climate and lush, unpolluted pastureland. The grass overlies a base of limestone, which produces the calcium needed for healthy bones. The native Irish horses are Connemaras, those cheerful animals that survive on saltmarsh grasses and seaweed in the far west. Romantic legends tell how Spanish Arab horses escaped from Armada vessels shipwrecked off the Galway coast in the 16th century and intermingled with the native stock, producing a taller, faster, and more elegant breed. The two other distinctively Irish equines are the powerful draft horses, used to plough fields and draw carts, and the charismatic creature of the turf, the long-limbed thoroughbred. Crossbreeding between draft and thoroughbred produces the sturdier but athletic animals used for hunting or show-jumping.

The lure of the turf Horse-racing is more than a mere sport in Ireland; it is a passion, consuming and generating vast sums of money. On-course betting turnover amounts to about €115 million a year, and thousands are avid studiers of form. The breeding industry turns over staggering amounts, aided by favourable government tax breaks. Racing, however, was known in Ireland many centuries ago. The legendary Red Branch knights of Ulster raced, as did later Gaelic warriors, although it was then mainly a sport of kings. The Normans and Elizabethans loved it; Cromwell, with his characteristic lack of *joie de vivre*, tried to ban it as the work of the devil—possibly one of his least popular moves in Ireland. During the 18th century racing was all the rage, and two neighbours in County Cork coined a new phrase with their epic cross-country dash between the spires of Buttevant and Doneraile churches—"steeple-chasing."

Today, racing "over the sticks" still has a great following, although not nearly as much money is involved as in flat-racing. Jumpers are usually gelded, so when their sporting days are over they cannot retire gracefully to sire lucrative strings of winning progeny, as flat-racers do. Nonetheless, the courage and stamina needed of both horse and rider in steeple-chasing make it an exciting and highly respected sport.

Ireland has nearly 30 racecourses, and meetings are held somewhere on approximately 245 days of the year, including Sundays. They vary enormously from state-of-the-art Leopardstown, just outside Dublin, to the quaint Laytown Races (see panel). Ireland's most celebrated flat-racing venue is the Curragh in County Kildare, 2,300ha (5,700 acres) of gorsy plain where visitors will see strings of racehorses testing their paces on the springy turf. The great national hunt (steeple-chasing) courses are at Fairyhouse (where the Irish Grand National is held), Punchestown, Navan, and Galway. You can find full details of the racing calendar in any Irish paper, or from the tourist board. The most valuable race is the Irish Derby; the winner, whose progeny will be closely watched for hereditary swiftness, commands a guaranteed place in the annals of racing history.

The tack room at one of Ireland's many riding schools; this is at Donacomper, near Celbridge in County Kildare

103

RACING IN IRELAND
Racing in Ireland is a popular sport with many of the 27 racecourses holding festivals at various times during the year. Summer is predominantly a flat-racing season, with the major races being held at the Curragh, Co. Kildare, or Leopardstown, in the southern suburbs of Dublin. National Hunt racing continues throughout the year, and among the most popular venues are Punchestown, Co. Kildare, which hosts a three-day festival meeting in spring; Fairyhouse in Co. Meath, which plays host to the Grand National; and Galway, which has a six-day meeting in the summer.

Inside Malahide Castle highlights include the Oak Room, full of intricate panelling from the 16th and 17th centuries

NEWBRIDGE
Beyond Malahide, in Donabate, lies the former home of the Cobbe family. Designed by George Semple, Newbridge is an 18th-century house set in wooded parkland (*Guided tours* available). The drawing room is an authentic example of Georgian decor, and the areas "below stairs" contain original utensils and equipment. More unusually, the much-travelled Cobbes built up a charming little museum of curiosities from many foreign places. Craft workshops and period transportation displays are on show in the courtyard.

▶▶ Malahide Castle   863C
Malahide, Co. Dublin, tel: 01 864 2184
Open: Apr–Sep, Mon–Sat 10–5, Sun 2–6
Admission: moderate

With the exception of a brief spell under Cromwell, this romantic-looking building was the seat of the Talbot family for nearly 800 years before it was bought by Dublin County Council in 1976. The Talbots were Jacobite supporters and fared badly in the Battle of the Boyne. It is said that the 14 cousins who sat down to breakfast at Malahide on the morning of the battle were all dead by nightfall. The tour of the building enables you to see its transition from a simple fortification to a charmingly domestic country house in elaborate Gothic style; the present turrets and battlements are ornamental. It contains many original furnishings, mostly 18th-century, and a fine collection of portraits that now form Ireland's National Portrait Gallery. The structure dates from several periods, the oldest section being its 14th-century tower. The beautiful gardens around the castle contain a remarkable botanical collection; beyond lies an expanse of well-kept parkland. In the castle yard is the **Fry Model Railway Museum▶**, with engines and rolling stock handmade by a Dublin railway engineer, Cyril Fry. The O-gauge railway is an amazing scale model with stations, bridges, barges, the Liffey River, and the Hill of Howth.

▶ Marino Casino   863C
Malahide Road, Marino, tel: 01 833 1618,
www.heritageireland.com. Open: Feb–Mar and Nov, Sun and Thu 12–4; Apr, Sun and Thu 12–5; May and Oct, daily 10–5; Jun–Sep, daily 10–6. Admission: inexpensive

If you are on your way to Malahide or Howth, this little Georgian gem is worth tracking down in Dublin's northern suburbs. The Casino has nothing to do with gambling, but was built for Lord Charlemont (who lived in what is now the Hugh Lane Municipal Art Gallery, see page 56) as an exuberant bit of neoclassical frivolity, a skittish aside to a villa in which he planned to house some of the works of art he brought home from a grand tour. The villa no longer exists, but the Casino survives, flamboyantly decorated with urns concealing chimneystacks. Nearby Marino Crescent (also known as Folliot's Revenge) was built out of spite to block Lord Charlemont's view of the sea. The backs of the houses were made particularly hideous, with ill-proportioned windows and scruffy sheds.

▶ Maynooth 862C

If you are touring west of Dublin you will probably drive through Maynooth at some point, a pleasant Georgian town with a ruined castle and, nearby, the famous seminary and lay university of St. Patrick's College (tel: 01 708 3576; *open* by appointment. *Admission free*) that contains an ecclesiastical museum. During the Reformation the college was suppressed, but reopened in 1795 after the repeal of the harsh Penal Laws against Catholics. The town's main square is in Victorian Gothic style and was designed by Augustus Pugin. Close by is the large estate of Carton House, a fine Georgian mansion built for the dukes of Leinster in 1740.

▶▶ Mellifont Abbey 862D

Mellifont Abbey, Colon, tel: 041 982 6459
Open: May–mid-Jun and mid-Sep–Oct, daily 10–5;
mid-Jun–mid-Sep, daily 9.30–6.30. Admission: inexpensive
Remains of the first Cistercian church in Ireland, founded in 1142, are in a maze of quiet lanes by the Mattock River. Built by St. Malachy, Archbishop of Armagh, it was heavily influenced by the French Cistercian monastery at Clairvaux, where St. Malachy had stayed and befriended the abbot, St. Bernard. View the ruins from the parking area, or pay a small entrance fee for a closer look. The ruin's most striking section is the Romanesque octagonal lavabo, or washing place, about half of which is still standing.

A TASMANIAN CONNECTION

The late Lord Talbot de Malahide was also the owner of another Malahide, in Tasmania, where his relatives still live. Inspired by his family's interests there, and by his own fascination for botany, he wrote the definitive multivolume work on the plants of Tasmania. He also introduced to the Irish Malahide garden plants from his antipodean property, as well as others from Africa, North and South America, China, Australia, and Mexico—which makes it a botanist's paradise.

105

Portraits from the National Gallery in Dublin now hang in the imposing setting of Malahide Castle

Mount Usher Gardens make the most of their position on the Vartry River

The Hill of Tara, once a site of pagan importance, is one of many such places to have been "Christianized"

►► Monasterboice 862D

North of Drogheda, off the N1, is one of the best examples in Ireland of a carved High Cross. This is the 10th-century Cross of Muiredach, nearly 6m (20ft) high, which bears numerous biblical scenes in deep relief, such as Cain slaying Abel, David and Goliath, and the Last Judgment. The west face is devoted to the life of Christ, including the arrest in the Garden of Gethsemane, and the risen Christ returning to meet St. Peter and St. Paul. At the bottom of the cross is an inscription in Gaelic saying "A prayer for Muiredach by whom this cross was made." Two other more eroded High Crosses can be seen on the site, along with a fine Round Tower and a pre-Gothic sundial. Two ruined 13th-century churches stand within the enclosure.

►►► Mount Usher Gardens 863B

Ashford, Co. Wicklow, tel: 0404 40205,
www.mount.usher-gardens.com
Open: mid-Mar–Oct, daily 10.30–6. Admission: moderate
These lovely gardens stand in 8ha (20 acres) of land on the banks of the Vartry River. Water forms an essential part of the scenery, with cascades and bridges visible in just about every section. It is possible to get utterly lost if you forget which way the water is flowing. The grounds were laid out by Edward Walpole, a Dublin businessman, and his sons from 1868 as a wild garden, and contain about 5,000 species, including many rhododendrons and eucalypti. The gardens offer fine displays of colour throughout the summer. The maples in late September and October are especially striking. Several craft and clothing shops stand by the entrance, where there is a tearoom.

► Navan 862D

Navan occupies a strategic site on the Boyne. Not compelling in itself, it makes a good base for seeing several places in the area. Within the town, the most interesting

sight is **Athlumney Castle▶**, over the bridge. This 15th-century tower house was apparently burned down by its last owner, Sir Lancelot Dowdall, a devout Catholic who refused to let it fall into William's hands after the Battle of the Boyne. He is said to have watched his home blaze all night from the opposite banks, then set off into exile.

About 13km (8mi) south of the town is one of Ireland's most famous antiquities, the **Hill of Tara▶▶▶** *(tel: 046 25903; open May–mid-Jun and mid-Sep–Oct, daily 10–5; mid-Jun–mid-Sep, daily 9.30–6.30. Admission: inexpensive).* This shows evidence of occupation from many different periods, and was the symbolic seat of the High Kings until the 11th century. Its history is steeped in legends, but archaeological evidence suggests that some grim events must have taken place there. Various ring forts can be seen, although some were damaged in recent years by British Israelites searching for the Ark of the Covenant (see panel). The site has probably always been associated with religious cults of some kind, but its influence waned after the arrival of Christianity. It was from this hill that King Laoghaire and the Druids first noticed St. Patrick's defiant fire on the nearby Hill of Slane.

The Hill of Tara is now just a grassy flat-topped hill grazed by sheep, reached by a field path from the parking area. It rises only 90m (300ft) or so from the surrounding land, but the views over the plains are very extensive. Various inconclusive mounds and earthworks indicate the locations of the old palaces, banquet hall, and Bronze Age burial sites, and many artefacts have been unearthed. Tara's most significant event in modern times was a mass meeting called by the nationalist leader Daniel O'Connell (see page 42), which is said to have attracted over a million people. This alarmed the British government, which suppressed O'Connell's activities and thus put one more nail in the coffin of a peaceful Anglo-Irish settlement.

A Hill of Tara interpretative centre has been established in an old church on the hillside, which really helps visitors to get to grips with the complex history of Tara and to identify the many different earthworks.

Today, visitors to the Hill of Tara are more inclined to appreciate the views than dig vainly for the Ark of the Covenant

107

THE ARK OF THE COVENANT
In 1899, the purchase of a book on Charing Cross Road in London led a group known as the British Israelites to the belief that the Ark of the Covenant lay buried on the Hill of Tara. One of them, a Mr. Groome, went off to Ireland to excavate in furtherance of his biblical quest. When he found nothing, some locals took pity on his disappointment and placed some Roman coins where he would dig on the morrow and where, inevitably and to his own delight, he duly discovered them the next day. But after a singular lack of success in locating what he had set out to find, he packed his bags and returned to England. The Ark remains undiscovered on the Hill of Tara—or anywhere else.

The entrance to the passage-grave, with the roof-box above the lintel

The sparkling white of the quartzite lends added drama to Newgrange

►►► Newgrange 862D

Bru na Boinne, tel: 041 988 0300, www.heritageireland.com
Open: Jun–mid-Sep, daily 9.30–7; May, daily 9.30–6.30;
mid-Sep–Feb daily 10–4.30; March and Apr daily 10–5
Admission: expensive

Newgrange is unquestionably one of Ireland's most important archaeological sites, and perhaps the most spectacular passage-grave (the tomb takes the form of a long passage covered by a vast mound) in Western Europe. Dating from ca 3000 BC, it is possibly 1,000 years older than England's Stonehenge. The tumulus stands in a sloping field above the road, overlooking the glittering snake of the Boyne and a vast sweep of quiet farmland. It is easily spotted because the front retaining walls of the grass-covered mound are faced with brilliant white stones of quartzite. The nearest source for these stones is the Wicklow Mountains, south of Dublin, so thousands of tons of material must have been dragged huge distances. Egg-shaped grey stones are studded at intervals among the white ones, though the original pattern of these (if there was one) is a matter of speculation. The mound itself measures about 100m (330ft) across, and is about 10m (35ft) high at its central point. Over the years it had collapsed, but was reconstructed during the 1960s, using careful measurements to determine its precise dimensions. In front of the mound is a low entrance formed by slabs of rock, and above it another rectangular opening, the roof-box. This sophisticated device is constructed with a narrow slit in the stone so that once a year, for about 15 minutes on the morning of the winter solstice, the rays of the sun illuminate the interior of the tomb. All around the edge of the tomb is a low wall of large boulders, some carved with spiral shapes. The significance of these is unknown; they may have been purely decorative.

You can walk all around the mound (the white wall does not go all the way) to see what remains of a circle of standing stones. A guided tour takes you into the inner stone chamber of the tomb, from which three recesses lead; the dovetailed structure of the vaulted roof still keeps the water out. Mysterious patterns are carved on the inner stones, some invisible from outside and presumably for some cult purpose. Stone basins contained the bones of the cremated dead with offerings of beads and pins. At the end of the tour a light is switched on to re-create an approximation of the solstice phenomenon.

Newgrange is open all year, and is besieged by school groups and visitors in high season. During the winter solstice (21 December) and several days around that date, access is virtually impossible; places are booked many years in advance to see the phenomenon within the tomb. Tourism at this sensitive site is carefully managed, but even so, erosion is occurring. The Office of Public Works has constructed an interpretative centre near the site with a model to reduce the pressure of visitor numbers.

Newgrange is by no means the only local antiquity. The nearby mounds of Dowth and Knowth also contain passage tombs. As you look from Newgrange over the lush pastureland enclosed by this sheltered bend of the Boyne, the shapes of numerous strange humps and tumuli are visible—these are other burial sites, about 40 in all, some of which have not yet been explored. The Irish name for this giant graveyard is *Bru na Boinne*, the palace of the Boyne. Its builders were a farming community who were apparently fairly settled and peaceful, clearing forests and raising stock. The looping Boyne River furnished them with a useful artery of communication and a natural defence barrier.

Many aspects of the tombs are puzzling, and myths and theories abound. The fatally wounded Diarmuid, lover of Gráinne, is alleged to have been brought here "to put aerial life into him." Other legends declare these tombs (inaccurately) to be the burial places of the Kings of Tara, while the sun-cult rituals echo those discovered in ancient Egyptian tombs, although these graves probably predate the pyramids by several hundred years.

There are several inscribed stones at Newgrange; this one is at the back of the mound

TOMORROW NEVER COMES

In early Irish mythology, Newgrange was associated with the Dagda, the good god of the Celts, his wife Bóann (the divinized Boyne River) and his son Oengus—all supernatural beings belonging to the Tuatha Dé Danann (peoples of the goddess Danu), who had defeated the *Fir Bolg* people (see page 30) and had occupied Ireland before the Celts. The 12th-century *Book of Leinster* tells the tale of how Oengus used a verbal trick to get possession of the great mound at Newgrange from his father. The Dagda, it seems, was persuaded to let his son have it for a day and a night, and when he asked his son to return it the next day, Oengus replied that a day and a night meant forever—so he kept it. He probably argued, with impeccable Irish logic, that tomorrow never comes as every day is today.

DANIEL ROBERTSON

The terraces of Powerscourt Gardens were indelibly stamped by the unsteady hand of this gouty and eccentric architect who, in 1840, was commissioned by the 6th Viscount Powerscourt to draw up new plans for the garden. Apparently Robertson's *modus operandi* was to be trundled around the gardens in a wheelbarrow, directing staff while swigging intermittently at a bottle of sherry. Once the bottle was empty he ran out of ideas and all useful work for the day ground to a halt. Robertson's habits were expensive, and he was constantly in debt. Whenever the sheriff called, he used to hide in the copper dome of the house.

The Great Sugar Loaf Mountain forms a memorable backdrop to the gardens at Powerscourt

▶▶▶ **Powerscourt**   *863C*

Enniskerry, tel: 01 204 6000
Open: Mar–Oct, daily 9.30–5.30; Nov–Feb, daily 9.30–dusk
Admission: expensive

The pretty village of Enniskerry and the dramatic backdrop of the Wicklow Mountains add to the appeal of this vast estate, with its 1.6km (1mi) long drive. James I granted the land to the 1st Viscount Powerscourt, Sir Richard Wingfield, in 1609. A magnificent house was designed by Richard Castle, whose Palladian handiwork can be seen all over Ireland. Unfortunately, the great edifice had just been restored when it burned to a shell in a disastrous accident in 1974. The house now has a new use: It houses an exhibition on the history of the estate, shops, and a terrace restaurant, which overlooks the gardens. There is also a garden centre. All that can be seen now are the splendid **gardens**, laid out on the south-facing slopes in front of the house that overlook the Great Sugar Loaf Mountain. They were first created in the mid-18th century soon after the completion of the house, but redesigned in the 19th century by the redoubtable Daniel Robertson (see panel) with classical parterres and Italianate statuary. They contain glorious lakes with spouting fountains and winged horses, and magnificent specimen trees that grow to a prodigious height in this mild climate. Unusual touches include a Japanese garden (1908) on reclaimed bogland sporting little scarlet bridges, a pet cemetery dedicated to many faithful friends (Jack, Sting, and Taffy), mosaic terraces made of beach pebbles from Bray, and neat kitchen gardens.

An additional attraction about 5km (3mi) away (separate entrance charge) is the **Powerscourt Waterfall▶▶**, which plunges about 120m (400ft) in a mare's-tail plume down a jagged rock face (see panel opposite). There are excellent local walks around the valley below. To justify the entrance fee, take a picnic and make an outing of it.

►► Russborough House 862C

Blessington, tel: 045 865239
Open: May–Sep, daily 10.30–5.30; Apr and Oct, Sun
10.30–5.30. Admission: expensive

Like nearby Powerscourt, this grand Palladian mansion shows the Anglo-Irish ascendancy in the Pale at its most confident and powerful. It was designed by the ubiquitous Richard Castle (and, after his death, Francis Bindon) for the 1st Earl of Milltown, a wealthy Dublin brewer. The structure is palatial: Two huge semicircular wings stretch from the main body of the building to two side pavilions. Inside, the grandeur continues in magnificent plasterwork by the Francini brothers. Some of it, like elegant cake icing, swirls around exquisite oval sea scenes by Claude Vernet, commissioned specially for the house.

Today the house is owned by the nephew of Alfred Beit, the German co-founder (with Cecil Rhodes) of the De Beer Diamond Mining Company. Besides a multitude of antiques, tapestries, and valuable porcelain, his fabulous collection of art (strong on Spanish, Dutch, and Flemish schools) is now held at Russborough. At least, some of it is, for Russborough has suffered two major burglaries. The first was in 1974 when, in a *cause célèbre* that hit all the headlines, Dr. Bridget Rose Dugdale stole 16 paintings for her IRA lover (the haul was recovered, undamaged, later). In May 1986, another break-in occurred and this time the owners were not so lucky. Now the house is under a fair degree of surveillance and some important works have been donated to the National Gallery in Dublin. There is, however, still plenty that makes the house well worth a special visit. The grounds consist of woodland and a large artificial lake (actually a reservoir).

Nearby **Blessington**►► is one of the most charming villages in the Wicklow Mountains and a popular base for tourers. Its wide street is flanked by tall trees and dignified Georgian buildings. Dame Ninette de Valois, founder of London's Sadler's Wells Ballet Company, was born nearby.

Apart from a wonderful collection of paintings, Russborough House is also the home of some unusual dolls

A DRAMATIC DISPLAY
When King George IV announced his intention of visiting Powerscourt in 1821, a path was hurriedly laid out from the great house to the waterfall in the grounds, and an artificial lake with sluice gates created at the top of the fall to make a more dramatic cascade for the king to admire. But the delights of the luncheon table in the mansion gave His Majesty insufficient time to visit the waterfall, and when the sluice gates were subsequently opened, the great onrush of water destroyed the wooden platform on which the king should have been standing. So the British monarchy has reason to be thankful to Powerscourt—and a good lunch!

Skerries is so-called because of the islands lying just off the coast; the name means "sea rocks" in Gaelic

▶ Skerries

863D

This is one of the biggest resorts on the northeast coast, mostly visited by Dubliners. The strange indentations at Red Island are claimed to be the footprints of St. Patrick. Boat trips to St. Patrick's Island enable visitors to explore a ruined church where a national synod was held in 1148. Just south is the pretty fishing village of Loughshinny.

▶▶ Slane

862D

The town was built on the instructions of Viscount Conyngham in the 18th century, around a crossroads. For its modest size it has considerable historic interest, and is a pleasant grey-stone place of agreeable Georgian proportions. The estate of Slane Castle, former home of the Conynghams, lies behind firmly locked gates, although it can be glimpsed occasionally from nearby roads. Open-air rock concerts have been held in the castle grounds, but it is not generally open to the public. The Marchioness Conyngham was rumoured to have been George IV's last mistress, and he apparently spent a good deal of time there. Near the riverside is a mill. The four identical Georgian houses set at equal angles to the crossroads in the village centre have given rise to one of those appealing Irish tales that are almost certainly untrue.

THE ROAD TO SLANE
The reason, it is said, why the road from Dublin to Slane was made so straight (unlike most in Ireland) was to minimize the time it would take King George IV to reach his mistress in Slane Castle when he visited in 1821.

A shield set into the walls of Slane Abbey

The houses were supposedly built for four quarrelsome spinster sisters whose exasperated brother became so fed up with their wranglings under one roof that he insisted they live separately. Whether or not the story is true, the houses are fine examples and deserve a close look.

A humble labourer's cottage (now a museum) a short distance from the centre of Slane was the birthplace of the lyric poet Francis Ledwidge. A plaque outside displays one of his most haunting verses, written after his friend Thomas MacDonagh was executed for his part in the Easter Rising of 1916:

"He shall not hear the bittern cry
In the wild sky, where he is lain,
Nor voices of the sweeter birds
Above the wailing of the rain."

Ledwidge himself was killed soon after this—at Flanders, fighting on the British side. He was only 30 and is now lamented as a great loss to literature, though his work was not widely read at a time of such political upheaval.

Outside the village is the **Hill of Slane▶**, on which the ruins of a monastery stand. The site is famous as the place where St. Patrick lit Easter fires to challenge the pagan king, Laoghaire, who had forbidden flames to be kindled within sight of his palace at Tara (see page 107).

▶ Straffan   *862C*

This village on the banks of the Liffey has two visitor attractions, although both are open only in high season. The **Butterfly Farm▶▶** (tel: 01 627 1109; *open* May–Aug, daily noon–5.30. *Admission: moderate*) is the only one of its type in Ireland, with tropical species fluttering about in a hothouse full of exotic plants. The **Steam Museum▶** (tel: 01 627 3155; *open* Easter–May and Sep, Tue–Sun 2–6; Jun–Aug, Mon–Sat 2–6, Sun 2.30–5.30. *Admission: moderate*) documents the history of the steam age in Ireland, showing how it revolutionized industrial as well as agricultural practices such as butter churning and corn threshing. Working steam engines are on display, including Richard Trevithick's prototype steam-powered road vehicle. The engines stand in the courtyard of an 18th-century house. Phone in advance to attend a "live steam day." Straffan is also home to Ireland's most glamorous club, the **Kildare Hotel and Country Club** (tel: 01 627 3333. *Admission: expensive*), where Arnold Palmer designed the K Club, one of Ireland's most prestigious 18-hole golf courses and home to a future Ryder Cup—where Europe's top 10 golfers take on their counterparts from the US. The K Club is owned by multimillionaire Michael Smurfit, and the hotel itself is a splendid example of an early 19th-century, mansard-roofed manor built in the French style.

GARRICK CASTLE
Standing near the Boyne a short distance upriver from Slane is the ruined castle of Garrick. Close by was a weir and, so the story goes, fish caught in a net there touched a wire connected to the castle kitchen, so that the cook would know when to serve up the freshest of salmon on the menu.

113

Slane Abbey was founded in 1512 for four priests, four clerks, and four choristers

Christianity reached Irish shores during the late 4th century, not with Roman fire and sword, but through the persuasive urgings of an extraordinary band of missionary monks who brought the glad tidings to the pagan Gaels. Many of these early Christian teachers and founders of monasteries are now Irish saints.

ST. OLIVER PLUNKETT (1629–1681)

One of the most interesting of Ireland's saints was canonized as recently as 1976. St. Oliver Plunkett, Archbishop of Armagh and Primate of All Ireland, had the misfortune to live during the troubled years of the 17th century, when Catholicism was rigorously suppressed by English authorities. He was on friendly terms with the Protestant clergy of Ulster, who had a high regard for his sincerity and achievements, but false allegations by Titus Oates in 1678 over a "popish plot" to bring French soldiers into Ireland resulted in his arrest, although the charges were blatantly absurd. On 1 July, 1681, he was executed in London for "treason," his offence being simply that he was an unrepentant Catholic. At his trial the Lord Chief Justice declared, "The bottom of your treason was your setting up your false religion, than which there is not anything more displeasing to God." Plunkett's severed head was rescued from the flames and brought back to Ireland. It lies in a shrine in the Catholic Church of St. Peter, Drogheda.

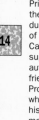

Saintly lives Innumerable saints are encountered on any visit to Ireland. Most of them are obscure (who now remembers St. Gobnet or St. Lurach?) and the patterns of their lives are often very similar—they renounced the world, founded monasteries, and did good works. The achievements of these early monks, however, are hard to overestimate. The trials they endured, the distances they travelled in uncharted terrain, and their dazzling artistic talents are truly staggering. Christianity was indeed a faith that moved mountains. The Christian message was mainly interpreted by men, just as it is now, and attitudes to women were extremely misogynistic. Just a few intrepid women saints braved this exclusive and hostile masculine preserve, among them St. Brigid, who founded one of the earliest of Ireland's nunneries at Kildare.

In today's Ireland, the saints still play an active role in the lives of many devout Catholics. You will find candles burning at every shrine, votive offerings in sacred places, and eager pilgrims praying for their intercession in everyday affairs or for the perpetual forgiveness of sins. Factual evidence about most of the early saints is sparse. Their lives are but shadowy, and wreathed in legends or miraculous tales. Some of them are composite figures or even Christian incarnations of pagan Celtic gods. The most famous Irish saint, of course, is St. Patrick, the most effective of all the early missionaries (see page 226 for details of his life, and places associated with him).

St. Columba (ca 521–597) Also known as Columcille, St. Columba was born at Lough Gartan in Donegal. He was a high-ranking member of the O'Neill clan, a scholar, poet, and natural leader. After training as a monk at Moville and Clonard, he founded the monasteries of Derry and Durrow, possibly also Kells. In 563 he left Ireland with 12 companions to found a monastery in Iona, an island off the Scottish coast, but retained his links with Ireland. He was a charismatic figure, tall and striking, well educated, persuasive, and ardently committed to his cause. Some of his actions seemed less than saintly. This endearingly human paragon was, by all accounts, a thief and a cheat—stealing a ceremonial cross from a neighbouring church and secretly copying a psalter he borrowed from a friend. This resulted in the deaths of thousands at the Battle of the Books (see panel on page 210).

St. Ciarán (ca 521–545) The founder of the great monastery of Clonmacnoise, St. Ciarán had an auspicious pedigree as a Christian leader—he was the son of a

carpenter. His first monkish years were spent on the Aran Islands with Enda, the islands' most famous saint. Later he went to Scattery Island, in the mouth of the Shannon, and finally to Clonmacnoise farther upstream, where he died soon afterward. Apparently he aroused such jealousy among his fellow clerics that they prayed he would die young—and he did! But his good works lived on, and the influence of Clonmacnoise spread far and wide, surviving until 1522, despite many Viking raids.

St. Brendan the Navigator (ca 486–575) This famous Irish saint was the founder of a monastery at Clonfert in County Galway, and also Ardfert in Kerry. His missions took place mostly in western Ireland, but he is best remembered as a great traveller. His epic voyage is chronicled in the 10th-century account, *The Navigation of St. Brendan*, in which he set sail with 12 disciples in search of an earthly paradise in the Atlantic Ocean. The journey lasted over seven years, and it has been suggested that his account of "crystal columns" (icebergs?) and "curdled seas" (migratory eels in the Sargasso?) may pinpoint him as the first to cross the Atlantic. St. Brendan's supposed voyage was imaginatively re-created in similar conditions by the modern explorer Tim Severin, and the wood-and-leather boat he sailed across the Atlantic in 1976 can be seen in the history theme park of Craggaunowen, County Clare (see page 183).

Clonmacnoise, founded by St. Ciarán, was for centuries the intellectual capital of Ireland

This little church at Glendalough is familiarly known as St. Kevin's Kitchen as the small bell tower resembles a chimney

ST. KEVIN (died ca 618)

Founder of the great monastery at Glendalough, County Wicklow, St. Kevin came from a noble Leinster family and was educated by monks from childhood. After his ordination he adopted a hermit's existence at Glendalough. His quest for solitude was in vain, however, for crowds of disciples soon gathered around him and he became the leader of a great and influential community. He is alleged to have murdered a woman who attempted to seduce him, shoving her from his rock-ledge cave into the lake below. The tale conveniently bolsters the early fathers' belief that women were the source of all corruption.

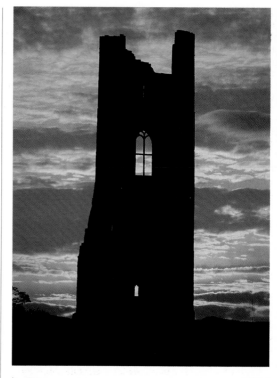

The stark silhouette of the Yellow Steeple; nearby stands a section of Trim's town walls

MICHAEL DWYER'S ESCAPE
The year 1798 witnessed great upheavals against English rule, especially in the southeast. During the harsh winter of 1798–1799 the Wicklow-born rebel Michael Dwyer took refuge in a cottage in Derrynamuck, in the Glen of Imaal. More than 100 English soldiers surrounded it, but he declined to surrender, although he requested that the owners of the house be freed. The army allowed this, then battle commenced. A fellow rebel, Sam McAllister, sustained a broken arm and could fight no longer, so offered to sacrifice himself to give Dwyer a chance to escape. He showed himself at the door and drew the English fire. He was immediately killed, but while the soldiers were reloading their muskets, Dwyer was able to slip away. The cottage is now a museum.

CAPTAIN ROBERT HALPIN
Robert Halpin (1836–1894) was one of Wicklow Town's most prominent citizens. His main achievement was as commander of the *Great Eastern*, the iron steamship that laid the first transatlantic telegraph cable. A granite obelisk commemorates him in the town, and a plaque at the church of St. Lavinius, but for further insights, head for his former home, Tinakilly House, 3km (2mi) north of town, now a luxury hotel and restaurant.

▶ Trim   *862D*

Trim Castle is one of the most imposing Anglo-Norman fortresses in Ireland, and as it stands in the centre of the town by the Boyne River, it is easy to get a good idea of its size and layout. The ruins cover about a hectare (2½ acres) and include a vast keep flanked by rectangular towers. Sections of curtain wall are interspersed with battle gates. The original castle was built by Hugh de Lacy in 1172, although the present structure dates from a later period. The ruins are freely accessible. Nearby are the ruins of the Royal Mint and a gaunt skeleton called the Yellow Steeple, dating from the 14th century, the last remnants of an Augustinian abbey, destroyed in 1649.

Bective Abbey▶▶, between Navan and Trim, is one of the earliest examples of a Cistercian foundation in Ireland. Hugh de Lacy was buried here in 1195, and it was obviously a place of some significance (its abbot sat in the English House of Lords). Most of the surviving ruins date from the 15th century and stand in a gloriously peaceful setting in a field by the Knightsbrook River.

▶ Wicklow   *863B*

The county town of this much-visited area is small and unassuming, but it makes a pleasantly unstressful base, as its name, meaning "Viking meadow," suggests. Its history, however, has been far from untroubled. In AD 432, St. Patrick had an unfriendly reception when he landed at Travilahawk Strand. One of his entourage had his teeth knocked out and became known as Mantan (the toothless one). Irish clans (O'Byrnes and O'Tooles) slugged it out with the Anglo-Norman Fitzgeralds for centuries, and after the rebellion of 1798 many of the participants were tried in the town's courthouse; those who evaded capture took to the hills. Wicklow's main features of interest are the scanty remains of the Black Castle by the road above the harbour, a fine headland for coastal walks, a ruined 13th-century friary, and a heritage centre in the town gaol (local history and genealogical research). The Protestant **Church of St. Lavinius▶** (*Open* daily 10–6. *Admission free*) topped by a Byzantine dome, has several unusual details, including a Romanesque doorway and a fine roof. In Norman times the slopes to the Vartry River were planted with vines, a testimony to Wicklow's comparatively sunny climate. The harbour area is oddly severed from the main town; beyond it stretches a long, shingly beach trapping a brackish lagoon (Broad Lough), which makes a sheltered habitat for wildfowl.

▶▶▶ The Wicklow Mountains 862B

These wild hills on Dublin's doorstep are a great boon to city dwellers. From the southern suburbs you can gaze at them on clear days; by public transportation or a car they take just half an hour to reach. If you have time enough you can even walk there on the 132km (82mi) Wicklow Way, starting just outside Dublin in Marlay Park. The route is not very clear in places, and the mountains can be dangerous in misty conditions. The rounded hills of ice-eroded schist and granite enfold a strange mixture of bleak, awesome glens and boggy plateaux, interspersed with welcoming Shangri-La valleys like Glendalough or the Vale of Avoca. The improbable cones of the Great and Little Sugar Loaf mountains protrude suddenly from the surrounding contours, their granite caps more resilient than the rest. The wildness and emptiness of the mountains made them good hiding places after the 1798 rebellion, and during those troubled times they were full of insurgents. One of the main arteries through the region, the military road linking Rathfarnham and the garrison at Aghavannagh, was constructed by English forces in yet another attempt to impose control on recalcitrant Ireland.

THE DUKE OF WELLINGTON
A monument in Emmet Street, Trim, commemorates Arthur Wellesley, who lived here as a boy before becoming, as the Duke of Wellington, the victor at Waterloo. He had been born in Dublin in the same year as his great adversary, Napoleon. But he had very low regard for the capital city of his birth, if we can judge by the answer he gave when asked what he thought of Dublin: "If a man is born in a stable, that does not make him a horse."

117

Wicklow was one of the bases used by the Vikings on the east coast of Ireland

Southeastern Counties

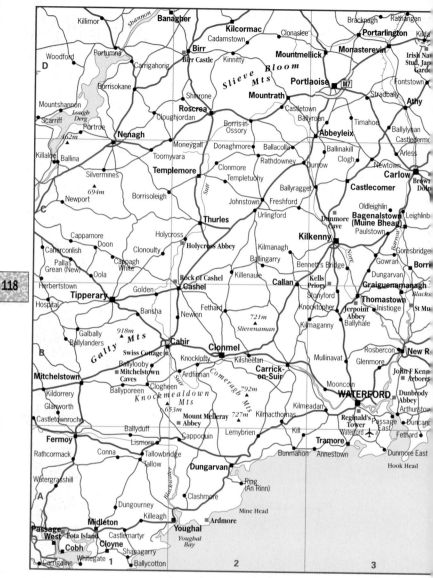

D

Killimor · Banagher · Bracknagh · Rathangan
Shannon · Kilcormac · Clonaslee · Portarlington · Kilda
Woodford · Cadamstown · Mountmellick · Monasterevin
Portumna · Birr · Kinnitty · Mountmellick · Irish Nat
Carrigahorig · Birr Castle · Mountmellick · Stud, Jap
Borrisokane · Slieve Bloom Mts · Portlaoise · Fontstown
Mountshannon · Shinrone · Mountrath · M7 · Stradbally · Athy
Lough Derg · Cloughjordan · Roscrea · Castletown · Ballyroan · Timahoe · Ballylynan
Scarriff · Portroe · Borris-in-Ossory · Abbeyleix · Castledermo
462m · Nenagh · Moneygall · Donaghmore · Ballacolla · Ballinakill · Arles
Killaloe · Ballina · Toomyvara · Rathdowney · Durrow · Clogh · Newtown
Silvermines · Templemore · Clonmore · Ballyragget · Castlecomer · Carlow · Brow
Newport · 694m · Borrisoleigh · Templetuohy · Freshford · Oldleighlin · Bagenalstown · Leighlin
Johnstown · Urlingford · Dunmore · (Muine Bheag) · Dolm

C

Cappamore · Thurles · Holycross · Kilkenny · Paulstown · Goresbridge
Caherconlish · Doon · Clonoulty · Holycross Abbey · Kilmanagh · Bennett's Bridge · Gowran · Borri
Pallas · Cappagh · Ballingarry · Kells · Dungarvan
Green (New) · Oola · White · Rock of Cashel · Killenaule · Priory · Graiguenamanagh
Herbertstown · Golden · Cashel · Callan · Stonyford · Blacks
Hospital · Tipperary · Bansha · Fethard · Knocktopher · Thomastown
Galbally · Newinn · 721m · Kilmaganny · Jerpoint · Inistioge · St Mu
Ballylanders · 918m · Slievenaman · Abbey · Ballyhale
Galty Mts · Cahir · Clonmel · Rosbercon · New R
Swiss Cottage · Knocklofty · Kilsheelan · Mullinavat · Glenmore
Mitchelstown · Ballylooby · Carrick-on-Suir · John F Kenn
Mitchelstown Caves · Ardfinnan · Comeragh Mts · Mooncoin · Arboret
Kildorrery · Clogheen · 792m · WATERFORD · Dunbrody
Glanworth · Ballyporeen · Knockmealdown Mts · Kilmeaden · Abbey
Castletownroche · 653m · Mount Melleray · 727m · Kilmacthomas · Reginald's · Arthurstow
Abbey · Tower · Passage
Fermoy · Ballyduff · Lemybrien · Kill · Waterford · East · Fethard
Rathcormack · Lismore · Sappoquin · Tramore
Conna · Tallowbridge · Bunmahon · Annestown · Dunmore East
Watergrasshill · Tallow · Dungarvan · Hook Head
Dungourney · Killeagh · Ring (An Rinn) · Mine Head
Passage West · Midleton · Castlemartyr · Youghal · Clashmore · Ardmore
Cobh · Fota Island · Cloyne · Youghal Bay
Carrigaline · Whitegate · Shanagarry · Ballycotton

1 · **2** · **3**

A · **B**

An attractive thatched cottage at Kilmore Quay; throughout modern Ireland, you are more likely to see whitewash than thatch.

Far right: ship's figure-head in the maritime museum found in the old Lightship, Kilmore Quay

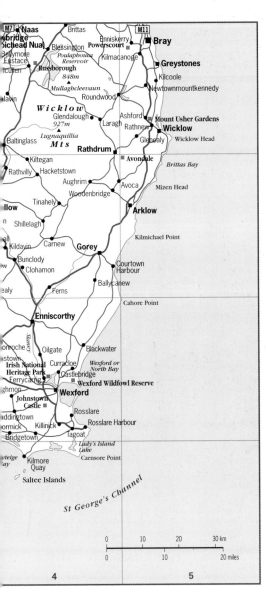

SOUTHEASTERN COUNTIES

In contrast with the scenic wildness of western Ireland, the landscape of the southeast is mostly low-lying and docile. Rich pastureland watered by brimming rivers extends gently to a quiet coastline of long sandy beaches, estuarial mudflats of wading birds, and low cliffs fringing deep bays. Ireland's most fertile farmland lies in the Golden Vale, making Tipperary one of the most prosperous inland counties. There is a great deal to see and do, although to reach all its scattered attractions you will need a car. The sunny, drier climate of southeastern counties attracts both Irish and foreign visitors for summer holidays, and there is an excellent choice of beaches.

Tacumshane, near Kilmore Quay, has the rarity of a thatched windmill in working order

120

TOWN AND CULTURAL ATTRACTIONS Development here remains low-key; Tramore is the largest built-up resort, offering amusement parks and a costly multimedia attraction themed on the Celts. If this atypical brashness doesn't appeal, it is easily avoided. The southeast's other resorts are all small and villagelike, even the county town of Wexford. Waterford is the only "towny" place, a thriving port and commercial centre where derricks unload cargoes on the wharves and industrial complexes hum. Most famous is the crystal factory about 2km (a mile) out of town. This is the largest of its kind in the world, and its annual turnover is astounding. There is no shortage of visitors on the free guided tours, even if few leave clutching a chandelier (see page 143).

The other sizeable towns of the area are medieval Kilkenny, a smart visitor town with enough attractions to act as an excellent base, and Tipperary's prosperous county town, Clonmel, where Georgian influences are more noticeable. Carlow, however, is disappointing: neither the town nor the county have much to detain you.

County Tipperary's great visitor honeypot is the Rock of Cashel. Bus tours flock to this atmospheric outcrop of limestone in the middle of lush plains to admire the majestic ruins clustered on its summit. If abbeys and monasteries interest you, this is a good area to explore— the great settlements at Holycross (County Tipperary), Duiske, Jerpoint (both County Kilkenny), Dunbrody, and Tintern (both County Wexford) are some of the finest. Castles, too, stud the bridging points in these great river valleys—no significant town is without some bristling fortress or other. Cahir, Kilkenny, Lismore, Nenagh, and Enniscorthy are among the most impressive.

SPORTS AND FITNESS BREAKS As well as for seaside breaks or conventional touring, the southeast is a splendid area for exercise. The flatter coastal terrain makes walking and biking holidays less strenuous than in some parts of the country, though inland the hill ranges of the Comeragh, Blackstairs, or the splendidly named Knockmealdown Mountains have plenty of visual drama. The South Leinster Way through Carlow and Kilkenny takes in some of the most beautiful scenery around the Nore and Barrow rivers. The Munster Way meanders along the borderland of Tipperary and Waterford over the spectacular high point known as the Vee Gap, and the lovely valley of the Nire. You can link the two routes (they meet at Carrick-on-Suir), or pick up the Kildare Way along the Barrow River towpath from Graiguenamanagh. Bird-watchers should head for the reclaimed Wexford Slobs, Hook Head Peninsula, or the Saltee Islands.

For fishing holidays the region is excellent; the rivers teem with brown trout, salmon, and all kinds of other fish, particularly the Blackwater River. Dungarvan and Dunmore East are the best centres for deep-sea fishing. Lough Derg in the far northwest of County Tipperary is another good location for water sports, including cruising, though the main centres are in Clare or Galway (Killaloe, Mountshannon, and Portumna). Equestrian sports are popular in this horsey country; hacking (hiring horses) and fox-hunting can be arranged. Tipperary breeds some of Ireland's finest racehorses, and the interest in racing is evident from no fewer than four racecourses, while greyhound racing centres on Clonmel. Competitive sport is a passionate preoccupation throughout Ireland, but the traditional games of Gaelic football and hurling are played in Tipperary with special enthusiasm. It is no surprise to discover the Gaelic Athletic Association (GAA) was founded here by the sportsmanlike Archbishop of Cashel.

A TURBULENT HISTORY The Vikings held sway over this region for many years, finding those broad estuaries and inviting harbours easy landings from which to torment the native Celts with pillage and nose taxes ("Pay up or we'll cut your nose off!"). Following their example, Strongbow invaded Ireland for the Anglo-Normans via Waterford in 1169, ostensibly to aid Dermot MacMurrough in regaining his Leinster throne. In return, Strongbow received the hand of Dermot's daughter, the first dynastic alliance between Irish and Norman. But the Normans stayed on and their power grew. The Gaelic MacMurrough Kavanaghs resented the curtailment of their influence, and remained a thorn in the English side, rebelling every so often with unexpected ferocity. Cromwell finally broke their resistance, and is unaffectionately remembered in this part of Ireland for his slaughter of hundreds of unarmed citizens at Wexford. The southeast was relatively peaceful through the 18th century, but the surface calm disguised many ill feelings. When a confrontation with the yeomanry fanned smouldering passions in 1798, the people of Carlow and Wexford erupted in fury, wielding pikes in a brave but hopeless stand against English cannon fire at the decisive battle of Vinegar Hill, Enniscorthy.

The Vee Gap, near Mitchelstown in County Tipperary, looks especially dramatic in "Irish weather"

Ardmore's Round Tower; it is one of the finest (and latest) in Ireland

ARDMORE'S ROUND TOWER

"The tower…is said to have been built by St. Declan in one night; that when it had arrived at its present height, a woman coming to gather herbs, looking up, asked the Saint what he was doing, upon which he threw down his trowel and killed her, and coming down he threw her upon the top of the tower, where a part of her remained till a few years ago. It is certain, however, that the tower was never raised higher than it is, which it is said it would have been, had not the woman interrupted the Saint in his pious work."

P. D. Hardy: *The Holy Wells of Ireland* (1836)

▶▶ Ardmore   *1182A*

Ardmore (roughly 13km/8mi east of Youghal) is an attractive little resort at the foot of high cliffs, where simple hotels and a guesthouse or two command awesome views over the bay. A blue-flag award for its clean beach and a "tidy town" commendation indicate a sense of local pride. One of its best-known residents is the popular novelist Molly Keane. An ancient place, Ardmore saw the foundation of Ireland's earliest Christian settlement when St. Declan arrived here from Wales, some 30 years before St. Patrick. His bell and vestments were miraculously borne across the water by a glacial boulder, now tilted on a little spur of rock on the beach. It promises wondrous healing powers for all agile enough to creep beneath it.

Excellent views can be seen from the monastery. Most of the remains date from after Declan's time; a well-preserved 30m (100ft) Round Tower and cathedral are largely 12th century. The cathedral displays clear and vigorous carvings of biblical scenes, such as the Judgment of Solomon and the Weighing of Souls. Inside are several ogham stones (see page 16). St. Declan's Oratory is an older structure that may contain the saint's remains, the surrounding earth much pillaged for its restorative properties. St. Declan's Well and a ruined church where the saint spent his final years can be found along the cliff walk leading from the village.

▶▶ Cahir   *1181B*

The fortress in the centre of this small town on the Suir River is in fine condition after restoration work. **Cahir Castle**▶▶ (tel: 052 41011; *open* Apr–Jun and late-Sep–mid-Oct, daily 10–6; Jun–mid-Sep, daily 9–7.30; late-Oct–Mar, daily 10–1 and 2–4.30. *Admission: moderate*) dates mainly from the 15th century with later alterations, and was formerly a stronghold of the powerful local Anglo-Norman Butler family, dukes and earls of Ormonde. Queen Elizabeth I's favourite, the Earl of Essex, rammed a

few cannonballs into its masonry in 1599, but it survived Cromwellian times little scathed. The huge walls enclose three separate "wards," outer, middle, and inner, the inner one guarded by a gate with a portcullis. Rooms in the keep are whitewashed and contain armour displays and period furnishings from the 16th and 17th centuries.

Cahir's fortunes waxed and waned through the centuries, but in peacetime it developed an important milling industry introduced by local Quakers. The town is something of a time warp, and some of its shops and houses appear little changed for decades. One of them, Keating's Draper's Shop, traded in predecimal currency until it closed down a few years ago. Another agreeable feature of the town is its evident lack of religious or political bigotry. Protestants and Catholics used to worship simultaneously in its ruined church, separated only by a curtain wall. Somewhat unusually, in the main square is a war memorial dedicated to the many local men who fell in the Great War. Throughout most of the Republic, the World Wars seem unmarked, and the people who gave their lives in these conflicts are forgotten.

The other curiosity in Cahir is the **Swiss Cottage**▶ (*Open May–Sep, daily 10–6; Oct–Nov, Tue–Sun 10–4.30; Dec–Mar Tue–Sun 10–6; Apr, Tue–Sun 10–5. Admission: moderate*), lying just outside the town on the Clonmel road. This quaint thatched building with its eyebrow windows and corkscrew timbering looks like something out of Hansel and Gretel rather than the Swiss Alps. It was designed in about 1810 by the royal architect, John Nash, for a scion of the Butler family, in a then-fashionable genre known as a "cottage *orné*," a sort of rustic summer-house or hunting lodge in which the wealthy gentry relaxed and amused themselves in what they imagined to be rural simplicity. The cottage was rescued from dereliction by various enthusiastic conservationists and extensively restored, the original handpainted French wallpapers and fabrics have been faithfully copied, and it is now elegantly furnished with many fascinating period details.

St. Declan's Well, Ardmore

Cahir Castle was once thought to be impregnable, but Cromwell took the castle in 1650

At around 100 tons, the capstone of Brownshill Dolmen weighs heavy upon its supporting stones

124

An intriguing shop-front in Carrick-on-Suir

▶ Carlow 1183C

Though a county town, Carlow is disappointingly lacklustre apart from a few nice old shop-fronts (Cigar Divan on Dublin Street is a fine example of authentic Victoriana). It lies on the east bank of the Barrow in the once tempestuous borderland at the edge of the Pale, old warehouses lining its former quays. Its castle, standing in the grounds of a mineral-water bottling plant, is perilously ruinous after the misguided attempts of a Dr. Middleton in 1814 to reduce the thickness of the walls in order to convert the castle into a lunatic asylum. Unfortunately he understood little of the explosives he was using for the purpose, and the walls were well and truly modified, becoming so unsafe that some parts later had to be demolished. Also worth a brief look in the town is the county museum which has various reconstructed farm interiors. The 19th-century Gothic cathedral is easily spotted by its unusual lantern spire, looking like a crown of thorns. It contains an elaborate pulpit and a finely sculpted marble **monument to Bishop Doyle▶**, or JKL (James of Kildare and Leighlin). The story goes that the artist, John Hogan, forgot to include the bishop's ring, and was so mortified by this omission that he committed suicide.

Some 3km (2mi) east is the **Brownshill Dolmen▶**, clearly visible across a field, though it stands some way from the road. The tilted granite capstone is enormous, weighing around 100 tons, and is thought to be the largest of its type in Europe. It poises on its supporting stones as delicately as a ballerina. A fenced path leads from the parking place around the edge of the field.

▶▶ Carrick-on-Suir 1182B

A border town straddling the counties of Tipperary and Waterford, Carrick is noteworthy for its beautiful Tudor mansion. This is all the more remarkable because such buildings are a rarity in Ireland, in comparison with

125

Ormond Castle, one of the finest examples of an Irish manor house

literally hundreds of fortresses and abbeys. Despite its name, **Ormond Castle▶▶**, the house is completely unfortified, perhaps in misplaced expectations of less turbulent times (tel: 051 640 787; *open* mid-Jun–Sep, daily 9.30–6.30. *Admission: moderate*). The building was commissioned by "Black Tom," the swarthy-faced 10th Earl of Ormond, in anticipation of a visit by his cousin Queen Elizabeth I (who didn't come). Tom was a great favourite of the Queen's, a potent reason for an attempted poisoning by his rival, the Earl of Leicester, which he survived. Tom remained an ardent royalist and contributed greatly to the maintenance of English rule in Ireland during this troubled period.

Behind the grey-stone, gabled exterior pierced with many mullioned windows lies lovely stucco work, particularly fine in the 30m (100ft) Long Gallery where royal coats of arms surmount the fireplace. The timber roof contains no bolts, only carpentry joints. Marks can be seen in the attic-room beams, where garrisoned soldiers would stick their knives before retiring for the night.

There is probably no truth in the legend that Anne Boleyn (Queen Elizabeth's mother) was born at Carrick. Today the town is much prouder of a more recent hero, Sean Kelly, the bicycle racer, who was ranked number one in the world throughout the late 1980s. He won many of the sport's major events. A square in the town is named after him.

Just outside Carrick (on the N24) a well-signed thatched roadside showroom indicates the factory of **Tipperary Crystal▶** (tel: 051 641 188; *open* Mon–Fri 10–3.30). Visitors are welcome to look around the production plant and, of course, buy the hand-decorated glassware. The founders of this enterprise learned their trade at the much more prestigious Waterford factory, but were laid off during hard times and used their severance pay to set up a rival company, using similar techniques. Prices are slightly lower, and Tipperary Crystal has been successfully competing with Waterford—a gratifying piece of vengeance for those laid-off workers.

A LITERARY RANSOM
The Butler family of Carrick Castle had many notable warriors, but it also included men of letters, particularly one Émonn mac Risderd Butler. He employed scribes to write for him, and one of their manuscripts, dating from the middle of the 15th century, is now preserved in the British Library in London. So highly prized were his manuscripts that two were given to the Earl of Desmond in ransom for Émonn's life after he had been defeated in the Battle of Pottlerath in 1462.

GAELIC ATHLETIC ASSOCIATION

This largely rural movement was first founded in 1884 in Thurles, 16km (10mi) north of Cashel, under the sponsorship of the Archbishop of Cashel, Thomas William Croke (1824–1902). The GAA's purpose was ostensibly to popularize traditional Irish pastimes such as hurling, handball, and Gaelic football, and today it remains Ireland's most important sporting association. Though not party political, it has proved a fertile recruiting ground for Republican activists, and in the past has been suspected of IRA sympathies.

The Rock of Cashel rears up from the fertile plains of County Tipperary

▶▶▶ Cashel   1182B

Rock of Cashel: tel: 062 61437
Open: mid-Mar–mid-Jun, daily 9–5.30; mid-Jun–mid-Sep, daily 9–7.30; mid-Sep–mid-Mar, daily 9–4.30
Admission: moderate

Stories tell how the devil bit a huge chunk out of the Slieve Bloom Mountains, then spat it out in disgust here in the Golden Vale when he saw St. Patrick preparing to build a great church. This erratic outcrop of limestone among the patchwork plains of rich cattle pasture looks almost freakish enough to justify such a tale. The Rock of Cashel is a mere 61m (200ft) high, but approached from below, the craggy outline of towers and gables crowning the hilltop looks most ethereal, especially in certain conditions of light or weather. Close up, the romantic image fades a little under the pressure of tourism. It is one of Ireland's most popular sights and is always besieged by visitors in high season. The little town of Cashel has managed to avoid the worst excesses of commercialized religiosity, however, and remains a pleasant country town.

Cashel has long been a place of great significance, and rivalled Tara as a royal seat for the kings of Munster from the 4th century AD. St. Patrick arrived in about AD 432 and converted King Aengus, who became Ireland's first Christian ruler. Among many legends associated with this event, St. Patrick is alleged to have used a shamrock leaf to illustrate the nature of the Holy Trinity. During Aengus's baptism, St. Patrick accidentally drove his sharp crozier

through the king's foot, but the king did not complain and his wound was discovered only after the ceremony, when he said he had assumed the suffering was some sort of initiation rite, emulating the pain of Christ.

The buildings visible on Cashel date mainly from the 12th and 13th centuries. Earliest of these structures is probably the **Round Tower▶**, well preserved, with an entrance doorway 3.5m (12ft) above ground level. **Cormac's Chapel▶▶**, ornately carved with beasts and human figures, begun in 1127, is in excellent condition and displays the Irish Romanesque style clearly. A sarcophagus in the chapel is said to be the tomb of Cormac, the bishop-king of Munster, who presided during Cashel's great time of influence in the 12th century. The roofless 13th-century **St. Patrick's Cathedral▶▶**, the largest building on the Rock, with tall lancet and quatrefoil windows and a later central tower on Gothic arches, witnessed a particularly unpleasant act of Cromwellian barbarism when Lord Inchiquin besieged the town in 1647. The citizens fled to sanctuary in the cathedral, whereupon turf was piled up around the walls and set on fire, roasting hundreds of unfortunate townspeople to death. Attempts were made to repair the building but it declined, and in 1749 Cashel's main place of worship was moved to the town. The **Hall of the Vicars▶**, a 15th-century residence for privileged members of the choir, at the foot of the Rock, has a museum with St. Patrick's cross and coronation stone. The Brú Ború heritage centre promotes Celtic studies and performing arts.

In the town, a small **folk village▶** attracts many visitors (*Open* Mon–Sat, 9.30–7.30. *Admission: inexpensive*). It features reconstructions of 18th-century buildings and displays artefacts of the period. The **GPA-Bolton Library▶▶** in the grounds of the Protestant Cathedral is an unusually gripping collection of old tomes; it contains over 12,000 volumes, including part of Chaucer's *Book of Fame*, printed by Caxton, and a collection of church silver (tel: 062 61944; *open* Mar–Oct, Mon–Sat 9.30–5.30, Sun 2.30–5.30. *Admission: inexpensive*). Take a look at **Cashel Palace▶**, a splendid brick edifice, former home of the Archbishop of Cashel and now a luxury hotel (see Hotels and Restaurants, page 272). Visitors can take advantage of the basement Buttery Restaurant, one of the best places in town for a hearty meal or quick snack.

AN INFLAMMATORY PRIEST
The building of the cathedral on the Rock of Cashel began in the 13th century, but funds must have run out, as the nave was curtailed very considerably and its western end was constructed as a palace for the archbishop. The cathedral was set on fire during the 15th century by Gerald Fitzgerald and, when asked by King Henry VII why he had done such a thing, he replied that he thought the archbishop was inside!

St. Patrick's Cross

MILER MAGRATH
Buried in the cathedral at Cashel is Archbishop Magrath, a noted pluralist who enjoyed the best of both worlds. Born around 1523, he began his religious life a Franciscan friar, soon becoming Catholic Bishop of Down and Connor, an office he later combined with being Protestant Archbishop of Cashel. At his death (1622) he had amassed 70 parishes, four bishoprics, two wives, and numerous offspring.

Inside the museum at the Rock of Cashel

CHARLES BIANCONI

This adopted citizen of Clonmel was born at Tregolo in northern Italy on 24 September, 1786. He was dispatched to Ireland by his father to avoid a scandal at the age of 16 after he had fallen in love with a neighbour's daughter who was destined for a marriage with the nobility. On 6 July, 1815, he began a one-horse cart service between Clonmel and Cahir, which rapidly grew into a thriving mail-coach business and reputedly the world's first public transportation system. His vehicles were known as "bians" (after Bianconi) and ran thousands of miles each day all over Ireland, despite competition from the railroads. His headquarters were in Hearn's Hotel on Parnell Street and he became mayor of Clonmel twice.

The attractive harbour at Dunmore East continues…

►► Clonmel   1182B

Clonmel is Tipperary's county town, a prosperous and pretty place with plenty of life and, if home-grown novelist Laurence Sterne's writings are anything to go by, some whimsical goings-on. Sterne lived during the 18th century and is best known for his novel, *Tristram Shandy*. Other novelists have connections with the town; Anthony Trollope worked for a while in the local post office, and George Borrow, the 19th-century traveller and writer, was at school here. There are no outstanding sights in the town, but it has lots of pleasant shops and eating places and stands on the edge of some extremely picturesque touring country. The **circular drive►►** to the south, along the Nire and Suir valleys, is well worth taking on a fine day. So are trips into the unspoiled Comeragh Mountains.

The town was once an important stronghold of the powerful Butler family. Its Main Guard replaced the court-house destroyed in the Cromwellian siege. The West Gate dates from 1831 and stands on the site of an earlier medieval gateway. Near St. Mary's Protestant church are sections of the old 14th-century walls that defended the town against Cromwell for longer than any other Irish town. Several churches have eye-catching, 19th-century, "streaky bacon" coloured brickwork.

Clonmel is famed for its field sports, notably fox-hunting and hare-coursing (sending dogs after hares). It is a great centre of the greyhound world, and the slim animals can often be seen being exercised along the road, much as racehorses are in Kildare.

► Dungarvan   1182A

A bustling fishing port and resort on the Colligan estuary, Dungarvan is surrounded by low cliffs and gentle hills. The setting is rather more appealing than the town itself, but it caters well to simple family stays with an excellent beach at Clonea Strand. The centre of the town is Grattan Square, flanked by stately buildings. Down by the harbour a maze of tiny alleyways laces between warehouses towards the quayside, where several attractive old inns serve good seafood. Old Market House contains a museum of local history, where the sad tale of the *Moresby*, shipwrecked in Dungarvan Bay, is recounted. Close to the town the remains of Dungarvan's Castle, built by King John, can be seen, and on the east bank of the Colligan is an Augustinian abbey overlooking attractive **Helvick Head►►**. The drive around the bay to this headland leads through the tiny Gaelic-speaking village of **Ring►►**, with some fine coastal views on the way.

►► Dunmore East   1183A

This substantial village at the seaward end of Waterford harbour is now a popular resort and sailing centre, but tourism is a secondary interest. Dunmore has its own *raison d'être* dating from 1813, when it was

128

chosen as Waterford's mail packet station. Bright fishing boats crowd the pretty harbour of what is obviously still a well-used port. Visitors are warned that they approach the waterside at their own risk; ropes and steel hawsers bestrew the workmanlike quays. The setting is lovely—red sandstone cliffs, topped with vivid emerald turf and golden gorse, catch the sun, while beneath lie sheltered coves of soft sand. A lighthouse guards the headland. The picturesqueness has encouraged an influx of well-heeled visitors and the village has been used more than once as a film location. Waterford residents retire or escape here in spacious architect-designed bungalows, and more transient holiday-makers stay in thatched homes. The core of the old community is still visible closer to the harbour, in a pleasing assembly of well-kept Georgian and Victorian cottages. The village boasts an exceptionally good range of reasonably priced accommodation and unpretentious eating places, and is an excellent place to stay to explore Waterford City or any of this attractive coast.

MASTER MCGRATH

At a fork in the road 5km (3mi) northwest of Dungarvan stands a splendid commemorative monument—to a greyhound. It was erected by local sportsmen to Master McGrath, winner of the Waterloo Cup three times (1868, 1869, and 1871) and victor in all but one of the 37 courses he ran. Doubtless they were keen to honour both his triumphs and the bets he won for his backers.

…to be the mainstay of the local economy

129

From the County Wexford Museum in Enniscorthy

130

AN IMPOSTOR
The Round Tower that dominates the Irish National Heritage Park at Ferrycarrig gives the impression that the hill on which it stands was the site of an early Irish monastery, to which Round Towers normally belonged. However, a plaque in the wall gives the game away; the tower is a 19th-century copy commemorating the men of Wexford who died in the Crimean War (1853–1856).

▶ **Enniscorthy** *1194B*

The market town of Enniscorthy on the banks of the Slaney River is remembered for a terrible battle in the troubled year of 1798. On 21 June about 20,000 rebels, including many women and children, armed with agricultural implements and metal bayonets or swords, gathered on Vinegar Hill just outside the town. They had held it for nearly a month, but English troops under General Lake, finally losing patience, strafed the insurgents with continuous cannon fire. Exactly how many were killed is not known (many slipped quietly down the far side of the hill), but the massacre remains vivid in the minds of Irish people. The Battle of Vinegar Hill effectively marked the end of the 1798 uprising, but Enniscorthy played an active anti-British role in the Easter Rising of 1916. A fascinating collection of items connected with the battle can be seen in the **Wexford County Museum▶▶** (tel: 054 35926; *open* Apr–Sep, Mon–Sat 10–6,

In its heyday, Jerpoint Abbey was surrounded by a small town, but few, if any, traces of this now survive

Sun 2–5.30. *Admission: inexpensive*), housed in the sturdy square-towered castle. This impressive Anglo-Norman building was briefly leased to the Elizabethan poet and politician, Edmund Spenser, during his inglorious period of office in Ireland. From the castle you can see the slopes of Vinegar Hill, golden with gorse most of the year, and crowned with the stump of an old windmill that served as the rebels' HQ. The town is the centre of the southeast's soft-fruit industry, and every July a Strawberry Fair is held. Enniscorthy's other noteworthy building is its Gothic cathedral of St. Aidan's, designed by Pugin.

A few miles up the road lies **Ferns►**, now a village but formerly the capital of Leinster. Its ruins are the remains of a 13th-century castle and an Augustinian abbey.

►► Ferrycarrig   *1194B*

Just where the Slaney River broadens into tidal mudflats west of Wexford is the **Irish National Heritage Park►►**, which re-creates aspects of life in Ireland through about 9,000 years of history up to the Anglo-Norman period (tel: 053 20733; *open* mid-March–mid-Oct, daily 9.30–6.30. *Admission: moderate*). Full-scale models of lake settlements, ring forts, burial places, and a complete Norman castle lie hidden among hazel groves and reed beds in a large park. This is "theme-park Ireland," but of its kind it is well done, informative, and naturalistic, helping to put into context many of the scattered antiquities you will find as you travel around Ireland. An audio-visual presentation is available at the visitor centre.

► Holycross Abbey   *1182C*

Holycross, tel: 050 443241
Open: daily 9–5 and during services. Admission free
Holycross Abbey is set in peaceful water meadows by the Suir River. It was founded in 1169 and restored in the 15th century. It fell into decay until 1971, when much rebuilding and interior whitewashing made it usable again as a parish church. The abbey's great treasure that attracts thousands of pilgrims to its wall shrine is an alleged splinter of the True Cross, thought to have been given to Murtagh O'Brien, King of Munster, by a 12th-century pope. The Ulster clan chiefs O'Donnell and O'Neill stopped off to pray here on their way to Kinsale, but fate was against them (see page 162). The interior contains a rare wall painting of a Norman hunting scene and some fine stonework.

►► Jerpoint Abbey   *1183B*

Thomastown, tel: 056 21755
Open Mar–May and mid-Sep–mid-Oct, Wed–Mon 10–5;
Jun–mid-Sep, daily 9.30–6.30; otherwise obtain key from the on-site caretaker. Admission: moderate
These evocative Cistercian ruins seem to have a much more authentically medieval ring about them than somewhat commercialized Holycross, the stone tower and battlements erupting suddenly on a quiet bend south of Thomastown. Peer through the gaps in the walls, but if the visitor centre is open it is worth the modest entrance charge to wander around the cloisters and chancel for a close-up of the vivacious carvings of medieval figures and beasts on capitals and tombs. The **glassworks►** at Jerpoint produce a plainer style than most Irish crystal factories.

131

Characterful figures adorn the tombs at Jerpoint Abbey

*The Long Gallery in
Kilkenny Castle includes
portraits by Van Dyck
and Lely*

DUNMORE CAVE
These caverns can be
found just north of
Kilkenny town in craggy
limestone farmland, with
an entrance lying down a
long flight of steps. One
has a thick stalagmite
pillar and lots of tiny ceiling straws like icicles. A
collection of items and
geological material is on
display at the visitor
centre by the ticket office.
One grisly find included
the bones of more than
40 people, many of them
women and children, who
are believed to have taken
refuge in the caves,
perhaps to elude the
Vikings. Their undamaged
bones suggests they
died of starvation, or
may have been suffocated
by smoke.

▶▶▶ **Kilkenny**   *1183C*

One of Ireland's most delightful towns, Kilkenny stands on
a bend in the Nore River. It is packed with history (in
summer, with visitor traffic, too) and its medieval heritage
is particularly well preserved. Discerning visitors will find
a number of high-quality craft studios and good restaurants. One of the most popular times to come is during the
Arts Week festival in the last two weeks of August. The
beautiful countryside around Kilkenny makes it an excellent touring base. The most striking building is the
castle▶▶ (tel: 056 21450), a stronghold of the Butler family
until the 20th century, which began life as a Norman
fortress and gradually became more domesticated through
the centuries. It saw conflict, however, when anti-
Treatyites occupied it briefly during the Civil War in 1922.
After massive restoration, the castle is once again on show.
The hammer-beamed picture gallery, lined with portraits
and elaborate ceiling decorations, is the most memorable
room. The well-proportioned 18th-century buildings
opposite the castle have now been converted into an imaginative enterprise called the Kilkenny Design Centre,
where local artists produce high-quality crafts. A large
retail outlet fronting the street supplies some of the best
goods on sale in Ireland and is an attractive place to do
some shopping, though prices are steep.

Kilkenny's historical importance formerly rivalled
Dublin's, and several significant political events took
place there. The Statutes of Kilkenny, passed in 1366,
were a notorious and crude attempt to assert English
authority in Ireland by what was essentially a form of
apartheid. The Anglo-Norman settlers were prevented
from intermarriage or social intercourse with the native
Celtic Irish, on pain of death. Gaelic names were banned,
the language was suppressed, and the native population
was forced to live outside the city walls. Understandably,

the Irish grew restless at this repressive regime. After the Reformation had suppressed even their religious beliefs, the "Old English" and Gaelic aristocrats (both Catholic factions) formed an uneasy alliance called the Confederation of Kilkenny, a parliamentary assembly that aimed to resist the ferociously unjust anti-Catholic laws imposed by Protestant England. Cromwell's invasion brutally put a stop to this and thus drove an iron stake through the heart of Anglo-Irish integration, which, if left to itself, would, over time, probably have resulted in a harmonious community.

Many other interesting buildings are scattered through the old town. **St. Canice's Cathedral**▶▶ (tel: 056 64971) is its most notable church and one of the finest 13th-century buildings in Ireland, despite Cromwell's use of it to stable his horses in 1650. The monuments of the black limestone known as Kilkenny marble are particularly impressive—one female statue wears a traditional Irish cloak. Next to the cathedral are a **Round Tower**▶, which can be climbed for splendid town views, and the valuable **St. Canice's Library**▶ containing many rare early volumes. St. Mary's Cathedral is the Catholic counterpart built in 1849. Other medieval churches include the Black Abbey, the ruined St. John's Priory, and St. Francis's Abbey.

One of several Tudor buildings is **Rothe House**▶▶ (tel: 056 22893). This stone mansion belonged to the merchant John Rothe and his growing family of 12 children, which necessitated the addition of several wings rambling around cobbled courtyards. The restored building has now become a museum run by Kilkenny Archaeological Society. The Tourist Information Centre is housed in a **Tudor almshouse**▶ (tel: 056 51500, www.southeastireland.com) built by lawyer Sir Richard Shee in 1594. A *son-et-lumière* presentation is held upstairs. The Tholsel (town hall) and courthouse date from the 18th century.

ALICE KYTELER

The medieval home of Dame Alice Kyteler is now a popular old tavern in Kilkenny. In 1324, she was charged with witchcraft and the poisoning of her four husbands, all of whom had died painfully in quick succession, leaving Alice somewhat wealthy. Whether there was any truth in the accusation is unknown, but Alice was a sly character, and she fled to Scotland, leaving her poor maid, Petronella, to take her place at the stake.

KELLS PRIORY

The countryside south and east of Kilkenny is pretty. If you head south you will find the romantic remains of Kells Priory, a walled monastery looking like some medieval city standing in a sloping field. A short way south of the tiny medieval village are a Round Tower and a High Cross.

St. Canice's Cathedral

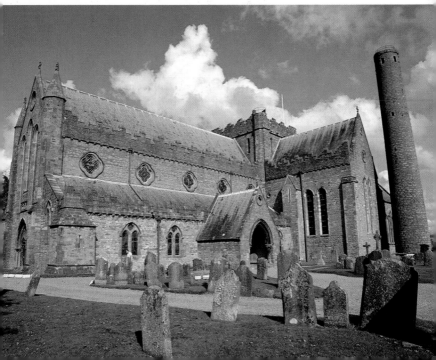

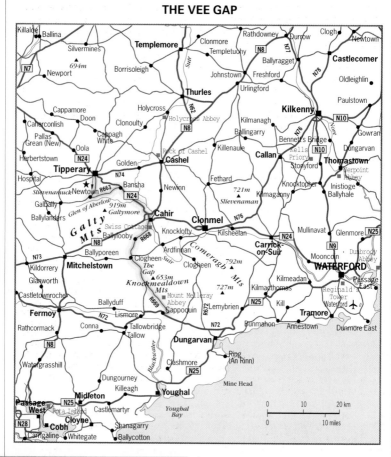

THE VEE GAP

134

The Vee Gap

A roller-coaster drive between southern Tipperary's two ranges of hills, with panoramic views of fertile plains.

From the mundane agricultural town of **Tipperary**, an important dairy farming centre, a scenic route is marked via the **Glen of Aherlow▶▶**. A road through dappled woodland meanders up to a sharp hairpin bend, giving a breathtaking vista down the Aherlow Valley. This beautiful glen is about 16km (10mi)

long, following the course of the Aherlow River. Shortly afterwards it joins the Glen of Aherlow road, with grand glimpses of the Slievenamuck Hills to the north, and the shallow-pitched ridge of the Galty Mountains on the southerly side. The highest summit is Galtymore Mountain, at 919m (3,015ft). The Cahir Way and numerous forest trails lead through the hills, past ancient cairns and glacial tarns. The region is noted for its traditional farmhouse cheeses, Galty bacon and sausages, hams, and even venison. **Mitchelstown▶** is a good place to buy these products.

From **Bansha** the N24 leads southeast to **Cahir▶▶** (see pages 122–123). At Cahir the minor R668 runs down towards the old market town of **Clogheen▶**, where you can join the spectacular **Vee Gap Drive**►► through the Knockmealdown Mountains. The Vee road winds steeply up through larch and rhododendron, and at its most dramatic loop several safe parking bays offer irresistibly photogenic views. Far below, the Suir Valley and the Golden Vale of emerald fields lie as flat and placid as an embroidered quilt beneath vast skies. Black-and-white cattle graze amid a sprinkling of farmsteads. Just south of these viewpoints the road climbs over heather-, bracken-, and gorse-covered slopes to the V-shaped pass that forms the boundary between Tipperary and Waterford counties. A tarn is visible below the road, and a couple of stone shepherds' shelters. Beyond the pass, the road descends past **Mount Melleray Abbey** (see page 136) to **Cappoquin**.

► Kilmore Quay   1194A

Just offshore lie the Saltee Islands, Ireland's largest bird sanctuary. Boats run from the harbour from May until mid-July, the nesting season for thousands of seabirds. The pretty village of thatched and whitewashed cottages vies with Kinsale by hosting a seafood festival in July—the Wooden House pub is one of the better bars offering traditional music. An old lightship moored in the harbour contains a small maritime museum. The westerly sandspit of Ballyteigue is another important nature reserve, with rare plants.

►► Lismore   1181A

The **castle**►► (tel: 058 54424), looming above the dense woodland of the Blackwater Valley, is one of Ireland's most evocative fortresses. Built by Prince John in 1185, it was extensively remodelled in the 19th century, when Joseph Paxton (designer of the Crystal Palace in south London) was commissioned to re-create a Tudor-style residence for the 6th Duke of Devonshire from the medieval ruins. It was planned on an opulent scale; the gorgeous **gardens** are open to the public during the summer (although you can't see inside the castle). Sir Walter Ralegh lived there for a time, later selling it to Richard Boyle, father of the famous pharmacist who was born in the castle. It also functioned as an archbishop's palace, eventually passing in 1753 to the Cavendish family, the Dukes of Devonshire, whose Irish seat it remains to this day. For many years Lismore Castle was the home of Fred Astaire's sister, Adele, who married a Cavendish.

The other main buildings of interest in Lismore are the two cathedrals. **St. Carthage's**►►, the Anglican one, is mostly 17th century, its notable features including the splendidly carved MacGrath tomb dating from 1548, and two bright lancet windows by the pre-Raphaelite artist, Sir Edward Burne-Jones. The Catholic Cathedral, built in 1881, contains many ornate decorations in Italian Romanesque style.

An award-winning **heritage centre**►► (tel: 058 54975) has appeared in Lismore's stone courthouse. An excellent audio-visual production on the history of the town and area dwells particularly on its importance as a monastic settlement and university in the 7th century. Today Lismore is proud of another local celebrity, the travel writer Dervla Murphy, who acquired her wanderlust by cycling around this beautiful wooded valley where she was born.

SURPRISING LISMORE
Lismore Castle is a place of surprises. James II, on looking out of the window over the Blackwater River in 1689, was so amazed at the drop that he started with a fright; the spot is pointed out to this day. In 1814, when workmen were repairing the castle, they found a crozier dated around 1100 in a wall, and a later medieval manuscript containing the lives of early Irish saints. Both were probably hidden when the castle was besieged and burned in 1645. They are now in the National Museum, Dublin.

135

A figurehead at the Maritime Museum, Kilmore Quay

▶▶▶ Mitchelstown Caves 1181B

Burncourt, tel: 052 67246, www.mitchelstowncaves.com
Open: Jul–Sep, daily 10–6; Oct–Jun, daily 10–5
Admission: moderate

These caves are believed to be the largest system of river-formed limestone caverns in Ireland. Though privately owned, they remain pleasantly uncommercialized. You buy your ticket at a roadside farmhouse, and the 3km (2mi) tour around a small section of the caves is conducted on an amateur family basis. Minerals in the rocks have caused spectacular colourations. The caves served as a hiding place for the Earl of Desmond during the 16th century. Occasional special events take advantage of the acoustics.

▶ Mount Melleray Abbey 1182B

Mount Melleray, tel: 058 54404
Open: daily 9–6. Admission free

This austere, grey monastery was founded in 1832 by the Cistercian order, who have industriously turned a barren hillside into fertile and productive land. The community of mostly Irish monks was expelled from its original home in France and granted land here. Visitors are welcome in the main church and can stay in the guest lodge by prior arrangement. Just south of the monastery is a grotto shrine where miraculous visions of the Virgin have been seen, and the faithful gather to light candles and pray.

▶ New Ross 1183B

There are few reasons to visit New Ross specifically, but you will almost certainly find yourself driving through it if you are in the southeast. It commands the lowest bridging point on the Barrow River, so you must either take the car ferry between Passage East and Ballyhack, or pass through New Ross to travel between counties Wexford and Water-

Mitchelstown Caves lie in a limestone trough between the Knockmealdown and Galty mountains, and are the unexpected home of a very rare spider, Porrhoma Myops

The J. F. Kennedy Arboretum, near New Ross

ford. Views of the town from either of the stepped hills rising sharply from the waterfront overlook its busy wharves. It is a very old settlement, founded in the 13th century by Strongbow's son-in-law, William le Marshall, on an ancient monastic site. Part of the ancient city gates remain. The waterfront can be pleasantly explored from a boat deck; river cruises up the Barrow are organized in summer on the Galley Cruising Restaurant. There are also many rewarding excursions, particularly north, towards Inistioge and St. Mullin's. Flower-dappled lanes wander through ancient villages studded with crumbling castles and abbeys. Sparkling rivers snake through the meadows, and the gentle contours of the Blackstairs Mountains, brown, green, or heather-coloured, rise in the background.

The drive northwest through the beautiful Nore valley leads past **Inistioge▶** to **Thomastown▶▶** and **Jerpoint Abbey▶▶** (see page 131). Inistioge is a picturesque little town, with linden trees planted in its main square beside the bridge, a pretty riverfront, and a jumble of 18th- and 19th-century houses on the lane twisting up from the town centre. There are ruins of a Norman castle and an Augustinian monastery. Thomastown, once a medieval walled town of importance, is now a lovely place with mellowed grey-stone buildings and a few ruins. The **Kilfane Glen and Waterfall▶** is an 18th-century woodland garden. Return to New Ross via **Graiguenamanagh▶▶** and **St. Mullin's▶** (see page 141). Graiguenamanagh, in a spectacular position beside the river, is a little market town, famous for **Duiske Abbey▶** (*Open* daily 9–5 and during services. *Admission free*), a much-restored 13th-century Cistercian foundation, once the largest in Ireland. The effigy of a knight stands beside the abbey's entrance.

South of New Ross lies the **J. F. Kennedy Arboretum▶▶**, occupying an area of forest and landscaped gardens with about 5,000 types of specimen trees and shrubs (tel: 051 388171; *open* May–Aug, daily 10–8; Apr and Sep, daily 10–6.30; Oct–Mar, daily 10–5. *Admission: inexpensive*). Nature trails lead through the grounds and visitors can drive to a viewpoint on the summit of Slieve Coillte. Much botanical and arboreal research is carried out there.

IRISH-AMERICAN PRESIDENTS
Two recent US presidents have roots in southeast Ireland. President John F. Kennedy's great-grandfather was born in a cottage in Dunganstown, just south of New Ross in County Waterford, and descendants of the family still live there. A memorial arboretum to President Kennedy has been planted close by. President Ronald Reagan's folk probably hailed from the tiny, one-horse town of Ballyporeen, near Mitchelstown in County Tipperary. President Reagan visited Ballyporeen in 1984 and brought great fame to it.

"As long as Ireland produces men with sense enough to leave her, she does not exist in vain." George Bernard Shaw's remark is unkind, but apt. Irish-born people or, more broadly, people of Irish descent, have had a most disproportionate influence in many fields, particularly in the arts, media, sports, and politics. But they have often shown this after they have left the island.

Top: a stylized depiction of Ireland's most famous 20th-century exile— James Joyce

THE FLIGHT OF THE WILD GEESE
After the final victory of William III's forces at the Battle of Limerick in 1691, many Jacobite officers accepted the terms of surrender at the Treaty of Limerick and sailed away down the Shannon to join the armies of Catholic Europe (perhaps with the hope one day of returning to defeat the old enemy). Among these aristocratic mercenaries was the hero of the Battle of Limerick, Patrick Sarsfield, Earl of Lucan. Like the earlier Flight of the Earls in 1607, this exile of leaders dealt a great blow to Gaelic power in Ireland. Their estates and castles were quickly snatched by Protestant settlers.

A constraining influence Many periods in Ireland's history have worked against pioneering spirits; the long doldrum since the Irish Free State was formed in 1922 is one of the most noticeable of these in recent times. After English shackles were shaken off, Ireland had everything to play for—high ideals, a young and vigorous population, and a new nation to form. Under de Valera's rule and the constricting influence of a peculiarly oppressive form of Catholicism, Ireland remained fossilized in a twilight zone of romantic mythology, social divisiveness, and economic gloom. Many people have left Ireland since, ironically for the land whose rule they have so roundly rejected.

Artists and Ireland Artists and writers have deserted Ireland for centuries in search of havens where their work would receive a better reception than in the reactionary climate of their birthplace. Since World War II, the Irish government has tried to stem the tide by offering artists (including writers) tax-free status in the Republic. The hugely successful novelist Frederick Forsyth was one of the most notable acceptors of this bribe, though other writers found it odd that a government should encourage literary enterprise with fiscal measures and then censor it on religious or moral grounds. An enormous number of Irish writers have made their homes abroad. One, Cecil Day-Lewis, even became an English poet laureate. The novelist Edna O'Brien, herself an exile in London from Tuamgraney, County Clare, described the claustrophobia of Irish provincial life. "Hour after hour I can think of Ireland, I can imagine without going too far wrong what is happening in any one of the little towns by day or by night." For a visit, for a holiday, the pace of Ireland is refreshing, endearing, delightful. However, for a lifetime, many have found it stultifying.

Enforced emigration Reasons for the steady departure of Irishmen to lands abroad range from general "grass is greener" aspirations to the most dire and desperate emergencies. Most drastically, the Famine years of the late 1840s resulted in massive emigration, mostly from the west. Whole communities were decimated and many have never recovered. In earlier times, religious persecution was often the spur, famously in the exile of leading Catholic families after the confiscation of their lands

(The Flight of the Earls in 1607, see pages 34–35), or after defeat in battle ("The Wild Geese," after the Battle of Limerick in 1691, see panel). The Ulster Presbyterians emigrated in great numbers in the late 18th and early 19th centuries in order to seek their fortunes in the New World. One of the best places to learn all about this fascinating phase of Irish history is at the **Ulster American Folk Park** in County Tyrone (see page 234).

The Kennedy homestead in the J. F. Kennedy Arboretum near New Ross shows what early American homesteads looked like

Influential exiles To see evidence of Ireland's influence abroad, you need look no further than the list of US presidents. Over a quarter of them are of Irish descent—mostly of Ulster Protestant stock. More recently, John F. Kennedy and Ronald Reagan have partly redressed the balance with their origins in counties Waterford and Tipperary. Canada has had Brian Mulroney as prime minister. Today more than 40 million US citizens can claim Irish ancestry.

The excellent Ulster American Folk Park near Omagh, County Tyrone, Northern Ireland

Irish representatives overseas can be found in just about any field you care to mention: John Field, the composer; John Philip Holland, inventor of the submarine; James Hoban, architect of the White House; the writers F. Scott Fitzgerald and Eugene O'Neill; Sir Hans Sloane, founder of the British Museum; John McEnroe, the tennis star—and a host of others whose influence can be found across the globe.

▶ **Oldleighlin** — *1183C*

A few minor sights make this village worth a brief stop. One is the squat crenellated tower of the 13th-century Anglican church known grandiosely as St. Lazerian's Cathedral, with, nearby, a 7th-century monastery and Lazerian's well, which attracts many pilgrims. The simple cathedral has a Gothic door and two fonts. Leighlinbridge to the east, as its name suggests, is a bridging point over the Barrow (the original bridge here dates from 1320). The scanty remains of the Black Castle can be seen on the east bank, one of the earliest Norman defences in Ireland.

▶▶ **Ring of Hook** — *1183A*

The quiet peninsula on the east side of Waterford Harbour is a strange low-lying place full of deserted villages and migrant birds. The straight, empty roads lead through Ballyhack, where a small shuttle ferry cuts out the long trek inland via New Ross, then through **Duncannon**, a peaceful small seaside resort with a sandy beach and a reputation for fine sea fishing. Military remains indicate its former strategic importance; a fortress built by the Anglo-Normans stands by the water-front, strengthened to guard against the Spanish Armada in the late 16th century, and during Napoleonic times the British built three Martello Towers to deter the French. The big house here, Loftus Hall, was built by the 4th Marquis of Ely for his bride-to-be, Victoria, the Princess Royal, who called off her engagement for mysterious reasons. It later became a hotel, capitalizing on a ghostly legend that the Devil once escaped through the roof here after a game of cards, leaving cracks that are impossible to repair (a good excuse for leaving them alone, anyway!).

At the craggy, desolate tip of the peninsula stands an ancient lighthouse, the oldest in Ireland. Warning lights for shipping have been kept here for some 1,400 years, but the present, zebra-striped version dates from Norman times. Even earlier than that, a Welsh monk called Dubhand is thought to have kept a form of lighthouse by hoisting a cauldron of burning pitch to a high platform. On stormy days the sea sends dramatic columns of spray through blow holes in the rocks. During high season some enterprising families seek out

BY HOOK OR BY CROOK
The origin of this phrase is much disputed, but Cromwell is alleged to have used it when he was planning his assault on Waterford, declaring he would take the city "by Hook ..." (on the eastern side) "... or by Crook" (just below Passage East on the west side of the harbour).

140

The lighthouse on Hook Head has ancient origins; it was built by one Raymond le Gros in 1172. The sea at Hook Head is also noted for the beauty of the corals found growing on the limestone

A cannon still guards the busy port of Rosslare

these quiet beaches around Fethard and Booley Strand; at other times of year you can enjoy them almost unchallenged. The village of Slade is especially charming and is a well-known scuba-diving centre. The remains of some 18th-century salthouses can be seen on the pier (where salt was extracted from seawater by evaporation).

▶ Rosslare   1194B

Well known as a ferry terminal for traffic from Normandy and Wales, Rosslare is actually 8km (5mi) north of its harbour. It is a popular seaside resort capitalizing on its long, sandy beach and relatively sunny climate. However, there is little of interest in the place, except perhaps for golfers (it has an excellent links course).

Just south of Rosslare is Our Lady's Island, connected to the mainland by a causeway, where the ruins of an Augustinian priory and a Round Tower can be seen (the tower leans more precariously than that at Pisa). There is an annual pilgrimage to the Marian shrine from 15 August to 8 September. Some pilgrims crawl around the site on their knees; others walk with one foot in the water.

▶ St. Mullin's   1183B

A monastery was founded here in the 7th century by St. Moling, a monk of high birth and apparently artistic talents. The watercourse that he dug with his own hands to power a mill is still there, but the monastery buildings have disappeared and the remains date from medieval times. In the churchyard are a penal altar, used surreptitiously when Catholic services were banned, and the graves of several Leinster kings, including the warrior Art MacMurrough, scourge of the Anglo-Normans. St. Mullin's is scarcely worth visiting for its remains alone, which are minimal and hard to track down, but the village itself is at a most beautiful spot by a stream with the Blackstairs Mountains rising behind. Many places around here, or in Graiguenamanagh (see page 137), upstream where the more impressive monastery of Duiske Abbey stands, are ideal for walks and picnics.

CAPTAIN MYLES KEOGH
Captain Keogh, from Leighlinbridge, was an adventurous soul. He fought for the pope in the 1860s when Garibaldi was uniting Italy, then joined the American Civil War on the Union side. His third military adventure was with Colonel Custer's 7th Cavalry, where he fought gallantly at the Battle of Little Big Horn against the Sioux Indians in 1876. He was apparently one of the last to die, and as a mark of respect was not scalped after the battle. His horse Comanche was the only survivor on the army's side.

Waterford City has been a bustling centre since the Vikings settled there in the middle of the 9th century

WATERFORD MUTINY
The citizens of Waterford were a fairly pugnacious lot, it seems. Mayor Briver had to be rescued by his wife in 1641 when a riot took place. Mrs. Briver wrote that when she heard swords being drawn against her husband, "I ran oute into the streete without hatt or mantle and laid my handes about his necke and brought hem in whether he wud or no." Later this same mayor lost three fingers from his hand—bitten off by an angry mutineer.

►► Waterford   1183B

Waterford is by far the largest town in the southeast and one of the few prospering industrial centres in the Republic. It is most famous for its glassworks, benefiting again after suffering badly during the last recession. Other industries include light engineering, electronics, paper manufacture, and brewing. Some visitors find the overtly workmanlike quaysides a turnoff after rural towns in Ireland, but Waterford has a grand history and plenty to explore.

Waterford is essentially a Viking city, with many reminders of this period of its history among the buildings lying immediately behind the waterfront. **Reginald's Tower►** (tel: 051 873501; *open* Jun–Sep, daily 9.30–6.30; Easter–May and Oct, daily 10–5. *Admission: inexpensive*), was built in 1003 as part of the old city walls by a certain Reginald (an unlikely sounding name for a Danish city governor), and served subsequently as royal residence, fortress, mint, prison, and air-raid shelter. It is now the Civic and Maritime Museum, containing many municipal documents and regalia.

The most interesting churches are **St. Patrick's** Catholic church of 1750, well restored after being used as a corn store during penal days, and the Protestant **Christ Church Cathedral**, built in 1770 and containing a weighty colonnade of Corinthian columns and fine stucco ceiling decorations. A grim memorial to James Rice, a mayor who died in 1490, depicts the process of posthumous decomposition in graphic detail. The Catholic **Holy Trinity Cathedral** also has a remarkably sumptuous interior.

Later civic buildings worth a glance are the 1849 courthouse with a massive classical portico, the **city hall►** (tel: 051 873 501) of 1788 with magnificent Waterford crystal glittering in the public assembly rooms, and the **Chamber of Commerce►** (tel: 051 875 788. *Admission free*), a town house of 1795 with a spectacularly beautiful stairwell.

Housed in the old granary beside Merchant's Quay, **Waterford Treasures►** (tel: 051 304500; *open* Jun–Sep, daily 9–9; Apr–May, daily 9–6; Oct–Mar, daily 10–5. *Admission: moderate*) is a heritage centre and city museum in one. The audio-visual displays guide you through 1,000 years of Waterford history.

A visit to the crystal factory on the N25 Cork road, near the city centre, is the most popular visitor activity Waterford has to offer. Free factory tours take place every weekday during the mornings. At busy times of year you should reserve a place.

The tours are indeed interesting, and take about 40 minutes (a good plan for a wet day: to reserve a place contact Waterford Crystal on 051 332500, www.waterford-visitorscentre.com. *Admission: moderate*). You are taken around each stage of manufacture. Basic ingredients of glass are silica and potash; lead crystal also requires a significant quantity of lead oxide in powder form (safety regulations must be strictly adhered to with this toxic substance). The lead gives the glass its qualities of brilliance and capacity to refract light, and also makes it very heavy. The ingredients are heated to about 1,200°C (2,200°F) over many hours, then hand-blown and skillfully shaped before cooling. Finally the glass is cut with deep grid-like patterns, the air filling with minute particles and the screech of carborundum and diamond wheels. You will see Waterford crystal in grand houses throughout Ireland; today, a modern version of one of those glittering droplet chandeliers costs several thousand Euros.

The plant now covers a site of about 15ha (38 acres). By far the largest market for Waterford crystal is the United States, and American tastes are therefore strongly reflected in the ornate designs. Waterford now has many home-grown rivals throughout Ireland, although Waterford still claims the edge for its high quality (no inferior produce is ever sold; it is simply smashed and melted down again), its purity of colour, and its deep cut. Certainly, if you want to find out about crystal, this is the place to do it. Prices start at over €25 for a tiny liqueur glass.

THE HISTORY OF WATERFORD CRYSTAL

The history of Waterford glass started in the late 18th century, when George and William Penrose set up a factory there in 1783. It flourished for 68 years, before the disastrous economic conditions of 1851 caused its closure. A century later, Waterford once again became home for a glassworks, modest at first, but expanding to prodigious dimensions within only 40 years.

143

A master cutter concentrates on his task

The county town of Wexford lies where the estuary of the River Slaney meets Wexford Harbour

WEXFORD OPERA FESTIVAL
This event has been held during October at the Theatre Royal for over 40 years, now attracting opera buffs from far and wide, as well as many international stars. It tends to favour rare or neglected works, and so has a pleasantly off-beat, avant-garde tinge. If you manage to get tickets, you may of course discover why some of these works are rare and neglected! For all that, it's the social event of the year in Wexford, festive but unsnobby, where local people dress up and drink champagne. Book well ahead for seats; they are gold dust (box office tel: 053 22400). If you can't get a ticket, many other events will be going on, too—concerts, revues, recitals, jazz in pubs, etc. Many travel companies offer package tours to the opera festival.

▶▶ Wexford   1194E

For all its bloody history, Wexford has a peaceful air. First glances may suggest it is all too dull, basking in its muddy estuary like some somnolent reptile. But it is by no means moribund. Present traces of a proud past are admittedly vestigial, but a bustling small-town charm and sense of life outweigh any initial disappointment. If you catch it during October when the acclaimed opera festival is in full swing, you will be left with no doubt that Wexford rates itself pretty highly, and why not, achieving full-page write-ups as it does in all the national papers?

The Viking name *Waesfjord* (harbour of the mudflats) is appropriate. The Slaney River and several tributaries empty their silt-laden waters into the sea there, and Wexford's practicality as a deepwater port has long since been overtaken by its rival in the next county, Waterford. But the mud is not all bad. North and south of the town, large areas on either side of the estuary provide a habitat for many thousands of wading birds. The **Wexford Wildfowl Reserve▶▶** is a must for ornithologists (tel: 053 23129). The "Slobs," as the mudflats are known locally, are "polders," or reclaimed land lying lower than sea level. Follow the signs for the reserve from Wexford's coastal exit roads and you will reach a research station with a visitor centre, a lookout tower, identification charts, and hides (like hunting blinds). Entrance is free. The neighbouring dunes around Raven Point are also an important nature reserve with rare plants and insects.

The town itself straggles along the waterfront, several blocks deep. The helpful tourist office can be found right in the centre of the seafront, where Crescent Quay takes a bite from the shore. The bronze statue outside commemorates Commodore John Barry, the brilliant naval officer who avenged his Irish ancestors by emigrating to Philadelphia and trouncing the English during the Revolutionary War. Wexford is best explored on foot (historic walking tours are advertised) when narrow alleys and one-way streets provide no obstacle. The old centre of town is a cheerful mix of agreeable pubs, old-fashioned shops, and plenty of decent down-to-earth eating places. The main historic monuments are the **Westgate Tower▶** (tel: 053 46506), dating from 1300 (*The Wexford Experience*, a short film, is shown inside), and the remains of **Selskar Abbey▶**, where the Anglo-Irish treaty was signed after the Norman invasion, and where Henry II spent many Lenten hours atoning for the murder of St. Thomas à Becket. A couple of modern Gothic churches can be seen, interesting only because they are virtually identical. In the Bull Ring Cromwellian troops slaughtered 300 hapless citizens as they prayed for mercy. Many others were put to the sword in one of the most appalling massacres of the Ironside invasion. When Ireland rebelled again in 1798, Wexford's inhabitants were among the most vigorous pike-wielders, as the statue in the Bull Ring indicates.

Two other sights are well worth a visit if you are in the vicinity of Wexford. The **Irish National Heritage Park▶▶** is described on page 131 (see **Ferrycarrig▶▶**). Towards Rosslare is another museum, in the massive Gothic-revival building called Johnstown Castle, constructed as a private residence around the core of a 15th-century tower house. This contains the **Irish Agricultural Museum▶▶** (tel: 053 42888); the rest of the building serves as an agri-cultural college. It is the largest collection of its kind in Ireland, full of attractive displays of intriguing imple-ments like furze rooters, barley hummlers, and turnip knives. The veterinary section displays fearsome horse gags and drenching horns. Little workshops have been re-created showing how the tools would have been arranged and used by wheelwrights, and coopers, among others. There are also displays of ancient domestic appliances and butter-making equipment. The grounds around this imposing castellated and mullioned grey-stone building are beautifully landscaped and open to the public.

is described on page 131

WHITE-FRONTED GEESE
The Wexford Slobs attract 40 percent of the world's population of Greenland white-fronted geese for about eight months of the year. Farmers are not too thrilled by this, since, protected from all preda-tors, the geese munch their way through the same amount of grass as a herd of several hundred cattle. Their diet is supple-mented with specially provided helpings of sugar beet in frosty weather. The film at the research station shows how the birds are tagged to study their lifestyles and migration patterns. Many other species join the Greenland geese on the Slobs at various times of year.

The Irish National Heritage Park

Southwestern Counties

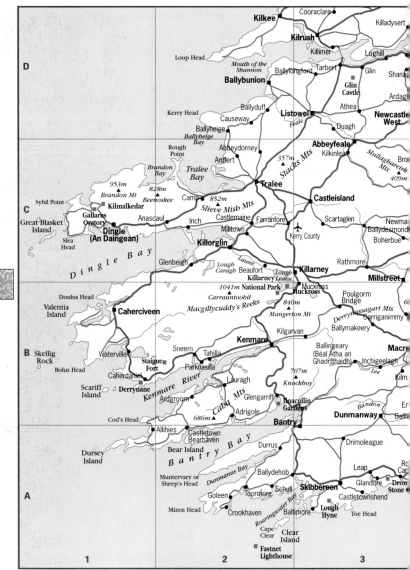

RAIN IN THE WEST?
"When the glass is up to thirty
Cork and Kerry will be dirty;
When the glass is high O very
There'll be rain in Cork and Kerry;
When the glass is low, O Lork!
There'll be rain in Kerry and Cork."
"Thirty" refers to high barometric pressure, normally assuring dry weather!

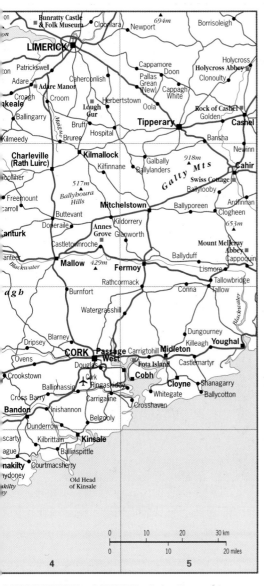

147

SOUTHWESTERN COUNTIES Ireland's southwestern corner ranks high with most visitors, and for many people the counties of Cork and Kerry represent the best that Ireland can offer, with striking scenery, charming towns, a mild climate, and many places of interest. There is a huge variety of things to do and see for just about anyone, young or old, active or sedentary. To see much of it, you will need your own transportation, as elsewhere in Ireland. If you prefer to see things slowly and in more detail, that could mean a bicycle, or a Romany (Gypsy) caravan. If you can afford to pamper yourself, the region has a fine collection of country house hotels (including a few stately homes) and many excellent restaurants.

FUNGI THE DOLPHIN
This half-tame creature has captured the hearts of thousands in the past few years. His behaviour suggests he may have escaped or been released from a marine park at some stage. He cavorts in Dingle Bay to the delight of all onlookers and the great pleasure of the tourist authorities, and has apparently no fear of humans or their boats. He will frolic beside wetsuited swimmers, jump over boats, and really gives the impression that he enjoys company. Fungi seems to have become completely fixated by his human visitors and will chase off any rival dolphin who encroaches on his territory. Boat trips from Dingle harbour virtually guarantee a sighting in summer.

148

Page 146: Slea Head, Dingle

The predictable, but pleasant, face of tourism on the Muckross Estate near Killarney

Events such as Kinsale's annual gourmet festival raise both standards of cuisine and the region's popularity with international visitors. The high quality of local ingredients helps; seafood, good beef, and rich dairy products now available everywhere belie the terrible sufferings of the southwest during the Famine years.

The massive emigration from these counties to the New World has resulted in a backwash of third- or fourth-generation visitors migrating back to the land of their forebears searching for roots. Shannon Airport welcomes transatlantic visitors, who converge on Limerick and Killarney. Many foreigners from continental Europe approach via Cork and some have settled there permanently, adding new influences to the area's restaurants and bringing fresh artistic talents with them.

A WARM WELCOME English attempts to subjugate this old Irish province of Munster produced a mass of fortifications all along the coast, ever-watchful for Catholic plots from Spain and France using Catholic Ireland as an unlocked back door from which to invade Britain. Today, however, the tricky Anglo-Irish interface leaves little mark here.

The southwest has two of Ireland's largest cities, Cork and Limerick. These are certainly worth seeing, but the rural areas are far more appealing. The coastline is, in places, particularly beautiful, and generally more exciting than the lush inland scenery, cut by its great easterly flowing rivers. An exception is Killarney's National Park, a high spot in any itinerary. Less well known, but also worth exploring, is the forest park of Gougane Barra, on the remote inland borders of Cork and Kerry. It is a place of wildlife, of tumbling streams, and the hermitage of St. Fin Barre. Founded probably in the 6th or 7th century, although the ruins beside the modern church date from

Youghal beach, Cork

the 18th century, the hermitage of Cork City's patron saint is set on an islet in the beautiful Gougane Barra Lake, the source of the Lee, which eventually reaches the sea at Cork. The county of Limerick is the Cinderella of the three, with little to lift its flattish landscapes from mediocrity. Killarney and Blarney are perhaps the only blatant examples of mass tourism in the region. Elsewhere, the tourist scene is low-profile. Kinsale, Kenmare, Dingle, Youghal, and Bantry all make charming and much classier bases for exploring the coast.

A MILD AND VERDANT LAND Few would argue that the islet-strewn peninsulas that trail westwards to the Atlantic are the places to visit for the best scenery, where the blue water of never-distant sea sets off the brilliant rain-washed emerald of fields and mountains. There the pace of life is slow and gentle, and the ambience profoundly Irish, perhaps most noticeably in the Dingle peninsula, one of the largest Gaeltacht (Irish-speaking) regions. Traditional Irish music can be heard all over the region, particularly in Dingle and some of the villages of south Cork, such as Leap and Clonakilty.

The influence of the Gulf Stream keeps frost permanently at bay and, although Atlantic storms can be severe, sheltered regions lend themselves to superb subtropical gardens and a great range of flora and fauna. Even the least botanically minded can scarcely fail to be impressed by the lush fuchsia hedges dripping scarlet all summer, the rhododendrons in profusion, or the arbutus trees that grow wild in the valleys of Iveragh. Water lilies and rare bog plants colonize the reedy pools of Cork's quieter peninsulas. The southwest is a good place for birdwatchers, too—the region is first landfall for the myriad exhausted migrants in spring and autumn on Clear Island or the wild Skellig Islands, the moors, mountains, and lakes of Kerry, and the sheltered, muddy estuaries around Timoleague on the south Cork coast.

ROSE OF TRALEE FESTIVAL
This is held in the last week of August and is a great attraction for the region. Six days and nights of merriment take place, including pipe bands and parades. The main event is a beauty contest that any woman of Irish origins can enter. Visitors from around the world compete for the honour of being crowned Rose; details from the Festival Office in Lower Castle Street, Tralee (tel: 066 7121322).

The enormous, conical, whitewashed beacon near Baltimore acts as a marker for boats

An enterprising bar in Bantry has erected this elaborate and informative advertisement for its wares

1796

NOTICE

THIS ANCHOR WAS TAKEN IN A TRAWL
BY THE MOTOR TRAWLER 'SAOIRSE',
SKIPPERED BY PAT DEASY ON THE 11th
SEPTEMBER, 1964. EXPERTS BELIEVE
THAT IT IS ONE OF THOSE ANCHORS LEFT
BEHIND WHEN THE FRENCH FLEET UNDER
WOLFE TONE, WHICH WAS COMING TO
ASSIST THE IRISH REBELS IN 1796, WERE
FORCED TO CUT THEIR ANCHORS IN A GALE
AND RETIRE. THE ANCHOR WEIGHS 17 CWT.
NOT QUITE SO HISTORICAL BUT EQUALLY
INTERESTING IF YOU ARE DYING OF THIRST IS
THE ANCHOR BAR WHICH ERECTED THIS SIGN

▶ Baltimore   1463A

Baltimore combines salty fishing-village charm with a sturdy castle and several good restaurants. Trips are also available to Sherkin Island, where there is a 15th-century friary, and to the Fastnet Lighthouse on the outermost scrap of Irish territory. In June 1631, Baltimore witnessed a curious and tragic incident when Algerian pirates stole into the harbour and attacked the village, killing a number of residents and abducting about 200 as slaves to North Africa. Some believe the raid may have been orchestrated by the fierce O'Driscoll clan to frighten off English settlers. If so, it worked: many of them moved upstream where they felt less threatened. The poet, Thomas Davis, wrote a rollicking poem about the raid in 1844:

"The yell of 'Allah' breaks above the prayer and shriek and roar,
Oh Blessed God! The Algerine is Lord of Baltimore."

▶ Bantry   1463A

Most people who tour south Cork pass through this fishing and market centre on the main coastal road. The town stands at the head of the long haven of Bantry Bay, sheltered by two of the hilly peninsulas that trail southwest from Cork's mainland. A statue of St. Brendan gazes seaward from its square by the harbour. Bantry was twice an unsuccessful target for French invaders hoping to establish a base in a friendly Catholic enclave from which to overthrow the English. In 1689, a French fleet sailed in, offering support for James II, only to be rebuffed by Williamites. In 1796, the revolutionary Wolfe Tone arrived with another French fleet (see panel), but was driven back by fierce storms. An alert local landowner, Richard White, sent urgent warnings to the English forces and was rewarded for his loyalty by a peerage.

His descendants still live in **Bantry House**▶▶ (tel: 027 50047, www.bantryhouse.ie; *open* Mar–Oct, daily 9–6. *Admission: expensive*), one of the most beautifully sited houses in Ireland. The terraced Italianate gardens overlook a gorgeous sweep of Bantry Bay, and the house's sumptuous rooms are full of fascinating contents. The hospitable present owners offer a classy brand of B&B in a separate wing of the house, and another attraction is the **Bantry 1796 French Armada Exhibition Centre**▶▶ in a renovated side courtyard. This lively museum recounts the history of Wolfe Tone's failed rebellion and displays articles recovered from the wreck of the frigate *La Surveillante*, which sank during the storms and was excavated in 1982.

Minor diversions in the town itself are a museum of local history and the **Kilnaruane Pillar Stone**▶, carved with mysterious early Christian symbols.

▶▶ Blarney   *1474B*

Everyone has heard of Blarney and, when bus tours clog the village, it seems as if everyone has come to see it, too. Visitors come for two reasons— to kiss that stone in **Blarney Castle**▶▶ (tel: 021 438 5252; *open* May and Sep, Mon–Sat 9.30–dusk, Sun 9–5.30; Jun–Aug, Mon–Sat 9–7, Sun 9–5.30; Oct–Apr, Mon–Sat 9–dusk, Sun 9.30–dusk. *Admission: moderate*) and to visit the large gift and craft centres that have sprung up nearby. Why the Blarney Stone exercises such fascination is hard to fathom, but the belief that kissing it endows you with Irish eloquence is certainly appealing.

The stone is an oblong block of limestone set high among the battlements of a fine 15th-century tower house, once a stronghold of the MacCarthys, former kings of Munster and lords of Blarney. A Cormac MacCarthy supposedly strung Queen Elizabeth I along with promises and prevarications, until she exclaimed in exasperation, "What he says he does not mean," and thus the word entered the language. To reach the stone, you must clamber up the tower steps (more than 120 of them), join the inevitable line (in high season, at least), and then lie down and lean backward over a sheer drop. It looks awkward but is actually quite safe, even without the two strong-armed retainers there to grab your ankles. The stone is swabbed down regularly enough to prevent transmission of any nasty ailments. Some locals will offer to take your photograph while you are kissing the stone, but be warned, it isn't a flattering angle (see above)!

The lush water gardens by the Lee River and the 19th-century Rock Close (a rock garden with fanciful wishing

WOLFE TONE'S INVASION
On 16 December, 1796, a French Armada of 43 ships set sail from Brest, bound for Ireland. The French intended to aid Wolfe Tone's rebellion and to deal a blow to the British. From the start, it was a disaster, storms disrupting communications between the fleet. Only 16 battered crews reached Bantry Bay with Wolfe Tone. On Christmas Eve he was ready to attack, but decided to wait for Hoche, the French commander. By the next day his chance of a landing had gone; savage gales had blown the ships out of the bay. Tone wrote in his journal, "We were close enough to throw a biscuit ashore…The elements fight against us."

151

Whatever one gains from kissing the Blarney Stone, one loses one's dignity

FASTNET LIGHTHOUSE
This perches like a fairy-tale castle on its rocky bastion to warn shipping off the treacherous coast. Recreational sailors use it as their westerly target during the biennial Fastnet Yacht Race, starting from Cowes on the Isle of Wight.

There's more to Blarney than the stone

THE SINKING OF THE *LUSITANIA*
Speculation about this has made disturbing reading. In World War I the ship, sailing from New York to Liverpool, was sunk off Cobh by the Germans, who claimed that she was carrying arms as well as civilians. This was denied, but evidence now suggests that it was true. More disturbing is the theory that the Allies contrived the episode to hasten US entry into the war. The German government had placed advertisements in New York papers warning passengers not to take the sailing, implying that the vessel was not a random wartime target. Both suspicion and casualties were increased by the unusual absence of patrolling British warships. She sank in 20 minutes, leaving passengers floundering in the water. Some survived by clutching floating debris, one sitting in a cane chair. The submarine that had sunk the ship did nothing to save passengers, although knowing many were US civilians, and not a remotely legitimate target.

steps and druidical associations) make an attractive foil for the romantic ruin, and behind the castle is an elaborate Scottish baronial mansion called **Blarney House** (visitable on a joint ticket), furnished in Victorian style.

In the village, craft and knitwear shops catch the purse strings, the most advertised being Blarney Woollen Mills, now a colossal hypermarket with a restaurant, hotel, and large parking area. The smaller shops are more enjoyable than this bargain basement, but there's certainly a wide range of merchandise from all over Ireland.

▶▶ Castletownshend   *1463A*
The literary cousins, Edith Somerville and Violet Martin, lived in Drishane House and are both buried in the greystone church of St. Barrahane, where Edith was organist. They are better known as Somerville and Ross, authors of the *Irish RM* stories. The village is pretty, its main street sloping steeply up from the quayside. If you careen down it too fast you are in danger of hitting a tree carefully preserved in the middle of the road. Nearby is an excellent, quaint old pub called Mary Ann's. The Townshend family still live in the local castle, where an idiosyncratic B&B evokes the atmosphere of the *RM* books.

▶▶▶ Clear Island   *1462A*
The frayed coastline at Ireland's bottom left-hand corner disintegrates into a scattering of islets around Baltimore. From there, or from Schull further along the coast, you can take a boat to Ireland's most southerly community, Clear Island, where the Irish-speaking population of fewer than 200 is greatly outnumbered by the birds. An observatory enables visitors to delight in the multitude of streaming migrants—all kinds of gulls, shearwaters, storm petrels, and rare songbirds, even an occasional disorientated albatross. Other sights pale beside the birdlife: the well and church dedicated to St. Ciarán, born here in the 6th century, a wind-driven electricity generator financed by the EU, and a small heritage centre. It is possible to stay on the island, although amenities are spartan.

►► Cobh

1475B

For many Famine emigrants, the scenic panorama of **Cork Harbour►►** and the colourful houses of Cobh must have been their last glimpse of the Emerald Isle. Many perished en route in the dreaded "coffin ships." The name Cobh (pronounced "cove") means "haven" in Irish. Besides emigrant ships, Cobh berthed some of the great transatlantic liners, including the ill-fated *Titanic* and the *Lusitania*, torpedoed offshore on 7 May, 1915, with the loss of 1,198 lives (see panel). Many victims are buried in the local cemetery. Cobh's history is presented in **The Queenstown Story►►** (tel: 021 481 3591; *open* Feb–Nov, daily 10–6. *Admission: moderate*) at a local heritage centre. Today Cobh is a fishing port, seaside resort, and sailing centre, its well-restored buildings and slightly raffish air giving it great character. **St. Colman's Cathedral►►** (tel: 021 481 3222; *open* daily at varying times. *Admission free*) is the most striking landmark, set high on the hilltop, its spire honed to an impossibly slender point. It was designed by Pugin in 1868 and is an exuberant masterpiece of Victorian high Gothic. Harbour trips are available in summer.

In the estuary at the mouth of Cork harbour and connected by bridges to the mainland, **Fota Wildlife Park►►** (tel: 021 481 2678; *open* mid-Mar–Oct, Mon–Sat 10–6, Sun 11–6. *Admission free* for gardens and arboretum; wildlife park: *expensive*) can be reached via the Cork–Cobh railroad line. This huge estate includes a park where cheetahs and wallabies breed and an important arboretum with many rare specimen trees.

BUILT TO LAST?

A 16th-century tower house at Castlehaven near Castletownshend was built by the O'Driscolls, who gave it to the Spaniards before the Battle of Kinsale in 1601. When the Spanish were defeated, they yielded the castle to the English. Before *they* could occupy it, the O'Driscolls retook it and were about to blow it up when in turn they were surprised by the English, who prevented the destruction. It survived until 1926, when Edith Somerville, one of the literary combination of Somerville and Ross, was out for a walk; she heard a rumble, and found that the castle had collapsed into a heap of rubble behind her.

St. Colman's Cathedral sits perkily on top of the Georgian seafront

The Anglo-Saxon bishop and historian known as the Venerable Bede remarked on Ireland's clement weather: "Ireland is far more favoured than Britain by latitude, and by its mild and healthy climate…there is no need to store hay in winter…and no lack of vines." The typical Irish "soft day" of gentle drizzle and sunshine is ideal for plants, and Ireland contains a fine collection of gardens of all types in which many rare species flourish.

154

STRAWBERRY TREE

This plant is most closely identified with Killarney and the lush countryside of south Kerry, where it grows to prodigious heights. It is also known as the arbutus tree, *Arbutus unedo*, and has waxy white flowers and dark green glossy leaves. It flowers in the autumn and is then hung with slow-ripening strawberry-like fruits. A song of 1890 commemorates the tree:

My love's an arbutus
By the borders of Lene,
So slender and shapely
In her girdle of green.

ILNACULLIN GARDENS

Annan Bryce, a Belfast-born MP, purchased Ilnacullin from the British War Office in 1910. His dream to build a mansion and lay out gardens on this bare island off Glengarriff in County Cork was ambitious: the soil was shallow and infertile, the terrain exposed. To realize his project he enlisted the help of Harold Peto, an advocate of the Italian style of garden design and architecture in an age when less formal wild gardens were all the rage. Ilnacullin is a blend of both styles, containing a wide range of oriental and southern hemisphere plants, and many architectural features complementing the splendid natural setting.

A long tradition In early Christian times a major activity of any monastery was gardening—mostly for food or medicines, but also for decorating churches. With the arrival of the Normans horticulture became much more complex and widespread, with new and varied foodstuffs. Sir Walter Ralegh's foreign travels introduced important plants from the New World—tobacco, cherries, and, of course, the potato. His friend, the Earl of Cork, laid out one of Ireland's first Renaissance pleasure gardens in the estates of Youghal. During the latter part of the 17th century gardening was on a grand scale, influenced by the gardens of Versailles, designed by Le Nôtre. Exotic plants began to arrive from abroad, and Dutch immigrants brought innovative botanical techniques. The 18th century was a great age for gardening, as for most aspects of civilized living, passing from baroque formality to the naturalistic landscapes of "Capability" Brown. The Royal Horticultural Society of Ireland was founded in 1816.

During Victorian times botanical tastes diversified, many gardeners concentrating less on design and more on accumulating specimens; several important botanic gardens were planted at this time. Two great gardeners of the age were Daniel Robertson (see page 110) and William Robinson, who introduced a new style of "natural" gardening based on a close observation of landscape. Many smaller, intimate gardens appeared, too, some influenced by the English style of Gertrude Jekyll—two gorgeous creations are Heywood (County Laois) and Butterstream (County Meath). During the early 20th century a passion for oriental gardens developed; the Japanese Gardens at Tully, Kildare, are one such example (see page 101).

Period landscapes One of Ireland's most interesting gardens, historically, is Kilruddery, outside Bray (see page 93), which retains its 17th-century canals, parterres, and statuary. Representing an earlier era, the lovely gardens around Lismore Castle were laid out in Jacobean times. Greatest of the Georgian gardens surround houses such as Florence Court, County Fermanagh (see page 230) and Castletown, County Kildare (see page 94). A fascinating late 18th-century example is Emo Court, County Laois, where lawns dotted with neat, clipped yews and statues provide a foil for James Gandon's neoclassical mansion.

Spectacular gardens Despite its latitude, Ireland has some celebrated gardens in the north, several in the care of the National Trust, among them Mount Stewart and Rowallane (see page 231). In the southwest, Anne's Grove near Castletownroche represents some of the best work of William Robinson—shrubs, magnolias, rare mallows, and water plants flourish in hedged compartments and walled gardens. The Italianate gardens of Bantry House, set by the sea, are a must for keen gardeners, too, as are the castle gardens of Timoleague and the grounds of Muckross House in Killarney's National Park, where vast rhododendrons and exotic trees (including the strawberry tree, see panel) grow against a mountain backdrop. Derreen Gardens, on the road between Kenmare and Castletown Bearhaven, luxuriate in woodland with many subtropical species, tree ferns mingling with bamboo and eucalyptus. Nearby are the gardens of Dunloe Castle, with more rare trees (Chinese swamp cypresses and the pungent "headache tree," *Umbellularia californica*). One of the most enjoyable of all the southwest's gardens is Harold Peto's masterpiece, Ilnacullin, on an island reached by boat trips from Glengarriff, in County Cork (a landing charge). On a fine day in May or June, this Italian garden of Grecian temples and an orderly jungle of flowering shrubs makes a marvellous excursion (see panel opposite).

Bord Fáilte produces a useful leaflet with information about Ireland's best gardens.

Ilnacullin Gardens on Garinish Island

The glorious colours of Rowallane Gardens

St. Fin Barre's Cathedral looks down over the southern branch of Cork's Lee River

THE *EXAMINER*

Cork's daily newspaper seems to epitomize the independent spirit of the city. The *Examiner* (just called "the paper" locally) is a distinguished piece of journalism that has gone national. The first edition appeared in August 1841, shortly before the potato famine. Many of the population were illiterate and certainly too poor to afford newspapers, so it was a brave venture. The first edition proclaimed it devoted "to the welfare and interests of the whole community," and that it seems to be, read by all classes of society. It survived attacks by anti-Treaty demonstrators in 1922 when the machinery was smashed, and has never lost a day's printing through strikes, wars, or technical problems.

▶▶ **Cork** *1474B*

Cork has no compelling sights, nor is it especially beautiful, and an initial reaction to the Republic's second city may be one of disappointment. Nonetheless, visitors generally go away well pleased with the place, perhaps infected by the vehement enthuasiasm of its inhabitants for their city. The way *not* to enjoy Cork is to drive through panicking about the check-in time at the airport or harbour. A map shows why the city, the first bridging point on the Lee estuary, is a bottleneck. Traffic is invariably congested during working hours, and parking is regulated: Leave the car in one of the official parking areas and walk.

Cork takes pride in being the cultural and economic centre of the southwest, constantly challenging Dublin's supremacy. It has always favoured ousting British rule, becoming known as "rebel Cork" after supporting Perkin Warbeck (a Flemish impostor who, in 1492, claimed to be Duke of York), and was a base for the Nationalist Fenian movement in the 19th century. Its prosperity was based on trade in hides, textiles, butter, and wine. Industries such as shipbuilding and engine manufacturing are no more, replaced by skills such as the computer business. The centre's streets reveal Cork's mercantile past—tall 18th-century bow-fronted houses and fine warehouses.

The centre is built on reclaimed marshes ("Cork" comes from the Irish meaning "marshy place") and the older part of the city is on an island embraced by two arms of the Lee River. The land rises steeply towards the heights of Shandon; several imposing church spires pierce the skyline, Victorian Gothic being the prevailing style. **St. Fin Barre's▶** (tel: 021 496 3387) was designed by William

Burges in a flourish of white limestone steeples. Inside it is richly decorated, with angels gazing down from a starry apse. On the Shandon side of town is **St. Anne's Church▶▶**, which soars to a red and white pepper-pot tower surmounted by a golden weather vane in the shape of a salmon. It houses the famous eight-bell carillon immortalized in the corny ballad known as "The Bells of Shandon." You can climb the tower and, for a fee, "play" the bells. The nearby neoclassical **Shandon Craft Centre▶** (tel: 021 450 7487) contains several craft studios, making jewellery, ceramics, and traditional porcelain dolls.

On the island, Cork's commercial heart beats along the main thoroughfares of Grand Parade and St. Patrick's Street. Old-fashioned department stores flank trendy clothes boutiques, but the newer and most chic shops are around the pedestrianized area near St. Paul's Street. Classy Donegal rainwear and equestrian clothing are also sold in these side streets. To the west lie elegant Georgian malls and the university. The **Cork Public Museum▶▶** (Republican history features prominently, tel: 021 427 0679) is in the grounds of Fitzgerald Park by the Mardyke Walk, an attractive riverside breathing space.

Cork has plenty of nightlife, from raucous pub discos to avant-garde theatre. Its opera house (not a pretty sight) is a 1960s addition to municipal culture; other arts venues are the **Triskel Arts Centre▶** (tel: 021 427 2022) and the **Crawford Art Gallery▶** (tel: 021 427 3377, and worth a visit just for its restaurant—see Hotels and Restaurants, page 281). At the end of October, the city is thronged for its acclaimed international jazz festival. Eating in Cork is a pleasure, with plenty of choice, from imaginative, cheap organic foods to gourmet French cuisine. The **English Market▶** off Princes Street has excellent food stalls. Accommodation in Cork ranges from civilized Georgian town houses to well-run, good-value hostels.

▶▶▶ Dingle Peninsula   *1461C*
See pages 158–159.

ELIZABETH ALDWORTH
This young lady from County Cork achieved fame as the only woman ever to be accepted into the bizarre and secretive world of Freemasonry. The local lodge met at her family home in Doneraile (her father was a Mason), but naturally she was always banished during the proceedings. One day in 1712 curiosity got the better of her and she hid in a clock-case to find out what went on, but was discovered. Once the Masons got over their anger, they decided the only way to keep her quiet was to enroll her, and so she became the order's one and only female member. Her grave is in St. Fin Barre's Cathedral.

157

BETTER THINGS TO COME
"Limerick was, Dublin is, and Cork shall be
The finest city of the three."
Recorded in 1859 as "the old prophecy."

The Coal Quay open market in Cork City

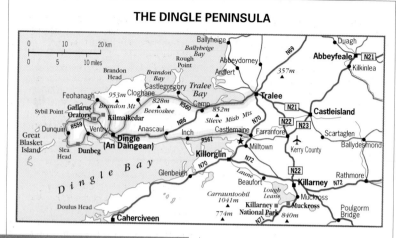

THE DINGLE PENINSULA

Drive

The grandeur of the Dingle Peninsula

A tour of this remote, Irish-speaking westerly extremity offers many things: superb coastal scenery with peaceful beaches and scattered islands; grand mountains and lush, fuchsia-splashed countryside; a fascinating assortment of antiquities; and a lively scene of music and excellent seafood

The shrine at Slea Head

restaurants based on the charming fishing port of Dingle.

Starting points for this drive are Castlemaine (north of Killorglin) or Tralee. For scenic drama go clockwise (although the scenery at first is quiet and undramatic) with good dune beaches at Inch and small hamlets like **Anascaul▶**; the strange, secretive tarn (small mountain lake) to the north, **Anascaul Lake▶**, is worth a brief detour.

Dingle▶▶ is the peninsula's main tourist centre, constantly lively during the summer. It is by no means undiscovered, as anyone arriving during its festival season (July–August) will note, but it never seems as overcrowded or touristy as Killarney, and it's a great deal classier. Off-season, though, many of its good restaurants, craft shops, and hotels are closed, and no boat trips run. The town is extremely well kept, with restored shop-fronts and colourful inn signs. The harbour is particularly appealing, its bright fishing vessels moored in a lovely natural haven. In former centuries smuggling was a major source of income.

Beyond Dingle is **Ventry▶**, where you may see upturned *currachs* (canvas-covered canoes) on the beach. Follow the road marked Slea Head Drive around Ireland's most westerly point. The whole area is riddled with forts, souterrains, standing stones, and crosses; you need a good detailed map to explore them all. On the hillsides you will pass a number of strange little stone huts known as beehives or *clochans*. There are more than 400 in the area altogether. Some farmers may charge you to visit these, and the more perfect specimens may have been reconstructed from the original stones as storage places (or for their more recent value as visitor attractions). **Dunbeg**►►, near Ventry, is one of the best sites (an Iron Age clifftop fort with beehive huts nearby).

If archaeology does not thrill you, the scenery certainly will, especially when the wild **Blasket Islands**►► appear as you round the **Slea Head** promontory. The Blaskets are now occupied by a handful of summer visitors, including the former Irish prime minister, Charles Haughey, and there are plans to renovate some of the abandoned houses. The last native inhabitants moved to the mainland in 1953, the local women no longer willing to confine their marriage prospects within this tiny community. The Blaskets have inspired a thriving literary tradition: Maurice O'Sullivan's *Twenty Years a'Growing* and Tomás Ó Crohan's *The Islandman* are two of the best-known accounts of island life. Summer boat trips visit the islands from **Dunquin**►, where the film *Ryan's Daughter* was made. The Blasket Centre at Dunquin (*Dun Chaoin* in Irish) contains an exhibition on island life and literature.

Towards the ragged northwest of the peninsula are two interesting historic monuments. One is the **Gallarus Oratory**►►, a tiny but perfectly preserved church built of neatly packed unmortared stones. It dates from between AD 800 and AD 1200 and still keeps the rain out, although its roof-line is sagging slightly. A short distance up the road is **Kilmalkedar**►, another early church from about the 12th century, roofless but bearing fine Romanesque carvings in purplish stone. By returning to Dingle again, you can start the final dramatic leg of this drive, over the **Connor Pass**►►► (most spectacular on a clear day), past the 953m (3,127ft) summit of Mount Brandon. Once over the pass, you see **Brandon Bay**►► opening in a fantastic geological model of lakes, rivers, and rock-strewn contours. The seafaring monk St. Brendan set sail from these shores in the 5th century. In 1976, Tim Severin re-created this voyage in a similar craft of wood and leather to discover whether St. Brendan could have reached America before Columbus (see the Craggaunowen Project, page 183). The northern coastal strip, back at sea level, is a quiet and easy drive past long beaches and humdrum farmland.

159

Dunbeg promontory fort, Ventry, dates from between 400 BC and 50 BC

ROSS CASTLE

Ross Castle is a fine ruin dating from the 15th century; a tower house and later dwelling house still remain containing 16th- and 17th-century furnishings. Home of the local chieftains, the O'Donoghues, Ross Castle was the last place in Munster to fall to Cromwellian forces in 1652. The story goes that General Ludlow, hearing of a superstition that Ross Castle would never be taken by land, bought ships to sail up the lake, whereupon the defenders, hitherto defiant, immediately gave up their arms.

From Ross Castle, it is possible to take boat tours of the lake (these are non-stopping) or, alternatively, to hire a rowing boat for a landing on Innisfallen Island. Here, against a landscape of gentle valleys and dark woods, are the ruins of Innisfallen Abbey dating from AD 600.

KATE KEARNEY

A well-known pub on the way up to the Gap of Dunloe, Kate Kearney's Cottage is named after the colourful local beauty who dispensed illegal *poteen* (home-brewed liquor) to travellers passing through the gap during the mid-19th century. She was apparently in constant trouble with the law, but was finally vanquished by the potato blight that made *poteen* distilling impossible. One night, she simply vanished.

KILLARNEY ENVIRONS

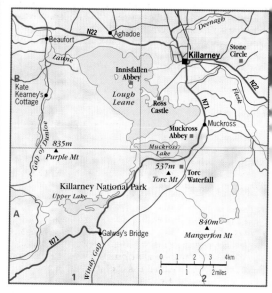

▶▶ Killarney   1463C

Every visitor to the southwest has to see Killarney. The town itself, however, is disappointing. Once a seemly little place with a soul of its own, it is now given wholly over to tourism. It becomes hopelessly congested in summer, is very commercialized and, apart from the tall-spired Catholic **cathedral of St. Mary's▶**, designed in flamboyant high Gothic in 1842, has no outstanding features of interest. However, the immediate surroundings of the **Killarney National Park▶▶** (tel: 064 31947) are not to be missed and, if you can evade the milling tour buses and wheedling "jarvey-men" (pony-trap drivers), it takes on the grandeur of genuine wilderness. Macgillycuddy's Reeks, Ireland's highest mountains, lie just outside the National Park, but are clearly visible on fine days. Killarney is the usual starting and finishing point for the popular excursion drive known as the Ring of Kerry (see pages 170–171), although if you have your own transportation you can just about avoid the town centre. The tourist office, however, is very helpful with maps and detailed local information. The Kerry Way is a 56km (35mi) footpath leading through the mountains from the National Park towards Glenbeigh on the Iveragh peninsula.

Once out of the town, the choices for exploration are bewildering. To the south (the east shore of Lough Leane) lie the Muckross estate and various well-known beauty spots on the Kenmare road up to the pass called Moll's Gap. On the way, you may be diverted by the 15th-century **Ross Castle▶▶** (tel: 064 35234, see panel) by the lakeshore, and **Muckross Abbey▶**, a 15th-century ruin surprisingly well preserved after a Cromwellian visit in 1652. The main attraction, however, is **Muckross House▶▶** (tel: 064 31440) and the surrounding gardens and parkland. No cars are allowed within the estate, but you can park near the house. To explore the extensive grounds, you can either accept a ride from one of the jarvey-men (negotiate the fare carefully before you set off) or hire a bicycle. Muckross House is a furnished 19th-century neo-Tudor mansion designed by William Burn. Attached to it is a folk museum, where craftsmen demonstrate their trades, and several reconstructed farmhouses. The lakeside gardens have wonderful rhododendrons and azaleas, best in early summer. The Meeting of the Waters is a popular spot between the Upper Lake and Lough Leane, where arbutus trees flourish in the mild climate. Lake boats "shoot the rapids" there, and close by is the **Torc Waterfall**▶▶, plunging 20m (66ft) down a mountainside. All these make excellent picnic sites if you can avoid the crowds.

Beyond Muckross House the road winds on through woods, heather moors, and mountains, becoming ever more beautiful, but you'll need to be careful at hairpin bends and tunnels. **Ladies' View**▶▶ is a place to pause for an unforgettable vista across the lakes of the National Park toward the Gap of Dunloe. (The "ladies" were Queen Victoria and her ladies-in-waiting, who presumably caught this view on a fine day and were duly impressed.)

The **Gap of Dunloe**▶▶▶ is Killarney's other great visitor attraction, a rugged glacial pass between the mountains, providing magnificent views of tarns and cliffs. It lies on the west side of the lake and is reached by heading north from the centre of Killarney. Once again, the jarvey-men will be only too happy to stir their bored nags into action from the centre of town, but you will save time and money by driving at least as far as touristy Kate Kearney's Cottage (see panel opposite). From there vehicular traffic is banned, so you must walk or hire a pony or jaunting car. Most of the visitors head no farther than the Gap itself, but if you want more seclusion you can continue on foot through the lonely Black Valley down past Lord Brandon's Cottage (a tea-shop) to the lakeshore and pick up a boat past the caves of Middle Lake and over to Ross Castle.

KILLARNEY WILDLIFE

Ireland's last wolf was killed near Lough Leane in 1700, and the wild mountain landscape of the National Park, backed by Macgillycuddy's Reeks, has always been home to many species of wildlife, some quite rare. A herd of red deer may be found there, together with wild goats, Japanese sika deer, otters, badgers, foxes, hares, and hawks. The remote Black Valley attracts many birds. Whooper swans, with their shiny black legs, yellow-and-black bills, and whooping, buglelike call, visit every winter; hooded crows and the rare chough can also be seen.

161

Ladies' View, near Killarney, justly one of Ireland's most famous panoramas

1474A

KINSALE GOURMET FESTIVAL

During the first week in October, Kinsale is even more packed than usual, although its visitors may look more sleek and well-heeled than at other times of the year. Kinsale's Gourmet Festival extends the normal tourist season nicely and is well publicized throughout Ireland, attracting a good many discerning foreign palates, too. This is a time for eating, when the town's excellent pubs and restaurants vie with each other to produce gastronomic delights. The emphasis is on local seafood, and the places to look for clearly display the Kinsale Good Food Circle sign.

▶▶▶ Kinsale

Kinsale has attractions out of proportion to its modest size and so is very popular, though it has managed to maintain a more exclusive image than Killarney. Its setting is seductive, with tall slate-roofed houses sprinkled among the steeply wooded estuary slopes of the Bandon River. Its historic interest and fishing-village charm make it an appealing place both to stay and to eat (see panel). From Kinsale you can easily explore both Cork City and the glorious coastal or inland scenery of south Cork. It is also a notable sailing and fishing centre.

During 1601–1602, a Spanish force occupied Kinsale and was besieged by English troops. Irish allies of the Spaniards were routed, a significant step towards the establishment of the English order (and the decline of Gaelic power) in 17th-century Ireland. Soon afterwards the main players in this struggle, the O'Neill and O'Donnell clan chieftains, fled to Europe and abandoned their lands to English settlers. The town was spared a Cromwellian hammering, wisely backing the winning side. Later that century, James II landed at Kinsale with French forces in an attempt to regain his throne, and from here he finally left Ireland, defeated. Kinsale became an important English naval base, and Desmond Castle (now a heritage centre) held many French prisoners in Napoleonic times. The town is proud of its history, which is well recorded in the local **museum▶** (tel: 021 477 2044; *open* Mon–Sat 11–5, Sun 3–5. *Admission: moderate*), a Dutch-style 17th-century town hall in the centre of town. Some of its most interesting exhibits relate to the sinking of the *Lusitania* (see page 152).

Of Kinsale's two fortresses the more interesting is **Charles Fort▶▶** (tel: 021 477 2684; *open* Jun–Sep, daily 10–6; Apr–May and Oct, Mon–Sat 9–5, Sun 9.30–5.30; Nov–Mar, Mon–Fri 8–4.30. *Admission: moderate*), on the east side of the estuary, built in the late 17th century to guard the harbour entrance. One of the best-preserved examples of a star fort in Europe, you can clamber over the ramparts (keep an eye on children) and visit a military exhibition. On sunny days the signposted Scilly Walk is a wonderful stroll along the edge of the sea to the village.

Kinsale fishermen tend their nets

From Kinsale to Mizen Head is by no means undiscovered, but seems far less obligatory and overdone than excursions such as the Ring of Kerry, when you take your place in a convoy of tour buses. Meandering along tiny coastal roads through small villages, and undoubtedly getting lost amid Irish signposting, is one of the most delightful ways to enjoy the Emerald Isle.

he Old Head of Kinsale is a lonely headland on which stands a ruined fortress; offshore is the wreck of the *Lusitania* (see page 152). From Timoleague to Clonakilty—the Seven Heads peninsula—is a massively convoluted shoreline. **Timoleague▶▶**, known for its beautiful gardens, is also remarkable for its skeletal Franciscan abbey. There the coast is utterly peaceful, but beautiful. Wading birds paddle in the estuary, and the shores are full of unusual plants. **Clonakilty▶** is an engaging place. There's little to see, but it has a lively feel, the main street lined with painted shop-fronts and old-fashioned bars. Traditional music, street theatre, festivals, and crafts add to its attractions. Outside town is the birthplace of Michael Collins (see page 43), whose exploits are recounted in O'Donovan's Hotel. Seemingly endless, unspoiled sand graces the vast beach at **Inchydoney▶▶**.

The drive through the fuchsia-splashed villages of Ross Carbery, Glandore, and Unionhall is glorious; creeks and lagoons mirror wooded slopes and fishing cottages with sandy coves tucked biblike under their chins. Leap is famous for Irish music, which is based at Connolly's Bar. Beyond lie the pretty village of **Castletownshend▶▶** (see page 152), tidal Lough Hyne, and a scatter of islands in Roaringwater Bay. After **Skibbereen▶** are the colourful villages of **Ballydehob▶**, **Schull▶▶**, **Goleen▶**, and the spectacular 220m (722ft) cliffs of **Mizen Head▶▶**, guarded by an O'Mahoney stronghold. Barleycove is a fine beach. To the north, Sheep's Head peninsula is a lovely tour if time permits. The Beara peninsula is unfairly neglected in favour of the Ring of Kerry, but is as rewarding and less crowded. Highlights include the rugged copper-mining country around **Allihies▶** and the **Healy Pass▶▶**.

A MODERN SHRINE
Between Glandore and Ross Carbery, and not too difficult to search out, is the Drombeg Stone Circle, a good example from the early Bronze Age. Charred bones were buried in the middle of this stone circle. Nearby is a *fulacht fiadh*, or cooking trough, which would have been heated with stones from a fire.

163

The lighthouse at the Old Head of Kinsale

Many of Ireland's historic houses fell into decay or were destroyed during the 20th century, but a heartening number have survived, and those too large to make comfortable family homes have been converted for other purposes. Some of them are now splendid hotels, giving many visitors a chance to experience a grandeur granted at one time to only a privileged few.

A taste of the past These hotels are all highly individual, but fall into several types. The ultra-wealthy favour the great baronial castles (mostly more or less latter-day fakes, but nonetheless with some interesting history and contents, and palatial comfort). There is the legacy of the Georgian era, spanning 170 of Ireland's most prosperous years. These may be mansions in rolling parkland or pleasingly modest rectories. Then there are Victorian properties with famous family histories. Just a few examples can be mentioned; for further suggestions see Interesting Places to Stay (pages 242–243) and Hotels and Restaurants (pages 269–283).

Grand castles Shannon Airport attracts many well-heeled transatlantic visitors who desire nothing more than to stay in a real Irish castle. This need is satisfied by several large, expensive, luxury hotels within easy reach. Nearest, 13km (8mi) from the airport, is **Dromoland Castle**, a vast mock-Gothic mansion on a 150ha (370-acre) estate. The estate dates back to the 16th century, when it was the seat of the O'Brien family, descendants of the great High King, Brian Ború, but the original house was replaced in the 1820s and the interior has been given a New York-style facelift by society decorator Carlton Varney. **Ashford Castle** is another Hollywood dream also under American ownership, this time on Lough Corrib, predictably furnished in sheer luxury and with superb grounds. Once the home of the Guinness family, it incorporates a 13th-century castle

A CRICKETING PRINCE IN IRELAND
Set in glorious countryside beneath the Twelve Bens in Connemara, but far, far away from any cricket pitch, is Ballynahinch Castle, now a comfortable hotel. At the beginning of this century, when still a private residence, it was owned by Prince Ranjitsinhji, a characterful Indian nobleman who played cricket for England on many occasions.

Top: Bantry House
Below: Ashford Castle, County Mayo

Adare Manor, County Limerick

and a later French-style château in its opulent 19th-century shell. Also within reach of Shannon is **Adare Manor**, past seat of the earls of Dunraven. Again it is Victorian and grandiose with vast mullions and fireplaces and colossal state rooms. On a somewhat smaller scale is **Markree Castle** in Sligo, home of the Cooper family since 1640, and last altered substantially in 1802. Its hotelier owner is a member of the original family, and an accomplished restaurateur. The castle has welcomed literary lights such as Lady Gregory and W. B. Yeats. **Waterford Castle** has a special brand of seclusion. It is set on an island in Waterford harbour, and reached only by private car ferry. The core is a genuine 17th-century castle, with oak panelling, antique furniture, and tapestries.

Elegant country houses One of the earliest period houses in Ireland now open as a hotel is **Assolas Country House** in Kanturk, County Cork. This peaceful place was built about 1590, but is now largely 17th-century in style, with gorgeous gardens and fishing rights. If Georgian elegance is to your taste, one fine example is **Enniscoe House**, near Crossmolina (Mayo), a mid-18th-century mansion with fascinating period features. The perfectly proportioned facade conceals an earlier structure with a different layout of floor levels and room sizes. Its owner, Susan Kellett, is a descendant of the original family. **Carnelly House** (Clare) is also Georgian but was built in Queen Anne style by Francis Bindon. The tall windows, Francini ceilings, and Corinthian pillars give a gracious air to this creeper-covered brick house. **Cashel Palace** is an exceptional building of the same period (1730) and for 200 years was a bishop's palace. It stands beneath the Rock of Cashel, and has an ancient mulberry tree on the lawn. **Coopershill** in County Sligo dates from 1774, but echoes earlier times in its utterly relaxing rooms. Regency-period **Marlfield House** (1820) is in Gorey, Wexford. This formed part of the Courtown Estate, later the seat of the Earl of Courtown and a great focus of social life. It retains the tradition of lavish hospitality amid elegant and sumptuous furnishings.

TINAKILLY HOUSE, WICKLOW
This is one of the most interesting Victorian houses in Ireland. It was built in the 1870s for Captain Robert Halpin, commander of the *Great Eastern* steamship that laid the first telegraph cable linking Europe and America. Halpin was granted a substantial pension by a grateful government, and retired here to this grand mansion in 3ha (7 acres) of sheltered gardens by the sea. Unfortunately he barely lived long enough to enjoy it. After a dangerous life of shipwrecks and dubious escapades in the American Civil War he succumbed to blood poisoning at 58, after cutting his toenails! A splendid staircase, mahogany inlaid doors, Italian fireplaces, oil paintings, and seafaring memorabilia preserve something of the atmosphere of this flamboyant house and its larger-than-life owner.

Southwestern Counties

LOUGH GUR

Limerick's countryside is not especially noteworthy, but there is one little jewel tucked away in the southeast. Lough Gur is a beautiful crescent-shaped lake around which evidence of early civilizations has been found. Antiquities include a wedge tomb and a large stone circle at Grange. Cartloads of remains were discovered after the partial draining of the lake in the 19th century. An interpretative centre has been set up overlooking the reedy lake, with a visitor centre and museum in two replica thatched *crannóg* huts of the neolithic era.

▶ Limerick
1474D

Limerick is a significant city in terms of industry and population, currently vying with Galway for third place in the Republic. It has a rich historical background and plenty of interesting sights, and, as a result of its strategic location at the lowest bridging point on the Shannon, most visitors to the southwest wind up here at some point during their stay. With relatively dull scenery on its doorstep, Limerick's attractions as a long-term base are limited. Until recently, it was a run-down and oddly surly city with a high rate of unemployment and crime. (Readers of Frank McCourt's memoirs, *Angela's Ashes,* will know just how rough and depressed Limerick once was.) However, energetic multimillion-pound efforts to revitalize the centre are at last showing some success, particularly around its historic quaysides. Wharves and warehouses have been transformed into new business premises, its Norman and Georgian heritage is now carefully restored, and the air of neglect has been banished with attractive shops, restaurants, and cafés. It is certainly worth half a day's time, more if you are interested in Irish history. Limerick was originally a Viking settlement, due to its strategic location at the mouth of the Shannon. Brian Ború, High King of Ireland, eventually conquered the Danes, many of whom settled down quite happily in Ireland and intermarried with native Gaels. The Norman era was important for Limerick. The Normans expanded the town and built huge fortifications with curtain walls, King John's Castle being one of the most impressive. In Cromwellian times it suffered terribly under the onslaughts of General Ireton, Cromwell's son-in-law and commander of Ireland, who besieged the city walls for more than six months. Later that century, Limerick was one of the last Jacobite bastions after the Battle of the Boyne, the hero of the period being Patrick Sarsfield, who made a daring raid on William's ammunition wagons and supply trains.

King John's Castle is unusual in that it has no keep

Eventually, however, Limerick capitulated, and the infamous Treaty of Limerick was signed in 1691. Few incidents in Ireland's history illustrate the role of "perfidious Albion" more clearly than this. Within two months the English reneged on their promises to grant the Catholic population religious and property rights and instituted draconian measures against them. **The Treaty Stone►**, on which the agreement was signed, became a symbol of all that was hateful about English rule. It can still be seen at the west end of Thomond Bridge, now sandblasted clean in an attempt to erase the memories. Today Limerick is a vehemently Catholic and nationalist city.

Within the town centre the most notable monument is **King John's Castle►►** (tel: 061 411 201), near Thomond Bridge. First built in 1200, it still looks the part of a medieval Norman fortress, though much restored after its 17th-century battering during the Siege of Limerick and subsequent alterations. The tower is the oldest section, and housed a British garrison until the birth of the Irish Free State in 1922. An excellent and imaginative visitor centre now reconstructs the story of Limerick and its castle, while outside in the castle yard lie re-creations of various curious engines used in medieval siege warfare—find out what the mangonel and trebuchet were and how they worked.

For more history, Limerick's **City Museum►** (tel: 061 417 826) in two restored 18th-century houses documents the city's prosperity in Georgian times, when it produced fine silverware and lace. Even more worthwhile is the **Hunt Museum►►** (tel: 061 312 833), outside the centre in the university campus area at Plassey. The art historian and antiquarian, John Hunt, donated a magnificent collection of Celtic and medieval art, including the Antrim Cross and a Bronze Age shield. Only the National Museum in Dublin can better it for early Celtic and medieval art. **St. Mary's Cathedral►** (tel: 061 416 238), in the centre, is the city's most appealing religious building and its oldest, founded in 1168 but dating mainly from the 15th century. Unexpectedly in this strongly Catholic city, it is a Protestant church. Its most interesting features include black oak choir stalls with carved 15th-century misericords (see photograph and caption, above right).

An ornately carved misericord from St. Mary's Cathedral. They were so-called because they afforded clerics some form of rest when standing through lengthy services (misericordia is Latin for pity). They perched on these small seats, rather than standing unsupported

167

Inside St. Mary's Cathedral

Old Midleton Distillery even had its own fire engine

THE MOUTH OF THE SHANNON

W. M. Thackeray thought the undulating grounds that border the Shannon estuary enjoyable, if not beautiful: "though the view is by no means a fine one, I know few that are pleasanter than the sight of these rich, golden, peaceful plains, with the full harvest waving on them and just ready for the sickle."

WHISKEY

Whiskey (*uisce beatha*—the water of life) has an interesting pedigree. It was probably invented by Irish missionary monks with their arcane knowledge of the Middle Eastern alembic, a still used for making perfumes. Thirteenth-century soldiers were fortified with a dose of the stuff before battle and Queen Elizabeth I herself is said to have been partial to a drop—probably a taste acquired from Sir Walter Ralegh, who was presented with a handsome 120 litre (32-gallon) cask of whiskey by the Earl of Cork. In introducing tobacco and possibly whiskey, it seems Ralegh was responsible for popularizing more than one addictive substance!

▶▶ **Old Midleton Distillery**   *1475B*

Midleton, tel: 021 461 3594, www.whiskeytours.ie
Open: Mar–Oct, daily 9–4.30; Nov–Feb, tours only, Mon–Fri 12.30 and 3, Sat–Sun 2 and 4. Admission: moderate

In the pleasant little town of Midleton, an impressive 18th-century industrial complex of stone mills and warehouses has been restored to enlighten visitors about the fine art of whiskey distilling. The Jameson Heritage Centre is an entrepreneurial venture by Irish Distillers, emulating the successful Northern Irish attraction at Bushmills. For a fee (which includes a tasting) you can tour the modern distillery together with the Old Midleton Distillery, in use for 150 years from 1825 to 1975. The world's largest pot still, with a capacity of more than 178,200 litres (40,000 gallons), stands by the reception building. Despite the heritage centre's name, it was the brand known as Paddy, rather than Jameson's, that was distilled in Midleton from the 19th century; John Jameson's whiskey was always produced in Dublin.

▶ **Rathkeale and environs**   *1474D*

Castle Matrix▶▶ (tel: 069 64284; *open* mid-May–mid-Sep, daily 11–5, rest of year by appointment. *Admission: moderate*), just outside Rathkeale, is a 15th-century tower house containing an important collection of documents connected with the Flight of the Wild Geese, the exodus after the Battle of Limerick. The farmland of west Limerick and the Shannon estuary is tame compared with the grandeur of Cork or Kerry, but if you have been around the Dingle peninsula you could well find yourself driving through it. A few sights are worth a detour. **Ardfert**▶, north of Tralee, has some restored monastic remains. The beach nearby is Banna Strand, where Roger Casement's abortive adventure took place (see page 43). Hugging the Shannon coast is **Glin Castle**▶▶ (tel: 068 34173, www.glincastle.com; *open* May–Jun, daily 10–noon and 2–4, rest of year by appointment. *Admission: expensive*), seat of the Knights of Glin and a fine 18th-century house with Victorian Gothic additions (open only to group tours). Part of the house is a B&B where you can stay in luxurious accommodation. Further along, and probably the most worthwhile stop of all, is **Foynes Flying Boat Museum**▶▶ (tel: 069 65416; *open* Apr–Oct, daily 10–5. *Admission: moderate*), in the terminal of the original Shannon Airport. During the 1930s and 1940s, Foynes was the operational headquarters for seaplanes travelling to and from the United States, and with its fascinating collection of film footage, instruments, photos, and logs, the museum is a must for any aviation buff. **Adare►**, a notably pretty village of thatched cottages on the main Limerick road, contains the ruins of three ancient abbeys and of 12th-century Desmond Castle. Adare Manor, a lavish Gothic mansion, is now a country house hotel.

►► Youghal   *1475B*

Youghal stands by the winding Blackwater estuary, right on the border between counties Waterford and Cork. Pronounced "yawl," this ancient walled seaport has a rich history and several interesting buildings. Its resilient, salty character is striking, and in 1956 it impressed the director, John Huston, sufficiently to use it as a film location for *Moby Dick*. Its most illustrious resident was Sir Walter Ralegh, once mayor of the town. A Potato Festival is intermittently held to commemorate Ralegh's supposed introduction of the Virginian tuber to Irish shores. A citizen with a more genuine claim to the town's attention was Richard Boyle, father of the famous scientist who formulated Boyle's Law, and builder of the almshouses in the town. The **Youghal Heritage Centre►►** (tel: 024 92447) is a great introduction to the complex history of the town and its environs; an audio-visual display and guides to walk you through the town are available. **St. Mary's Collegiate Church►** (tel: 024 92350) is Youghal's most impressive building, containing many tombs and effigies, including one to the fantastically wealthy Earl of Cork and his 16 children (by three wives). Other privately owned buildings to look for are the Georgian **clock tower►** bridging the main street; the tower house, **Tynte's Castle►**; and the **Red House►**, a Dutch-style merchant's house. The **town walls►►** are some of the best examples in Ireland, with large sections still in fairly good condition. Another good reason to pause in Youghal is its excellent seafood restaurant, Aherne's (see Hotels and Restaurants, page 281).

ROSE OF TRALEE

The pale moon was rising
above the green
mountain,
The sun was declining
beneath the blue sea;
When I strayed with my
love by the pure crystal
fountain,
That stands in the beautiful Vale of Tralee.

She was lovely and fair as
the rose of the summer;
Yet 'twas not her beauty
alone that won me;
Oh no, 'twas the truth in
her eyes ever dawning,
That made me love Mary,
the Rose of Tralee.

William Mulchinock

169

The lighthouse at Youghal

THE RING OF KERRY

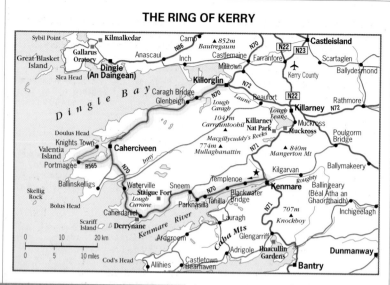

Drive

The spectacular Ring of Kerry

Perhaps the most popular of all tourist routes in Ireland, this drive offers a mix of dramatic scenery, sights, and eating places, some geared towards the bus-tour trade. Allow a full day to see everything.

Sneem caters well to tourists

Many of the tour buses that ply this route start from Killarney, so if you have your own transportation you stand less chance of being held up in traffic convoys if you do the Ring clockwise, starting in **Kenmare►►**. There are advantages either way; if you prefer to save the best till last, follow the bus route. As a variation, you could take the high mountain road that runs down the spine of the Iveragh peninsula through Macgillycuddy's Reeks. Several roads connect this with the coastal route. From Kenmare, the coastal road begins pleasantly enough through Templenoe and Blackwater Bridge, with peaceful estuary views to the south. At Parknasilla the lush gardens of the Great Southern Hotel give some idea of how mild the climate is, with palms and tender shrubs growing profusely. **Sneem►** is a pretty village of colour-washed houses clustered around village green. Farther on, don't miss **Staigue Fort►►**, perhaps the best example of a stone *cashel*, or ring fort. It probably dates from about 500 BC and its stout walls must have been a sturdy defence for the inhabitants huddled within. Now all you will find are a startled sheep or two perched on the walls. An honesty box requests a small fee to compensate the farmer for "trespass." On the southwest tip of the Ring is the Derrynane Estate at **Caherdaniel►**, where the Irish statesman Daniel O'Connell lived. The wooded grounds are part of a **national park▶▶**, and encompass lovely rock-and-sand beaches and dunes. The house is now a museum commemorating O'Connell.

Waterville▶▶ faces the Atlantic gales bravely, its short holiday season attracting many visitors to a long sandy beach. Golf and fishing are additional attractions. As you approach Waterville you may spy a brief but unforgettable glimpse of the jagged **Skellig Rock▶**, some way out to sea. These inhospitable islets provided a penitential home for Celtic monks who founded St. Finian's Abbey there in AD 560. Oratories, crosses, and beehive huts are among the ruins visible on Skellig Michael, the larger island. Little Skellig is a notable haven for seabirds, especially gannets. Boat trips run in summer from various points along this coast, but landings on the islands are now very limited because of erosion and damage to the sites, not to mention bad weather. Choose a calm day in these waters! The **Skellig Experience▶▶**, an interpretative centre near the modern bridge at **Portmagee▶** (tel: 066 947 6306;

open Apr–Jun and Sep, daily 9.30–5; Jul–Aug, daily 9.30–7. *Admission: moderate*) linking mainland Kerry with Valentia Island, provides lots of multi-media information about the hardy Skellig monks, the local seabirds, and various aspects of coastal life. A guided cruise among the Skellig Islands is available.

Valentia Island▶ is a strange place of tame hills and a domesticated patchwork of walled fields and fuchsia hedges. The first transatlantic tele-graph cable to the United States was laid from there in 1866. Knightstown is the main village, with fishing and tourism its principal concerns. If you decide to stay overnight, you can enjoy some excellent traditional music and dancing there.

Cahersiveen▶, on the mainland, was the birthplace of Daniel O'Connell. From here the north coast road leads past grand mountain slopes and sea vistas to the town of **Glenbeigh▶**. A detour inland past the lushly wooded slopes of Lough Caragh makes an interesting variation to the coast road, which is fairly unex-citing from here as far as **Killorglin▶**.

Looking across Valentia Harbour

Western Counties

RED MARY

Máire Rua (Red Mary) O'Brien, who lived in the 17th century, was apparently a perfectly harmless person, although one tale described her as a woman of great lust who had many suitors. Before giving her hand, she would demand that a suitor should prove his worth by riding her fierce stallion—which then promptly raced out over the Cliffs of Moher and deposited his rider in the Atlantic below. All perished except one, who succeeded in bringing the stallion back to Máire Rua whereupon she closed the gates of her castle. In trying to leap over the gateway the horse died, thus explaining the name of her castle—Leamaneagh (*Léim an Eich*, or horse's leap), though neither history nor legend records that she married the brave horseman.

172

A Celtic cross is silhouetted against the darkening sky on Inishmore, the largest of the Aran Islands

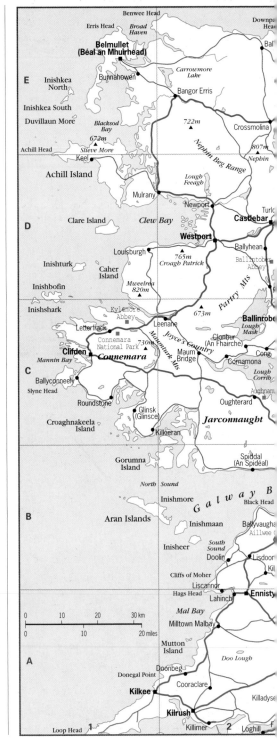

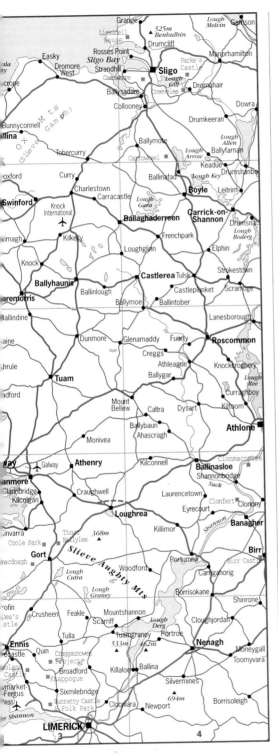

Grange
525m
Benbulbin
Garrison
Lough Melvin
Lissadell House
Drumcliff
Rosses Point
Manorhamilton
Easky
Dromore West
Sligo Bay
Strandhill
Sligo
Parke's Castle
crope
Carrowmore
Lough Gill
Ballysadare
Creevelea
Dromahair
Dowra
Collooney
ala
y
Bunnyconnell
Drumkeeran
illina
O X
(Slieve Gamph)
Ballymote
Lough Allen
Ballyfarnan
Tobercurry
Lough Arrow
Carrowkeel
Keadue
Lough Key
Drumshanbo
oxford
Curry
Ballinafad
Charlestown
Carracastle
Lough Gara
Boyle
Leitrim
Swinford
Knock International
Ballaghaderreen
Carrick-on-Shannon
Drumsna
Lough Boderg
imagh
Kilkelly
Frenchpark
Elphin
Knock
Loughglinn
Castlerea
Tulsk
Strokestown
Ballyhaunis
Ballinlough
Castleplunket
Scramoge
aremorris
Ballymoe
Ballintober
Lanesborough
allindine
Dunmore
Glenamaddy
Fuerty
Roscommon
aine
Creggs
Knockcroghery
hrule
Athleague
Lough Ree
Tuam
Ballygar
Curraghboy
adford
Mount Bellew
Caltra
Dysart
Kiltoom
Ballybaun
Ahascragh
Athlone
Monivea
Clonmacnoise
ay
Galway
Athenry
Kilconnell
Ballinasloe
anmore
Shannonbridge
Clarinbridge
Suck
Kilcolgan
Craughwell
Laurencetown
Clonfert
Clonony
Eyrecourt
Loughrea
Banagher
invarra
Killimor
Shannon
Coole Park
Thoor Ballylee
368m
Gort
Portumna
Birr
nacdoagh
Slieve Aughty Mts
Woodford
Carrigahorig
Birr Castle
Lough Cutra
Borrisokane
Shinrone
Lough Graney
ofin
Crusheen
Feakle
Mountshannon
Cloughjordan
ea's
Scarriff
Lough Derg
Portroe
stle
Tulla
Tuamgraney
Nenagh
Ennis
533m
462m
Moneygall
castle
Quin
Craggaunowen Project
Toomyvara
oland
Castle
Broadford
Killaloe
Ballina
market-
Fergus
Knappogue
Silvermines
hnon
Sixmilebridge
694m
Bunratty Castle & Folk Park
Cloonlara
Newport
Borrisoleigh
r Shannon
LIMERICK
3
4

CONNEMARA PONIES
The qualities of this versatile breed make it popular with horse-lovers all over Britain and Ireland. At most times of year they can be seen roaming the harsh terrain of Connemara, surviving on a diet of brackish grass and seaweed. In August many are brought to Clifden for the Connemara Pony Show to be examined by local dealers. Resilience is an obvious characteristic, but these ponies are also good-tempered and easily taught. A subtle mixture of Arab blood lends style to the sturdy native stock and, when well groomed and smartened up, they are handsome, elegant creatures in any show ring.

174

WESTERN COUNTIES Oliver Cromwell's famous declaration that Irish rebels could go "to Hell or to Connaught" suggests he didn't think much of this western region. In times when soil fertility and accessibility were important considerations, these rain-swept, isolated outposts of barren limestone or waterlogged bog must have held few attractions. Famine struck western Ireland particularly hard and emigration from counties Galway, Clare, and Mayo has been high. Until the 18th century, British influence was minimal, and the area is still firmly Gaelic in outlook, its population mostly in tiny, scattered rural communities rather than towns and villages. The traditional Irish spirit is evident in local speech, music, crafts, and sports. Now, it is the west's very distinctiveness that many visitors find so appealing, and, above all, its scenery. These three counties encompass a colossal variety of landscapes and sights. Scenic highlights are unquestionably the ghostly grey-white expanses of bare limestone in the Burren, and the wild coast and mountains of Connemara, where the Twelve Bens loom over flattering mirrors of water amid moorland and blanket bog. Mayo, to the north, is quieter and less popular, although its peaceful scenery has always appealed to a discerning minority. Achill Island is one of its loveliest (and most visited) spots. Céide Fields, near Ballycastle, is an imaginatively displayed neolithic settlement long preserved in peatland (tel: 096 43325 and ask for visitor information).

VISITOR ATTRACTIONS Tourism, low-key at first, has boomed and become much more commercialized since

Dún Aengus, on Inishmore, the most imposing ruin in the Aran Islands

IRISH CABINS
During the early 19th century standards of living in Connaught were extremely poor due to overpopulation and the oppressive land laws of the time. A description in 1823 gives an idea of how many people lived: "a room fifteen feet by nine, no window, no chimney, not even the sign of a fireplace, a mud floor sunk considerably below the level of the road by the side of which it stands, originally ill made and in this wet season covered by almost one foot of water, in one corner are a few lighted sods of turf which, while they afford but little warmth to the wretched group around them, fill the room with volumes of smoke."

the opening of Shannon Airport, near Limerick. This is still an important, though no longer mandatory, stop for all transatlantic passenger aircraft flying into Ireland. Worryingly, the importance of tourism to the region's economy may threaten some of its most sensitive sites. The Office of Public Works planned to build a new visitor centre in one of the most remote parts of the fragile Burren. This plan, at least, was rejected by the Irish Supreme Court, but there will doubtless be others.

Off-season (Oct–Apr) most of the west is quiet, with everything except the busiest attractions being closed and less choice of accommodation available. In order to tour the area in any depth, it is essential to have a car. If you are unable to drive, the best base is rapidly expanding Galway City, which offers plenty to do all year round and opportunities for nearby excursions. One of the most interesting trips is to the Aran Islands—it is advisable to stay a day or two, if you can, and see them all. The west provides ample opportunities for golf, riding, fishing, and relaxing.

The ideal time to visit the Burren is May or June, when its fantastic variety of flowers are at their best. For birdwatching, however, spring and autumn are good times, particularly on the Cliffs of Moher and Downpatrick Head. Inland, huge expanses of water also attract thousands of wildfowl. Pontoon, between loughs Conn and Cullin, is an especially good place to watch them. So, too, are the lonely bogland and mountains of the Connemara National Park and the strange turlough lakes of Counties Galway and Clare—one month, a sheet of water, the next, just a vivid emerald patch of freshly watered vegetation, brilliant with flowers, as the giant underground aquifers steadily fill.

Knappogue Castle in County Clare runs medieval banquets in season

CURRACHS

These traditional rowboats, with no keels, are made of tarred canvas stretched over a light wooden frame (originally made of hazel rods and cowhide). The stern is flat, the prow high, so the boats ride high in the water and are extremely buoyant in the roughest seas, though very fragile. Most carry three oarsmen. They are carried to and from the water's edge upside-down over the crew's heads to avoid damage by rocks, which gives a very strange insectlike impression to a spectator. They are still used for inshore lobster fishing and collecting seaweed, but the popular sport of *currach*-racing on the west coast of Ireland also helps to keep these unusual craft afloat. (See photograph on page 194.)

Typical Aran cottages, with the ubiquitous dry-stone walls marking the field boundaries

▶▶ Achill Island   1721D

Mayo's western seaboard seems on the verge of disintegration, its straggling peninsulas anchored to the mainland only by a thread. Achill is the largest of these semi-islands, a rough triangle with sides about 24km (15mi) long, linked to Curraun (itself a peninsula) by a modern road bridge over Achill Sound. Its quiet beaches and spectacular mountain scenery make it an appealing destination; touring, by car or bicycle, surfing, and fishing are the main activities and in summer boats make trips to coastal caves or in pursuit of the harmless basking sharks that haunt this coast. A rash of uniform visitor cottages threatens to blight the island's beauty. Keel is the main village, boasting shops, simple accommodation, and a splendid sandy beach, with some dramatic formations known as the Cathedral Rocks at its farthest end. The most scenic parts of the island can be seen from the Atlantic Drive (signed from the main road near the bridge), which leads past awesome cliffs, heather and gorse moors, and white cottages sprinkled against dark rocks. Beyond Keel, the road stretches towards Achill Head, rearing towards the Atlantic like a sea monster.

▶▶▶ Aran Islands   1721B

The cracked limestone terrain of the Aran Islands, lying about 48km (30mi) out in Galway Bay, links them geologically with the Burren, in County Clare. The islands are flattish, but tilt towards massive sea cliffs in places. Making a living on these bleak rock platforms, virtually treeless and exposed to the full brunt of Atlantic storms, has always been a struggle. Large areas have no natural depth of soil and the islanders have painstakingly created fields from a mixture of sand and seaweed compost, protecting them with an intricate network of dry-stone walls.

Today's dwindling population of islanders (about 1,500) subsist on their age-old livelihoods of fishing and farming, and, increasingly, on tourism. Many speak Gaelic, and a very few still wear traditional Aran dress. The canvas fishing boats called *currachs* are used, although now they often have outboard motors. The Arans have inspired a strong

Traditional shop-front, Bunratty Park

CASTLES AND ABBEYS

The Shannon region has many ancient buildings, often carefully restored to achieve full tourist potential. Besides well-known Bunratty, there are tower houses at Knappogue, a MacNamara stronghold, and Dunguaire, near Kinvarra. Less touristy are Aughnanure, on Lough Corrib, and Portumna, on Lough Derg. Some of the best monastic sites include: the Franciscan friaries of Quin and Ennis; Clonfert, which has a lovely Romanesque doorway; Ballintober, founded by a Connaught king; Ross, near Headford; and the remains at Kilmacdoagh, with its leaning Round Tower and cathedral. Cong Abbey, in Mayo, housed the great processional Cross of Cong, now in Dublin.

tradition of literature and oral storytelling; J. M. Synge set his play *Riders to the Sea* here, and the film, *Man of Aran*, made by the Irish-American director, Robert Flaherty, in 1934, depicted the harsh life on the island.

Most visitors, on a day-trip to one island, only get a faint whiff of Aran's cultural background; by staying in the islands' simple accommodation, you will absorb far more. Two ferry companies serve the Aran Islands from Galway City, Rossaveal, and Doolin (County Clare). Aer Arann flies tiny aircraft to all three islands from Galway. All transportation services may be affected by weather.

Inishmore►►► is the largest and most visited island. You can explore by bicycle, on foot, take a minibus, or a pony-trap ride along its 11km (7mi) spinal road. Inishmore has a wealth of ancient monuments, notably one of Ireland's outstanding prehistoric sites, the remarkable cliff fort of Dún Aengus. Three concentric horseshoe rings of stone perched atop mighty cliffs seem an odd place of refuge, so exposed to the elements and with a sheer drop to the roaring sea below. Its precise age and purpose are still a mystery. The smaller islands are **Inishmaan►►** and **Inisheer►►**, both of which have small fortresses, churches, and folk museums to visit.

►► Bunratty Castle and Folk Park   1733A

Bunratty, tel: 061 361 511, www.shannonheritage.com
Open 8 Sep–May, daily 9.30–5.30; Jun–Aug, daily 9.30–7
Admission: expensive

Bunratty, on the main visitor route from the west coast to Shannon Airport, is now a highly commercialized venture, dragging in bus tours by the thousand for "medieval" banquets and "traditional Irish nights" of fiddle music and Irish stew. For all that, the 15th-century castle is genuine enough and well worth seeing.

Set in the castle grounds, the Folk Park re-creates rural Irish life at the turn of the 20th century by means of a series of "typical" village buildings of the sort you will rarely see in Ireland outside folk theme parks. Extraneous attractions include exhibitions, gift- and tearooms, and the famous tourist pub, **Durty Nelly's►**, obligatory viewing for any tour.

STONE GATES

Despite there being a high density of fields and walls on the Aran Islands, wooden gates are very rare, since trees are scarce. The islanders' answer is to use small gaps in the wall, filled with stones. When access is needed the "gate" is dismantled and then reassembled. Some gates are topped with a branch of thorn to dissuade the occupant of the field from pushing the gate over. See above for a typical example.

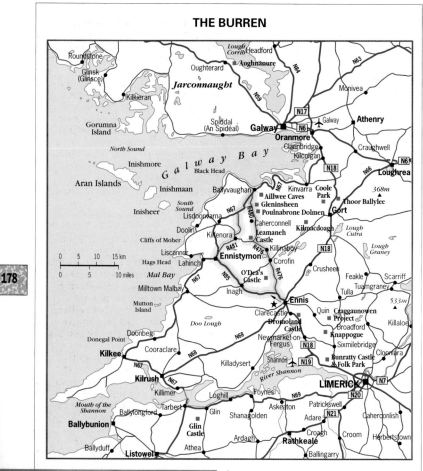

THE BURREN

The eerie beauty of the Burren

A moon buggy may seem better suited to this eerie landscape than a car. Geologists, botanists, and antiquity-hunters will be in their element.

From a distance, parts of this treeless limestone plateau in north Clare look bleak, but a closer exploration reveals that the area is astonishingly rich in plant life, playing host to more than 1,100 of the 1,400 species found in Ireland. Although the stone surfaces have been scraped clean by the elements, every crack and hollow contains some fragile vegetation. Alpine species flourish next to those from Mediterranean shores: rare saxifrages, gentians, maidenhair ferns, and orchids. The best time to visit the Burren for flowers is in May or June.

Within a couple of hours you can drive across the Burren on the major road from Ennis to Ballyvaughan, and get an idea of the landscape of ancient domed hills and grey-white "flagstones." But this moonscape reveals its real charms only to the sharp-eyed observer on foot, so take a picnic and leave your vehicle at some stage. Walkers on the Burren should wear sensible footwear and take great care. A 32km (20mi) marked trail, the Burren Way, runs from Ballyvaughan towards Doolin.

Bloody cranesbill, which grows commonly all over the Burren

Ballyvaughan▶▶ is an attractive centre from which to explore the Burren; other bases with accommodation are **Killinaboy**▶, **Corofin**▶, and **Ennistymon**▶. The southern section of the Burren is characterized by seasonal lakes called *turloughs*, which ebb and fill as the region's water table changes. Gradually, rainwater falling on this limestone plateau finds its way underground into a maze of caves and subterranean channels. Most are too dangerous for novice investigations, but one has been opened and is worth a visit: **Aillwee Caves**▶▶ (tel: 065 707 7036, www.aillweecaves.ie; *open* Mar–Jun and Sep–Oct, daily 10–6; Jul–Aug, daily 10–7. *Admission: moderate*) south of Ballyvaughan, is a commercial operation, but the cavern itself is left reasonably natural apart from pathways and illumination. Near the cave entrance a shop sells local cheeses and other produce.

Parts of the Burren are reasonably fertile, yet others seem inhospitably bare, a shock after the lushness of most of Ireland. For centuries before the advent of tourism, the population of the Burren lived in poverty.

The best way to find out more about the Burren's unique flora and geology is to visit the **Burren Display Centre**▶▶ (tel: 065 708 8030; *open* Jun–Aug, daily 9.30–6; Mar–May and Sep–Oct, daily 10–5. *Admission: moderate*) at Kilfenora, by **St. Fachtnan's Cathedral**▶▶. Other sights to look for as you cross the central spine of the Burren are ancient tombs, such as the 4,500-year-old **Poulnabrone Dolmen**▶, or the **Gleninsheen wedgetomb**▶, easily spotted beside the R480 near Caherconnell. The ruins of **Leamaneh**▶, a 17th-century mansion owned by the O'Briens, are a prominent landmark near Kilfenora.

Another curiosity is a weatherworn *sheila-na-gig* on the ruined church at **Killinaboy**▶. These carvings of female figures in indelicate poses were perhaps an ancient fertility symbol, or a dire warning of the sins of the flesh.

179

Glen Inagh, where the Burren meets the sea

There are no snakes in Ireland, as every Irish schoolchild knows. But its national parks, national nature reserves, bird sanctuaries, and forest parks provide a remarkably varied collection of habitats for a vast number of other species, including creatures that are now very rare in Britain, such as corncrakes and otters.

THE BURREN
This unusual terrain soaks up the rays of the sun and releases it gently throughout the winter, keeping temperatures a vital fraction higher than the surrounding area. It supports an amazing variety of plants, including many fragile, low-growing types that would be swamped in the average meadow. Species to look for include the deceptive fly orchid (resembling an insect); gentians, and alpine saxifrages. Mountain avens and wild thyme grow everywhere on the Burren, forming colourful sheets in early summer. Needless to say, visitors are requested not to pick or uproot any of the area's plants.

Fly orchid

An unspoiled land Ireland is a predominantly rural country, but like everywhere else, is steadily becoming more built up. Land use is changing, usually to the disadvantage of native flora and fauna, but there are still huge tracts of unspoiled countryside where ancient farming patterns prevail. Migrant birds return year after year to safe haunts, rare orchids and obscure insectivorous plants flourish in specialized niches, and lichen grows thick on walls or tree trunks in unpolluted air. Birdwatchers and botanists, or anyone who appreciates country life, will much enjoy a break in Ireland. Remember your binoculars, and a reference book for identifying unusual species. If you plan to walk any of the long-distance footpaths of Ireland, or visit specialist regions like the Burren, check what to look for at an information or visitor centre before you set off. Bord Fáilte's leaflet, *Ireland Naturally*, outlines the main nature reserves and places of interest.

Abundant wildlife Practically any part of Ireland offers the keen-eyed naturalist a good selection of species, but a number of locations are especially noted for unusual wildlife. Ireland has fewer mammals than Britain (no moles, for instance), but those that are there can often be found more abundantly. Otters colonize many rivers and streams, even quite near towns. Pine martens, red deer, and red squirrels can be found in the newly designated forest parks. The last remaining native woodlands can be seen in the national parks of Killarney and Glenveagh.

Exotic plants If you are interested in plants, the best region to head for is the mysterious limestone wilderness of the Burren in County Clare (see panel, and pages 178–179). Other areas special for plants are the sand-dune habitats, such as the Raven National Nature Reserve in County Wexford (wild asparagus, round-leafed wintergreen, and lesser centaury), and the lush, subtropical oceanic lands of Kerry and Cork, where wild fuchsias bloom and the strawberry tree grows to unusual size. Mosses and ferns thrive in the moist, mild air. Ireland's boglands support a unique ecosystem of wetland plants, including sundews and butterworts (see pages 24–25).

Rare birds Birdwatchers have an immense choice of habitats. There are many exciting coastal reserves, first landfall for rare migrants that cross the ocean to breed or winter in Ireland. Spring nesting seasons begin early for native birds, followed by an influx of species from Africa.

THE IRISH YEW
Every example of this tree ultimately comes from cuttings taken from the mutant discovered in the gardens of Florence Court in County Fermanagh. The branches have an unusual upright habit instead of the normal spreading growth. The original tree was identified and first propagated in 1767, and the Irish yew is now planted widely in graveyards and formal garden settings.

MARINE RESERVES
For marine habitats, head for Strangford Lough near Belfast, or Lough Hyne in south Cork, where sheltered sea inlets have fostered unique colonies of creatures usually found in more tropical waters. Giant skate and basking shark glide through the narrow straits, carpeted with bright corals and sponges.

There are pine martens in the forest parks, but you will be lucky to see one

Corncrake

In autumn, rare American waders appear in ones and twos, and in winter great numbers of waterfowl fly in from northern Europe and the Arctic or Canada. Manx shearwaters glide close to Belfast towards dusk, with an eerie cry that once unnerved the Vikings, and nest on Light House Island. Greenland white-fronted geese arrive in huge flocks on the "slobs" (reclaimed *polder* mudflats) of Wexford. Puffins nest in a few rocky places on the west and southwest coast (the Cliffs of Moher, Clear Island, or Puffin Island). Terns colonize the sheltered inland sea of Strangford Lough. Several of the most famous bird reserves are islands: Ireland's Eye, just off Howth near Dublin, the Copelands near Belfast, and the wild Skellig Rock off the southwest tip of Cork. Clear Island and the Saltees are both accessible by boat at the most interesting times of year. Other good birdwatching locations are the quiet estuarial coast of Waterford and Wexford (particularly around Hook Head, Kinsale Old Head, and Kilmore Quay), the muddy flats of Timoleague, and the wild rocky fastnesses of Clare, Mayo, Rathlin Island, and Donegal, where seabirds gather in vast numbers on cliff ledges, at spots such as Horn Head (Donegal), the Cliffs of Moher (Clare), or Downpatrick Head (Mayo). Inland, many of the larger lakes and river systems support huge colonies of waterbirds—godwits, avocets, and swans. Birds of prey can be seen wheeling in lonely circuits around the Wicklow Mountains, the Slieve Blooms, the Sperrins (in the north), and Macgillycuddy's Reeks.

181

EDWARD SYNGE

During the dreadful Famine days, some Protestant landlords attempted to lure their starving tenants away from the Catholic church with offers of soup, education, and other blandishments if they would convert. In Clare, Edward Synge was one such individual; he aroused such passionate antipathy that an attempt was made on his life. A stoutly bound leather Bible in his breast pocket diverted the bullet aimed at his heart, thus finally convincing many of his unbelieving flock that God was very definitely on his side! The Bible (complete with hole) is displayed at the Clare Heritage Centre in Corofin.

A justifiably famous Irish viewpoint shows Clifden in its glorious setting by the Twelve Bens, most of which are visible below. Leaving Clifden on the Sky Road (on a clear day) and looking back after a short while reveals the full panorama

▶▶ Clifden   *1721C*

The "capital of Connemara" occupies a glorious position at the head of Clifden Bay, with the Twelve Bens mountain range a dramatic backdrop. Clifden is little more than a large village, but its location makes it a popular base, and it is now a major music and tourism centre. It is also an agricultural and market town, but much of the land around it is too poor to farm, and the region's income derives mainly from tourism. It has a range of affordable accommodation, lively bars, and fine sandy beaches. An arts festival is held in late September, though a more traditional event is the August Connemara Pony Show.

Cottages and bungalows have sprung up all around the 19th-century core of the town, founded in 1812 by the local landowner, John d'Arcy, descendant of an Anglo-Norman family who converted from Roman Catholicism to avoid dispossession under the Penal Laws. He built the ruined Gothic castle visible from the Sky Road.

The best views of the town and the surrounding landscape are seen from the Sky Road, a narrow circuit around the Kingstown peninsula to the northwest. This scenic corniche skirts the hillsides, overlooking plunging vistas of white farms, emerald fields, and sapphire sea.

▶▶▶ Cliffs of Moher   *1722B*

Sheer, dark walls of rock stretch dramatically for 8km (5mi) along the coast of Clare, an even-topped curtain, in places as much as 200m (700ft) high. These remarkable cliffs are home to a variety of seabirds, including a colony of puffins. On clear days there are splendid views of the Aran Islands and the mountains of Connemara. A cliff path leads to the southerly extremity of Hag's Head, fenced as the cliffs are so friable. The rocks are basically limestone of the same sort as the Burren, but shale and sandstone have formed on top, and are subject to rainfall erosion and the pressure of many feet; keep back from the edge. You can park near the highly commercialized visitor centre (tel: 065 708 1171,

www.shannonheritage.com. Visitor Centre *open* Feb–Apr, daily 10–5; May–Jun and Sep, daily 10–6; Jul and Aug, daily 9.30–6.30. *Admission free*). Close by is a folly viewpoint built by the 19th-century politician Sir Cornelius O'Brien, where a telescope gives a close-up of the huge rock faces and sea stacks in the lazily moving waves.

➤ Corofin   1733A

This village amid the pretty lakes of the southern Burren is a fine base for exploring the area. Accommodation consists mainly of B&Bs, with one good private hostel in the centre. Even if you don't stay, visit the **Clare Heritage Centre**➤➤ tel: 065 683 7955; *open* Apr–Oct, daily 10–6; Nov–Mar, Mon–Fri 9–5. *Admission: inexpensive*), housed in the former Protestant church. It has a moving exhibition connected with the Famine period, when this part of Ireland suffered particularly badly. In a building close by, a genealogical centre has been set up, containing half a million baptismal records of more than 2,500 families. Descendants of émigré families come to find their roots (see pages 74–75).

➤ Craggaunowen Project   1733A

Kilmurry, Sixmilebridge, tel: 061 367 178, www.shannonheritage.com
Open: mid-Apr–Oct, daily 10–6. Admission: expensive
This historic reconstruction brings to life Ireland's pre-Christian past and is one of the best of its kind, well explained with a good visitor centre, coffee shop, and picnic area. The art historian and archaeologist, John Hunt, restored the 16th-century tower house of Craggaunowen Castle during the 1960s. A Bronze-Age *crannóg* (island dwelling) stands in a reedy lake; other exhibits include a ring fort and a stretch of Iron-Age timber road. Also on display is the leather-covered boat called the *Brendan*, in which Tim Severin and his crew sailed the Atlantic in 1976–1977, in a putative repetition of St. Brendan's 6th-century voyage to the Americas (see page 115).

CONNEMARA

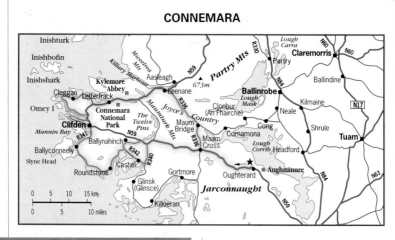

Mountains, beaches, untouched bogland, and a fiord

If you're lucky with the weather, this magnificent drive offers superb coastal and mountain scenery, a 2,000ha (5,000-acre) national park, and one of Ireland's best areas of blanket bog.

Connemara is the westernmost section of County Galway, beyond Lough Corrib. Inland are moors and looming hills, lakes and streams fringed by vivid green vegetation, and a massively

indented but placid coastline. One main road, the N59, leads through the centre of Connemara and around the northern area, but it's best to deviate from this for at least part of the way to take in some of the coast. If you start at Galway, take the main road for the first section (via Oughterard).

Oughterard►► is some way inland, but is surprisingly a great fishing centre, serving the resort area of Lough Corrib, Ireland's second-largest lake (40km/25mi long), which virtually splits the county in half. If you have time, a detour along the lush lakeshore towards Curraun is a pleasant option. From Oughterard it's a straightforward and beautiful trip past

Roundstone, a quiet village on the peaceful Connemara coast

mirror-like pools to **Maam Cross►**, where the monthly cattle fair is about the only sign of life. There you have a choice between exploring the mass of islets along the coastal peninsulas, or pressing on to the small, unremarkable settlement of Recess. Further on, stop at **Ballynahinch Castle►►** (now a luxury hotel, see panel on page 164). A detour via the peaceful coastline of **Cashel Bay►►** is a recommended alternative here. Sheltered from Atlantic gales and storms, this quiet bay sprouts luxuriant subtropical vegetation.

Roundstone► has a particularly attractive setting at the foot of Errisbeg with wonderful views of the Twelve Pins; its tourist industry is taking over from fishing. If you cut across the peninsula instead of following the coast you will see at close quarters one of the best remaining stretches of Irish blanket bog. It's a lonely road with some bad pot-holes, so drive carefully, especially towards nightfall. The bog is haunted by the ghost of a traveller murdered by two old women who offered him shelter—no advertisement for the local B&B trade!

Clifden►► is the "capital" of Connemara, a lively, popular town with magnificent scenery all around, best seen from the wonderfully scenic **Sky Road►►**, signed to the northwest. Just past the seemly Quaker village of **Letterfrack►►** is the entrance to the **Connemara National Park►►** (tel: 095

Dramatically sited Kylemore Abbey

41054, www.heritageireland.ie; *open* Apr–May and Sep, daily 10–5.30; Jun, daily 10–6.30; Jul–Aug, daily 9.30–6.30. *Admission free*), containing some of the West's finest mountain scenery. There's a visitor centre (*Admission: inexpensive*) with an exhibition on local natural history and bogland. Staff can suggest short hikes through the park; guided walks are organized in summer. For more challenging walking, follow one of the routes given in *The Mountains of Connemara; a Hill-walker's Guide*, on sale in local tourist offices. A little farther on stands **Kylemore Abbey►►►** (tel: 095 41146, www.kylemoreabbey.com; *open* Easter–Nov, daily 9–dusk. *Admission: expensive*), whose fairy-tale towers are reflected in a clear lake. Kylemore, a 19th-century folly, now houses a girls' boarding school, but welcomes visitors to its chapel, gardens, main hall, and craft shops. The road to **Leenane►** is especially scenic, running past the long inlet called Killary Harbour. Leenane achieved cinematic fame as the setting for the film, *The Field*. A brief drive over the bridge to **Aasleagh►** gives a view of a series of waterfalls, a salmon leap, and the gateway to County Mayo. If you want to return towards Galway from Leenane, a couple of routes wind through Joyce Country (so named because nearly everyone there has the surname Joyce) around Lough Corrib.

Western Counties

Oysters and Guinness at the International Galway Oyster Festival, held in late September each year

THE LYNCH MEMORIAL
This marble plaque over a Gothic doorway can be found near the Collegiate Church of St. Nicholas in Market Street. It commemorates a poignant, though almost certainly fictional, legend that a former city mayor, James Lynch FitzStephen, tried and convicted his own son, Walter, of killing a Spanish rival for the affections of his beloved. The boy confessed to the crime and Judge Lynch felt morally obliged to condemn his son to death as he would any other citizen guilty of murder. But no one would carry out the sentence, so he was forced to hang his son himself. After the execution the mayor retired into seclusion, a broken man.

CLADDAGH RINGS
These ornaments of silver or gold originated in The Claddagh, once a close-knit fishing community just outside Galway's old city walls, now a neat suburb. Claddagh rings depict two hands holding a heart surmounted by a crown, symbolizing a promise, or a hope, of eternal love and friendship. The precious heirlooms were handed down the female line and, depending which way the ring was worn, showed whether a girl was engaged, or still on the marriage market.

▶▶ **Galway**   *1733*

Galway is in the midst of an economic and cultural renaissance. The little city in the west is now the fastest growing urban centre in the country. Despite its size, it has an intimate, villagelike atmosphere and everyone seems to know everyone else, although this may be an illusion, as much of its population consists of temporary visitors (tourists or students). Besides its prestigious 19th-century university, where students can take their degrees in Gaelic, Galway has several Irish-language schools. None of its sights is essential viewing, but the city seems to add up to more than the sum of its parts, and is a good centre for entertainment and shopping (especially second-hand books and classy crafts).

There is always plenty going on, both low- and high-brow—a festival just about every month, an innovative theatre, concerts, lively pubs, and restaurants. In short, it is perhaps Ireland's most enjoyable and upbeat city, full of vivacity and character, and increasingly frequented by younger visitors in search of "good crack" (fun). It hosts high-calibre Irish folk groups and its sporting prowess is a source of pride, particularly in traditional games such as Gaelic football and hurling. The Galway Races (a six-day meeting in July) and its Regatta Festivals are some of the oldest regular events. Beside its own attractions, Galway is a good base for exploring local areas—Connemara, Lough Corrib, the Aran Islands, and the Burren.

Galway's prosperity was founded on its strategic location at the lowest bridging point of the Corrib River, a waterway once used by many vessels, now mainly by the spring salmon that leap the falls by the **Salmon Weir Bridge▶▶**. Founded by the Anglo-Normans in the 13th century, Galway became known as the City of the Tribes, a reference to the 14 leading families who held sway quarrelsomely in its early history. In its heyday, Galway was a significant port and European trading centre; it traditional vessels, the elegant lateen-rigged Galway hookers, traded food and fuel for livestock from the Aran Islands, or smuggled contraband from France and the Channel Isles. By the western mouth of the river are the remains of a Gaelic-speaking fishing community known as **The Claddagh▶** (see panel). The cottages have now been replaced by tidier municipal housing, but old photographs and artefacts displayed in the city's **museum▶▶** (tel: 091 567 641) show how it looked. The museum is in a stone structure called the **Spanish Arch▶**, erected by the harbour to protect ships unloading Iberian cargoes of wine and brandy.

Up towards the centre of town, the most striking monument is the unattractive **Roman Catholic Cathedral of Our Lady Assumed into Heaven and St. Nicholas▶** (tel: 091 563 577), a vast limestone structure in neo-Renaissance style, all seeping copper and flashy marble. The amorous behavior of its former bishop (Eamonn Casey), which raised eyebrows in 1992, has failed to dent local faith. More attractive buildings lie in the medieval quarter of the city, where wandering through its delightful streets of well-restored shop-fronts and stone town houses is recommended. Sixteenth-century **Lynch's Castle▶**, now an Allied Irish Bank building, was once the seat of the Lynch family and its mullioned facade is decorated with exotic escutcheons and gargoyles. The dignified **Collegiate Church of St. Nicholas▶** (tel: 091 564 648) has seafaring associations, including a legend that Christopher Columbus prayed there. Eyre Square is a welcome space after the confinement of the tiny old lanes. Dedicated to President Kennedy, it contains several monuments, the most interesting being the crested Browne Doorway, a disembodied portal dating from 1627, removed from a grand mansion in 1905. Bits of the city walls are incorporated into the Eyre Square shopping centre. Nora Barnacle, James Joyce's wife, hailed from Galway, and her house can be visited in the Bowling Green.

OYSTERS AND ALE

Galway's native oysters raised in the calm tidal waters around Clarinbridge are world famous, and it is an ideal place to acquire an expensive taste—whenever there's an "r" in the month. In fact, most Galway oysters are perfectly affordable, being farmed ones from Portuguese stock which, unlike the native oysters, can be eaten in any month. Though carefully prepared, these are served with no pretentious ritual. Wash them down with a pint of Guinness if you like. Each year in early September, the Clarinbridge Oyster Festival is held, and the end of September brings the Galway International Oyster Festival. The best place to try them is Paddy Burke's pub in Clarinbridge. They take about four years to reach maturity.

The beach at Salthill, west of Galway, looks south towards the Burren

MYSTIC VISIONS

Shrines and grottoes throughout Ireland, most still in constant use, declare the absolute faith many Irish people have in miracles, that is, in otherwise unexplainable religious experiences. These miracles can take the form of visions or statues that move, weep, or bleed. The testimony of these people is often unshakeable, even under rigorous cross-questioning. Grotto shrines can be seen at Ballinspittle, near Kinsale, and Mount Melleray, in County Waterford, among others.

Knock's position on the world pilgrimage trail was confirmed by the visit of Pope John Paul II in 1979

CROAGH PATRICK

The brooding, conical outline of this mountain dominates the skyline all around southwest Mayo. It is associated with St. Patrick, the site of his Lenten fast and legendary banishment of the snakes. Each year, on the last Sunday in July, pilgrims make an arduous ascent, some barefoot. On clear days, the summit gives magnificent views over Clew Bay to the Partry Mountains and Connemara. If you have sensible shoes, you can climb Croagh Patrick in a couple of hours. (See also page 226.)

▶ Knock

Knock's pedigree dates back over a century, when it was suddenly transformed from a humdrum little bog village into one of the most revered Marian shrines in Christendom. It is now the "Lourdes of Ireland," with a vast new basilica, constantly thronged by pilgrims. Its present high profile in the Catholic world is due in large part to the energies of a local priest, Monsignor James Horan. He battled with the authorities for an airport which, despite early descriptions as "a foggy, boggy white elephant," has greatly opened up the northwest region to visitor traffic since its eventual inauguration in 1986, seven years after Pope John Paul II made a celebrated visit to Knock. The commercialized religiosity of innumerable souvenir stalls may offend the purist, but today Knock attracts more pilgrims than ever, around 1.5 million a year.

On a stormy night in 1879, two village women saw a vision of the Virgin Mary, with St. Joseph and St. John, on the gable of the parish church. Unable to believe their eyes, they called other villagers, who also saw the vision before it gradually faded away. All 15 witnesses were interviewed and cross-examined by a commission of inquiry. Some 50 years later, three surviving witnesses were again independently interviewed, and firmly maintained every detail of what they had seen, giving an unnerving veracity to their story.

The original church still exists, the gable where the vision had appeared now preserved behind a glazed oratory. It has fine features inside, notably stained glass by the ubiquitous Harry Clarke (1889–1931). The new church, designed to hold a congregation of many thousands, was completed in 1976. Though fairly hideous to an unpartisan eye, the hexagonal building contains interesting examples of modern art and architecture. Its

2 ambulatory pillars each contain stone from a different Irish county, and the windows represent each of the four provinces: Connaught, Leinster, Munster, and Ulster.

Knock's religious significance dwarfs any other reason to come here, but there is a good little **folk museum▶** (tel: 094 88100, www.knock-shrine.ie; *open* May–Jun and Sep–Oct, daily 10–6; Jul–Aug, daily 10–7; Nov–Apr, by appointment only. *Admission: moderate*) in the village, illustrating life in the west of Ireland and giving some background on the shrine.

▶▶ Lisdoonvarna   *1722B*

Ireland's only spa stands in this curious village on the edge of the Burren, emitting sulphurous and radioactive iodine-filled springs alleged to cure numerous ills. The bathhouse facilities may seem primitive, but the old-fashioned bathtubs and massage rooms have a certain historic fascination. Needless to say, the water tastes terrible.

Grandiose spa hotels and villas indicate the spa's one-time popularity, but today the village is more renowned for its Matchmaking Festival, held annually in September after harvest time. The festival has an honourable history: Wealthy farming families used to pair off their eligible sons and daughters via a "matchmaker" for appropriate dowries of cattle or horses. Later the festival became a dating agency for the famously shy and sexually repressed bachelor farmers of rural Ireland, who often had few social outlets and little opportunity to meet potential brides. Many failed to marry until very late in life, if at all. These days, however, the festival has become a tawdry and depressing event, at which lonely singles turn up for a drunken grope and a one-night stand rather than a soulmate. Unusually in organized dating circles, the proportion of men is far higher than women (about three to one). There's plenty of good "crack" (fun), though, and it's certainly worth a visit as a social curiosity. If you're on the lookout, you may get lucky!

At the **Burren Smoke House▶** (tel: 065 707 4432. *Open* daily 10–7. *Admission: inexpensive*), signed from the village centre, fish is smoked, amid a choking salty fug of charring wood chippings. Women deftly fillet and trim massive sides of salmon (wild and farmed). A free video show explains the process. You can buy some of the products here, or try them in the Roadside Tavern next door.

This Lisdoonvarna house has turned a few heads

MONSIGNOR JAMES HORAN

The guiding light behind Knock International Airport may ultimately be of heavenly origins, but its earthly inspiration took the shape of Mgr. James Horan, an indefatigable local priest. He first raised the idea of upgrading the grass airstrip to jumbo-jet capacity. After the Pope's visit to Knock in 1979, Mgr. Horan was convinced the shrine would draw vast numbers of pilgrims. Decried by many as a foggy, boggy white elephant, the airport nevertheless opened in 1986, soon proving popular with both visitors and pilgrims. Indeed, the Lourdes–Knock run is used by many French visitors wishing to fish in the lakes of the West!

CAPTAIN CHARLES BOYCOTT

The man whose surname has entered the English language as a word meaning "to ostracize" was land agent for Lord Erne in County Mayo in the late 19th century. He lived at Loughmask House, on the lough's eastern shore. During the 1879–1882 Land War (Parnell's campaign to reduce land rents by 25 percent) he was isolated by the local community "as if he were a leper" for his refusal to cooperate. No one would work for him, or even speak to him, and eventually he was forced to leave Ireland.

Thoor Ballylee, Yeats's retreat from the frantic events of 1920s Ireland

COOLE PARK
Yeats's patron lived there—the redoubtable Lady Augusta Gregory (1859–1932), a wealthy widow who encouraged many writers and artists at the turn of the century. The house fell into neglect after her death and was demolished during World War II, but the splendid grounds are now open to the public as a national park and are a marvellous place for walks and picnics. The "autograph tree," a copper beech on which many famous visitors carved their initials, can be seen behind railings in the peaceful walled garden. In the park is the lake that inspired Yeats's poem *The Wild Swans at Coole*.

▶▶ Thoor Ballylee   1733B
North of Coole Park, tel: 091 631 436
Open: Easter–Sep, daily 10–6. Admission: moderate

> An ancient bridge and a more ancient tower,
> A farmhouse that is sheltered by its wall,
> An acre of stony ground,
> Where the symbolic rose can break in flower.
>   (*Meditations in Time of Civil War*)

In 1917, W.B. Yeats found this evocative "ivy-covered tower," conveniently close to his friend and patron, Lady Gregory, who lived at Coole Park. Thoor Ballylee was a fortified residence built by the Anglo-Norman De Burgo family during the 14th century. Then in his 50s and newly married to his young bride, George Hyde-Lees, Yeats purchased the derelict tower house for IR£35 and spent intermittent periods of the next decade there with his new family, converting the interior into simple but stylish living and sleeping quarters. The "winding stair" image that repeatedly appears in his poetry refers to the stone steps leading up the tower. From the battlemented rooftop, views extend over the placid meadows by the nearby millstream to the Slieve Aughty Mountains. Many of Yeats's more mystical writings were produced there, notably *The Tower* and *The Winding Stair* (not generally his most admired work); by this stage his disillusion with the Irish political scene was taking effect and he sought relief in seclusion and mythology. By 1928, Yeats had abandoned the damp tower for warmer climes; he died in France in 1939. The Kiltartan Society took over the decaying tower in 1961 and restored it fully. The audio-visual show gives a good background to the poet, the house, and the turmoil of the times.

Setting the world to rights in Westport

▶▶ Westport   1722D
One of the most charming towns in Ireland's western region, Westport shows its Georgian origins clearly in its broad streets and river, which flows in tidy canals along a lime-fringed avenue called The Mall. It is set on an inlet of Clew Bay, where the Carrowbeg River flows into the

...ea. Many of its fine buildings remain, some carefully ...estored. The Protestant church is late Victorian (about ...880) and has charming art nouveau influences.

Westport was originally laid out as part of a great estate ...nd, at the turn of the 18th century, prospered greatly ...rom its textile industry. In 1801, though, the Act of Union ...nade local businesses collapse as cheaper products ...looded in from England. By 1825, Westport's linen indus-...ry was virtually finished. Today, Westport is a market ...own and fishing centre, with a few good beaches nearby.

Westport House▶▶ (tel: 098 25430, www.westport-...house.ie; *open* Apr–May, Sun 2–5; Jun, daily 1.30–5.30; ...ul–26 Aug, Mon–Fri 11.30–5.30, Sat–Sun 1.30–5.30; 27 ...Aug–1 Sep, daily 1.30–5.30; 2 Sep–1 Oct, daily 2–5. *Admission: expensive*) stands in parkland just outside the ...own, near Westport Quay. Designed by James Wyatt and ...Richard Castle, it is the seat of the Brownes, Marquesses of ...Sligo, and is County Mayo's only stately home open to the public. Though highly commercialized in an attempt to meet the colossal running costs, it is still a remarkable house, beautifully furnished inside with Irish Georgian and Victorian silver and antiques, Waterford crystal, Chinese wallpapers, and a fine collection of paintings, including a *Holy Family* by Rubens. The doors are of Jamaican mahogany (the 1st marquess spent time as a governor there, apparently one of its more benevolent rulers, freeing many slaves). The dungeons beneath the house date from an earlier dwelling, allegedly a castle belonging to the pirate queen, Grace O'Malley. These now provide but one of the many attractions and sideshows in the park and grounds, which include a zoo, boating lake, a model railway, and horse-drawn caravans. The Browne family has lived in Westport House for over 400 years.

Westport Quay, just outside the main entrance gates to the house, has several good restaurants, and there is a range of accommodation in the town. A couple of summer festivals (arts in October and a street festival in July) and good music pubs are other reasons to head here. The Wyatt Theatre (in season) puts on some amateur productions of Irish drama.

"MY WIFE GEORGE"
W. B. Yeats was something of a pessimistic visionary at times, foreseeing the places he lived in going to rack and ruin after he left. On a plaque set into the wall of the tower at Thoor Ballylee, he inscribed the following verse:

I, the poet William Yeats,
With old mill boards and
    sea-green slates
And smithy work from the
    Gort forge,
Restored this tower for my
    wife George;
And may these characters
    remain
When all is ruin once
    again.

191

Westport House also has an attractive modern church in its grounds

Any glance at Ireland's antiquities—its great churches, the jewellery worn by the Celts, the intricacies of illuminated manuscripts like the Book of Kells—will show what a long tradition of sheer artistry exists there, what a delight in pattern, shape, and texture. This continues today, encouraged strongly by tourism.

BOG-WOOD CARVINGS

An artist with a highly individual product is Michael Casey, who works at Barley Harbour in County Longford and has achieved an international reputation. He has made an art of carving bog wood (blackened timber preserved for thousands of years beneath boglands) into imaginative sculptures of figures or animals. It is a long process. First the wood has to dry out—taking almost two years. Then it is carved, and finished carefully with sandpaper and beeswax to a remarkable sheen. The wood used is mostly yew, pine, or oak.

The labour-intensive and highly skilled craft of lace-making, here practiced in Monaghan

Souvenir hunting Ireland's craft industries are a major source of revenue. They vary from huge enterprises employing hundreds of workers, like Waterford Crystal, to tiny artisan studios where one person practices wood-carving or jewellery-making. Some crafts are still cottage industries—much knitting or lace-making, for example, is still done at home. Most visitors will want to take at least one reminder of Ireland home, and there is now a wide and attractive choice of souvenirs to suit all purses; shop around for price and quality. Prices can be high in Ireland with VAT at its currently high rates. If you live outside the EU, consider reclaiming this tax on anything valuable.

Many craft centres and even factories now welcome visitors, and free tours are provided at several large enterprises, such as Waterford Crystal, Tyrone Crystal, Belleek Pottery, Foxford Woollen Mills in County Mayo, Donegal Parian China, and Magee's tweed factory in Donegal Town. These are often elaborately set up with guided tours, audio-visual shows, refreshments, and showrooms where you can inspect, and of course buy, the product. Packing and shipment arrangements can also be made if you live abroad.

Kilkenny is an attractive place to buy crafts. The Kilkenny Design Centre, set up in old stables opposite the castle, provides a high-quality outlet for many of Ireland's best producers.

Craft villages Smaller studios have developed (mainly in the west of Ireland, notably in Donegal, Connemara, and Dingle) where economic conditions have justified a special focus of attention on employment opportunities. Artists can rent small workshops in these "craft villages" to produce jewellery, knitwear, pottery, woodwork, hand-weaving, etc. Connemara marble, a greenish stone, is fashioned into innumerable souvenirs near Moycullen. Several potters in Cork and Kerry have been particularly successful; Stephen Pearce's modern pottery in terra-cotta colours with abstract stripes of white is a typical example. Produced at Shanagarry, east of Cork City, it is now available in fashionable stores in Dublin or the West End of London. Robin and Jane Forrester's Bandon pottery is also very popular—in blue with a fruit pattern.

Glass and crystal Few visitors will be able to take a stained-glass window home, but in many of the churches of Ireland you will see the work of artists Harry Clarke or Evie Hone, who brought about a revival of this craft in the earlier part of the 20th century. There are good examples

at Carrickmacross in Monaghan, Ardara in Donegal, and at Kingscourt, Cavan. Ireland's brand of deep-etched, brilliant lead crystal is most famously produced at Waterford, but now has many competitors—in Tipperary, Cavan, Athlone, Donegal, Tyrone, and Galway. Jerpoint Glass, made in County Kilkenny, is plainer.

Linen and wool Textiles have always been a staple of Ireland's craft industry, linen and wool being the two main fibres used. Today's flax production is quite limited, but high-quality dish towels and tablecloths are available all over the island, subtly woven in damask patterns or more crudely stamped with shamrock motifs. Lisburn has linen trails and a linen museum. Centres of the lace industry are Carrickmacross and Clones in the border counties of Cavan and Monaghan (see panel on page 246) and Limerick. Both produce "mixed lace," which is sewn onto cotton net. Genuine handmade lace is expensive. Knitwear is ubiquitous. The classic Aran sweater is now produced all over Ireland in many different designs.

One of Ireland's most famous products is tweed. Manufacture still centres on Donegal, where those classic, hard-wearing fibres in soft peaty colours are woven in factories such as Magee's. Other natural fabrics are woven by Avoca Handweavers (see page 92). They are one of the most high-profile of Ireland's craft enterprises, producing soft worsteds and mohairs in bright, jewel-like colours of blues and pinks, mostly for women's fashions.

Limerick, too, is renowned for its lace

STEPHEN PEARCE

Stephen Pearce's pottery is at Shanagarry, near Cork, and is open to visitors. Only three designs are made, each in a simple, yet sophisticated style, from local clay. One is a black-and-white glazed earthenware range called Shanagarry, another a terracotta range, and the third a blue-and-white design. There may be only three ranges of pottery, but in all these contain over 400 separate items.

GLASS FACTORIES

Many of Ireland's lead-crystal manufacturers welcome visitors to look around and watch the glass being blown and cut by hand. Most famous is Waterford (see page 143), but other companies such as Tipperary Crystal, Tyrone, Galway, and Cavan will also allow visitors (contact local tourist offices for details). If you prefer a more modern, plain form of glass, one of the most interesting studios to visit is Jerpoint Glass, at Stoneyford in Kilkenny (tel: 056 24350).

193

Belleek Pottery dates back to 1857

Northwestern Counties

LOUGH DERG

This lake, set in desolate bog and moorland east of Donegal, is a highly popular destination for pilgrims who converge in droves on a tiny island, ostensibly for inner peace and solitude, although Station Island is now virtually covered by buildings—an octagonal basilica and several hostels.

St. Patrick is said to have spent 40 days praying and fasting there, and now the island receives up to 30,000 visitors a year. During a three-day summer vigil of prayer and contemplation only black tea and dry toast may be consumed; no sleep is allowed on the first night. Pilgrims walk barefoot around the island's shrines. If this sounds like an interesting weekend break, be warned that penitents come here from all over the world. Book early to avoid disappointment!

Traditional currachs are still widely used on the west coast

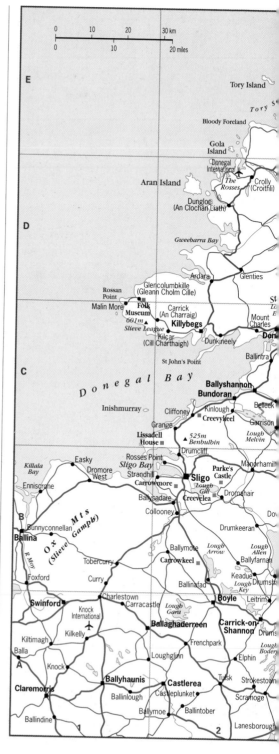

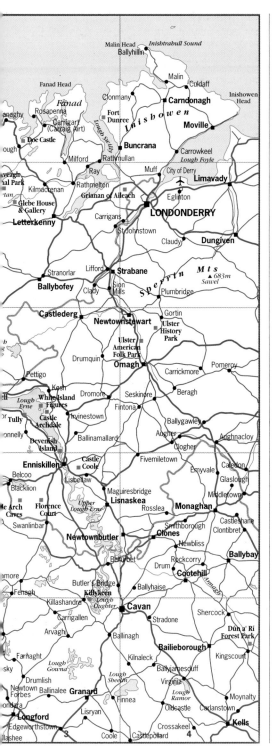

THE STOLEN CHILD

"Where the wave of moon-
   light glosses
The dim grey sands with
   light
Far off by furthest Rosses
We foot it all the night,
Weaving olden dances,
Mingling hands and
   mingling glances
Till the moon has taken
   flight;
To and fro we leap
And chase the frothy
   bubbles,
While the world is full of
   troubles
And is anxious in its
   sleep.
Come away, O human
   child!
To the waters and the wild
With a faery, hand in hand,
For the world's more full of
   weeping than you can
   understand."

196

W. B. Yeats (1865–1939).
(See page 201 for The
Rosses.)

NORTHWESTERN COUNTIES Donegal's spectacular scenery is often considered the best in Ireland, although its location keeps it remote. Outside a brief, intense summer season, when visitors flit through like butterflies, these northern regions (counties Sligo, Donegal, and Leitrim) can seem forlorn and windswept. All through the year clouds scud rapidly in from the Atlantic, bringing lashing horizontal squalls or drizzling sea mists. Just as suddenly these are followed by shafts of sunlight and vivid rainbows that transform its glens, cliffs, mountains, and beaches into the landscapes of Irish travel brochures. Here, in these far-flung peninsulas, you will find that elusive rural idyll—softly domed ricks of hand-turned hay and whitewashed thatched cottages with scarlet doors. The postcard scene disguises a history of constant struggle against the elements and economic deprivation. In many of these areas emigration is chronic. Until an increase in US investment there was little industry other than the old cottage-based crafts of knitting and weaving, although these are now organized to catch the visitor's eye in villagelike studio complexes or factories such as Magee's of Donegal Town. Most of the region's income comes from tourism and not all the side-effects are beneficial. On some sections of coastline, insensitive development has resulted in a garish outbreak of modern white bungalows that bear little relation to their surroundings. Numerous seaside resorts amuse those hardy enough to chance the weather. Bundoran's tawdry image evokes a socially conservative era. Today, some of these splendid and unpolluted beaches have achieved a new cachet as outstanding surfing spots.

NORTHERN EXTREMITIES

Somewhat tenuously attached to the Republic by a thin isthmus of land between the coast and its severed Ulster neighbours, Donegal waves its tattered banner even farther northward than the Six Counties, constituting Ireland's northernmost extremity. Its cliffs at Slieve League are the highest in Europe and

*The sturdy Irish Draught
is especially useful where
vehicles cannot venture*

several wild promontories make important habitats for sea birds. It scores not only with incomparable coastal scenery, but also with inland Glenveagh National Park, where massive glacial valleys carve through moors and blanket bog. Offshore lie several inhabited islands: Tory Island, where locals fish for lobster and paint naïve art; and Aranmore, more prosperous and biddable, welcoming visitors with holiday cottages.

Third-largest county after Cork and Galway, Donegal has the biggest Gaeltacht (Irish-speaking community) in Ireland and nationalist sentiments run high. This is the ancient Gaelic territory of Tir Chonaill—land of Conal. Even after the Flight of the Earls (see pages 34–35), the English never quite got their hands on Donegal's wilder regions, and after partition, though technically part of Ulster, they let it stay with the Republic. Road signs in rural areas may appear only in Irish. A significant proportion of the population on the eastern side of the county are Protestants, however, who look across the border from their prosaic farmland for their spiritual home.

LEITRIM AND SLIGO Farther south is Leitrim, which has a much lower tourist profile than Donegal, and few foreign visitors could pinpoint it on a map. It has pretty enough, but unspectacular, countryside, mostly mixed farmland, lakes, and moors on undulating low hills, with just a few dramatic limestone ridges near Manorhamilton. Lough Allen, the first lake on the Shannon, virtually bisects the county and provides most of its recreational attractions in the form of boating and fishing. Carrick-on-Shannon, the county town, is now a well-established cruise-boat centre. Leitrim has few significant historic sights.

Sligo, on the other hand, is rich in history, prehistory, and mythology, with ancient burial places and cairns. The distinctive shapes of Benbulbin and Knocknarea loom above the town, redolent of antique Celtic legends. The poet W. B. Yeats has strong links with the county, the scene of his childhood and his last resting place. The landscapes and myths of Sligo weave throughout his best work.

197

The very Irish Errigal Mountain looms above the white marble church of Dunlewy, County Donegal

198

▶ Ardara   *1942D*

Knitwear and tweed are the main concerns of this small town at the head of a deep sea-lough (saltwater lake). Outlets vie with each other on the main street, but you can, if you prefer, head for any one of half a dozen or so factory shops where you can watch the manufacturing process in action and probably visit a bar or tea-shop at the same time. Prices are generally cheaper here than in most retailers. The annual Weavers' Fair in midsummer is a popular local festival with plenty of traditional music and good "crack" (fun). A heritage centre has been set up in the old law courts. The Church of the Holy Family has a fine stained-glass rose window by the well-known artist Evie Hone.

▶▶ Carrowkeel, Carrowmore, and Creevykeel   *1942B–2C*

These confusingly named places are three of the most interesting and important prehistoric sites in the northwestern region. **Carrowkeel▶**, in the Bricklieve hills, is an ancient cemetery of circular mounds dating from the late Stone Age (2500–2000 BC). There are some splendid views from the exposed hilltop site. **Carrowmore▶▶** (tel: 071 61534; *open* Easter–Oct, daily 9.30–6.30. *Admission: inexpensive*), near Sligo, is the largest group of megalithic monuments in the whole of the British Isles. This site contains about 60 tombs, stone circles, dolmens, and other antiquities, the earliest of which are alleged to predate the famous passage-grave at Newgrange (see pages 108–109) by 700 years. Many have been damaged or removed, and incredibly, in 1983, plans were drawn up—and luckily abandoned—to turn the site into a dump. **Creevykeel▶▶**, near Mullaghmore, is a fine example of a neolithic court tomb, dating from about 3000 BC, with a double burial chamber surrounded by a wedge-shaped mound of stone. Polished stone axes, worked flints, and some bronze Celtic artefacts found there are now in the National Museum in Dublin.

One of the crafts demonstrated at the Donegal Craft Village is the production of tweed

▶ Donegal   *1942C*

Surprisingly, Donegal is not the county town of County Donegal (an honour granted to the somewhat unprepossessing town of Letterkenny), but it is nevertheless an attractive and strategic base for exploring the northwest and, more especially, for shopping. Its main store, Magee's (see panel opposite), is one of the best-known places to buy Donegal tweed. A short way out of town, on the southern side, is a collection of workshops producing a variety of high-quality crafts—jewellery, handweaving, ceramics, batik,

and crystal (look for signs indicating the Donegal Craft Village on the N15, the main road from Ballyshannon). Several other factory shops can be visited in the area, including those at Ardara (see page 198). **Ballyshannon▶**, a garrison town to the south, specializes in the region's brand of china, known as Parian ware (because it resembles the clear, white Greek marble from the island of Paros). The **Donegal Parian China Factory▶▶** (tel: 072 51826, www.donegalchina.ie; *open* May–Sep, daily 9–5.30; Oct–Spr, Mon–Fri 9–5.30. *Admission free*) and visitor centre are on the Sligo road. On the Ballyshannon–Belleek road is Celtic Weave China, producing basketware rather similar to the traditional Belleek pottery produced over the border in Northern Ireland (tours of the factory are free).

Donegal (*Dún na nGall*) means "fort of the foreigners," a reference to its history as a Viking stronghold. After the Vikings left, the town became the headquarters of Tír Chonaill, the territory of the O'Donnell clan. "Red Hugh" O'Donnell built a fortress and a Dominican abbey there in the 15th century. Early in the 17th century, the Gaelic chieftains left Ireland in the exodus known as the Flight of the Earls (see pages 34–35), and their lands and castles were appropriated by English and Scottish settlers. Sir Basil Brooke took over Donegal Castle in 1610 and enlarged it to a comfortable, if well-defended, Jacobean home with mullioned windows and imposing fireplaces. Today the castle remains are Donegal's most interesting sight. Sir Basil set about making his mark on the town in other ways, too, and Donegal displays typical characteristics of Ulster planning, including a classic Diamond (actually a triangular "square") in the city centre, where a monument stands to the Four Masters. To the south of town is a lovely stretch of coastline where several rivers flow into Donegal Bay. There the sun sets amid a maze of tranquil islets and sheltered creeks. St. Ernan's Island, reached by a causeway, is one of the best places to enjoy this scenery.

The Diamond, Donegal Town

MAGEE'S
This large department store on the north side of the Diamond is an Irish legend, still run by the family who established it in 1866 (the firm has passed to cousins of the original Magees, the Temples). In the late 19th century, handwoven Donegal tweed was produced on wooden looms, some of which are still in use. Magee's is the only company still weaving and tailoring handwoven tweed in Donegal. High-quality men's clothing and suit fabrics are produced under the Magee's label for worldwide export, in light worsteds as well as the hard-wearing, traditional tweed in the soft colours of the Donegal landscape. More than 600 work in two factories using advanced technology, and visitors are welcome for a short, free tour during opening hours. The upstairs café makes a good place for a coffee or light lunch.

THE ATLANTIC COAST

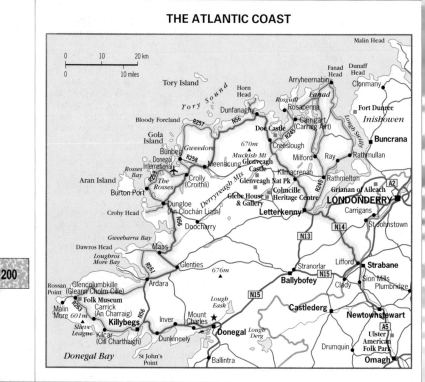

Map: The Atlantic Coast. Scale 0–20 km / 0–10 miles.

Locations shown include: Malin Head, Tory Island, Horn Head, Fanad Head, Dunaff Head, Clonmany, Arryheernabin, Rosguill, Rosapenna, Fort Dunree, Inishowen, Bloody Foreland, Dunfanaghy, Doe Castle, Garrtan (Carraig Airt), Buncrana, Gola Island, Creeslough, Gweedore, Muckish Mt, Glenveagh Castle, Milford, Ray, Rathmullan, Bunbeg, Meenacung, Donegal International, Crolly (Croithli), Glenveagh Nat Pk, Kilmacrenan, Rathmelton, Aran Island, Rosses Bay, The Rosses, Glebe House & Gallery, Colmcille Heritage Centre, Grianan of Aileach, LONDONDERRY, Burton Port, Dungloe (An Clochán Liath), Letterkenny, Carrigans, St Johnstown, Crohy Head, Doocharry, A2, Gweebarra Bay, Dawros Head, Maas, N13, N14, Loughros More Bay, Glenties, Stranorlar, Lifford, Strabane, Rossan Point, Glencolumbkille (Gleann Cholm Cille), Ardara, Ballybofey, N15, Sion Mills, Plumbridge, Folk Museum, Carrick (An Charraig), Mount Charles, Lough Eask, Clady, Malin More, Slieve League, Killybegs, Inver, Donegal, Lough Derg, Castlederg, Newtownstewart, A5, Kilcar (Cill Charthaigh), Dunkineely, St John's Point, Ballintra, Drumquin, Ulster American Folk Park, Omagh, Donegal Bay, Lough Swilly, Derryveagh Mts, Tory Sound.

Drive

The Atlantic Coast

So complex is north Donegal's coastline that any tour can take many variations depending on how much time
you have. Best views are from minor
roads rather than the N56, but skirting
the peninsulas is time-consuming, and
roads may be poorly surfaced.

The highlights of the journey are the
sculpted rocks at **Crohy Head**►► near
Dungloe, the fiery headland known as
Bloody Foreland►►►, and the
panoramic seascapes around **Horn
Head**►►► and **Rosguill**►►. If you
still have time and a taste for this
gorgeous scenery, **Fanad Head**►► by
the calm fiord of Lough Swilly, or the
pastoral **Inishowen Peninsula**►, from
which Malin Head relays weather

reports, are diverse and unspoiled.
Inland, the beautiful and lonely routes
through the **Glenveagh National
Park**►► are well worth exploring (see
page 203).

The weather in Donegal is always
uncertain, but its very unpredictability

is exhilarating, and compensations include amazing sunsets and glorious rainbows. Facilities for visitors along the Donegal coast are limited but steadily increasing.

The section between Dungloe and Crolly is known as **The Rosses▶** (*Na Rosa* means "the headlands"), a bleak, rocky, and fragmented coastline, sometimes worn into stacks and arches. Inland, the terrain is poor, consisting of boulder-strewn bogland waterlogged by myriad tiny lakes and streams. If you have time, you may be able to take a summer boat excursion to **Aran Island▶** (also known as Aranmore, but not to be confused with the Aran Islands off Galway Bay)—a 25-minute trip from Burton Port. There's not much to see except bog and lakes, but there are beaches and quiet walks. Boats now regularly visit **Tory Island▶** to the north, a treeless wilderness with 150 or so inhabitants who supplement their income from fishing by running a school of naïve art. Summer ferries leave from several local ports (such as Bunbeg and Falcarragh), but you may be marooned in bad weather. Balor, Celtic god of darkness, is said to have lived on the island's eastern cliffs.

Gweedore▶, the next peninsula, is scenically austere but densely populated, with new cottages and even some industry springing up along the coast. The most scenic stretch is **Bloody Foreland▶▶**, a mass of red granite that glows a brilliant colour at sunset. The sheer, quartzite cliffs of **Horn Head▶▶** provide terrific views and a windy ledge for thousands of seabirds. Sheep Haven is particularly attractive, and several roads lead to popular resorts. Marble Hill Strand has a fine beach. **Dunfanaghy▶** is the main resort, a gentle seaside village near an excellent sandy beach offering windsurfing and canoeing, and a blowhole called **McSwyne's Gun▶** that "explodes" periodically in rough weather. Beyond Dunfanaghy look for **Doe Castle▶▶**, a 15th-century fortress rebuilt in Victorian times. Views from the battlements overlook a wide expanse of Sheephaven Bay. Lackagh Bridge provides another vantage point. Inland, the barren, rocky landscape is scattered with lakes. The next outcrop is **Rosguill▶▶**, where an 11km (7mi) circular tour called the **Atlantic Drive▶▶▶** is signed past dunes and beaches. Highlights of the **Fanad Peninsula▶▶** include the neat plantation villages of **Rathmelton▶** and **Rathmullan▶**, where "Red Hugh" O'Donnell, Earl of Tyrconnell, was treacherously lured onto an English merchant ship for a drink, whereupon he was seized and taken to Dublin prison. On the **Inishowen peninsula▶▶**, don't miss the stone forts called **Grianan of Aileach▶▶**, **Fort Dunree▶** (The Guns of Dunree), and **Malin Head▶▶** (see pages 206–207 for more details).

201

The splendour of the Donegal coast

Derek Hill gave Glebe House to the nation in 1980. It makes a short but worthwhile detour from the Glenveagh National Park

ARTHUR KINGSLEY PORTER
The castle of Glenveagh was once owned by the American art historian Arthur Kingsley Porter, a specialist in medieval sculpture. One day in 1939, he set off on a fishing trip in Donegal; later his boat was found abandoned on an island without a trace of its former occupant. Wagging tongues said he feigned his disappearance to escape an unhappy domestic life; claims that he had been spotted subsequently in the French port of Marseilles and as a Buddhist monk in the Himalayas have never been substantiated, and his real fate remains tantalizingly unknown.

One of the early-Christian standing stones in or near Glencolumbkille

►► Glebe House and Gallery 1953D
Church Hill, tel: 074 37071
Open: Easter and May–Sep, Sat–Thu 11–6.30
Admission: moderate

This Regency building on Lough Gartan, a rectory dating from 1828, was for 30 years the home of the landscape and portrait artist, Derek Hill, who hailed originally from England. He furnished the house with immense taste and care, using a great mix of styles and art from all over the world, including Asian and Middle Eastern tapestries and ceramics, Victoriana, and original William Morris papers and textiles. Donegal folk art is also well represented, and in the adjacent gallery are works by Picasso, Bonnard, Kokoschka, Renoir, Augustus John, and other leading 19th- and 20th-century artists. A particularly interesting part of the collection contains works by the naïve school of painters on Tory Island, notably James Dixon. Temporary exhibitions are held in summer.

►► Glencolumbkille 1941D

The scenery is the great draw here; the drive along the north shore of Donegal Bay beyond the fishing port of Killybegs, past the grand cliffs of Slieve League, is thoroughly spectacular, through sheep-strewn moorland, heather, and turf-cut bog to a boiling mass of rocks and sea stacks by the shore. A detour by the coast, for example to the picturesque Gaelic-speaking estuary village of Teelin, is especially rewarding. Glencolumbkille, as its name suggests, has many other associations with St. Columba (Columbcille), the 6th-century saint from Lough Gartan who lived there for a time. On the saint's day (9 June), pilgrims conduct a barefoot procession.

A more recent benefactor, as yet uncanonized, was the energetic priest, Father James MacDyer, who made strenuous efforts to alleviate the area's chronic poverty and unemployment. He was responsible for setting up a number of collective enterprises to provide work. The most high-profile of these is the **Folk Village►** (tel: 075 41704; *open* Easter–Sep, Mon–Sat 10–6, Sun 12–6). *Admission: inexpensive*), on the edge of town. It is a small project using reconstructed cottages to simulate life in bygone Ireland. Three small dwellings are replicas of those typical in the area during the 1720s, 1820s, and 1920s, furnished with items of he period. The reception building sells craft souvenirs from all over Ireland, and the Shebeen café offers a variety of curious beverages, including some made from fuchsia or seaweed. A "famine pot," filled daily with an unenticing brew of the type of corn porridge eaten during the hungry years, stands in the yard.

▶▶▶ Glenveagh National Park   1953D

Church Hill, tel: 074 37088, www.heritageireland.ie
Open: Mar–Nov, daily 10–6. Admission: moderate

Some 10,000ha (25,000 acres) of wild scenery make up this park of glaciated valleys and open moorland around Lough Beagh. Parts of the park are wooded with native oak and birch or imported rhododendron and spruce. The approach via Dunlewy at the foot of Mount Errigal gives some of the most spectacular views. Off the main road, an expedition to the Poisoned Glen (so called because of a toxic variety of spurge, a shrub that grows by the waterside) is worth taking. Beside Lough Beagh stands the estate of Glenveagh Castle, created during the mid-19th century by John George Adair, who built the mansion in about 1870. He is remembered mostly for the harsh eviction of all his tenants after the murder of one of his estate managers in 1861. He later emigrated to the United States. His wife returned to Glenveagh after her husband's death and created the glorious gardens around the castle.

During the Civil War, the castle was occupied by the IRA and the Free State Army, then restored by a benevolent American owner who later transferred the land to the Irish National Parks Service. The estate contains the largest herd of red deer in Ireland, believed to number about 600 at present. A visitor centre is located on the estate (free minibus service to the castle in summer).

TORY ISLAND
A story about the Tory islanders claims that in 1884 a British gunboat, *The Wasp*, was dispatched to reprimand the inhabitants and to collect unpaid taxes. The islanders apparently called upon the forces of Balor, the one-eyed Celtic god of darkness, by circling the wishing stones in the centre of the island, and the gunboat promptly sank with all but six hands.

203

Glenveagh Castle and gardens

The Irish film industry is undergoing a revival, attracting film-makers from around the world. Ireland has a great stock of cinematic talent, and its history and political troubles are providing inspiration for Neil Jordan and Jim Sheridan, two home-grown directors, but there are many delightful films in a lighter vein.

Top: John Wayne and Maureen O'Hara starred in The Quiet Man, *roughly a cross between* The Taming of the Shrew *and* Much Ado about Nothing, *set in rural Ireland*

204

Richard Harris in pensive mood in the immensely successful The Field. *Critics, however, could never quite decide whether the plot lived up to the dramatic scenery*

Ireland stars In many films, Ireland itself is the star of the big screen. Directors of many nationalities have used Irish locations for movies—even ones not set specifically in Ireland—the soft beauty of its landscapes overcoming the vagaries of its climate. Earliest films included *Life on the Great Southern and Western Railway* (1904) and *In the Days of St. Patrick* (1919). Better remembered is Robert Flaherty's *Man of Aran*, made in 1934. This documentary of the harsh lifestyle endured on the Aran Islands has now become a classic, though it was not accurate in all respects—shark fishing, for example, had not been customary on the Aran Islands for over 60 years. It is regularly shown in Kilronan, the largest community on Inishmore, during the summer tourist season. *The Dawn*, set in Killarney, was made in 1937 by Tom Cooper, a story of the Revolutionary War using highly effective location sequences. In 1947, a British film was made about the story of Captain Boycott (see panel on page 189), villain of the struggle for tenants' land rights during the 19th century, starring Cecil Parker and Stewart Granger.

A stunning backdrop Several films of the 1950s used Irish backdrops, too. Most notable of these was probably *The Quiet Man*, a John Ford movie of 1952 with John Wayne and Maureen O'Hara. Much of the filming was done around Cong, in County Galway, and some of the stars stayed at the local posh hotel, Ashford Castle. It's a rollicking love story of an American who returns to Innisfree to find a bride, and good-naturedly perpetuates many Hollywood myths about the Irish. Yet another version of *Moby Dick* appeared in 1956, and the director, John Huston, chose the picturesque Cork town of Youghal for his harbour scenes. Rock Hudson is said to have sampled all the bars of Trim, County Meath, in 1955 during the filming of *Captain Lightfoot*, where the old Norman bridge played a leading role.

The National Film Studios were established at Ardmore in 1975, although lack of capital made this indigenous enterprise still largely dependent on foreign investment. Only

John Boorman's production *Excalibur* (both produced and financed in Ireland) could be described as an "Irish film" of the 30 or so that were made there between 1975 and 1980. Stanley Kubrick used Caher Castle, Tipperary, and Huntington Castle, in County Carlow, for *Barry Lyndon*, a gorgeously photographed, if rather static, version of Thackeray's tale about an Irish adventurer.

1980s and 1990s Many more recent films have featured Irish locations. *Cal*, by Pat O'Connor, dealt sensitively with IRA conflicts; *Far and Away* used the Temple Bar district of Dublin to represent 19th-century Boston; and *Educating Rita* found Trinity College a more suitable icon for an English university than either Oxford or Cambridge. *The Commitments* and *My Left Foot* (the moving story of a severely handicapped writer) were also set in Dublin. So was *The Lonely Passion of Judith Hearne* (though Brian Moore's novel was set in Belfast), a poignant tale of a genteel spinster music teacher, played by Maggie Smith, who falls disastrously in love with a gold-digging ne'er-do-well—Bob Hoskins. Some of Neil Jordan's best-known films include *The Miracle*, *The Crying Game*, *Michael Collins*, and *The End of The Affair*. *The Snapper* and *The Van*, by Stephen Frears (completing Roddy Doyle's "Barrytown Trilogy" begun with *The Commitments*), are both set in Dublin. In sharp contrast, the lush location photography of *The Field*, filmed in the Connemara village of Leenane, provides the sort of Irish green that almost hurts your eyes. Leenane, full of tiny fields and looming hills, was a natural choice for this grim tale written by John B. Keane. John Hurt and Richard Harris starred, and once again, the film created a local legend, with many residents—and pubs—earning bit parts as extras. *Hear My Song*, starring Ned Beatty, is also set largely on Ireland's west coast. *December Bride*, a spare tale of nonconformist passion, is one of the few nonterrorist movies to be set north of the border.

RYAN'S DAUGHTER

The blockbuster in 1970 was unquestionably David Lean's emotive love story, *Ryan's Daughter*. For this an entire village was built on the beautiful far western tip of the Dingle peninsula, at Dunquin. Few vestiges of this remain today, but the film still lives on in the imaginations of local people, many of whom were used as extras, and for a while had a taste of Hollywood glamour. The story, by Robert Bolt, is set at the time of the Easter Rising and tells of an Irish woman who falls for a British officer, to the horror of all. The film had a star cast (John Mills, Sarah Miles, Robert Mitchum) and had great box-office success, if dismissed as overromanticized by the critics. Certainly Lean picked his set with care—Dunquin is a magical place.

Local extras stare down the street of the specially built village in Ryan's Daughter. *One critic, Pauline Kael, wrote of the film, "Gush made respectable by millions of dollars tastefully wasted"*

FORT DUNREE (THE GUNS OF DUNREE)

A short way north of Buncrana is Fort Dunree Military Museum, an example of a coastal defence battery. The building was originally constructed in 1880 to guard the entrance to Lough Swilly. Martello towers augmented a series of heavy guns. At the beginning of World War I, a British fleet of 40 warships assembled at Dunree Head to protect the convoys that gathered here for the North Atlantic run. In 1917, a US base was established there, but 21 years later it was handed over to the Irish Republic and was last manned in 1952.

206

Some believe that the Grianan of Aileach was designed for sun-worshipping rituals, with hundreds watching the goings-on from the terraces

▶▶ Grianan of Aileach   *1954D*

This remarkable circular fortress lies about 13km (8mi) south of Buncrana, perched on a hilltop and reached by a small winding lane. Aerial photographs of it, such as the one below, show the stone ring fort in an emerald pool of grassland amid scrubby tufts of brownish heather and gorse. The name means "stone palace of the sun." Similar *cashel* forts can be seen elsewhere in Ireland, such as Staigue Fort in County Kerry. Its precise age is disputed, some authorities dating it well before the Christian era (to about 1700 BC), others rather later. Its suspiciously neat appearance is due to enthusiastic restoration during the 1870s by Dr. Walter Bernard, a Derry historian. The round enclosure measures about 23m (75ft) across, with walls 5m (17ft) high and 4m (13ft) thick. A single gate allows access to the interior, which contains four tiers of steps and various passages or storage places. It was recorded by Ptolemy in the 2nd century AD, and was used as a stronghold by the O'Neill kings for several centuries before its gradual destruction. If you are lucky enough to visit it on a fine day the views from this hilltop are amazing, stretching for huge distances over Derry, the Fanad and Inishowen peninsulas, and the Swilly estuary.

▶▶ Inishowen Peninsula   *1954E*

Ireland's most northerly point lies in the Republic on this ragged triangular headland, not in Northern Ireland as most people would expect. Lough Foyle and Lough Swilly virtually isolate Inishowen from the rest of the county. The interior is a mix of low white farms and cottages huddling against the wind, and grand brown mountains rising toward Slieve Snaght. The scenic 160km (100mi) route around the edge of Inishowen takes in Malin Head, castles, churches, High Crosses, and pre-Christian antiquities. None of these is essential viewing, but the tour, which takes a full day, is a dramatic and varied drive.

Buncrana▶▶ is the main centre, a popular holiday resort much favoured by inhabitants of Derry. Through-

ut the centuries it witnessed many clashes between English and Irish. Ireland's remote extremities were always feared (not without reason) as a potential Achilles' heel in English defences against invading Catholic forces from Spain or France, and any hints of disaffection were dealt with ruthlessly. In 1602, the O'Dohertys prepared to welcome a second Spanish armada here, and a couple of centuries later Wolfe Tone was held in Buncrana Castle after his abortive rebellion in 1798. Buncrana also has a Vintage Car Museum.

Malin▶ is a 17th-century plantation village built around a green, its most striking feature a long bridge of stone arches. Malin Head relays weather reports from the fishing village of Ballyhillin, sheltered from the worst of the storms by the rocky promontory. Several minor historical sights, such as crosses and stone circles, are clustered around Carndonagh.

▶ Letterkenny   *1953D*

Donegal's county town is now the main commercial centre of the Republic's northwest region and, as such, has several bustling shopping centres. It guards the lowest bridging point on the Swilly River, just before it widens into the scenic fiord known as Lough Swilly. There are few especially attractive views of this from the town itself, however, which is on the whole not all that interesting. Its main claims to fame are the longest main street in Ireland and the lofty spire of the Victorian neo-Gothic St. Eunan's Cathedral, which has a handsome altar of Carrara marble and rich stained glass. Look for the Four Masters carved on the pulpit. The Irish patriot Wolfe Tone was captured in Letterkenny in 1798 after his foiled invasion with French allies, and taken to Dublin under heavy guard. The county museum is housed in the old workhouse and the regional tourist office just out of town on the N56. Letterkenny makes a useful base for exploring inland Donegal, including the Blue Stack Mountains and the Glenveagh National Park.

St. Eunan's Cathedral, Letterkenny, was built by Donegal masons using Donegal sandstone

207

THE LAKE ISLE OF INNISFREE

"I will arise and go now,
  and go to Innisfree,
And a small cabin build
  there of clays and
  wattles made:
Nine bean-rows will I have
  there, a hive for the
  honey-bee,
And live alone in the bee-
  loud glade."

W. B. Yeats (1865–1939)

208

Parke's Castle stands on the shores of Lough Gill, considered one of Ireland's most picturesque loughs. About 8km (5mi) long, Lough Gill resembles a smaller version of the Lakes of Killarney

▶▶ Lough Gartan

1953D

Donegal's local saint, Columba (or Colmcille/Columbcille in Irish), was born by the beautiful shores of Lough Gartan in AD 521. A modern building on the eastern shore houses the **Colmcille Heritage Centre▶** (tel: 074 37306; *open* May and Sep–Oct, Mon–Sat 10.30–6.30, Sun 1–6; Jun–Aug, Mon–Sat 10–6.30, Sun noon–6.30. *Admission: inexpensive*), which outlines the saint's life (see page 114) and the rise of Christianity in Ireland. An interesting feature is an exhibition on the preparation of illuminated manuscripts, using parchment and natural pigments. At the saint's alleged birthplace are two sacred stones around which various superstitions have spread. Pregnant women pray at the Natal Stone to ensure a safe delivery, while the Stone of Loneliness warded off the anguish of homesickness and was a place of pilgrimage for those about to emigrate.

▶▶ Parke's Castle

1942B

Fivemile Bourne, tel: 071 64149, www.heritageireland.com
Open: Apr–Oct, daily 10–6 Admission: inexpensive
A fortified manor house with an interestingly chequered history stands by the calm waters of **Lough Gill**. Built in 1609 by an Ulster settler, Captain Robert Parke, it occupies the site of a much earlier tower house belonging to the O'Rourke clan, rulers of the kingdom of Breffni. The last unfortunate O'Rourke lord sheltered a shipwrecked Spanish Armada officer and was executed in London for treason. Features of the medieval structure can be seen in the later house. Beyond the outer defences near the water's edge lies a little beehive hut of stone. This is a sweatbox, or early Irish sauna, used to alleviate various ailments. Exhibitions and an audio-visual show about the castle and many local places of interest, including Sligo's range of antiquities, can be seen inside; free guided tours are available. From the jetty you can take a boat around Lough Gill, calling at the Yeatsian island of Innisfree (see panel).

The eerie light of dawn on Lough Gill

Rathmelton   1953D

This dignified plantation town is all stately warehouses and seemly Georgian buildings on a salmon river. It was built by Sir William Stewart for settlers during the early 17th century. The Leannan River was once an important waterway, and in earlier times Rathmelton was a significant port exporting grain, salmon, butter, and linen (a more unusual product was iodine, made from local seaweed). A new heritage centre in the former Presbyterian meeting house displays information both on the town's history and on the founding of American Presbyterianism.

209

An exhibit from the Flight of the Earls Heritage Centre, Rathmullan

Rathmullan   1953E

The eastern side of the Fanad peninsula, overlooking the fiord-like scenery of Lough Swilly, is the most appealing drive, and this fortified harbour village is one of the most interesting places to visit. Before the battery was constructed by the English to ward off Napoleonic attacks, Rathmullan figured twice in Irish history. First, it was the place where "Red Hugh" O'Donnell, the Ulster chieftain, was treacherously lured on board a disguised merchant ship for a convivial drink, only to find himself in chains on his way to Dublin Castle, where he languished for six years. Twenty years later, the earls of Tyrone and of Tyrconnell finally left Ireland from Rathmullan in the incident known as the Flight of the Earls (see pages 34–35). Initially they had hopes of raising support against the English from Spanish allies, but their plans came to nothing and they died in exile, leaving their great estates and castles to be occupied by Ulster settlers. A heritage centre in the old fort tells the history of this period. Another of Rathmullan's attractions is a country house hotel, Rathmullan House (see Hotels and Restaurants, page 282), one of Donegal's most comfortable bases, with a good restaurant.

The Dominican Friary, more usually known as Sligo Abbey

THE BATTLE OF THE BOOKS

A tragic storm in a teacup —but an important principle of copyright—lies at the heart of this curious incident, which took place at Cooldrumman, north of Sligo. In AD 561, St. Columba borrowed a psalter from St. Finian and surreptitiously copied it. When St. Finian found out he angrily demanded the copy. St. Columba refused and the pair went to arbitration at the court of the High King, Diarmuid. He decided in favour of St. Finian, with the famous judgment, "To every cow its calf; to every book its copy." St. Columba refused to accept the ruling and raised an army against St. Finian; more than 3,000 men were killed. St. Columba was the victor, but, stricken with remorse, he went to live in exile in Iona off the Scottish coast, where he died in AD 597.

The eye-catching monument to W. B. Yeats, winner of the Nobel Prize for Literature in 1923, in Sligo Town

▶ Sligo   1942B

Sligo is one of the largest towns in the northwest, a lively market town and centre for music pubs and eating places designed more for its own 18,000 inhabitants than for visitors. Colourful houses stand alongside the Garavogue River, and the town still has many characterful old quarters and shops. Its literary associations give it a cultural cachet and it now draws an annual influx of scholars and students on the Yeats trail, especially during August when a Yeats summer school is held.

Sligo was sacked by the Vikings in 807 and, situated as it is on the fringes of Connaught and Ulster, later became a key location for warring clans. The Anglo-Norman Fitzgeralds held sway in the 13th century when the castle (now vanished) and abbey were built. Later the O'Conors and O'Donnells fought for supremacy, and in Cromwellian times the town was one of the last Jacobite strongholds. During the Famine the population fell drastically and massive emigration occurred.

Sligo's main sights are its 13th-century Dominican abbey, sacked in 1641, and its **museum and art gallery▶** (tel: 071 45847; *open* Mon–Sat, 10–5.30. *Admission free*), which houses many documents relating to W. B. Yeats, together with paintings by his brother, Jack. The town has two cathedrals, the Church of Ireland St. John's, designed by Richard Castle in 1730, and the 19th-century Catholic cathedral. Hargadon's pub is a local institution. It now allows women inside, but otherwise firmly retains its old-world character and decor, with tiny dark booths and swivelling windows around which drinks could be passed with ease.

Outside the town loom the great hulks of Benbulbin 525m (1,722ft) and Knocknarea 330m (1,083ft), like upturned ships. Both hills can be climbed, but can be treacherous in the mist because of the deep fissures in the rain-eroded limestone. Benbulbin is the legendary death site of Diarmuid, who eloped with Gráinne. Knocknarea to the southwest, is supposed to be the burial place of the warrior Queen Maeve (though she died elsewhere), and is surmounted by a massive cairn of 40,000 tons of rock.

YEATS COUNTRY

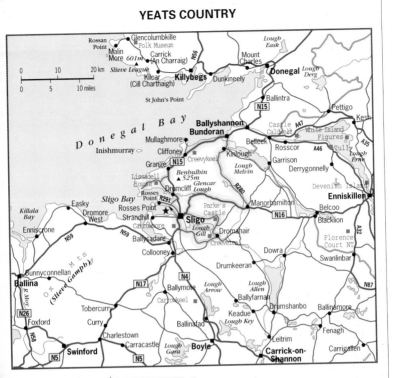

Yeats Country and Benbulbin

You're never far from **Benbulbin** on this tour, the mountain that so inspired Yeats. The coast is quiet and much broken; inland are lakes and pastures.

This area is called "Yeats Country" as the poet passed much of his childhood and was eventually buried here (his adult life was mainly spent in Dublin and County Galway). Above Sligo Town the curious hulk of Benbulbin looms like a capsized ship, its flat limestone top scored by erosion. Off the N15 north of Sligo is **Drumcliff churchyard▶**, where Yeats's tomb lies. Minor roads from the N15 lead past the headland of **Rosses Point▶**. Farther up, follow the coastal turning to **Lissadell House▶** (tel: 071

63150; *open* Jun–mid-Sep, Mon–Sat 10.30–12.30 and 2–4.30. *Admission*: *moderate*), 19th-century home of the Gore-Booth family. Sisters Eva Gore-Booth and Constance Markiewicz, friends of Yeats, took part in the Easter Rising. The house, in need of restoration, is surrounded by rampant vegetation. On the promontory of **Mullaghmore▶** is Classie Bawn (private), former home of Lord Mountbatten, who was killed in 1979.

From the resort of **Bundoran▶**, a well-marked drive to Manorhamilton passes typical limestone ridge scenery. From there, go west around the north shore of **Glencar Lough▶▶**, where a waterfall drops 10m (33ft) through ferny rocks to a pool (in Yeats's poem *The Stolen Child*). Return to Sligo, then strike east for a drive around **Lough Gill▶▶**, famous for the lake-isle, Innisfree. Summer cruises are available from Sligo, Dromahair, or Parke's Castle (see page 208). Other sites on the lough are the ruined Creevelea Friary and the Deer-park Monument, a series of stone burial chambers dating from 3500 BC.

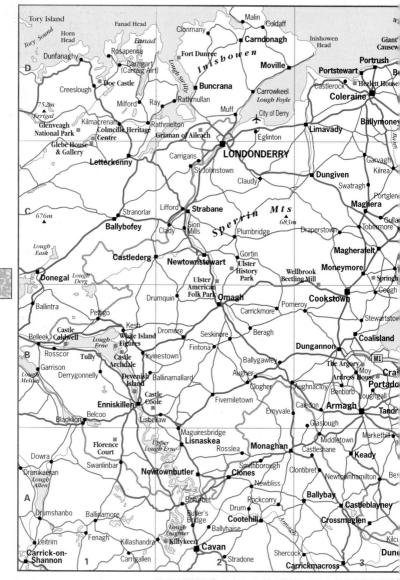

Victorian homage to the art of drinking: the Crown Liquor Saloon in Belfast

Northern Ireland

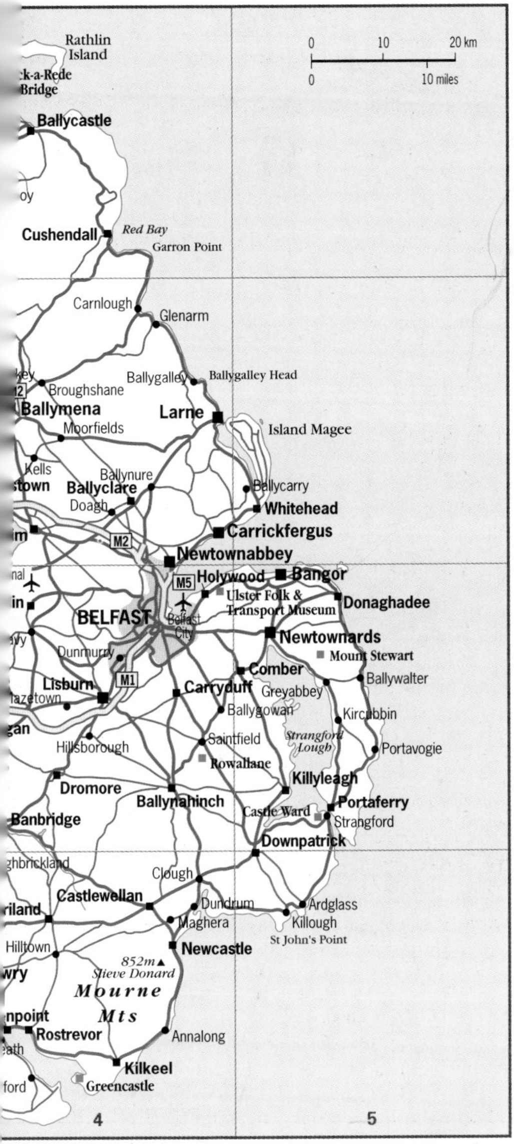
Rathlin Island
0 10 20 km
0 10 miles
Bridge
Ballycastle
Cushendall
Red Bay
Garron Point
Carnlough
Glenarm
Broughshane
Ballygalley
Ballygalley Head
Ballymena
Larne
Moorfields
Island Magee
Kells
Ballynure
Ballyclare
Doagh
Ballycarry
Whitehead
Carrickfergus
M2
Newtownabbey
M5
Holywood
Bangor
Ulster Folk & Transport Museum
Donaghadee
BELFAST
Belfast City
Newtownards
Mount Stewart
Dunmurry
Comber
Ballywalter
M1
Lisburn
Carryduff
Greyabbey
Ballygowan
Kircubbin
Saintfield
Strangford Lough
Portavogie
Hillsborough
Rowallane
Dromore
Killyleagh
Ballynahinch
Castle Ward
Portaferry
Banbridge
Strangford
Downpatrick
Clough
Castlewellan
Dundrum
Ardglass
Maghera
Killough
St John's Point
Hilltown
Newcastle
852m
Slieve Donard
Mourne Mts
Rostrevor
Annalong
Kilkeel
Greencastle
4
5

NORTHERN IRELAND For many years, the Troubles have been a significant factor in any decision to visit Northern Ireland. Yet, for over five years now a cease-fire has held while the politicians try to make a power-sharing agreement work. For the visitor Northern Ireland is, most of the time, in most places, as tranquil as anywhere in the South—and that makes it pretty quiet. In fact, the reduction in the military presence, and relative peace, has allowed the more "normal" street crimes such as theft to reassert themselves. However, this doesn't mean you shouldn't keep your wits about you, particularly in sensitive zones such as west Belfast, Derry, Armagh, or Newry.

The relief of Derry

CROSSING THE BORDER
Don't pick up hitchhikers near the border. Before driving in Northern Ireland, check your insurance. If you have hired a car in the Republic you must inform the company when you pick up the car that you intend travelling in the North (and vice versa). Major hire companies are fully covered for North and South Ireland, and make no extra charge.

Cars are best parked in official parking areas or otherwise in pay-and-display areas (where you buy a sticker allowing you to park for a certain length of time). Some towns and cities have signposted control zones where vehicles must not be left unattended, and illegal parking may cause a security alert. Outside the trouble spots, Northern Ireland feels, and is, entirely peaceful. Wherever they come from, visitors receive a warm welcome. Local people, whether Catholic or Protestant, are extraordinarily hospitable. Most of them are on perfectly good terms with their neighbours of whatever creed, and it is often baffling to imagine where the tension lies. The majority of people here are simply interested in getting on with their lives in peace.

SCOTTISH CONNECTIONS The closeness of Scotland to Ulster (a mere 20km/13mi at its narrowest point) has always influenced the province strongly, even before the plantation years (see pages 34–35). Waves of invaders made the short sea crossing, most notably Edward Bruce, brother of the famous Scottish leader, Robert, who first arrived at Carrickfergus with his "gallowglasses" (mercenaries) in 1315. Settlement hasn't always been one-way. During the 4th and 5th centuries AD, Irish Celts made their way to various westerly parts of Britain. But the people who returned during the reign of James I were mostly Scottish Presbyterians—tough, industrious, and determined to the point of intransigence.

Northern Ireland has been supported since the plantation years by massive financial support from Britain, but its economic success could not have been achieved without the settlers' Protestant work ethic and resourcefulness. These characteristics show in the many pioneers who left Ulster to seek their fortune in the New World the "Scotch-Irish" who emigrated to the United States of America have achieved an influence out of all proportion to their numbers. Presidents Kennedy and Reagan were of Irish Catholic stock, but about a dozen former presidents were of Ulster Scottish descent. Theodore Roosevelt was one of these, and his mother described her Antrim forebears in these telling terms: "grim, stern people…relentless, revengeful, suspicious…also upright, resolute and fearless, loyal to their friends and devoted to their country."

TOWN AND COUNTRY The scenery of Northern Ireland is its primary attraction and most tourism is concentrated in a few clearly defined rural areas: the Mountains of Mourne, the Glens of Antrim, the Causeway Coast, and the Lakes of Fermanagh. Other less well-known areas such as Lough Neagh and the wild Sperrin Mountains are now becoming more popular destinations for walking and fishing, and several forest parks have been created. The Ulster Way is one of Ireland's best long-distance footpaths, leading through the province's most scenic and beautiful landscapes in all six counties. But it is the cities of the North, especially Belfast and Derry, that give a complete picture of the province and cannot be ignored if you want to see more than surface prettiness.

The North is particularly strong on museums, and boasts a fine collection of stately homes and gardens (its Georgian houses are generally better preserved than in the Republic). In many ways Northern Ireland's landscapes are similar to the Republic's, however the North—for years the more prosperous region—has fallen behind economically, and this is reflected in the slightly jaded look of some of its infrastructure.

Checkpoints aside, it's easy to get around. Roads are generally good and the traffic regulations, like the telephone and postal systems, are the same as in the rest of the UK. The euro is accepted in some places, but most take only sterling.

215

The strange, regular formations of the Giant's Causeway make a fascinating viewpoint along the beautiful Antrim coast

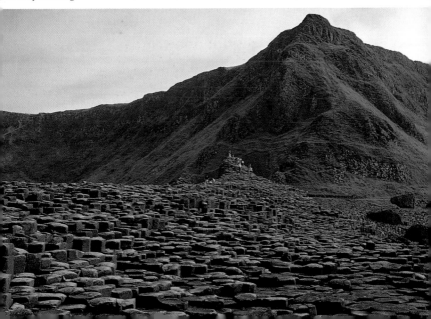

BELFAST

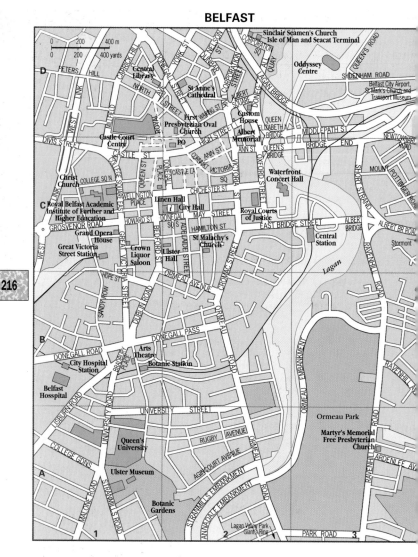

Right: the welcome at Larry's Bar is warmer than the ghostly images might imply

► **Belfast**   213M

Since Partition in 1921, Belfast has been the official capital of Northern Ireland. Stormont is now home to the new powersharing government. With a population of around 400,000, Belfast is much smaller than Dublin, and a large exodus of the younger middle classes during the past two decades to dormitory suburbs has unbalanced the city centre's demography, although it is still a transient home for over 8,000 university students. Apart from its two best museums, none of its sights is hugely compelling, but there is certainly plenty to do for a day or two, and the city has a highly distinctive atmosphere.

Few people unfamiliar with the city will immediately warm to the prospect of a stay there. Religious bigotry, sectarian violence, and deliberately high-profile security

measures have in the past given the impression to outsiders that Northern Ireland's capital is a war zone. Like many things in Ireland, however, the reality is a surprise. If anything, Belfast has always been less of a risk for the average visitor than Dublin. Security checks and searches (much less stringent since the 1997 cease-fire) are endured with the stoicism that prevailed during World War II, when Belfast's dockyard targets caused many civilian casualties. Belfast hosts one of the UK's liveliest and most acclaimed arts festivals at Queen's University each November, as well as an impressive year-round series of concerts, exhibitions, opera, and drama. Restaurants along its Golden Mile bustle; sports events flourish.

The great engineering works that once made Belfast so prosperous are in sad decline, and unemployment figures in the province are among the highest in the UK. Its earliest industries included rope- and linen-making, cotton-spinning, and printing. In 1859, the UK's largest shipyards were established here by the Yorkshire engineer Edward Harland and a marine draftsman from Hamburg, Gustav Wilhelm Wolff. Two vast yellow cranes with the initials "H&W" still dominate the dockland skyline as powerfully as any cathedral and are affectionately known as Samson and Goliath. The decision to close these mighty

Like Dublin, Belfast lies close to hills, in this instance Cave Hill, north of the city

217

Northern Ireland

shipyards was a great psychological blow to the city, as well as an economic one. Other firms closely associated with Belfast are Shorts, the aircraft manufacturers, and Gallahers, the tobacco giant.

Belfast's setting is often praised more than the city itself. The name derives from the Gaelic *beal feirste*, meaning "mouth of the sandy ford," and Belfast stands at the head of a deep seawater lake surrounded by unspoiled hills, the Lagan River cutting through its heart. Belfast has abundant parks and open spaces, all documented by the tourist authorities (pick up leaflets in their office on North Street). Within minutes fast roads can take you beyond the city to scenic areas such as the Ards Peninsula or Strangford Lough; it is a slightly longer trip to the Mountains of Mourne or the Glens of Antrim.

The city's commercial centre and university area lie close to the river on its western side; prosperous residential districts are to the east and south. On the far west of town, beyond the dividing pale of the Westlink motorway, are the notorious sectarian ghettos that have given the city its worst reputation. The overcrowded run-down areas of Ballymurphy, Falls, and Shankill are depressing and can easily be avoided. To some, however, they are fascinating, and intrepid visitors venture

Belfast's City Hall was designed by Crumwell Thomas in 1906; the staircase in the entrance hall is lit by seven stained-glass windows depicting scenes from the city's history

there to see their vivid and sometimes highly artistic displays of street mural propaganda. If you want to visit these areas, you can take one of the black cabs that assemble in lines at the edge of the city centre, plying strictly within either Catholic or Protestant territory. To see the Catholic Falls area (Andersonstown), pick up a cab at Castle Street; to visit Shankill, go to North Street. On the Falls route you will pass the last remnant of the notorious Divis Flats, some of the saddest housing in Europe, and St. Peter's Catholic Cathedral in 19th-century Gothic. The Peace Line is a barricade of iron dividing Protestant and Catholic areas. On the

The City Hall, in the background, is built around a central quadrangle

THE *GIRONA*

Legend has it that one of the strange formations along the Causeway Coast confused the sailors of the Spanish Armada, fleeing after their defeat, who believed it to be Dunluce Castle (3km/2mi west). The galleass *Girona* was wrecked in 1588 at Port-na-Spaniagh with all but five hands—a loss of about 1,300 lives. Artefacts salvaged from the ship in 1967 are now on display at Belfast's excellent Ulster Museum, including cannon, rings, coins, and a quaint gold salamander ornament, set with rubies.

The Palm House at Belfast's Botanic Gardens is one of the oldest examples of a structure made of cast iron and curved glass, dating from 1839 to 1852

THE RED HAND OF ULSTER

A grisly myth explains the presence of a hand on Ulster's coat of arms. Two great warriors raced each other to the shores of Ulster; whoever touched land first would be king. Neck and neck they sped, until at the last moment one pulled ahead. The other, desperate to win, struck off his hand with his sword and hurled it ashore, so claiming victory. The red hand still stands on the province's coat of arms, a fittingly gory symbol.

The Grand Opera House had fallen into such disrepair that it closed in 1971, eventually reopening in 1980 after five years of restoration. Since then it has sadly become a victim of terrorist bombs, being badly damaged in both 1991 and 1993

Protestant side, murals can be seen all along the Shankill and Donegall roads, the most famous image being King William on a white steed, rearing from the waters of the Boyne.

MAIN SIGHTS

Belfast is essentially a Victorian city, modelled on those robust mercantile centres such as Liverpool and Manchester across the water. The poet John Betjeman found much to admire in the city's civic architecture, notably its **Custom House▶** near the docks (not open to the public), several palatial bank buildings near the High Street, and the **City Hall▶▶** (tel: 028 9032 0202. *Guided tours* are available Wed mornings) on Donegall Square, a flamboyant structure of white Portland limestone. Inside, the City Hall has many interesting features and rich decorations of marble and glass. Donegall Square contains gardens, statues, and several other noteworthy buildings, such as the **Linen Hall Library▶** (tel: 028 9023 1707), with a fine collection of volumes in its old-fashioned interior. The Albert Memorial Clock, on Victoria Street, was built in 1865 by William Barre and depicts Prince Albert in the robes of the Order of the Garter. The tower now leans slightly from the vertical

Also in the city centre (large parts of which have been pedestrianized) is **St. Anne's Cathedral▶** (tel: 028 9032 8332), on Donegall Street. Belfast's Anglican cathedral is austere neo-Romanesque, enlivened inside by mosaics and a floor made of stone from all parts of Ireland. Sir Edward Carson, architect of Partition, is buried there **St. Malachy's▶▶**, in Alfred Street, was built in 1844, the plain red-brick exterior of this Roman Catholic church disguising a glorious inner riot of plasterwork

in Strawberry Hill Gothic style. **Sinclair Seamen's Church▶** in dockland is another of Belfast's most striking churches, with a jaunty nautical theme. The oval **First Presbyterian Church▶**, opened in 1783, has an unusual interior designed by Roger Mulholland. For a truly unforgettable flavour of Belfast, head for the Martyrs' Memorial Free Presbyterian Church, also east of the river, where the Reverend Ian Paisley presides each Sunday.

Belfast has some extremely florid architecture, which is particularly apparent at the start of its Golden Mile, stretching along Great Victoria Street towards the university. The **Crown Liquor Saloon▶** (tel: 028 9024 9476) is a splendidly ornate, gaslit Victorian pub now in the care of the National Trust, all coloured marbles, tiles, mirrors, and panelled booths. Good Irish food is served, but lunchtimes can be busy. The **Grand Opera House▶▶** (tel: 028 9024 1919) is a beautiful Victorian theatre, badly damaged in bomb attacks in 1991 and 1993. It contains a typically lavish auditorium and presents performances of many kinds. Of the same era, but in a different style, is **Queen's University▶** (tel: 028 9033 5252) on University Road. The main building boasts an impressive facade of Tudor Gothic red brick and stone mullions. Close by are the **Botanic Gardens▶▶** (tel: 028 9032 4902) in Stranmillis Road, a beautiful oasis of lawns and gardens sloping down to the river. Its two main structures are the **Palm House▶** and the **Tropical Ravine House▶**.

On the grounds of the Botanic Gardens is a modern building housing what is certainly one of Ireland's best museums. The **Ulster Museum▶▶▶** (tel: 028 9038 3000) has a varied and extensive collection, though anything but wearisome. Schoolchildren delight in its dinosaurs; others may prefer its sparkling minerals or exquisite ceramics. The sections devoted to Belfast's industrial heritage are excellent, as is its clear and unpartisan summary of Ulster's history. One of its most

Queen's University, with its Tudor-style building, was founded in 1849

Belfast's tropical jungle can be found at the Botanic Gardens, south of the city

Belfast Castle (completed in 1870) was built in the style of Balmoral, the Queen's Scottish residence, and designed by W. H. Lynn

Flamingos cope with unfamiliar weather at Belfast Zoo

popular sections contains treasures and artefacts from the Spanish Armada ship, *Girona*, wrecked on the Causeway Coast. It has a fine collection of paintings, too, including some interesting 18th-century representations of the Giant's Causeway by Susanna Drury.

Outside the city centre lie several other sights. **Belfast Castle▶** (tel: 028 9077 6925), some way north on the lower slopes of Cave Hill, is a Victorian Scottish baronial house, with attractive gardens and fine views of the harbour area. Belfast's **zoo▶** (tel: 028 9077 6277) is pleasantly set in former gardens near to the castle and is just one of many parks and open spaces in and around the city boundaries. **Lagan Valley Park▶▶** (tel: 028 9049 1922) is one of the largest of these parks, with 16km (10mi) of towpaths and locks. Close by there is a prehistoric earthwork called **The Giant's Ring▶**. On the A20, 6.5km (4mi) east, is **Stormont▶** (tel: 028 9052 0700), a grand, classical building, which once housed the Northern Ireland parliament and now serves as administrative offices. It stands proudly at the top of a sweeping drive through neat parkland. The Scottish baronial Stormont Castle nearby contains the office of the Northern Ireland secretary of state, the British cabinet minister (senior member of the British Parliament) responsible for the province. Both can be viewed only from outside for obvious reasons. See page 235 for details of Ulster's Folk and Transport Museum in Cultra, on the Bangor road.

If you want to stay in Belfast, the best area to head for is the university area to the south of the city centre. In the seemly residential streets of Stranmillis, Malone, and Botanic there are a number of moderately priced guesthouses—safe, clean, and respectable. Several well-known hotels in the central areas have been terrorist targets in the past.

▶▶ Armagh 2123B

Armagh has often been the scene of battle, and today, this close to the border, security precautions are in force. County Armagh is predominantly Catholic, especially in the south, but the city itself is a Protestant stronghold. The two rival cathedrals, both dedicated to St. Patrick, scowl at each other from two of Armagh's seven small hills. The Protestant one has to be kept locked for security reasons, but instructions for obtaining the key are posted on the door. Solid, squat, and square, it is mostly 19th century, in perpendicular Gothic style, with a fringe of grotesque heads around its otherwise plain exterior. It is the burial place of Brian Ború, the warlike king who finally drove the Vikings out of Ireland. The Roman Catholic cathedral, completed in 1873, stands proudly twin-spired at the top of a long flight of steps. The interior is astonishingly ornate—walls and roof covered with rich mosaics of saints and angels. The Mall, a broad, tree-lined square, is surrounded by some of Armagh's finest Georgian buildings, including the courthouse and the Royal Irish Fusiliers and County Museums. Armagh's most unusual sights are the 18th-century **Observatory▶** (tel: 028 3752 4725) and neighbouring **Planetarium▶▶**, where computer displays and models track down heavenly bodies. **Navan Fort▶**, now just a huge mound to the west, was the ancient palace of Queen Macha, a site that rivalled Tara, and the court of Ulster's chivalrous Red Branch Knights.

PEATLANDS PARK
This nature reserve in County Armagh, near the southern shore of Lough Neagh, was set up by the Irish Peat Development Company and covers about 240ha (600 acres) of lakes, orchards, woodland, and virgin bogland. A visitor centre explains the fragile bogland ecosystem, and various sections of the reserve can by visited on foot using carefully marked pathways or by means of a narrow-gauge railway. Demonstrations of turf-cutting are always interesting. Further information is available from the park (tel: 028 3885 1102).

223

There are few remaining signs of Eamhain (or palace of) Macha, at Navan Fort, County Armagh. The site is thought to be 4,000–5,000 years old, and is associated with Cuchulainn, the Ulster hero

BULLETS, OR ROAD BOWLS
This ancient game is played along the local roads near Armagh (a version of it can also be seen in Schull, County Cork). A heavy iron ball, about the size of a baseball, is hurled along the lanes and the aim is to reach the end of the winding 4km (2.5mi) course in the fewest number of throws. Betting is fierce. Ask for details in local pubs if you want to see a game—most take place on Sunday afternoons. The first Sunday in August is championship day.

▶ Carrickfergus 2134C

The main landmark of this small seaside town is its vast Norman **castle▶▶** (tel: 028 9335 1273), still mostly intact, on a basalt ledge by the shore. Displays of its history are housed inside, and today the castle plays amiably to the gallery by hosting medieval banquets and a Lughnasa festival in August. William of Orange entered Ireland via these shores in 1690 and a Williamite trail can be followed around the town. Just to the east is the **Andrew Jackson Centre** (tel: 028 9366 6455), an 18th-century cottage with re-created period interiors and displays relating to the seventh US president, whose parents lived nearby.

The fine, underrated city of Derry

▶▶ Derry (Londonderry)   2122C

This historic city, nestled in the Foyle Valley, is now officially known by its original name, Derry, although its Loyalist population still refers to it as Londonderry—an allusion to James I's gift of the city to the livery companies of London. (To add to the visitor's confusion, the county name remains officially Londonderry.) Derry's notorious Bogside district has seen much unrest, for it is there that Catholic/Protestant tribalism is most sharply polarized. Catholics, unwillingly stranded right on the Republic's border, have suffered much discrimination under gerrymandered Protestant control, while Loyalists find it impossible to cast off their atavistic siege mentality. On a freestanding gable-end near the Bogside (once an IRA no-go area and the scene of "Bloody Sunday," when 13 Catholic civilians were killed in 1972 during a civil rights march) are the giant words "You are now entering Free Derry." Protestants reply a few streets away with the defiant slogan "No Surrender."

For all its political ill-feelings, Derry is a fascinating city, retaining intact the **17th-century walls▶▶** that have played such a significant role in its history. These sturdy ramparts, 8m (25ft) high and up to 9m (30ft) thick, have never been breached. Five of the cannons that defended the city during its long siege stand above Shipgate Quay. Walkways lead along parts of the city walls, giving excellent views of both the inner city and the lower city with its great modern bridge spanning the Foyle River. Within the walls are an extraordinary little enclave of old-fashioned shops and bars, the Protestant cathedral of St. Columb in "Planters' Gothic" style, and a typical Ulster central square known as the **Diamond▶**. A hopeful sign of constructive community spirit is the Derry Craft Village, showcasing modern artisanry.

▶ Downpatrick   2135A

In contrast to Derry, the market town of Down has lengthened its name, in honour of its most distinguished visitor, St. Patrick (see page 226). Down Cathedral stands in the highest part of the town amid seemly Georgian buildings. It is small, mostly 18th century and, perhaps surprisingly, is Anglican, not Catholic. Inside, the original Regency box pews have been preserved.

Not far down the hill is Downpatrick's other major sight, the **Down County Museum▶▶** (tel: 028 4461 5218), set in the local gaol. The **St. Patrick Heritage Centre▶▶** (tel: 028 4461 5218) is well worth seeing for a coherent version of what is known of the saint's life and times (detailed film and exhibition). There are also very good local history and wildlife sections. The old prison cells can also be visited. These grim, dark, cramped rooms once housed the leader of the United Irishmen, Thomas Russell, who was convicted and executed here in 1803 for his part in Robert Emmet's rebellion (see pages 38–39).

From Downpatrick the landlocked sea inlet called **Strangford Lough▶▶** and the **Ards peninsula▶▶** can be explored. Both of these shore roads are attractive, especially the easterly one, but to reach this it is necessary to take the car ferry across the straits between Strangford and Portaferry, where the tides rush with great force. The lake is an important wildlife habitat supporting many unusual species. To find out more details about this remarkable ecosystem, simply stop at Portaferry's **aquarium▶** (tel: 028 4272 8062), Exploris, near the quayside, which is devoted to local marine life. At Strangford, on the western side of the straits, is **Castle Ward▶▶**, built in a jarring mixture of styles (see page 230).

The gruesome figure of Death makes an appearance at the Derry Festival, held in February/March

St. Patrick is remembered in this stained-glass window (1937) at Down Cathedral

St. Patrick is Ireland's patron saint, and one of the best-known saints in Catholic hagiography. His importance to the island is evident from the number of places associated with him and from the many Patricks, Pats, or Paddys (including a whiskey) named after him.

THE SHAMROCK
This plant, *trifolium minus*, is a trifoliate, or cloverlike plant, thought to have been used by St. Patrick to illustrate the doctrine of the Trinity. It is one of Ireland's national emblems, traditionally worn on St. Patrick's Day (17 March).

The summit of Croagh Patrick—St. Patrick's mountain—appears to be perfectly conical from some angles

The saint is reputed to be buried in Downpatrick's cathedral graveyard, though the evidence for this is shaky. The rough granite slab that marks his "tomb" dates from about 1900 and was placed over the site of a large pit excavated by relic hunters eager to find his bones. Downpatrick is, nevertheless, the best place to learn about St. Patrick (visit the heritage centre in the Down County Museum).

St. Patrick, son of a minor Roman official, was born in western Britain at the turn of the 5th century AD. He was captured by Irish raiders at the age of 16 and spent six years in Ireland in slavery, working as a shepherd on Slemish Mountain, County Antrim. Eventually he escaped to France, where he trained as a cleric. Haunted by a vocation to convert the Irish to Christianity, he returned in about AD 432 and spent an energetic 30 years preaching and founding churches, mostly in Ulster, Leinster, and Connaught. In AD 433, he challenged Laoghaire, High King of Tara, by lighting the paschal (Easter) fires on top of the Hill of Slane against the pagan king's express command. Laoghaire was so impressed by Patrick's fiery sense of purpose that he let him continue his mission unhindered.

In County Mayo, the mountain Croagh Patrick is sacred to his memory. Legend has it that here the saint rang his bell and the snakes of Ireland fled. Of course there never were any snakes, but the mountain remains shrouded in mystery (and often mist), and is visited annually by countless devout pilgrims. The jewelled shrine said to contain St. Patrick's bell is held in the National Museum, Dublin.

▶ Enniskillen

2121B

The Belleek Pottery

This appealing little town owes much of its attractiveness to its setting on an island where the two sections of Lough Erne constrict to their narrowest point. Several routes converge on Enniskillen's strategic location and at busy times it can be a traffic bottleneck. Nevertheless, it makes a good base for exploring Fermanagh's lakeland, where boat trips, fishing, and several islands offer many diversions. In the town the main places of interest are the quaintly turreted Watergate and the castle, which contains two museums. One is a heritage centre devoted to Fermanagh life and customs, the other a museum dedicated to the Royal Enniskillen Fusiliers and Dragoons. The town's military associations with these famous regiments have made it a terrorist target. In 1987, Enniskillen suffered one of the IRA's most infamous attacks, when a Remembrance Day ceremony was bombed; 11 people were killed, 61 injured. Parking control zones are enforced within the town centre.

Many boat trips operate from various points on Lower Lough Erne (the northern lake), where several islands can be visited. **Boa Island▶**, **White Island▶**, and **Devenish Island▶** all have interesting Celtic or early Christian antiquities. Reached via the pretty lakeshore roads, Castle Archdale Country Park and Castle Caldwell Forest Park have good woodland walks and picnic sites. Near Enniskillen are the grand houses, Castle Coole and Florence Court (see page 230).

At the far western tip of the lake, straddling the border with the Republic, **Belleek▶▶** is famous for its pottery. Guided factory tours can be arranged and a museum and visitor centre display its wares. Belleek pottery is extremely elaborate, delicate, and expensive: Clay is extruded in thin strands which are laid over each other in complex lattice patterns to form the classic "basketware" style. The results command high prices.

MARBLE ARCH CAVES
These caverns, 14km (9mi) southwest of Enniskillen, are among the best in Ireland. The 90-minute tour takes place partly on foot, partly by boat. The impressive formations are given the usual fanciful names. Near the exit is a nature reserve where the Cladagh River emerges through a gorge into a bluebell wood.

Marble Arch Caves

CARRICK-A-REDE ROPE BRIDGE

If you arrive on the Causeway Coast between April and September, be sure to visit this curiosity linking the mainland with the salmon fisheries on Carrick-a-rede Island. The bridge is put up each spring and provides an exhilarating 18m (60ft) walk along planks with wire handrails, swaying alarmingly 24m (80ft) above a rocky cleft. You cross at your own risk (inadvisable in high winds), but the trip looks a lot more terrifying and perilous than it actually is, and it's great fun.

228

OLD BUSHMILLS DISTILLERY

In 1608, Sir Thomas Phillips was granted a licence to distill whiskey in the village of Bushmills, south of the Causeway Coast. Continuing the tradition today, Old Bushmills is the oldest continuously run (legal) distillery in the world. Now it is also a visitor attraction, offering tours (*Guided tours* Jul–Aug, Mon–Sat; rest of year Mon–Thu morning and afternoon, Fri morning only), with tastings of course (hot toddies in winter). Two blends and one malt are made. Reserve a place in high season (tel: 028 2073 1521).

The Giant's Causeway; the other end of Finn MacCool's construction is on the Scottish island of Staffa, where there is a similar (but smaller) causeway

▶▶▶ Giant's Causeway   2123D

This extraordinary phenomenon is Northern Ireland's most famous landmark, studied by the Royal Geographical Society as long ago as 1693. Visitors have flocked here from far and wide ever since. The Causeway is set on a cliff-lined coast of outstanding natural beauty and is now in the care of the National Trust. In April 1987 it was declared Ireland's only World Heritage Site.

The Causeway is a complex series of promontories, but the most spectacular section consists of about 37,000 polygonal columns of dark basalt, many tawny with lichen, packed so neatly together that it is easy to imagine them as building blocks of some supernatural hand. Most columns are hexagonal, forming a honeycomb pattern, but some have five, seven, or as many as ten sides. They measure about 30cm (1ft) across and may reach a height of 12m (40ft). Besides classic "threepenny-bit" stacks are other extraordinary formations, some like bulbous eyes, others like ramparts. All were formed about 55 million years ago, after a volcanic eruption poured molten basalt out above the chalky bedrock, crystallizing into these regular structures as it cooled. Legends have arisen about the origins of the Causeway; the main one tells how the Ulster giant, Finn MacCool, built it to walk across to Scotland.

At the top of the cliffs, a large modern visitor centre contains an interesting exhibition about the Causeway and the local history and wildlife. During high season a minibus shuttles visitors down the steep path to the Causeway, but this rather spoils the magic of the place; the best way to enjoy it is to walk along the North Antrim Cliff Path. Off-season, when no other visitors are around and the waves crash on these bleak, dark rocks, the Causeway is memorable.

THE GLENS OF ANTRIM

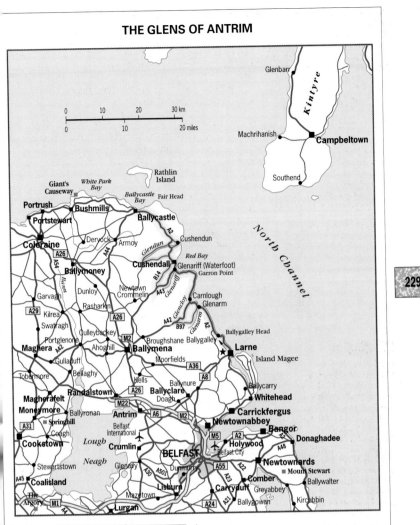

The Glens of Antrim

Road access to the glens is from the A2 from Ballycastle to Larne. The area is good for walking, with the Ulster Way running along the coast past all the glens. From Larne, **Glenarm►►**, heavily wooded with forest trails and picnic sites, and **Glencoy►**, near Carnlough, are the first glens you reach. Farther

north is the most popular of the glens, **Glenariff►►**, described by William Thackeray as a "mini-Switzerland," with waterfalls and a forest park. **Cushendall►►**, the "capital of the glens," has a number of minor sights, including a sandstone tower (the Curfew, or Garrison Tower), once used as a lockup for "riotous persons," the ruined 13th-century Layde Old Church, and Ossian's Grave, a Stone Age burial mound dating from 3000 BC. The pretty conservation village of **Cushendun►►** sits at the foot of **Glendun►**, wildest of the glens. North of Ballyteerim is the Tornamoney Cashel, a stone fort dating from AD 500–1000.

The properties and landscape owned by the Northern Ireland branch of the National Trust (NT) are an impressive collection. Besides the well-known set pieces such as Castle Coole and the Giant's Causeway, the National Trust also protects many minor and surprising sights—a lively Victorian pub in Belfast, a printing press and a beetling mill (used in the old linen industry) in County Tyrone, the curious rope bridge at Carrick-a-rede in County Antrim, and several follies and castles.

JOINING AND MEMBERSHIP

For an annual fee members of the National Trust (or National Trust for Scotland) gain free admission to almost all the properties managed by the Trust throughout the UK Contact the National Trust, P.O. Box 39, Bromley, Kent BR1 3XL, UK (tel: 020-8315 1111).

230

Country Houses The grand Palladian mansion of **Castle Coole**►►► (tel: 028 6632 2690), home of the earls of Belmore, is the most impressive house of its age in Ireland. A masterpiece by James Wyatt, completed in 1798, the house contains magnificent plasterwork and carved doors of ancient mahogany. Entrance to the landscaped parkland is free.

Ardress House► (tel: 028 3885 1236), in parkland near Portadown, dates from the 17th century. The interior contains paintings and good plasterwork. Livestock and farm implements are on show outside; visitors may explore the gardens.

Not far away from Ardress House is **The Argory►►** (tel: 028 8778 4753), very little changed since its construction in the 1820s. It has many original contents and a pretty, early-Victorian sundial garden. The interior is still lit by a rare acetylene gas plant surviving in the laundry yard. The surrounding wooded countryside offers many fine walks.

On the shores of Strangford Lough is **Castle Ward►►** (tel: 028 4488 1204), a mansion that clearly displays the diverse tastes of its 18th-century owners, Lord and Lady Bangor. He liked classical style; she favoured Gothic. Architecture was not all they disagreed on and eventually they separated. Despite its disparity of styles, the house and contents are of great interest, giving a vivid impression of Victorian life (see the laundry and the playroom). Within the 280ha (670-acre) estate are a 17th-century tower house, a wildfowl collection, and an exhibition about Strangford Lough.

Florence Court►►► (tel: 028 6634 8249) is a particularly fine mid-18th-century Palladian (classical) house. The seat of the earls of Enniskillen, it was superbly restored after a disastrous fire in 1956. Splendid plasterwork is the main feature, and is best preserved on the staircase and dining-room ceiling, which quick-thinking workmen saved from collapse by drilling holes to drain flood water. The grounds contain a water-powered

WELLBROOK BEETLING MILL

The last stage of manufacturing linen is known as beetling, when flax fibres are hammered to produce a smooth surface. The cultivation of flax was Northern Ireland's largest industry and many deserted mills can be seen. West of Cookstown, in County Tyrone, is Wellbrook Beetling Mill (above) where the machinery is still in working order.

wmill and a 220-year-old Irish yew tree, said to be the
arent of all Irish-type yews. The 3rd earl's fossil collec-
on is exhibited in one of the side pavilions.

A thatched "long-house" dating from about 1691, **Hezlett
ouse▶** (tel: 028 7084 8567) in County Londonderry was
obably first used as a parsonage. Its most unusual
ature is the cruck-truss (curved timber) roof. Inside, it is
mply furnished in 18th-century style and contains a
splay of early building and joinery methods. Farther south
 Springhill▶ (tel: 028 8956 1861), former home of the
onynghams, a military family of Ayrshire origins. The
lifice dates from the 17th century (with later additions).
utbuildings house a costume museum, while the gunroom
ontains weapons from Vinegar Hill and the siege of Derry.

ardens There are two fine gardens in County Down.
ount Stewart Gardens▶▶ (tel: 028 4278 8387) were
eated by the wife of the 7th Marquis of Londonderry in
e 1920s. The mild microclimate created by neighbour-
g Strangford Lough enables many rare and tender plants
 flourish. The house is richly furnished and contains
olitical memorabilia. One forebear was Viscount
astlereagh, the 19th-century politician who signed the
ct of Union. The county's other horticultural attraction is
 Rowallane▶▶ (tel: 028 9751 0131). This plantsman's
arden was created over the first half of the 20th century
 a drumlin (smooth glacial hills) site of 20ha (50 acres)
nd contains specimens from all over the world. Its pride
nd joy are the azaleas and rhododendrons in May and
arly June, but the gardens are worth seeing throughout
e opening season from April to October.

GRAY'S PRINTING PRESS
Strabane, in County
Tyrone, was an important
centre of the Irish printing
industry in the 18th and
19th centuries. The
National Trust now
preserves the only surviving printers, Gray's (*Open*
afternoons only in season;
closed Thu and Sun) on
Strabane's Main Street.
John Dunlap, printer of the
American Declaration of
Independence and
publisher of America's
first daily newspaper, *The
Pennsylvania Packet*, is
said to have learned his
trade here, as is James
Wilson, grandfather of
President Woodrow
Wilson. Visitors may
inspect an impressive
array of decorative printing
presses, all kept in
working order, and other
antique printing
equipment.

231

*Mount Stewart House
and Gardens, County
Down*

*With only one road
leading through the
Mountains of Mourne,
they can only be properly
appreciated on foot*

BESSBROOK
This neat little town
northwest of Newry was
built during the 19th
century by a Quaker linen
manufacturer, John Grubb
Richardson. It was
designed to house his
flax-mill workers, whose
living conditions must
have been much better
than many of their
colleagues at other mills.
They may have regretted
the absence of a pub,
however. The tidy, slate-
roofed houses are
grouped around two
village greens.

▶▶▶ The Mountains of Mourne   2134

These wild, steep-sided granite hills present an unforge
table aspect when seen across Carlingford Lough fro
the Republic. They reach to an average height of abo
600m (2,000ft) and are largely inaccessible except on foo
though the range is ringed by roads. Greencastle is
notable landmark near the entrance to Carlingfo
Lough. It changed hands many times, and now stand
gaunt and ruined near the rocky shore. Other places
interest along the coastal route are the marine park ar
restored 19th-century corn mill at Annalong, and th
Murlough National Nature Reserve, a stretch of san
dunes by Dundrum Bay providing an important habit
for many birds.

There is not much to recommend the town of Newry
a base to stay. If you want to explore the Mourne are
choose one of the eastern coastal resorts or stay in th
delightful village of Carlingford over the border in th
Republic. **Newcastle▶** is the main tourist centre for th
Mourne Mountains. The resort, though pleasantly set,
of no great interest, but it has a good sandy beach and
wide range of accommodation. There are many walks
the nearby forest parks of Tollymore and Castlewella

Slieve Donard is the highest Mourne pea
(852m/2,796ft) and it is said that on rare, clear days yc
can see all the countries of the British Isles from i
summit (a relatively safe and easy climb), where there
also a hermit cell. At one time the mountains were
remote and ungovernable area inhabited by smugglers.
maze of ancient tracks lead through open moorland ar
upland pasture that make excellent walking country. F
good maps and information, head for Newcastle's touri
office or the Mourne Countryside Centre at 91 Centr
Promenade. Rock climbing is popular on the steeper cl
faces. The most accessible section is a well-marked rou
called the Silent Valley that leads up to two reservoi

rving the Greater Belfast region. A visitor centre stands
ere and shuttle buses take people from the parking area
Ben Crom Reservoir (other traffic is banned). The
pper sections of the Mourne hills are characterized by
y fields and dry-stone walls. The Mourne Wall is the
rgest of these, 35km (22mi) long and more than 2m (6ft)
gh, enclosing the water catchment area around the
ent Valley. Many semiprecious stones have been mined
the mountains around Hare's Gap.

e Ulster Way Northern Ireland is excellent for walk-
g, and its interconnected paths form a magnificent
0km (435mi) long-distance footpath through all six
unties. For most of the way it hugs the perimeter of the
ovince fairly closely, ducking inland across the
errin Mountains and briefly touching the shores of
ugh Neagh. Obviously some sections are more scenic
d easier to follow than others. The paths running
rough the Mountains of Mourne, the Glens of Antrim,
e Causeway Coast, and the Lakes of Fermanagh are
e most popular and most clearly marked, and it is in
ese well-known tourist areas that you can most easily
d accommodation. At various points the Ulster Way
ks with other routes leading through the Republic.
ear the border areas it is advisable not to stray from the
arked paths.

For the most part walking in Northern Ireland is safe
d straightforward; no special equipment is needed
art from a good map and sensible footwear and cloth-
g. Route guides and detailed maps are both available
om various sources, notably the Sports Council for
orthern Ireland, House of Sport, Upper Malone Road,
lfast BT9 5LA (tel: 028 9038 1222). The Youth Hostel
ssociation of Northern Ireland (22 Donegall Road,
lfast BT12 5JN, tel: 028 9032 4733) also organizes
mbling and hiking holidays throughout the year.

SPERRIN HERITAGE CENTRE

The fascinating history, wildlife, and geology of the Sperrin Mountains is well documented in this visitor centre which can be found between Cranagh and Sperrin, 12km (7mi) east of Plumbridge (*Open* week-days 11–5 and Sun after-noons; longer in high season). Nature lovers can enjoy the sight of rare mammals and birds of prey in these glaciated hills on the northeastern border of County Tyrone. The Sperrins also contain significant deposits of gold. Commercial exploita-tion is causing concern to environmentalists, but small-scale panning expeditions are arranged for visitors. Multimedia presentations include a holographic storyteller and 3-D slide shows, and weary walkers along the Ulster Way may welcome its excellent coffee shop.

Newcastle nestles under the shadow of the Mountains of Mourne

ULSTER-AMERICAN PRESIDENTS

A dozen Americans of Ulster stock have made it to the White House, 11 as presidents, including three first-generation emigrants. Some of the more memorable include: Andrew Jackson, whose family came from Boneybefore, outside Carrickfergus; Ulysses S. Grant, the Civil War hero, with roots in Aughnacloy in County Tyrone; Woodrow Wilson, whose thatched ancestral home is at Dergalt near Strabane; and Theodore Roosevelt, whose maternal family hailed from Antrim. The 12th man was Major General Robert Ross, fighting for the English, who burned down the White House in 1814. Ulster émigrés also produced two prime ministers of New Zealand and a South Australian governor.

234

Past centuries are imaginatively re-created at the Ulster American Folk Park

▶ ▶ ▶ Ulster American Folk Park   2122

Omagh, tel: 028 8224 3292, www.folkpark.com
Open: Apr–Sep, Mon–Sat 11–6.30, Sun 11–7; Oct–Mar,
Mon–Fri 10.30–5. Admission: expensive

This theme park near Omagh, County Tyrone, has been set up with a generous endowment by the Mellon banking magnates who founded Pittsburgh, Pennsylvania. Thomas Mellon left Ulster in 1818 with his family and became vastly prosperous. The park has been re-created in the peaty bogs around his birthplace at Camphill, a modest whitewashed cottage, and traces the progress of those early Ulster émigrés from the Old World to the New. A guided walk takes visitors from a large reception and exhibition centre through birch groves. In the first section, reconstructed buildings create the atmosphere of a typical 18th-century Ulster village—a blacksmith's forge, a weaver's cottage, a dour Presbyterian meeting house where interminable sermons were preached. Costumed staff cook up griddle cakes over open peat fires, spin wool, and organize "lessons" in the village school (quill pens are used). One of the more imposing buildings is Hugh Campbell's house, where extracts from his journal of 1818, written during his emigration voyage, can be read: "During the night every moveable in the ship was put in motion by the great heaving…buckets full of all kinds of filth were hurled in the greatest confusion through the steerage to the great offence of our smelling organs!" On 12 July he wrote, "This day the anniversary of the Battle of the Boyne was commemorated by a certain part of our passengers to the no small annoyance of another part," which suggests that not much has changed in the intervening years. Visitors then pass through the Emigration Gallery, a replica emigration ship (complete with sound effects of creaking timbers and roaring seas) and onto the New World, where typical log barns, wagons, and farmsteads of the early settlers can be seen. Of its type, this theme park is highly successful without sacrificing historical authenticity. A café, craft shop, and genealogy library are also on site.

▶▶▶ Ulster Folk and Transport Museum   2134B

ultra, tel: 028 9042 8428, www.nidex.com/uftm
Open: Apr–Jun and Sep, Mon–Fri 9.30–5, Sat 10.30–6, Sun noon–6; Jul–Aug, Mon–Sat 10.30–6, Sun noon–6; Oct–Mar, Mon–Fri 9.30–4, Sat–Sun 12.30–4.30. Admission: expensive

The Ulster Folk and Transport Museum

This museum is located about 8km (5mi) east of Belfast in the extensive grounds of Cultra Manor on the Bangor Road. Typical Ulster buildings have been re-erected or reconstructed here. The exhibits include urban terraces, shops and cottages, farmhouses, a flax mill, forge, and school. Inside, demonstrations of local crafts such as spinning and weaving take place. An entertaining exhibition of domestic, social, and agricultural life in Ulster can be seen in the gallery that functions as an introduction to the park. The transportation galleries on the opposite side of the main road house the entire Belfast Transport Museum and include many exhibits from horse-drawn carts to the ill-fated De Lorean sports car (see panel). The Irish Railway collection is one of the best sections. Local engineering heroes, such as Harry Ferguson, receive due attention, as do the great Belfast transport firms such as Shorts, the aircraft manufacturers, and Harland & Wolff, the shipbuilders (one of their commissions was the *Titanic*).

The pioneering spirit lives on at the Folk Park

▶ Ulster History Park   2122C

Gortin, tel: 028 8164 8188, www.omagh.gov.uk/historypark.htm
Open: Apr–Sep, Mon–Sat, 10.30–6.30, Sun 11.30–7;
Oct–Mar, Mon–Fri 10.30–5. Admission: moderate

This attraction near the Gortin Glen Forest Park traces the history of settlement in Ireland, starting with prehistoric societies dating back to about 8000 BC (life-size replicas of *crannógs* and neolithic huts) through early Christian architecture (Round Towers and churches), Norman castles, ring forts, and 17th-century planters' houses.

A number of drives, parks, and beauty spots can be visited in the nearby Sperrin Mountains, a range of hills in which traces of gold have been found. The rare hen harrier flies high above the remoter uplands.

DE LOREAN
The famous gull-winged sportscar venture funded by public money to create employment in Belfast caused a major crisis in the Thatcher years when the enterprise crashed spectacularly, amid accusations of business malpractice and fraud. Investors and employees suffered greatly, and confidence in Northern Irish manufacturing projects took a sharp nosedive.

Lakeland Counties

THE CHILDREN OF LIR

According to Irish myth, the second wife of King Lir (not to be confused with Shakespeare's Lear) became inordinately jealous of her four step-children and turned them into swans, condemning them to roam for 900 years over the waters of Ireland—300 on Lough Derravaragh (Westmeath), 300 on the Sea of Moyle (the waters between Ireland and Scotland), and 300 on the Bay of Erris (Mayo). After their long enchantment the swans assumed human forms, but as ancient, wizened creatures who expired almost immediately.

Waiting for the racing results at Birr, County Offaly

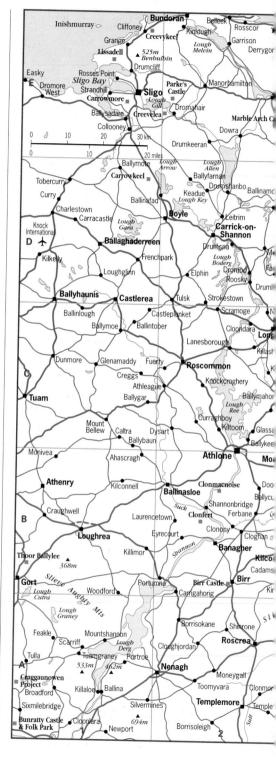

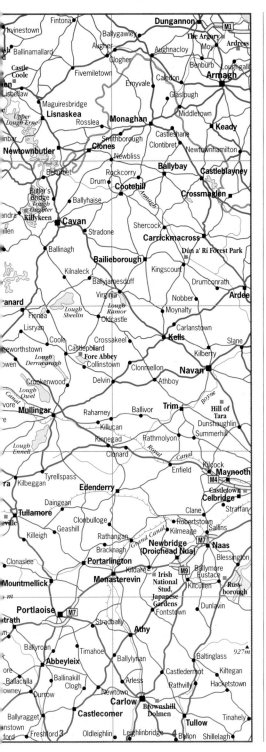

Lakeland Counties

Castle Island on Lough Key (County Roscommon) is named after a 19th-century folly

SIONNA AND THE SALMON OF KNOWLEDGE
This legend echoes the story of Adam and Eve. Sionna, granddaughter of the great King Lir (see page 236), desired the gift of knowledge, which was granted to men alone. She went to Connla's Well to search for the Salmon of Knowledge. Whoever ate the salmon would acquire its wisdom. As Sionna tried to trap the fish, it lashed its tail and the well overflowed. Sionna was swept away and drowned in the Shannon Pot (the source of the Shannon in Cavan).

GRAND CANAL
Until the early 19th century the Grand Canal, running from Dublin through these lakeland counties to the Shannon River at Ballinasloe, was a most important transportation route, and it carried freight until 1959. The heyday of the Royal and Grand Canals, however, occurred before the Act of Union in 1801, which effectively destroyed Ireland's ability to compete with the Industrial Revolution in Britain. Horses would gallop along the towpaths, hauling barges at speeds of up to 16kph/10mph. In recent years many canals have enjoyed something of a renaissance, thanks to their recreational use.

LAKELAND COUNTIES These small, watery counties—Cavan and Monaghan near the Northern Ireland border, and Westmeath, Laois, Offaly, Roscommon, and Longford—form the geographical heart of Ireland, yet are usually portrayed as places to get *through* on the way to somewhere more interesting. Initially they are unprepossessing. Dreary main roads blast through on radial routes from the capital, often slow with heavy traffic. Closer exploration of these unsung plains is surprisingly rewarding, however. There are historic towns, abbey ruins, and grand houses to visit, and masses of outdoor activities. Highlights include Strokestown House, Birr Castle Gardens, and the monastic ruins of Clonmacnoise.

Facilities for visitors are limited compared with parts of the more popular western or southeastern counties. Budget accommodation, especially campsites or hostels, is scarce, but the area has some highly distinctive country house hotels, offering good value. These central counties also offer a less stereotyped picture of the Emerald Isle. Visitors are welcomed with true Irish hospitality, with no pressure to buy sweaters or shamrock table linen.

WATERLANDS The landscape seems at first monotonous—a shallow saucer of endless unremarkable arable and pasture land, broken up by a maze of lakes and river systems. Few grand vistas can be seen; the eyeline generally stops at the first broken hedge. The small-scale, piecemeal landscape appears intimate and domesticated, although its most significant geographical feature, the Shannon River, is the longest in the British Isles, carving its ponderous course through the brimming flood plains and water meadows of several counties. It provides many things—scenic interest, wildlife habitats, an important navigable waterway, and a profitable playground for fishermen and boat lovers. As if more water were needed, long canals slice through the bogs, the Grand Canal in the heart of Offaly and the Royal Canal linking Dublin with the Shannon. These waterways and the massive lakes of the Shannon and its major tributaries are extensively exploited for recreational use. Myriad smaller pools dot the wavering horizons of Monaghan and Cavan.

acticed topographical eye will quickly identify this orderland area as drumlin country, where glacial deposits have been left in distinctive ridges, or eskers (the only geological term to be derived from the Irish language) and pear-shaped hills (drumlins) forming a classic "basket of eggs" landscape.

Laois has the highest hills, the Slieve Blooms, which rise to a modest maximum of 527m (1,729ft). Amid these low-lying plains, however, they seem grand indeed and the long-distance footpath called the Slieve Bloom Way attracts many walkers.

SETTLERS, INVADERS, AND BANDITS Patterns of settlement are complex. Invaders and adventurers throughout the centuries tramped across these mournful boglands to find out what lay beyond, and the fierce clans who established themselves here posed a constant threat to the Anglo-Normans walled up in the Pale around Dublin. The area is full of castles, dour planters' churches, and the estates of great families. In Elizabeth I's time many estates were confiscated from their original Gaelic owners and parcelled out to Scottish and English landlords.

The wild border counties of Monaghan and Cavan harbour further resentment. Once part of the old kingdom of Ulster, they were torn from their ancient allegiances by Partition. Complex geography makes a national frontier virtually impossible to police, and parts well deserve the sobriquet "bandit country." The bizarre course of the boundary between North and South seems to epitomize, by its perverse loops and twists, the irrationality of the present dividing line. There is not much reason to linger on this section of the border and, while here, it is prudent to adopt the local habit of remaining tight-lipped on political opinions.

BOG BUTTER

Butter has always been eaten in Ireland in great quantities. In medieval times it was sometimes flavoured with garlic or onions. Before the days of refrigeration, it was discovered that Irish peat-bogs conserved food remarkably well, and caches were often buried in wooden barrels where they were safe from plunderers. It developed a distinctive cheesy flavour but would last for hundreds of years. Bog butter from long ago is still occasionally unearthed during turf cutting.

239

14th-century Clough-outer Castle stands in Lough Outer (Cavan)

JOHN MCCORMACK
A legend in his own lifetime, John McCormack (1884–1945) is still regarded as one of the greatest lyrical tenors in recorded history and, fortunately, he lived in an era when his voice could be captured on early gramophone disks. He quickly achieved fame and was internationally recognized in Italy, England, and the United States. He spent his fortune from his repertoire of popular music on his other two oddly varied passions: horse-racing and the Catholic Church. For his charitable services he was awarded the unusual honour of being made a Papal Count.

The Anglo-Norman fortress of Athlone Castle

► **Athlone**
2362
The "capital of the Midlands" stands at one of Ireland's most central points, midway along the Shannon and an important rail, road, and river junction on the border between Leinster and Connaught. The town was besieged and badly damaged by Williamite forces after the Battle of the Boyne, when the defeated Jacobites retreated here and were finally routed at nearby Aughrim. Its strategic location necessitated a stronghold, and one of its most significant historic buildings is a **13th-century castle**►► (tel: 0902 72107; *open* May–Sep, daily 10–5; Oct–Apr by appointment. *Admission: moderate*) in the market square whose curtain walls, towers, and keep are still intact. The castle is used as the setting for a museum of local history; its most interesting section is an exhibition on the famous tenor, John McCormack, who was born in the town. Recordings of McCormack's voice can be heard on his own 78 rpm gramophone. Elsewhere in the town is his birthplace, on a narrow street called The Bawn. Apart from the castle, a handful of abbey ruins, and a fine Jacobean house (Court Devenish) dating from 1620, there is no very pressing reason to visit Athlone, but it makes a good base for boat excursions on Lough Ree and its various islands. Of these, Inchclearaun and Inchbofin both have churches and Early Christian grave-slabs; Inchclearaun is also associated with the legendary warrior Queen Maeve, who met her death here bizarrely, struck by a missile of cheese!

► **Birr**
2362B
This pleasant, quiet Georgian town was formerly known as Parsonstown, after the family name of the earls of Rosse, whose seat is **Birr Castle**►► (tel: 0509 20336, www.birr-castle.com; *open* Apr–Oct, daily 9–6. *Admission: expensive*). The building is 17th-century Gothic and not generally open to the public, but the 40ha (100 acres) of gardens are open all year and heartily reward a visit. They contain many rare specimen trees and shrubs and the tallest box hedges in the world (10m/33ft high). The gardens are

emorable in spring and autumn, when flowering trees, ulbs, and colourful foliage are at their best. Walks lead eside the lake and rivers, around which the grounds are andscaped. The most fascinating feature of Birr Castle, owever, is a remarkable early telescope, recently restored o its former glory. Built by the 3rd Earl of Rosse in the 1840s, t was then the largest and most powerful in the world, its 83cm (72in) lens enabling the aristocratic astronomer and is son, the 4th earl, to study the spiral nebulas and measure he heat of the moon. Massive supporting walls hold the nstrument in place; taped information provides back-round history. The stable block at the castle is home to reland's Historic Science Centre, which has exhibitions of stronomy, photography, and engineering.

Boyle   *2362D*

he main reason to visit Boyle is to see the ruined **Cistercian abbey▶** dating from 1161, founded by the ame group of monks who built Mellifont. Although entral and near one of the town's main streets, the abbey eems tranquil beside its rushing stream, and a good roportion of it is still intact, despite innumerable attacks y warring Irish clans. The restored 16th- to 17th-century ateway contains an exhibition. The 12th-century church vithin the compound shows Gothic and Romanesque rches and interesting carvings.

A short distance east of Boyle is the **Lough Key Forest ark▶▶** (tel: 079 62363, www.roscommon.ie; *open* daily lawn–dusk. *Admission free*), part of the enormous Rock-ngham estate that once belonged to the King family Edward King, drowned in the Irish Sea in 1636, was the ubject of Milton's elegiac poem *Lycidas*). Rockingham riginally belonged to the MacDermots, the local chief-ains and Lords of Moylurg, but was handed to the King amily in 1617. The big house in what is now the forest ark was burned down in 1957, but King House, the amily's town mansion in the main street, can be visited. rybrook House is another fine Georgian mansion. With he Curlew Mountains close by and its excellent opportu-ities for walking and fishing, Boyle is an increasingly opular touring base.

The grounds of Birr Castle straddle the boundary between counties Offaly and Tipperary

241

AN IRISH ROMEO AND JULIET

Castle Island in Lough Key, near Boyle, is tradi-tionally taken to be the burial place of two young lovers, Una MacDermot and Thomas Costello, the subject of a famous tradi-tional Irish poem (*Úna Bhán—White Una*). Her parents would not allow the match and Thomas departed grief-stricken from her home, promising to return only if he were recalled before he crossed a nearby river. He tarried at the ford, but finally crossed, too late to learn that Una had died of a broken heart. She was buried on Castle Island, where Thomas used to swim his horse each night to lament his lost love until he collapsed lifeless over her grave. Two ash trees grew above the tomb and entwined over this Irish Romeo and Juliet, united at last in death.

Ireland is one of the most hospitable countries in the world. Visitor accommodation is big business, and there is a vast range of places to stay at all price levels, from modest cottages to great castles. A genuinely warm welcome, a homelike atmosphere, and an excellent breakfast are features of many of them.

DISTINCTIVE HOUSES

Cheaper options include Blanchville in County Kilkenny, Bruckless House in County Donegal, Ballycormac House in Tipperary, and several Glebe Houses (once providing accommodation for Church of Ireland clergy)—those in Dowth, County Meath, and Ballinadee, County Cork are highly recommended. More modest but excellent value are Fergus View, convenient for the Burren, Church Villa or Dunmore Lodge (both in Dunmore East, County Waterford), Kille House in County Galway, Hanora's Cottage in County Waterford, Larchwood House in Cork, and Rosturk Woods in County Mayo.

The dining room at Tullanisk, near Birr, in County Offaly

Useful publications Anonymous business hotels or luxury castles will give you reliable hot water and TV, but little of the real Ireland of conversation and idiosyncrasy that you will find in more personally run places. To meet the increasing demand for places with something special, several useful listings have been made. Pick up the booklets in any tourist office. *The Blue Book* lists a fine range of country-house hotels and restaurants, often with some historic interest or culinary distinction. Staying in most of these places is a memorable, but generally expensive, experience.

The Hidden Ireland provides an even more interesting selection of homes offering hospitality (as opposed to commercially operated hotels). In many of these you may dine *en famille*, join a country-house party atmosphere, get to know the owners, or join in locally available sports such as hunting or fishing. All the places are rural and of some architectural distinction, many are fascinating and distinguished old houses filled with family mementos and antiques. *Friendly Homes of Ireland* is a personal choice (by John Colclough, a well-known journalist) of generally less expensive places offering family hospitality in interesting settings. (There is some overlap between these listings.) Many visitors base their whole holiday on these selected houses, and although not every establishment may be to your taste, they all have merit, and if you have little idea of where to start looking, are of great help.

Here are just a few places offering exceptional and typically Irish hospitality—informal, effortless, unsnobby, and warm. (For details see pages 269–283.)

Luxurious mansions At the more expensive end of the price range, **Hilton Park** in Clones, County Monaghan, overlooking extensive parkland that includes a golf course and three lakes, offers a splendid Anglo-Irish country-house stay. Fourposter beds, elegant furnishings, and lots of memorabilia add to the interest of the house, home of the Madden family for some 250 years. Organic produce from the gardens appears on its excellent dinner menus. **Bantry House** in Cork is a magnificent stately home still owned by descendants of the White family, who lived there in 1796 and helped to foil Wolfe Tone's invasion. The Whites were addicted to European fine art and furniture and had the money to support their habit; so the house has an impressive collection of paintings and tapestries. Don't miss the view of the bay from the rear of the house, said to be one of the best in Ireland. Accommodation is provided in a separate wing of newly refurbished rooms, all very comfortable, overlooking the lovely Italianate gardens. Concerts are a feature. The state rooms are open to the public, so don't expect complete seclusion. Slightly less expensive is **Ballyvolane House** (also in County Cork), dating from 1728, elegantly remodelled in early Victorian times. It has lovely peaceful grounds, private fishing, and excellent Irish country cooking. **Newbay House**, closer to the Wexford coast, is another cheerful, relaxing Georgian home in sweeping parkland. The high-Georgian Moyglare Manor, in County Kildare, is set on 5.5ha (14 acres) of rolling hills and pastoral meadows. Owner Nore Devlin decked the place out in period antiques and paintings. **Ballinkeele House** was designed by Daniel Robertson (of Powerscourt fame) in 1840, and is the ancestral home of the Maher family, who dispense effortless hospitality and excellent cooking amid 135ha (340 acres) of farmland. **Roundwood House** in Laois is one of the best of all Irish country houses for character and idiosyncratic charm. It is also one of Ireland's finest Georgian homes, in the Palladian style. **Tullanisk**, also in Lakeland (County Offaly) is the former Dower House of the earls of Rosse, who own Birr Castle.

BALLYMALOE HOUSE
This rambling, Georgian mansion with a Norman keep is in farming country east of Cork. Owned by the Allen family, produce from the 160ha (395-acre) farm is used to good effect, for Myrtle Allen is one of Ireland's most celebrated chefs, happy to pass on her skills in books, television broadcasts, and through the Ballymaloe cookery school, run by her son and daughter-in-law, Timothy and Darina Allen. The hotel has many facilities and is lavishly furnished, but retains the feel of a family home and is utterly relaxing.

243

Tullanisk, in the Birr Castle estate; guests are given free admission to the castle gardens

Clonalis House (1878), seat of the O'Conors

GOLDSMITH COUNTRY
The poet and playwright, Oliver Goldsmith (1728–1774) was born at Pallas, County Longford, and spent much of his childhood in Lissoy parsonage, near Auburn crossroads. Villages most associated with Goldsmith's writings (particularly his long poem, *The Deserted Village*) include Tang, where he went to school, and Ballymahon, his widowed mother's home. Most of his adult life was spent in London, but he recalled his Irish childhood and the gentle, humdrum lifestyle of this rural area in idyllic terms. The Three Jolly Pigeons pub, immortalized in *She Stoops to Conquer*, can be seen on the Ballymahon road near Athlone.

► **Castlerea** 2361D

The town itself is not in the least riveting, but **Clonalis House►** (tel 0907 20014. Call for opening hours and tour price), on the south-western outskirts, is worth a look. Guided tours are conducted by the family owners, and you can even enjoy an unusual, if expensive, brand of aristocratic B&B in its palatial bedrooms, or rent one of the nearby cottages. Clonalis House is a late-Victorian mansion in fine parkland whose main interest exists in its contents and its inhabitants. It is a rare example of a clan house, the seat of an ancient Gaelic family that can, it claims, trace its line back through 60 generations to the Kings of Connaught and the last High Kings of Ireland. The O'Conors have owned the local land for the best part of two millennia, and many castles and abbeys in the region are associated with the clan. The house is sumptuously furnished with antiques, and is full of archive material and family memorabilia, including silver, porcelain, costumes, and manuscripts. One of its most prized items is a harp belonging to the great 17th- to 18th-century harpist, Turlough O'Carolan.

►►► **Clonmacnoise** 2362E

Clonmacnoise, tel: 0905 74195, www.heritageireland.ie
Open: mid-Jun–Sep, daily 9–7; Oct–May, daily 10–6 or dusk
Admission: moderate

These extensive and impressive monastic remains stand in velvety, emerald water meadows by a rushy bend in the Shannon River, a place of almost tangible stillness, especially at dawn or dusk when the few visitors who venture here are absent. In earlier centuries it was even more isolated by the river and surrounding bogland, and was accessible only by boat, or along the esker (see caption opposite), known as the Pilgrims' Causeway. Founded by St. Ciarán (or Kieran) in about AD 548, this Celtic site became the most important religious establishment of its time in Ireland and was renowned as a place of art and learning throughout Europe. St. Ciarán himself died of plague at the age of only 33, just seven months after the monastery site had been established, but news of his good works eventually spread beyond Irish shores. Several ecclesiastical treasures produced here are now on display at the National Museum in Dublin. The gold and silver Crozier of Clonmacnoise, decorated with strapwork and animal patterns, is one of these. The *Book of the Dun Cow*, one of the earliest and most famous manuscripts in the Irish language, was also produced here.

Clonmacnoise was once a royal city and the burial place of the High Kings of Tara and Connaught, including the last

High King, Rory O'Conor (see Castlerea, left). Like most settlements of its type, it suffered depredations at the hands of Vikings and Normans, and was devastated by English forces in 1552. Still visible within its enclosing walls are the remains of a cathedral, eight churches, two Round Towers, many carved gravestones, and several High Crosses. The most interesting antiquities are displayed in the visitor centre. The splendid Cross of the Scriptures, erected in the 9th or 10th century, depicts, among the usual biblical scenes, King Dermot helping St. Ciarán erect the first cornerpost of the monastery at Clonmacnoise.

The Nuns' Church stands beside a quiet lane outside the main enclosure and is reached via a path through the modern cemetery and out onto the road beyond. It is worth making the short excursion to this pleasant spot; the tiny church with its finely carved arches is sheltered by tall trees in a peaceful little meadow. It was built by Dervorgilla, Ireland's equivalent of Helen of Troy, whose abduction by Dermot MacMurrough provided the excuse for Strongbow's Anglo-Norman invasion (see pages 32–33). On the other side of the monastic buildings, not far from the parking area, vestiges of a Norman castle stand on the slopes by the river. Rossana Cruises are a popular way of visiting Clonmacnoise from Athlone.

THE DEAD AT CLONMACNOISE

"In a quiet water'd land, a land of roses,
Stands Saint Ciarán's city fair;
And the warriors of Erin in their famous generations
Slumber there."

T.W. Rolleston (1857–1920); from the medieval Irish poem by Enóg Ó Gilláin.

Clonmacnoise, strategically sited on an esker beside the Shannon. (An esker is a winding ridge of gravel deposited by a meltwater stream running beneath a glacier)

245

Many of the sporting activities of this central region are based upon its rivers, lakes, and forests. Several forest parks have been created, to allow for recreation and to increase the region's tourism potential. Some of these designated parks have become rather overdeveloped, with plentiful picnic tables and similar amenities. If you prefer a slightly wilder scene, head for the Slieve Bloom Mountains.

LACE-MAKING

County Monaghan is famous for its lace industry. Carrickmacross and Clones are the two main centres and, in both cases, the craft was introduced during the 19th century by local rectors' wives, partly as a means of relieving the area's chronic poverty. The fortunes of the industry waxed and waned as a result of changing fashions and periodic overproduction. Lace is still made by hand in these centres, although the genuine article is extremely labour-intensive and expensive. Carrickmacross lace incorporates hundreds of intricate fine loops. Clones lace is crocheted and often features small raised knots known as Clones dots.

Lace-making, County Monaghan

Forest parks Lying just outside Boyle, in the grounds of the former Rockingham estate, the **Lough Key Forest Park►►** (tel: 079 62363) extends over about 340ha (840 acres) along a lakeshore, and includes a cypress grove, deerpark, ice house, temple, bog garden full of peat-loving plants such as azaleas, and many marked paths. Boats tour the lake from Rockingham Harbour, and rowboats can be hired. There are ring forts and islands to explore, and a vantage point called the Moylurg Tower can be climbed for views of the surrounding scenery. The gateway and lodge of the old estate still exist, though the main house, designed by Nash, was burned down in 1957.

Northwest of Cavan on the N3, the 240ha (593-acre) **Killykeen Forest Park►** (tel: 049 433 2541) is set amid the complex puzzle of water and islets that forms Lough Oughter. Marked walks and nature trails allow visitors to enjoy fishing, birdwatching, and exploring early fortifications.

Rossmore Forest Park► lies near Monaghan Town on the Newbliss road and consists of 280ha (692 acres) of gentle hills and lakes interconnected by forest walks through rhododendron plantations. Just beyond Newbliss is the Victorian Annaghmakerrig House, former home of theater director Sir Tyrone Guthrie, and now left to the nation as a centre for writers and artists. Visitors can picnic and walk in its beautiful surroundings.

Haunted by red squirrels, **Dún a' Rí Forest Park►►** provides 230ha (568 acres) of wooded walks southwest of Carrickmacross. From the hilltop parking area are views of the Mourne Mountains and a ruined Elizabethan fortress. A wishing well called Tobar na Splinnc is set into a rocky ledge above the Cabra River, and Sarah's Bridge supposedly commemorates a lady who was so startled by a belated proposal of marriage from a man she had been meeting for 30 years that she fell off and drowned!

Lough Muckno Leisure Park► is a former Georgian estate near Castleblayney. Set beside Monaghan's largest lake, it offers signposted walks through beautiful grounds of mixed woodland and gently undulating drumlins. Trailers and campers can be accommodated nearby.

The Slieve Bloom Mountains Though not particularly high, the **Slieve Blooms►►►** rise quite dramatically from the low-lying boggy plains that surround them, their looming purple shoulders a backdrop to many a view in this area. It is said that they are named after Bladhma, an ancient

Killykeen Forest Park lies on the shores of Lough Outer in County Cavan

ero, who once took refuge from his enemies in these ills. Later, in Cromwellian times, the Slieve Blooms gain became a place of hiding for men whose lands had een confiscated by the Parliamentary forces.

The slopes are rounded rather than steep, many overed in conifer plantations, and the high density of vell-marked paths and tracks (so unusual in Ireland) nake them ideal for walking. A long-distance footpath alled the Slieve Bloom Way runs for about 32km (20mi) round these hills, on a route past waterfalls and glens, hrough bog and moorland, conifer woods, and an ancient ore-Ice Age) river valley. Though the hills are mostly too entle for really dramatic views, the slopes do in some laces drop away sufficiently to reveal the great plains elow stretching mistily into the distance. Look for the are pine marten that haunts the mountains, together vith Irish hares, fallow deer, and mountain goats. Good tarting points for the walk are Glen Barrow or the tanding stone at Forelacka. Despite their unthreatening ltitude (maximum 527m/1,729ft), these hills can be reacherously misty and waterlogged, so adequate ootwear, clothing, and equipment are essential.

BOATING

An excellent way to enjoy the peaceful Midland scenery is from the deck of a boat, and you can charter boats in many centres on the 480km (300mi) of navigable lakes, rivers, and canals in the region. Tullamore, on the Grand Canal linking Dublin and the Shannon, is one of the most popular starting points for narrow boats, and the scenery spans flower-filled banks, gentle pasture, and open bogland (Celtic Canal Cruisers, tel: 0506 21861). Other good centres include Athlone (Athlone Cruisers Ltd., tel: 0902 72892, for boat trips around Lough Ree), Banagher, or Glasson.

Lough Key, a perfect place to enjoy some of Ireland's finest fishing

THE SEVEN WONDERS

Fore is famous for its seven wonders:
1. The monastery on a quaking scraw (a thin covering of grass grown on a bog).
2. A mill without a mill-race.
3. Water that flows uphill.
4. An ash tree that won't burn.
5. Water that never boils.
6. The great stone above the old church door.
7. The holy man in a stone (an anchorite's cell).
Many stories are told to explain the origin of these, but the grains of truth in some should be mixed with pinches of salt in others.

▶ Monaghan
2374

This garrison town shows a strong Scots Presbyteria influence, with solid mercantile buildings and a centra square known as the Diamond, similar to those in Derr and Donegal. Its position close to the Northern Iris border is not fortunate and, although it prospered fron the linen industry introduced mainly by Ulster settlers i the 18th century, it has been a hotbed of unrest from tim to time. Charles Gavan Duffy, one of its most famou inhabitants who eventually became premier of Victoria Australia, characterized the town's political awarenes by founding the Irish Tenant League and a nationalis newspaper called *The Nation*. The flamboyar 19th-century Gothic spire of **St. Macartan's Catholi Cathedral▶** lords it over the more sedate classical an Regency buildings of the town centre. In the Diamonc the elegant 1792 Market House, with its fine, carve decorations, is now the tourist office. The Rossmor Memorial, a huge Victorian drinking fountain, with eigh grey marble columns and a sandstone canopy, also in th Diamond, necessitated the removal from here of the ol 17th-century market cross, once a sundial, to anothe square in the town (Old Cross Square). The town's mos interesting sight is its **County Museum▶** (tel: 047 8292 www.countymonaghan.net/links/htm; *open* Jun–Sep Tue–Sat 11–5; Oct–May, Tue–Sat 11–1 and 2–5. *Admissio free*) on Hill Street near the tourist office, an award winning collection of local history and art. One of it prize exhibits is the beautifully embossed processiona Cross of Clogher, dating from about 1400.

▶ Mullingar
2373

This busy town is the centre of a prosperous commercia and cattle-raising area. Best of the museums is the **Militar Museum▶** (tel: 044 48391; *open* by appointment only *Admission free*), with a section devoted to the old IRA. Th modern **Cathedral of Christ the King▶** (tel: 044 48391; *open daily* 9–5:30. *Admission free*) contains two famous mosaic by a Russian artist, Boris Anrep, and an ecclesiastica

St. Brigid's Chapel in Mullingar Cathedral

The Old Gaol, Roscommon

ADOLPHUS COOKE
Not far from Mullingar on the road to Delvin is the small village of Reynella, where the graveyard contains a strange tomb in the shape of a beehive. This is the grave of a celebrated local eccentric, Adolphus Cooke, who believed that one of his flock of turkeys was his reincarnated father. He also tried his favourite dog, Gusty, for the crime of repeatedly straying and cavorting with the common dogs of Mullingar. The setter was eventually reprieved when the hangman claimed that the dog addressed him in a foreign tongue, thereby proving Cooke's theory of reincarnation. Market Hall Museum in Mullingar contains a few relics relating to this extraordinary person.

useum which houses the vestments of St. Oliver Plunkett ee page 114). North of Mullingar and near the underrated ough Derravaragh is **Tullynally Castle▶** (tel: 044 61159, ww.iol.ie/wmeathtc; *open:* gardens, May–Aug, daily 2–6; stle, mid-Jun–Jul and mid-Sep–27 Sep, guided tours aily 2:30–6. *Admission: expensive)* seat of the earls of ongford, with fine gardens. Inside is an interesting collec- on of domestic utensils and a celebrated private library, dicating the literary bent of the Pakenham family, whose .ions include the present Lord Longford's gifted daugh- rs, Antonia Fraser and Rachel Billington. Nearby is **Fore bbey▶**, founded in the 7th century by St. Fechin. This rge religious community was destroyed many times uring the Dark Ages, but a church dating from the 10th entury survives, along with a 13th-century Benedictine riory built by the de Lacy family.

Roscommon   *2362C*

ne huge **Norman castle▶**, standing in fields on the edge Roscommon, seems out of proportion to anything else this little county town. It dates from the 13th century, ough was much altered in later years, with refined udor mullions added in the 16th century. The quarrel- me O'Kelly and O'Conor clans seized it periodically, .t its last definitive remodelling took place at the hands Cromwellian troops and its drum towers now stand pped and hollow around a rectangle of neatly mown rf. In the town are the **Dominican priory ruins▶**, last rest- g place of the priory's 13th-century founder Félim 'Conor, a king of Connaught, whose tomb is decorated ith effigies of gallowglasses (Irish or Scots mercenaries). he main street, with attractively restored Georgian and ictorian shops, bifurcates around a copper-domed eorgian courthouse (now a Bank of Ireland branch). earby is the castellated county gaol, where oscommon's redoubtable lady hangman carried out her vic duty (see panel). Another curiosity is James J. arlow's Funeral Requisites and Furniture Stores, a beau- fully restored hardware shop and bar crammed with ousehold gadgets and nostalgic examples of advertising.

LADY BETTY
Roscommon's condemned prisoners faced a female executioner during the 18th century. Condemned to death herself, allegedly for the unwitting murder of her only son, she volunteered to step into the breach when the hangman was ill, on condition that her life be spared. She was subsequently appointed as the town's "hangwoman" with a salary and accommodation at the prison, and there she remained for about 30 years, performing her grisly duty with apparent efficiency and detachment. She drew charcoal portraits on her walls of some of her clients, whom she dispatched from a hinged board outside her third-floor window.

RICHARD CASSELS OR CASTLE

This architect (1690–1751) was one of the formative influences on Anglo-Irish architecture during Georgian times. Among his great works are Powerscourt and Russborough in County Wicklow, Westport in Mayo, Newbridge in Dublin, and Strokestown Park House in Roscommon. He came from a Huguenot family settled in Hesse-Kassel in Germany. He first arrived in Ireland in 1728 to work on a project in County Fermanagh and soon became known to Lord Burlington and his circle. Before long he was the most sought-after architect in Ireland. His style was Palladian, with heavy mouldings and muscular sculpted stonework. His name appears most often in its anglicized form—Castle.

The library at Strokestown Park House

▶▶ Strokestown   2362L

Many Irish towns and villages reveal their Georgian origins in wide streets, but Strokestown's is certainly exceptional; originally modelled on Vienna's Ringstrasse, which had greatly impressed one of the local landowners, it is said to be the widest provincial main street in Ireland. The village is little more than an adjunct to the enormous **Strokestown Park House**▶▶ (tel: 078 33013, www. strokestownpark.ie; *open* Apr–Oct, daily 9.30–5.30; by appointment rest of year. *Admission*: *expensive*), which lies beyond the Gothic triple arch on this main street. Home of the Pakenham Mahon family, their 17th-century farm house was reconstructed by Richard Castle (see panel) in the 1730s in Palladian style for the Anglo-Irish politician Thomas Mahon. Its most infamous proprietor was Major Denis Mahon, who presided over the Strokestown estate during the Famine years, and found himself so short of cash that he pressed his tenants to emigrate to the New World. Rumours spread that he was chartering the dreaded "coffin ships" in which so many Irish emigrants perished, and he was shot dead near Strokestown in 1847. In 1979 the house was sold to an enterprising local garage firm, who gallantly resisted the mood of the times to let all traces of "British imperialism" (including its superb Georgian heritage) lapse into ruin. The company restored the premises and parkland, and established the Famine Museum commemorating the tragic events of the 1840s.

Strokestown Park House is one of Ireland's finest and most authentic Palladian buildings and gives a real flavour of the life and times of the Anglo-Irish families and their tenants. One of its many fascinating features is the galleried kitchen in the south wing from which the lady of the house could drop menus and instructions to the kitchen staff without troubling herself by any close proximity. Tunnels allowing tradesmen and staff to perform their duties unseen link the main house to the kitchen and stables located in the wings.

At the far end of Strokestown, the **County Roscommon Heritage and Genealogical Centre**▶ offers presentations on local history.

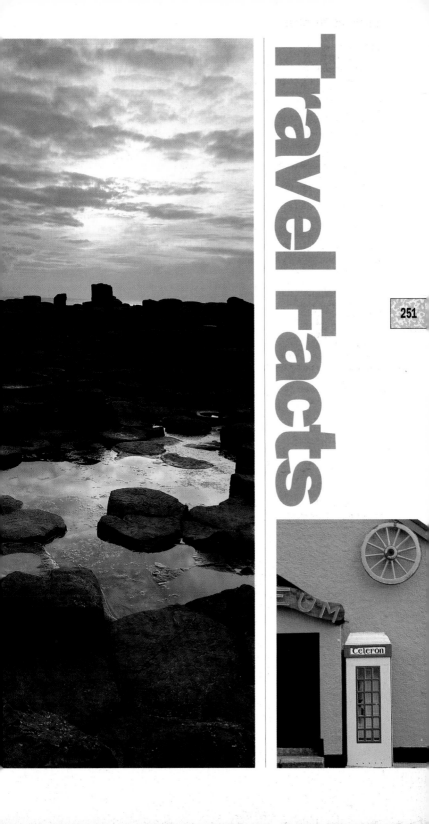

Travel Facts

Arriving

Entry formalities British visitors entering the Republic or the North do not need a passport. The best advice, however, is to take it anyway. It provides a useful means of identification for changing money, renting a car, or obtaining medical treatment. British nationals not born in the UK, or non-Caucasians, will find a passport cuts the red tape considerably.

EU and North American or Australasian visitors simply need a valid passport and can stay for up to three months. Other nationals should check to see if they require a visa.

In the North, British regulations apply. EU residents or those from English-speaking or Commonwealth countries can usually stay for up to six months with a passport or suitable identity documents.

252

By air Ireland's international airports are Dublin, Shannon, Cork, Belfast International (well linked by public transportation to the city centres), and Knock. Until 1994, all transatlantic flights to the Republic were required to land at Shannon, near Limerick, as part of a scheme to bring tourism and employment to the western regions. This is no longer mandatory, but if you are visiting western Ireland anyway, Shannon makes a convenient landing point. Most European flights land in either Dublin or Belfast, but other airports are served from the UK. Flying time from London is an hour to Dublin or Belfast (90 minutes to Shannon, Cork, or Knock). You can fly to Ireland from many regional UK airports.

The major airlines offer a range of tickets that can increase or decrease the price of any given seat by more than 300 percent, depending on the day of purchase. As a rule, the further in advance you buy the ticket, the less expensive it is but the greater the penalty (up to 100 percent) for cancelling. Check with individual airlines for details.

Charter flights offer the lowest fares but often depart only on certain days, and they are seldom on time. You may be able to arrive at one city and return from another; however, you

may lose all or most of your money if you cancel your trip. Don't sign up for a charter flight unless you've checked with a travel agency about the reputation of the packager. It's particularly important to know the packager's policy concerning refunds in the event of a cancelled flight; some agents recommend that travellers purchase trip-cancellation insurance if they plan to book charter flights.

One of the most popular charter operators to Europe is **Charter Scepter** in the US (tel: 516/255-9800). Other companies advertise in Sunday travel sections of newspapers.

From North America, it can be a cheaper option to fly to London and reroute from there, although this will add time to your already long journey. In the United States and Canada there are many discount fares available. Aer Lingus, Continental, and Delta operate scheduled services to Dublin; Aer Lingus also flies direct to Belfast. Boston–Shannon flying time is around five and a half hours.

Direct flights are also available from many European cities.

Aer Lingus offices can be found at the following addresses:
● Republic of Ireland: Dawson Street, Dublin 2 (tel: 01 844 4777)
● UK: Aer Lingus House, 83 Staines Road, Hounslow, Middlesex (tel: 020-8899 4747), and 223 Regent Street, London W1
● US: 122 East 42nd Street, New York, NY 10168 (tel: 212/557-1090)
● Northern Ireland: 46 Castle Street, Belfast (tel: 0845 973 7747)

By sea The Irish Sea is a notoriously uncomfortable crossing in bad weather. The main reason to opt for a sea crossing from the UK is to take a car, so cutting out the high costs of car rental in the Republic. Budget travellers may also use cheap rail/ferry or coach/ferry inclusive packages (student or youth reductions are considerable), though cheap air travel has severely dented even this market, and the Irish ferry scene has been marked by economic uncertainty in recent years. The main routes in the Republic are Holyhead to Dun Laoghaire (Dublin), Pembroke or Fishguard to Rosslare, or Swansea to Cork; in the

North you can travel from Liverpool or Stranraer to Belfast, and Cairnryan to Larne. A fast catamaran service runs between Stranraer and Belfast, Holyhead to Dun Laoghaire, and Fishguard to Rosslare. Services also operate from Cork and Rosslare to certain ports in Normandy and Brittany. In summer you need to book in advance for a place on many crossings. Ask your rail or bus travel centre about combined train/ferry or bus/ferry fares. London to Dublin coach fares can be extremely cheap, though it can be a very tiring and lengthy journey. Getting to the North is more expensive. Slattery's (tel: 020 7482 1604) and Eurolines (National Express, tel: 020 7724 0741) are the main operators, serving Ireland from many UK cities.

Quarantine Ireland is part of the British Isles quarantine area, which means that pets resident in Britain, the Channel Isles, or the Isle of Man for at least six months can be taken to Ireland without requiring isolation. Animals from other places, of course, will be placed in quarantine. The following breeds of dog must be kept under tight control:
● American pit bull terrier
● English bull terrier

Sited alongside working boats: the marina at Howth Harbour

● Staffordshire bull terrier
● ban dog
● bulldog
● bull mastiff
● Doberman pinscher
● German shepherd (Alsatian)
● Rhodesian ridgeback
● Rottweiler
● Japanese akita
● Japanese tosa.

Camping and caravanning
Lists of caravan (trailer) parks and campsites are available from both national tourist boards; those in Bord Fáilte's brochure are regularly inspected and graded. All these sites have facilities, including mains water and electricity, showers, restrooms, and sometimes restaurants and play areas.

Unofficial camping is widespread in Ireland, however, and as long as you have the landowner's permission and cause no disturbance you may camp in any field. You may be asked to pay a euro or two in tourist areas. Many hostels will allow cheap camping on nearby land with use of showers and kitchens. State-run forest parks in the Republic do not permit camping, whereas many in the North do.

Caravans can be rented, sometimes in conjunction with ferry deals. These vary from luxuriously furnished mobile homes to the picturesque,

253

horse-drawn Romany (Gypsy) caravans of the Irish brochures (see below for more information).

Horse-drawn caravans If you want to rent a horse-drawn caravan, it is best to arrange third-party liability insurance. Expect to cover no more than 16km (10mi) per day, and stick to the quiet, flatter lanes of rural Ireland. Most caravans are four-berth. Don't expect luxury facilities aboard (bed linen and simple cooking utensils are provided, but no toilets, for example; take your own towels and matches for lighting gas burners). Before you set off, rental companies give you full instructions on routes, and handling and looking after the horse. Prices are seasonal; a deposit is required, and you will have to pay for each overnight stop.

Riding horses can be rented to accompany the caravan. Some of the best-known companies specializing in this kind of touring are Slattery's Horse-Drawn Caravans, 1 Russell Street, Tralee, County Kerry (tel: 066 712 2364), Clissman's Horse-Drawn Caravans, Carrigmore Farm, Wicklow (tel: 0404 48188, fax: 0404 48288), and Kilvahan Horse-Drawn Caravans, Portlaoise (tel: 0502 27048).

The road between Glengarriff in County Cork and Kenmare in Kerry

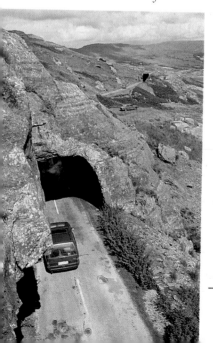

Car breakdown
If the car is rented, contact the rental company (their nearest contact number should be on your contract or other rental documents). Automobile Association (AA) members, or members of affiliated motoring organizations belonging to the AIT (*Alliance International de Tourisme*), may call on the AA rescue services (provided in the Republic by the Automobile Association of Ireland). Both the AA and the RAC operate a breakdown service for their members in Northern Ireland.

Car rental
Renting a car in the Republic is expensive; rates are among the highest in Europe, although they are cheaper in Northern Ireland. Tariffs vary and, as elsewhere, small local firms will often give you a cheaper deal than the major international companies. To offset this, the vehicle may in some cases be less roadworthy, pick-up points less convenient, and service less efficient. You may also have to return the car to the pick-up point rather than dropping it off in another town (check drop-off charges in advance). The large companies are geared to a nationwide operation, so if you rent in Dublin and break down in Donegal you won't have a problem. Just phone the nearest office. Major companies also insure you automatically to drive on either side of the border, though you should always specify this when you accept the car; check the booking conditions and insurance cover carefully. Most multinational companies have offices at the main airports and ferry terminals, as well as in large cities. Rental charges at Northern Ireland airports, however, may be higher than renting with the same firm in the city. The tourist offices or the Automobile Association will be able to offer advice on approved companies.

Avis/Johnson & Perrott (based in Cork but with offices in most airports and cities) are the largest operators in the Republic, supplying cars for several major travel firms, airlines, etc. They provide clean, reliable cars and a good backup service.

Other large firms include Hertz, Murray's/Europcar, and Budget. Rates are very seasonal. The cheapest way to book a rental car is to arrange an inclusive package deal in advance with a tour operator, airline, and ferry company (fly-drive or rail/ferry-drive) rather than waiting until you arrrive in Ireland.

To rent a car you must have a valid driver's licence (an international licence with an English translation if you are a non-EU resident). Some companies specify age limits for drivers (usually a minimum of 21 or 23 and a maximum of 70 or 75). Make sure you take out collision damage waiver (CDW) as well as the standard third-party insurance. Manual transmission vehicles are usually supplied unless automatics are specifically requested. Almost all rental cars use unleaded fuel. The best-value deals include unlimited mileage.

Climate
No one goes to Ireland for a tan. It has a fine climate (mild, free from extremes, good for plants), but perhaps too much weather. As the pressure systems sweep in from the Atlantic, Ireland gets it all—and rain follows sunshine with immense rapidity. Ireland's "soft days" of fine drizzle and low cloud are unavoidable, but it is unfortunate if you should happen to be touring the Ring of Kerry on one. Be prepared for the four seasons in a single day. The southeast is appreciably sunnier and drier than the west coast. July and August are the warmest months (average temperatures 10°C/50°F at night, 18°C/64°F during the day), but May, June, or September may well be drier. Ireland has the added advantage of being less crowded in late spring and early autumn. It is impossible to predict fine days at any time of year. If the sun comes out, enjoy it while you can. If it rains, cover up or head for the pub. It probably won't last long.

Crime
In general, rural areas of both the Republic and Northern Ireland are extremely safe. The main problems occur in cities, particularly in the deprived areas of Dublin, where car theft is pervasive. Limerick also has a significant problem of violent crime and theft. Large gatherings (festivals, markets, horse sales, and

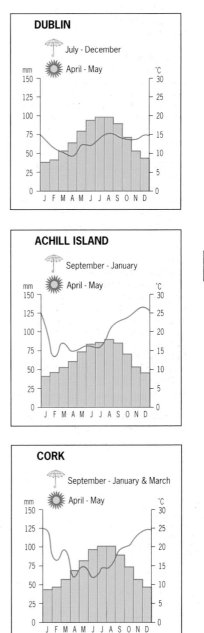

255

so on) attract a criminal element, as anywhere, and it is sensible to take precautions with your belongings. In particular, don't leave tempting valuables visible in a car. Personal violence or sexual assaults on strangers are fortunately rare, although women travelling alone should not take unnecessary risks (for example, by hitchhiking).

Customs regulations

Since 1993, EU travellers have been able to import the following quantities of *duty-paid* goods for personal use only: up to 50 litres of beer; 25 litres of wine; and 800 cigarettes. *Duty-free* allowances (not available when travelling within Europe) are lower: 200 cigarettes; 1 litre of spirits; 2 litres of wine, 50g of perfume and 250ml of toilet water, plus other dutiable goods to the value of €175 (tobacco and drinks allowances not available for travellers under 17). However, there are some restrictions on importing certain food items into both the Republic of Ireland and Northern Ireland (the latter if travelling from outside the UK). To obtain further information, get in contact with the Custom House either in Dublin (tel: 01 873 4555) or in Belfast (tel: 028 9035 2220).

The Irish are enthusiastic cyclists

Cycling

Cycling is without doubt one of the best ways to get around in Ireland, especially granted decent weather. The secondary roads are mostly empty, built-up areas limited, and open countryside all around. Most airlines will carry bicycles for free as long as you don't exceed your weight allowance. If you bring your own bicycle, take a spare tube and tyre with you, as Irish sizes are unusual. It is very easy to hire a bicycle when you arrive in Ireland. Raleigh (tel: 01 626 1333) is the biggest operator, with a nationwide organization of pick-up and drop-off points, but local dealers, hotels, and hostels can provide them, too. It is advisable to rent cycle helmets, available in some places but not everywhere. Check brakes and tyres and get a pump and repair kit. Bicycles can be carried on long-distance buses and trains, but there is a charge. You can get leaflets on cycling from Bord Fáilte or the Northern Ireland Tourist Board (NITB). Several companies in Britain and Ireland arrange cycling holidays, with accommodation, transportation of luggage, lunches, and guides, including: Celtic Cycling, Bagenalstown, County Carlow (tel: 0503 75282), Bike Tours (in Avon, England, tel: 01225 310859), and the Irish Travel Bureau, Manchester (tel: 0161-976 3887).

Visitors with disabilities

A number of associations for people with disabilities give advice on travel and mobility problems. Registered drivers with disabilities may park free of charge with an orange badge. The national tourist boards both produce useful literature (Bord Fáilte's *Accommodation Guide for Disabled Persons* is available free). Increasing numbers of hotels and guesthouses cater to people in wheelchairs, and access to many sights, museums, and other attractions, are being adapted. Addresses you may find useful :

● National Rehabilitation Board, 44 North Great George's Street, Dublin, (tel: 01 874 7503)
● Irish Wheelchair Association, 24 Blackheath Drive, Clontarf, Dublin 3 (tel: 01 833 8241; fax: 01 833 3873)
● Disability Action, 2 Annadale Avenue, Belfast BT7 3JR (tel: 028 9249 1011).

Driving

Motorists drive on the left in Ireland, although driving habits can be erratic, particularly in rural areas. Hazards for the motorist include slow-moving farm vehicles, often without lights, that lurch suddenly into the roadway from field gates, or equally suddenly turn into farm entrances without signalling. Herds of cows, flocks of sheep, seemingly endless loose gravel, and unexpected roadworks are all part of Irish driving. Farm dogs enjoy chasing passing cars. There is no need to swerve or brake for them; they know exactly how far to go. Poor public transportation networks and the importance of the pub in Ireland result in a high incidence of drivers on the roads with alcohol on board, though penalties for drinking and driving are severe. In short, a considerable amount of care is required at all times while driving on rural Irish roads.

Documents required A valid driver's licence is required (with an English-language translation if you wish to rent a car). Non-EU residents should obtain an international driver's licence from their country of origin. If you do bring your own vehicle to Ireland, take the registration document with you, and also a letter of authorization from the owner if he or she is not travelling with the vehicle. Both the car and any trailer or caravan should carry an appropriately sized nationality sticker. Insurance is compulsory; a Green Card is a well-recognized international proof of cover.

Regulations Irish residents are not insured to drive non-Irish visitors' cars, other than a garage hand with written permission. A red warning triangle or hazard lights should be used if you break down. Use low-beam headlights in poor visibility. Front seat belts should be worn at all times in the Republic; front and rear seat belts (if fitted) in Northern Ireland. Children under 12 must travel in the back. Offences such as speeding may attract an on-the-spot fine. Motorcyclists and passengers must wear helmets.

257

Speed limits Despite most signposts in the Republic being in kilometres, speed limits are defined on both sides of the border in miles per hour. In the Republic:
● 30mph (48kph) in built-up areas
● 60mph (96kph) in country areas unless otherwise indicated
● 70mph (113kph) on motorways

In Northern Ireland:
● 30mph (48kph) in built-up areas
● 40–60mph (64–96kph) in country areas
● 70mph (113kph) on divided highways and motorways
In both the limit for vehicles with trailers is 40mph (64kph).

Roads In the Republic there are more and more stretches of motorway as roads are rapidly improved with the aid of EU grants. There are three road classifications: National Primary (labelled N, plus a number between 1 and 50); National Secondary (N plus a number over 50); and Regional (R). These categories give little indication of how good the road actually is. Roads near large cities (Dublin, Cork, Waterford, and Limerick) may suffer from congestion in rush hours. Elsewhere roadworks may cause delays.

Generally speaking roads are busier than in the past, and driving in Ireland is no longer such a relaxing affair. Roads in Northern Ireland are of equal quality, whether A-roads, motorways, or B-roads.

Road signs In the Republic a single signpost may be cluttered with up to a dozen signs, in a mix of English and Gaelic. Distances are in kilometres on green Euro signs, but in miles on older black-and-white signs, and even in Irish miles (equal to 2.05km or 1.3mi) on some rare milestones, so the distance from your destination wavers as you travel! Part of the entertainment of driving in Ireland is finding your way in these circumstances, helped by local directions, often of the "I wouldn't be starting from here" variety.

Fuel Unleaded fuel is now widely used on both sides of the border. Filling stations usually stay open till around 8PM (later in built-up areas) in the Republic and some are open on Sundays. In the North they stay open longer, some 24 hours.

Parking Several larger cities in the Republic have a disk parking system. Buy a disk from local shops or garages to allow you to park for a specified time. Elsewhere, multi-storey or pay-and-display parking areas are the norm. In Belfast and other Northern Irish towns, park only in authorized places. Many towns have control zones where you may not leave a vehicle unattended. If you do, you may cause a security alert.

Crossing the border (See panel on page 214 for more details.) Since the 1997 cease-fire, border security measures have been relaxed, but there are still some checkpoints open. Be prepared to stop at checkpoints, state your destination, and show identification. A passport is useful, especially if you have rented a car with Irish Republic plates. Make sure that your insurance covers you across the border.

Automobile Association Offices The main AA offices in Ireland are at:
● 23 Suffolk Street, Dublin 2 (tel: 01 677 9950)
● 12 Emmet Place, Cork (tel: 021 427 6377)
● Unit 5, Newry Road, Dundalk (tel: 042 933 2955).

Electricity
The standard supply is 230 (240 in Northern Ireland) volts AC (50Hz), with mostly flat 3-prong sockets as in Britain (occasionally older round 2- or 3-prong ones may be found). North American appliances require both a transformer and an adaptor, which you should bring with you.

Embassies and Consulates
Embassies in the Republic:
● Australia: Fitzwilton House, Wilton Terrace, Dublin 2 (tel: 01 676 1517)
● Canada: 65 St. Stephen's Green, Dublin 2 (tel: 01 478 1988)
● UK: 29 Merrion Road, Dublin 4 (tel: 01 205 3700)
● United States: 42 Elgin Road, Dublin 4 (tel: 01 668 8777).

Consular offices for Northern Ireland:
● Australian High Commission: Australia House, The Strand, London WC2B 4LA (tel: 020-7379 4334)
● Canadian High Commission: Macdonald House, 1 Grosvenor Square, London W1X 0AB (tel: 020-7258 6600)

Dublin has a good suburban rail system

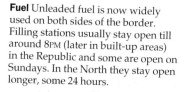

● New Zealand High Commission: New Zealand House, 80 Haymarket, London SW1Y 4TQ (tel: 020-7930 8422)
● United States: Queens House, 14 Queen Street, Belfast BT1 6WEQ (tel: 028 9032 8239).

Irish consulates abroad:
● Britain: 17 Grosvenor Place, London SW1X 7HR (tel: 020-7235 2171)
● Australia: 20 Arkana Street, Yarralumla, Canberra 2600, ACT (tel: 062 273 3022).
● Canada: 170 Metcalfe Street, Ottawa K2P 1P3, Ontario (tel: 613/233-6281)
● United States: 2234 Massachusetts Avenue NW, Washington DC 20008 (tel: 202/462-3939/40/41/42). There are also Irish consulates in Chicago, Boston, New York, and San Francisco.

Emergency telephone numbers
Dial 999 throughout Ireland for police, fire, ambulance, or rescue services (covering coastal, mountain, and cave).

Health
There are no special health requirements or recommended vaccinations for visitors to the Republic or to Northern Ireland, and no particular hazards or diseases.

EU residents are entitled to reciprocal health care (bring Form E111 or equivalent with you, obtainable from Post Offices). Make it clear you want to be treated under EU reciprocal arrangements if you need medical attention.

If you are a British citizen you are entitled to reciprocal free health care in the Republic; in practice this may be difficult to obtain unless you have an E111, and you may not find a doctor registered with the Health Board Panel who is prepared to treat you without charging. British citizens are entitled to free National Health Service treatment in Northern Ireland.

It is advisable for any visitor to take out adequate medical insurance. A good travel policy will cover loss and theft of property, cover you for any legal emergency, and get you home if you're stuck. If you need medical treatment, keep all bills and medical receipts for any subsequent claim. Be sure to take some convincing identification with you when you ask for treatment, and proof of insurance.

259

The International Association for Medical Assistance to Travellers
(IAMAT) offers a list of approved doctors whose training meets British and US standards. In the **United States** contact: 417 Center Street, Lewiston, NY 14092 (tel: 716/754-4883). In **Canada**: 40 Regal Road, Guelph, Ontario N1K 1B5 (tel: 519/836-0102). In **Europe**: 57 Voirets, 1212 Grandlancy, Geneva, Switzerland. Membership is free.

A detail from a mural at the Irish Life Centre in Dublin

Language

Everyone in Ireland speaks English, but officially the Republic is bilingual, and Gaelic (Irish) is the first language in areas of Cork, Waterford, and parts of the west (especially Dingle and Connemara) and northwest. Irish citizens can be heard in Irish if summoned to court, and it is an entry requirement for some universities. Radio, television, and newspapers have features in Gaelic. In practice, you don't need to speak Gaelic, but you may find a warmer welcome if you try. Pronunciation is difficult, bears no resemblance to spelling, and it is hard for a non-native to attempt some place-names without hearing an Irish speaker first. There are several dialects of Gaelic and pronunciation varies from place to place.

Lost property

Serious losses should be reported to the police, who should give you a copy of your statement if you wish to make an insurance claim. Inform your embassy if you have lost a passport, or a bank displaying the Eurocard symbol if you have lost credit cards or travellers' cheques

❏ Here are a few of the words and phrases you are most likely to come across:

Bord Fáilte (Irish Tourist Board, literally "board of welcomes")— pronounced "bord fawlcha"
Céad míle fáilte (literally, "a hundred thousand welcomes")— "kay-d mille fawlcha"
céilí (Irish dance night)—"kaylee"
Gaeltacht (Irish-speaking region)— "gale-tackt"
Garda Síochána (police)—"gawrda sheekawnah"
poteen (alcohol distilled from potatoes, illegal and often dangerous)—"potcheen"
sláinte (good health)—"slawn-cha"
slán (goodbye)—"slawn"
Taoiseach (Prime Minister)— "teeshock"
uisce beatha (whiskey, literally "water of life")—"ishka baha"
Most importantly, on entrance doors to public toilets, *Mná* means women and *Fir* means men.

And a few words that appear in place-names:
ard height (Ardmore, Ardglass)
ath ford (Athlone, Athlumney)
bal, *baile*, *bally* town (Ballymena, Ballinrobe)
carrick rock (Carrickfergus, Carrickmacross)
drom, *drum* ridge (Dromahair, Drumcondra)
dún fort (Donegal, Dungannon)
ennis, *inis* island (Enniskillen, Innisfree)
glen vale, glen (Glendalough, Glengarriff)
kil, *cille* church (Killarney, Kilkenny)
lios, *liss* mound, ring fort (Lismore, Lisdoonvarna)
rath fortified homestead, ring fort (Rathmullen, Rathkeale). ❏

The Irish seem very keen to get as much use as possible from their signposts, overloading them with countless signs— as seen here at Dromahair, County Leitrim

(keep a note of the numbers and your purchase receipt *separate* from the cheques in order to obtain replacements rapidly).

Media

Television broadcasting in the Republic of Ireland is operated by a state-sponsored body called RTE (Radio Telefís Éireann). It has five radio and three television channels (RTE1, Network 2, and the Irish-speaking TG4). There is also the privately owned TV3. You can receive them all over Ireland, including the North. In much of the Republic, you can pick up BBC (radio and television) and Ulster Television. Local radio, including many independent stations, offers blasts of Irish music, chat, and lilting Gaelic (also useful for traffic and weather reports, and events). British visitors will hear a new slant to Irish or world affairs, or the problems of the North, on Irish news broadcasts.

The main newspapers in the Republic are the *Irish Times* and the *Irish Independent*—both slim publications that are expensive by US standards, but a great insight into Irish life and politics. Another respected newspaper is the *Irish Examiner*, which comments on world affairs with *gravitas*. Sunday papers include the *Sunday Tribune* (good arts reviews and listings), *Sunday Independent*, and *Sunday Business Post*. The *International Herald Tribune* and the *Wall Street Journal* are available in Dublin and major cities. The most widespread local paper in the North is the evening *Belfast Telegraph*. In the mornings you have a choice of the nationalist *Irish News* or the loyalist *News Letter*.

Money matters: currency
Republic of Ireland
The unit of currency is the euro. Notes come in denominations of 5, 10, 20, 50, 100, 200, and 500 euros; coins come in denominations of 1, 2, 5, 10, 20 and 50 cents, and 1 and 2 euros.

Northern Ireland In the North the currency used is the pound sterling (as in the rest of the UK). Many shops in the North, especially in towns near

CONVERSION CHARTS

FROM	TO	MULTIPLY BY
Inches	Centimetres	2.54
Centimetres	Inches	0.3937
Feet	Metres	0.3048
Metres	Feet	3.2810
Yards	Metres	0.9144
Metres	Yards	1.0940
Miles	Kilometres	1.6090
Kilometres	Miles	0.6214
Acres	Hectares	0.4047
Hectares	Acres	2.4710
Gallons	Litres	3.7854
Litres	Gallons	0.2642
Ounces	Grams	28.35
Grams	Ounces	0.0353
Pounds	Grams	453.6
Grams	Pounds	0.0022
Pounds	Kilograms	0.4536
Kilograms	Pounds	2.205
Tons	Tonnes	0.9072
Tonnes	Tons	1.1023

MEN'S SUITS

UK	36	38	40	42	44	46	48
Rest of Europe	46	48	50	52	54	56	58
US	36	38	40	42	44	46	48

DRESS SIZES

UK	8	10	12	14	16	18
France	36	38	40	42	44	46
Italy	38	40	42	44	46	48
Rest of Europe	34	36	38	40	42	44
US	6	8	10	12	14	16

MEN'S SHIRTS

UK	14	14.5	15	15.5	16	16.5	17
Rest of Europe	36	37	38	39/40	41	42	43
US	14	14.5	15	15.5	16	16.5	17

MEN'S SHOES

UK	7	7.5	8.5	9.5	10.5	11
Rest of Europe	41	42	43	44	45	46
US	8	8.5	9.5	10.5	11.5	12

WOMEN'S SHOES

UK	4.5	5	5.5	6	6.5	7
Rest of Europe	38	38	39	39	40	41
US	6	6.5	7	7.5	8	8.5

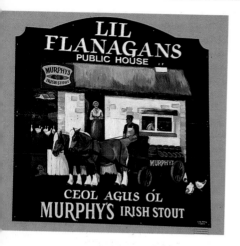

A Kilkenny pub sign

the border, will accept euros, but it's best to have a supply of both currencies ready if you are crossing the border.

Changing money This is best carried out at a bank; see **Opening hours**. Exchange facilities are also available at international airports, travel agencies, hotels, and some tourist offices, although the rates may not be as favourable at these places. Many ATMs will accept American bank cards on the Cirrus or NYCE systems.

Credit cards Major credit cards (those bearing the MasterCard and Visa symbols) are widely accepted all over Ireland, particularly in shops catering to visitors. Charge cards, such as American Express and Diners Club, are also acceptable in some outlets (less so in the North). You can use Visa to withdraw cash from banks displaying the card's symbol. Smaller retailers or restaurateurs and bed-and-breakfast owners prefer cash.

National holidays
New Year's Day, St. Patrick's Day (March 17), Easter Monday, Christmas Day, and St. Stephen's Day (December 26, known as Boxing Day in the North) are public holidays in both the North and the Republic.

The Republic has the following public holidays:
● first Monday in May
● first Monday in June
● first Monday in August
● last Monday in October.

Northern Ireland also takes these days as holidays:
● first Monday in May
● last Monday in May
● Orange Day (July 12)
● last Monday in August

Good Friday is not a statutory holiday, but is observed as a holiday, albeit marked by religious devotion, in most parts of Ireland.

Opening hours
Times given below are general and subject to local variations. In the Republic, particularly in rural areas, shop hours may be erratic, but shopkeepers are also flexible and may be willing to open up specially. In Dublin and Belfast, hours may be longer, with late-night shopping on either a Thursday or Friday.
  Museums and other visitor sights vary greatly: The largest stay open all year; others close from mid-September or October until Easter. Summer opening hours are usually longer than in winter. Some museums close on Monday; to avoid disappointment *always* check with the tourist office before making a long journey.
  Published times may be unreliable, or sights closed for renovation, or some other reason.

  The following opening hours apply in the Republic:
● shops: Mon–Sat 9–5.30; many stores stay open late on Thu and Fri
● banks: 10–4 (*Closed* national holidays). Many banks stay open until 5 on Thu in Dublin.
● post offices: Mon–Fri 9–5.30 or 6, Sat 9–1 (usually closed at lunchtime). Village post offices also close early one day a week
● pubs: Sun–Wed 10.30AM–11.30PM, Thu–Sat 10.30AM–12.30AM.
  Opening hours in the North are slightly different:

● shops: Mon–Sat 9–5.30, with one midweek early closing day (Wed or Thu). Some close for lunch, while many Belfast stores open late (until 9) on Thu

● banks: Mon–Fri 9.30–4.30. Some banks close 12.30–1.30

● post offices: Mon–Fri 9–5.30; Sat 9–1. Some close for lunch, or, alternatively, all day Wed

● pubs: Mon–Sat 11.30AM–11PM (some pubs in Belfast open until 1AM on Fri and Sat); Sun 12.30–2.30, 7–10 (at the landlord's discretion).

Pharmacies (chemists)
Besides medicines, these places also stock cosmetics and photographic products. When closed, they display a notice outside giving the list of pharmacists that stay open late. In an emergency, contact the local hospital. Contraceptives (condoms) are more widely available than they were a few years ago (when they were illegal), with many pubs having dispensing machines in the men's restrooms.

Places of worship
Ireland naturally has many churches, though it may surprise visitors to see how many are Church of Ireland (Protestant), not Roman Catholic. This "imbalance" is the result of the

The view from the Rock of Dunamase, County Laois

Penal Code (see page 36), which suppressed Catholic worship and encouraged Protestant church building. Some churches open only for services and are otherwise locked, but you can usually obtain the key by asking someone nearby where it is kept. If you cause no disturbance it is acceptable to slip in and out of a church during mass for a quick look around (don't barge about during the service, of course).

There are few non-Christian places of worship, but Belfast and Dublin have synagogues, and Dublin a mosque as well (check with tourist boards for details). Marian shrines, such as the one at Knock, or grottoes like Ballinspittle, attract many pious Catholics, the majority of whom are women.

263

Police
In the Republic, the police are called the Gardaí (pronounced "gardee"), wear blue-and-black uniforms, and are unarmed.

In the North, the police force has been renamed the Police Service of Northern Ireland (PSNI), and they wear green uniforms. They carry arms, and police stations all over the North have very tight security. It's hoped the on-going peace talks will lead to nationalists as well as unionists joining this new police force to make it truly reflect the community's diversity.

Post offices

These are easily identifiable, even in the Republic, by the word "Post" in green. The postal services in the Republic are expensive (postcards are cheaper than letters). In the North postal rates are the same as in the rest of the UK (a two-tier system is used: first and second class, the former purportedly buying speed). Post boxes are red in the north, green in the south. The correct stamps must be used either side of the border. The GPO in O'Connell Street, Dublin, is open longer hours than elsewhere, including Sundays and bank holidays. See also the opening hours section, page 262.

Public transportation

Local public transportation in the Republic is, in general, very limited, which is why you see so many young people hitchhiking. Things are better in the North, though it is still immeasurably more convenient to have your own transportation.

Air Regular air services connect Dublin with all parts of the country, and if money is no object, it is a very quick trip (30–40 minutes). Regular flights also connect Galway and the Aran Islands (15–25 minutes), operated by Aer Arann, weather permitting. Business travel and tourism have opened up a number of provincial airports with regular internal services and flights to the UK run by Aer Lingus and Ryanair.

Train The rail network in the Republic is controlled by the state-owned Irish Rail (Iarnrod Éireann), the rail division of CIE (Coras Iompair Éireann). Trains are fairly slow and infrequent, but generally reliable and comfortable. Most routes radiate from Dublin. The only service connecting the Republic and the North is the Dublin–Belfast Express (about six trains each way a day). Large parts of the country are not covered by the rail network at all, such as Donegal and the border counties, Clare, Connemara, and southwest Cork. Fares are complex and not especially cheap—consider a discount pass if you plan to do much rail travel (see Passes, opposite). The Dublin area has its own transportation system, DART (Dublin Area Rapid Transit), a suburban electric train service operating between Howth and Bray.

In Northern Ireland there are three routes run by Northern Ireland Rail. You can take a bicycle on mainline trains if there is room, but there is a charge.

Bus Bus Éireann and Ulsterbus respectively provide the Republic's and Northern Ireland's national express bus systems, supplemented by Dublin Bus in the Dublin area, and by many private bus lines (sometimes cheaper and faster than the national buses, though insurance cover may be dubious). Various bus operators offer sightseeing tours (such as Gray Line).

Bus travel in the Republic is often very slow, but fares are much cheaper than train fares. Off-season services may be very infrequent, but conversely weekend services may be over-subscribed. Small villages are sometimes served by only a couple of buses a week. Many bus indicators are in Gaelic, so check your destination carefully.

Midweek "single" (one-way) tickets can be used for a free return trip and remain valid for a month. Bicycles can be carried (for a charge) at the driver's discretion, if there is

Post boxes are green south of the border, and red to the north

The DART at Dun Laoghaire station

room. Bus travel in the North is generally reliable and serves most areas not reached by train.

Ferry or boat Three useful car ferries across estuaries cut down long detours inland. One is at Waterford (between Ballyhack and Passage East), linking counties Waterford and Wexford. The second is across the Shannon estuary between Killimer and Tarbert, linking Kerry and Clare and cutting out the bottleneck journey through Limerick. The third is between Strangford and Portaferry in County Down.

Most of Ireland's islands can be reached by ferry, too. There are regular services to the Aran Islands from Galway City, Rossaveal (farther west along the south Galway coast), and Doolin in County Clare. The islands off Donegal (Inishbofin, Aran Island) and those off Cork (Bear, Sherkin, and Clear Island) are also linked with regular ferries. Others can be reached by private charter services (such as the Blaskets, Skelligs, and Tory Island), usually in the summer only. Get the tourist office leaflet *Island Boat/Air Services* (No. IS50C) for further details. Rathlin is reached from Ballycastle.

Passes Many different discount schemes operate, but you need to assess your probable usage carefully before investing in a pass. Ask the tourist office which would be most appropriate for you.

Emerald Cards cover unlimited bus and rail travel throughout Ireland for 8 or 15 days.

Rambler or Rover Tickets buy you unlimited travel on Bus Éireann or Irish Rail for a certain number of days within a given period.

Runaround tickets are valid on Northern Irish trains. Check at tourist offices for the most up-to-date information.

More information Irish Rail (Iarnrod Éireann, tel: 01 836 6222); Bus Éireann (tel: 01 836 6111); Ulsterbus (tel: 028 9033 3000); Northern Ireland Railways (tel: 028 9089 9411). For guided tour information, contact CIE. Tours International, 35 Lower Abbey Street, Dublin (tel: 01 873 1100) or, in Northern Ireland, the Ulsterbus Travel Centre, Glengall Street, Belfast (tel: 028 9033 3000).

Restrooms
Public conveniences (restrooms) are generally available in towns and visitor sites throughout Ireland. You may see the Gaelic signs *Mná* (women) or *Fir* (men) on some, but ideograms usually leave you in no doubt which is which. Restrooms in traditional spit-and-sawdust bars may not be particularly well kept.

Security

Most of Ireland is extremely relaxed; even in the tension zones of the North security measures are less stringent than before. Nonetheless, be vigilant. Leave no baggage unattended and always park in authorized places (some central areas are controlled zones where any unattended vehicles will be removed or possibly detonated by security forces). If there is an alert, you may have to move very fast. Be prepared to show identification (a passport or driver's licence). Always stop at road checks. There are no public places to store luggage in the North, but lockers are usually available at bus and train stations in the Republic. It is generally illegal to take photographs of police or military barracks in the North and if you are noticed you may be suspected of terrorism. Security forces on both sides of the border are usually extremely polite to bona fide travellers, and if you have nothing to hide, you have nothing to fear.

Student and youth travel

Discounts are available for young people and students. Check fares through specialist agencies such as British-based STA Travel or Campus Travel, or ask ferry and airline companies direct. Tickets may be subject to availability (only bookable the day before you travel, for example), so you need to be more flexible than you might like during busy periods. Check youth fares against other types of discount tickets—there are many cheap fares available. You may need an international student identity card (ISIC), Youthcard, or Travelsave Stamp to obtain these low fares; in some cases a passport or driving licence will do. Eurail passes (for under-26-year-olds) are valid in Ireland.

Cheap travel concessions (such as combined accommodation and rail or bus tickets) are also available from The Irish Youth Hostel Association, An Óige, based at 61 Mountjoy Street, Dublin 7 (tel: 01 830 4555). It has about 50 hostels all over the Republic, some in attractive old buildings and beautiful settings. The Youth Hostel Association of Northern Ireland runs six hostels (YHANI, 22 Donegall Road, Belfast BT12 5JN, tel: 028 9032 4733). The 93 hostels of the Independent Hostel Owners group (IHO Information Office, tel: 073 30130) are run along rather more relaxed lines, with private double, single, and family rooms as well as traditional dormitory accommodation. Bord Fáilte runs an inspection scheme for independent hostels. Budget accommodation can become overcrowded during peak season.

Telephones

You can find public payphones in street booths and bars or shops (some with a sign saying "you can phone from here"). Older-style call boxes in the Republic are blue and cream and marked in Gaelic *"Telefón."* Some are quite old; follow the instructions carefully. Northern Irish phone booths are red. Newer automatic glass and metal boxes are replacing both types. Calls connected by the operator—dial 190 (100 in the North)—are much more expensive than direct-dial calls (cheaper after

The older style of Irish phone booth

6PM and on weekends); so are those made from hotels. Calls to Britain and parts of Europe (including EU countries) are cheaper after 6PM; to the US or Canada after 10PM; both are cheaper at weekends. Lower rates operate between the Republic and Britain than elsewhere (cheapest of all between midnight and 8AM—direct-dial from an ordinary phone only). Other countries have no reduced-rate call times. Cardphones are a convenient way of making long-distance calls (buy cards at newsdealers or post offices). A useful booklet summarizing telephone information and listing international codes can be picked up at airports, and post or tourist offices.

The greener form of transportation

❏ International Dialling

Omit the initial zero of the local code when dialling internationally.
Access codes to Ireland from:
- United States 011
- Canada 011
- Britain 00353 (for the Republic)
- Australia 0011
- New Zealand 00

followed by 353 for the Republic or 44 for Northern Ireland.

Access codes from the Republic:
- United States 001
- Canada 001
- Britain 0044
- Australia 0061
- New Zealand 0064.

- To dial the North from the Republic, dial 08, followed by the local code (in full, including the initial STD zero). Check in the phonebook or dial 11811 for local codes.
- To dial the Republic from the North dial 00, followed by 353, then the local code, omitting the initial zero. ❏

Time

Ireland is on Greenwich Mean Time (GMT) in winter; GMT plus one hour in summer (British Summer Time or Central European Time). "Summer" runs from March to October. When GMT is in effect, it is five hours later in Ireland than in New York, eight hours later than in California.

Tipping

If service is not included (it often is, at 12 or 15 percent), leave a 10–15 percent tip on restaurant bills. Taxi drivers, hotel porters, lounge bar waiters, and so forth like receiving tips as much as anyone, but in general help and advice to strangers is proffered as a natural courtesy in Ireland, without expectation of reward. Tipping is not customary in pubs.

Tourist information

A list of Ireland's tourist information offices can be picked up in any tourist office, North or South. These can supply maps, town plans, timetables, brochures, and information on local sights, events, sports facilities, and so on, though for many items a charge is made. Bord Fáilte's information sheets give summaries on many topics (such as fishing, car rental, horse-drawn caravans, Irish folklore). Maps of Ireland are often out of date and inaccurate, fine for general motoring, but not ideal for exploring in detail. Local maps, such as those produced by Tim Robinson, of Connemara, the Aran Islands, and the Burren, are the best bet for walking.

Northern Ireland has useful (free) information. Most tourist offices will book accommodation for you, though you have to pay a fee for the telephone calls; it is often better to get the lists and do your own phoning. A 10 percent deposit is taken at the time of booking, later deducted from your final bill. Accommodation unlisted by Bord Fáilte is not necessarily substandard.

Bord Fáilte (Irish Tourist Board)
● Britain: 150 New Bond Street, London W1Y 0AQ (tel: 020-7493 3201); also at All-Ireland Tourism, 12 Regent Street, London SW1Y 4PQ (personal callers only)
● Australia: 5th Level, 36 Carrington Street, Sydney, NSW 2000 (tel: 02 299 6177)
● Canada: 160 Bloor Street East, Suite 1150, Toronto, Ontario M4W 1B9 (tel: 416/929-2777)
● United States: 345 Park Avenue, New York, NY 10154 (tel: 212/418-0800)
● Northern Ireland: 53 Castle Street, Belfast BT1 1GH (tel: 028 9032 7888).

Northern Ireland Tourist Board
● Britain: Northern Ireland Business Centre, 11 Berkeley Street, London W1X 5AD (telephone enquiries only: 020-7766 9920); also at All-Ireland Tourism, BTA Travel Centre, 12 Lower Regent Street, London SW1Y 4PQ (personal callers only)
● Canada: 111 Avenue Road, Suite 450, Toronto, Ontario M5R 3J8 (tel: 416/925-6368)
● Republic of Ireland: 16 Nassau Street, Dublin 2 (tel: 01 679 1977)
● United States: Suite 701, 551 Fifth Avenue, New York, NY 10176 (tel: 212/922-0101).

Within the Republic there are about 100 tourist offices marked with the information symbol "i" on a green background. Those in major towns usually stay open all year, Monday to Saturday.

Dublin's main tourist office is on Suffolk Street (tel: 01 605 7700; www.visitdublin.com). The Irish Tourist Board is at Baggott Street Bridge, Dublin 2 (tel: 01 602 4000; www.ireland.travel.ie).

A Kinsale character

Northern Ireland has about 30 tourist information centres; NITB head office is at Donegal Square, Belfast (tel: 028 9024 6609; www.discovernorthernireland.com).

Useful things to bring
Warm clothes, comfortable footwear, and wet-weather gear are essential. Bring waterproof boots if you are planning to explore the boglands; sensible walking shoes and a compass if you are planning to do any serious walking. A flashlight can be handy for dark churches, caves, or castle ruins, or simply for finding your way home from the pub late at night.

Take a sleeping bag for staying in hostels. A good flower or bird identi-fication guide and binoculars are musts for keen naturalists.

Camera film is quite expensive in the Republic.

Bring any prescribed medicines or contraceptives you need; they may not be available locally.

Non-British visitors with electrical appliances will need to bring an adaptor and possibly a transformer.

Take your driver's licence if you want to rent a car. A passport pro-vides useful identification. Leave room in your suitcase, though, for an Irish sweater or some tweed clothing. You will certainly want to take home something from the Emerald Isle.

Hotels and Restaurants

HOTELS

Accommodation registered with the Irish Tourist Board (in the Republic) has a shamrock sign outside. All hotels in the North are inspected and graded by the NITB. This isn't always a guarantee of excellence, but it does indicate that some basic standards have been met. Standards of accommodation have risen dramatically. Many establishments have been totally renovated in the last few years, with modern bathrooms and all conveniences. Some visitors may feel that some of the old-style charm and period interest has consequently been lost.

There are many splendid country-house hotels in Ireland, and lots of good-value, friendly B&Bs. Middle-range places offering character and value are harder to find—there are many dull and shabby commercial hotels and seedy guesthouses with few attractions for the visitor. In high season all available accommodation can be very busy and it is advisable to book ahead, especially if some popular event or festival is taking place (the Kinsale Food Festival or the Cork Jazz Festival, for example). All the Bord Fáilte and Northern Ireland Tourist Board offices will call around to book a room for you for a small fee.

Three leaflets are well worth looking for: *The Blue Book* (fax: 046 23292), *The Hidden Ireland* (tel: 662 7166), and *Friendly Homes of Ireland* (tel: 01 668 6463). The Tourist Office publications *Town and Country Homes*, *Farm Holidays in Ireland*, and *Be Our Guest* also have useful if less discriminating selections. It is also worth getting hold of a copy of *Where to Stay in Northern Ireland*, published by the NITB, which lists all the recommended accommodation in the province. To stay really cheaply, look for the leaflet *Irish Hostel Guide*, a list of approved independent hostels, or contact An Óige, the Irish Youth Hostel Association (61 Mountjoy Street, Dublin 7, tel: 01 830 4555) in the Republic, and the Youth Hostel Association of Northern Ireland (22 Donegall Road, Belfast BT12 5JN, tel: 01232 324733) in the North. You need an international youth hostel membership card to stay in these hostels. *Self-catering*, listing cottage rentals, is also available. Irish Cottage Holiday Homes (4 Whitefriars, Aungier Street, Dublin 2; tel: 01 475 7017) offers inclusive self-catering vacations.

The list of accommodation that follows has been divided into three price categories, based on rates in high season (including tax):

● budget ($): you are likely to find a double bedroom for less than €75, including breakfast for two;
● moderate ($$): you are likely to find a double bedroom for between €75 and €125, including breakfast for two;
● expensive ($$$): you are likely to pay more than €125 for a double bedroom, including breakfast for two.

DUBLIN

(the code for Dublin is 01)

Butlers Town House ($$$)
44 Lansdowne Road, Ballsbridge, 4
tel: 667 4022 fax: 667 3960
www.butlers-hotel.com
This restored Georgian townhouse near the rugby ground has all the modern comforts: air conditioning, modem points, and good breakfasts.

The Clarence ($$$)
6-8 Wellington Quay, 2 tel: 407 0800
fax: 407 0820 www.theclarence.ie
The Clarence is one of the chicest, most expensive hotels in the city—it's owned by Bono and The Edge of U2 and Harry Crosbie, who refurbished it with superb contemporary design.

Herbert Park Hotel ($$$)
Ballsbridge, 4 tel: 667 2200
fax: 667 2595 www.herbertparkhotel.ie
The attractive and original décor and relaxing, informal atmosphere make this a popular choice. Excellent location beside the Royal Dublin Showground and overlooking Herbert Park.

Hibernian Hotel ($$$)
Eastmoreland Place, Ballsbridge, 4
tel: 668 7666 fax: 660 2655
www.hibernianhotel.com
Luxury hotel with country-house atmosphere, in a quiet area 15 minutes' walk from the centre.

Jury's Custom House Inn ($)
Custom House Quay, 1 tel: 607 5000
fax: 829 0400 www.jurysdoyle.com
This is the best of these good value hotels, close to the Financial Centre overlooking the Liffey. The tasteful accommodation includes all the latest facilities for both the business and tourist market. (Jury's Christchurch Inn, tel: 454 0000, on Christchurch Place is run on the same formula.)

Jury's Hotel Dublin ($$$)
Pembroke Road, Ballsbridge, 4 tel: 660 5000
fax: 660 5540 www.jurysdoyle.com
The Jury's Hotel provides comfortable, convenient accommodation. Facilities include parking, two restaurants, indoor/outdoor pool, and gym. The even grander adjacent sister hotel, The Towers (tel: 607 0000) has a separate entrance.

Le Meridien Shelbourne ($$$)
27 Stephens Green, 2 tel: 663 4500
fax: 661 6006 www.shelbourne.ie
The Shelbourne Meridien, Dublin's most famous hotel, was immortalized in James Joyce's novel *Ulysses*. The impressive interior is chic and comfortable and the location central (*see* also The Side Door, *restaurants* section, page 279). Good for morning coffee and predinner drinks.

Longfield's Hotel ($$–$$$)
Fitzwilliam Street, 2 tel: 676 1367
fax: 676 1542 www.longfields.ie
Attractively furnished Georgian townhouse with intimate basement restaurant, No. 10; near the city centre. Personalized service, a relaxed atmosphere, and good food.

Merrion Hotel ($$$)
Upper Merrion Street, 2 tel: 603 0600
fax: 603 0700 www.merrionhotel.com

Arguably Dublin's most luxurious hotel, this meticulously renovated terrace of Georgian townhouses lies opposite the Irish Parliament and is connected to the French Restaurant Patrick Guilbaud.

Mount Herbert Hotel ($)
*7 Herbert Road, 4 tel: 668 4321
fax: 660 7077 www.mountherberthotel.ie*
Expect welcoming service and comfortable, well-stocked rooms at the Loughran family's guesthouse. Facilities include a pleasant garden-level restaurant, children's outdoor play area, badminton courts, and lots of parking space.

Raglan Lodge ($$)
*10 Raglan Road, Ballsbridge, 4
tel: 660 6697 fax: 660 6781*
This attractive Victorian guesthouse is in a quiet residential area. All the bedrooms have private bathrooms.

Temple Bar Hotel ($$)
*Fleet Street, Temple Bar, 2 tel: 667 3333
fax: 677 3088 www.towerhotelgroup.com*
A classy, contemporary place in the heart of old Dublin, this hotel provides comfortable rooms and good service; food available all day.

EASTERN COUNTIES

County Kildare
Coursetown Country House ($)
*Stradbally Road, Athy tel: 0507 31101
fax: 0507 32740*
A charming Victorian country house set on a farm and bird sanctuary near Athy.

The Kildare Hotel & Country Club ($$$)
*Straffan tel: 01 601 7200 fax: 01 601 7299
www.kclub.ie*
Better known as The K Club, this is one of the most luxurious hotels in the country. It has fine grounds, including two championship golf courses.

Moyglare Manor ($$$)
*Moyglare, Maynooth tel: 01 628 6351
fax: 01 628 5405 www.moyglaremanor.ie*
Luxuriously furnished Georgian house set in extensive parkland; an easy run from Dublin (see also *restaurants* section, page 280).

County Louth
Ballymascanlon House Hotel ($$)
*Dundalk tel: 042 935 8200
fax: 042 937 1598*
A warm, comfortable hotel in its own grounds, which include an 18-hole golf course and health centre with gym, sauna, and Jacuzzi. Most rooms have excellent views. Woodland grounds covering 320ha (130 acres), screened from traffic noise, and the road. Restaurant.

Boyne Valley Hotel & Country Club ($$)
*Dublin Road, Drogheda
Tel: 041 983 7737 fax: 041 983 9188*
This rambling Victorian mansion, set in extensive grounds, has a traditionally comfortable interior. Conservatory bar and basement restaurant.

County Meath
Ardboyne Hotel ($$)
*Dublin Road, Navan tel: 046 23119
fax: 046 22355 www.quinnhotels.com*

Low-rise modern hotel on the outskirts of the town, overlooking pretty gardens. Simple accommodation and above-average food.

Conyngham Arms Hotel ($$)
Slane tel: 041 988 4444 fax: 041 982 4205
This unpretentious but comfortable stone-built village hotel has been renovated in Edwardian style with modern facilities. Good bar snacks.

Killyon ($)
*Dublin Road, Navan tel: 046 71224
fax: 046 72766*
Very comfortable, hospitable B&B opposite the Ardboyne Hotel, on the river side of the road.

Neptune Beach Hotel & Leisure Club ($$–$$$)
*Bettystown tel: 041 982 7107
fax: 041 982 7412 www.neptunebeach.ie*
This dashing new beachside hotel with old-world bar provides excellent leisure facilities and an interesting restaurant. Golf nearby.

County Wicklow
Ballyknocken House ($)
*Glenealy tel: 0404 44627 fax: 0404 44696
www.ballyknocken.com*
A simple 80ha (200-acre) working farm in the foothills of the Wicklow Mountains, with peaceful gardens. It is transformed by its welcoming hostess into a charming guesthouse. Tennis courts available. Walking holidays can be arranged.

271

Barraderry House ($)
Kiltegan tel: 0508 73209 fax: 0508 73209
A charming Georgian farmhouse, which has been refurbished to a high standard. Six golf courses and three race tracks within easy reach.

Brooklodge at MacCreddin ($$$)
*Macreddin Village tel: 0402 36444
fax: 0402 36580 www.brooklodge.com*
Where the ruins of an old village lay, imaginative developers have built a delightful country-house hotel with excellent food and adjacent "village," including a traditional pub and specialist shops.

Tinakilly ($$$)
*Rathnew tel: 0404 69274 fax: 0404 67806
www.tinakilly.ie*
Once the house of Captain Halpin, the Victorian seafarer who commanded the Great Eastern. Though now somewhat businesslike, the house retains the imposing dimensions specified by its creator, and overlooks lovely gardens to the sea. (See also *restaurants* section, page 280.)

Tynte House ($)
*Dunlavin tel: 045 401561 fax: 045 401586
www.tyntehouse.com*
A 19th-century farmhouse in the main street of this quiet country village, with farmland reaching up to the back door. Large, comfortable rooms overlook the Market House to the front and the farm at the back. This hotel is excellently situated for all the main tourist attractions in County Wicklow.

Woodenbridge Hotel ($$)
*Wooden Bridge, Vale of Avoca
tel: 0402 35146 fax: 0402 35573
www.woodenbridgehotel.com*
Dating from 1608, this is probably the oldest inn in Ireland. Two rooms have four-poster beds; some balconied rooms overlook an 18-hole golf course and there is fishing nearby.

Hotels and Restaurants

SOUTHEASTERN COUNTIES

County Kilkenny
Abbey House ($)
*Jerpoint Abbey, Thomastown tel: 056 24166
fax: 056 24192*
Strikingly modernized guesthouse that was once
part of, and located very close to, the abbey.
Berryhill ($$)
*Inistioge tel: 056 56434 fax: 056 58434
www.berryhillhouse.com*
This welcoming creeper-clad country house with
open fires, antiques, and home produce serves
excellent breakfasts.
Butler House ($$–$$$)
*16 Patrick Street, Kilkenny tel: 056 22828
fax: 056 65626 www.butler.ie*
This 1970s restoration of the former Dower House
of Kilkenny Castle, combines stylish modern con-
veniences with gracious 1770 proportions.
Mount Juliet ($$$)
*Thomastown tel: 056 73000 fax: 056 73019
www.mountjuliet.ie*
A luxurious and beautifully furnished 18th-century
house. The 600ha (1,500-acre) estate includes a
golf course and equestrian and health centres.
Newpark Hotel ($$)
*Kilkenny tel: 056 60500 fax: 056 60555
www.newparkhotel.com*
Set in grounds on the edge of town, this friendly
hotel has been made over in dashing, contem-
porary style. Facilities include a well-equipped
leisure centre, a good restaurant, comfortable resi-
dents' lounge, and plenty of parking.

County Tipperary
Aherlow House ($$)
*Glen of Aherlow, Bansha tel: 062 56153
fax: 062 56212 www.aherlowhouse.ie*
This chintzy interpretation of an old hunting lodge
is fitted out with antiques and modern furnishings.
This hotel is in the shadow of the Galtee
Mountains and surrounded by coniferous forest.
Ashley Park House ($–$$)
*Nenagh tel: 067 38223 fax: 067 38013
www.ashleypark.co*
This graciously proportioned 18th-century farm
house is set in wooded grounds, overlooking a
private lake; close to Lough Derg. Fishing, horse-
back-riding, and golf can all be found nearby.
Bansha House ($)
*Bansha tel: 062 54194 fax: 062 54215
www.tipp.ie/banshas.htm*
A pleasant Georgian guesthouse set in 40ha (100
acres) of farmland where brood mares and foals
roam. Modest modern furnishings.
Cashel Palace ($$$)
*Cashel tel: 062 62707 fax: 062 61521
www.cashel-palace.ie*
Architecturally imposing former bishop's residence
in quiet setting below the Rock of Cashel,
somewhat staid inside.
Inch House Country House & Restaurant ($)
*Thurles tel: 0504 51348 fax: 0504 51754
www.tipp.ie/inch-house/htm*
The 18th-century country house (on a 130ha/330-
acre farm) is furnished carefully in period style with
antiques and log fires; excellent breakfasts.

Legend's Townhouse & Restaurant ($)
*The Kiln, Cashel tel: 062 61292
www.legendsguesthouse.com*
This comfortable, brightly furnished guesthouse
and small restaurant lies adjacent to the Rock of
Cashel. Back bedrooms overlook the Rock.
Minella Hotel ($$–$$$)
*Clonmel tel: 052 22388 fax: 052 24381
www.hotelminella.ie*
Public rooms at Minella Hotel, an owner-managed
mansion in extensive grounds on the banks of
the River Suir, are in the main building, and the
comfortable, well-equipped bedrooms in the east
wing extension. Some have Jacuzzis; all have good
views. Sauna, Indoor pool.

County Waterford
Annestown ($$)
*Annestown tel: 051 396160
fax: 051 396474 www.annestown.com*
This comfortable Victorian house, complete
with wood fires and excellent food, is in a
superb location on the Waterford coast. Private
access to beach.
Diamond Hill Guest House ($)
*Slieverue, Waterford tel: 051 832855
fax: 051 832254 www.diamondhillhouse.com*
Though the rooms at this competently run town-
centre guesthouse are somewhat impersonal,
the Irish welcome and lovely gardens more
than compensate.
Foxmount Country House ($)
*Passage East Road, Waterford
tel: 051 874308 fax: 051 854906
www.iol.ie/tipp/foxmount.htm*
This 17th-century house, set in mature gardens
on a working farm, provides good value and is
convenient for exploring Waterford City or the
attractive harbour scenery. Delicious home cooking uses produce from the dairy farm and garden.
Granville Hotel ($$$)
*The Quay tel: 051 305555 fax: 051 305566
www.granville-hotel.ie*
This historic, centrally located hotel has been
totally renovated and now matches modern
comforts with real character.
Richmond House ($$–$$$)
*Cappoquin tel: 058 54278 fax: 058 54988
www.richmondhouse.net*
This interesting Georgian house was once part of
the Earl of Cork's estate. A lovely setting,
antiques, warm hospitality, and great food.

County Wexford
Ballinkeele House ($$)
*Ballymurn, Enniscorthy tel: 053 38105
fax: 053 38468 www.ballinkeele.com*
Delightful, welcoming house on a 140ha (350-acre)
working farm built (imposingly) in 1840, with early
Victorian feel and many interesting features. Fine
country-house cooking. Private fishing available.
Clonard House ($)
*Clonard Great, Wexford tel: 053 43141
or 053 47337 fax: 053 43141*
An above-average B&B in a Georgian farmhouse in
a peaceful location just outside Wexford. Some
four-poster beds. Unassuming hospitality. Serves
informal dinners—good value.

unbrody Country House & Restaurant
(5$–$$$)
rthurstown tel: 051 389600
ax: 051 389601 www.dunbrodyhouse.com
n impressive, luxuriously furnished Georgian manor
et in parkland. Croquet lawn, clay pigeon shooting,
nd horseback-riding available. Owner-run with
armth and professionalism. Outstanding food.

elly's Resort Hotel ($$$)
osslare tel: 053 32114 fax: 053 32222
ww.kellys.ie
his rambling, well-run, seafront family hotel has a
triking modern art collection. The rooms are very
omfortable (some with balconies) and leisure
acilities include sauna, gym, tennis, and croquet.
xceptional service and food.

emongrove House ($)
lackstoops, Enniscorthy tel/fax: 054 36115
large house in its own grounds surrounded by
ardens and plenty of parking space. Comfortable
nsuite bedrooms and public rooms. Near
osslare Ferry.

IcMenamin's Townhouse ($)
Auburn Terrace, Redmond Road, Wexford
el: 053 46442 fax: 053 46442
ww.wexford-bedandbreakfast.com
his popular, hospitable B&B, near Wexford and
osslare, serves good breakfasts. Golf nearby.

Marlfield House ($$$)
orey tel: 055 21124 fax: 055 21572
ww.marfieldhouse.com
pulently furnished with flair. Both bedrooms and
ublic areas of this aristocratic country house,
nce the residence of the Earl of Courtown, are a
nemorable experience (see also *restaurants*
ection, page 281).

albot Hotel Conference & Leisure Centre
$$$)
rinity Street, Wexford tel: 053 22566
ax: 053 23377 www.talbothotel.ie
a central quayside location. Extensive refur-
ishment has given all bedrooms attractive decor
nd new bathrooms. Day rooms include a
pacious foyer, lounge, and bar with an open fire-
lace. Informal cuisine in country-style kitchen.
hildren's room and beauty salon.

SOUTHWESTERN COUNTIES

County Cork

assolas Country House ($$$)
anturk tel: 029 50015 fax: 029 50795
ww.assolas.com
his is one of Ireland's most charming country
ouses—and one of the oldest (17th century in
arts)—on a tributary of the River Blackwater
fishing available). Expect serene surroundings,
eriod features, log fires, and antiques through-
ut. Welcoming atmosphere and lovely gardens
ith croquet lawn and tennis. Excellent food
available to residents only).

allymaloe House ($$$)
hanagarry, Midleton tel: 021 465 2531
ax: 021 465 2021 www.ballymaloe.com
well-loved hotel, offering peace and some
f the best food in Ireland (see also *restaurant*
ection, page 281). Part of the old Geraldine
astle estate, the keep of which stands by the
mellow, creeper-covered farmhouse. Several
outbuildings now house extra rooms.
Modern paintings include many works by
Jack Yeats. Superbly relaxing bedrooms. Family-
run with enthusiasm and enterprise. Golf
course nearby, outdoor heated swimming pool,
tennis courts.

Ballyvolane House ($$–$$$)
Castlelyons, Fermoy tel: 025 36349
fax: 025 36781 www.ballyvolanehouse.ie
An Italianate country house offering classy but
completely unpretentious hospitality in a fine
parkland setting. Beautiful park and gardens
and country-house cooking. House-party style
dining at one table. Fishing is available in the three
lakes, one of which is stocked with brown trout.
Croquet lawn.

Bay View Hotel ($$$)
Ballycotton, Cork tel: 021 464 6746
fax: 021 464 6075 www.bayviewhotel.net
Rebuilt to very high standards, reflecting
the owner's wish to retain the character of the
original building while providing modern comforts
and facilities. Comfortable bedrooms, some
with superb views over Ballycotton Bay. Friendly
and efficient staff. Horseback-riding, fishing, and
golf can all be enjoyed nearby.

Castle Hotel ($$)
Macroom, Cork tel: 026 41074
fax: 026 41505 www.castlehotel.ie
This classy stone-built hotel provides comfortable
rooms with en-suite bedrooms (some rather
small). The restaurant serves good food, and a
range of bar meals is also available. Facilities
include a relaxing lounge, private dining/meeting
room, and leisure centre which includes heated
indoor swimming pool, gym, steam room, pool
table, and solarium. Golf nearby.

Desert House ($)
Coast Road, Clonakilty
tel: 023 33331 fax: 023 33048
deserthouse@eircom.net
Desert House, a Georgian farmhouse overlooking
Clonakilty Bay, makes an ideal base for touring
West Cork and Kerry. Dogs accepted.

Glebe Country House ($–$$)
Ballinadee, Bandon
tel: 021 477 8294 fax: 021 477 8456
http//.indigo.ie/~glebehse/
Accommodation in this beautiful Georgian
rectory, with predominantly antique furnishings, is
both elegant and good value. The hosts are very
welcoming. Dogs accepted.

Hayfield Manor Hotel ($$$)
Perrott Avenue College Road, Cork
tel: 021 484 5900 or 021 431 6839
www.hayfieldmanor.ie
Cork city's premier hotel is set in its own gardens
in the university area and provides old-style comfort and service with modern convenience and
good food. Exclusive health club including indoor
swimming pool and gym.

The Heron's Cove ($)
The Harbour, Goleen tel: 028 35225
fax: 028 35422 www.heronscove.com
Beautifully located in a quiet position; rooms with
balconies overlook a small tidal harbour. Good
food (also open to non-residents).

273

Hotels and Restaurants

Innishannon House ($$$)
*Innishannon tel: 021 477 5121
fax: 021 477 5609 www.innishannon-hotel.ie*
This romantic 1720 "petit chateau" style house
(tastefully furnished, with an original art collection
and some unusual bedrooms, including two with
four-poster beds) lies in peaceful riverside setting.
Hospitable and comfortable, with good cooking by
the son of the house. Private fishing available.

Lancaster Lodge ($–$$)
*Western Road, Cork tel: 021 425 1125
fax: 021 425 1126 www.lancasterlodge.com*
A large, owner-run guesthouse convenient to city
centre. Overlooks the River Lee. Purpose-built to
a high standard; good breakfasts. Exceptional
value. Two ground-floor rooms available for
visitors with disabilities.

The Lodge & Spa at Inchydoney Island ($$$)
*Clonakilty tel: 023 33143 023 35229
www.inchydoneyisland.com*
Former winner of the Hotel of the Year for Ireland.
The bedrooms and public areas at this fashion-
able new hotel overlooking a sandy beach are
finished to a high standard. Most rooms have
sea views. The restaurant—built on the second
floor, with a view from some tables—is
quite ambitious. The health centre has a
thalassotherapy spa, indoor heated swimming
pool, gym, and sauna.

Longueville House ($$$)
*Mallow tel: 022 47156 fax: 022 47459
www.longuevillehouse.ie*
This is one of Ireland's most renowned country
manors, a grand building overlooking many acres
of parkland. The period features include an original Victorian conservatory, and the house has a
welcoming feel. Formal dining room with portraits
of all Ireland's presidents; superb food and hospitality (see also *restaurants* section, page 281).

Midleton Park ($$–$$$)
*Midleton tel: 021 463 1767 fax: 463 1605
www.kingsleyhotels.com*
This well-appointed modern hotel lies 10 miles
(16km) from Cork, off the N25 Cork–Rosslare
route. Spacious bedrooms, two with four-poster
beds, and comfortable public areas.

Old Bank House ($$)
*11 Pearse Street, Kinsale
tel: 021 477 4075 fax: 021 477 4296
www.oldbankhousekinsale.com*
Old Bank House, a discreetly elegant, well-run B&B
in tastefully furnished Georgian buildings near the
quayside, is stylish and comfortable.

Old Presbytery ($)
*43 Cork Street, Kinsale tel: 021 477 2027
fax: 021 477 2166 www.oldpres.com*
This welcoming B&B in a quiet (but central) loca-
tion is personally and interestingly furnished. The
breakfasts are especially good here. Sailing and
sea fishing available.

Sea View Hotel ($$–$$$)
*Ballylickey, Bantry tel: 027 50073 fax: 027
51555 seaviewhousehotel@eircom.net*
A large old house in lovely gardens, hospitable and
well furnished in traditional style. The rooms are
large and light, some with views. Good food is
served in the restaurant where diners can enjoy
wonderful sea views. Dogs accepted.

Trident Hotel ($$–$$$)
*Kinsale, Cork tel: 021 477 2301 f
ax: 021 477 4173 www.tridenthotel.com*
This blocky modern hotel at the harbour's edge
has its own marina with boats for rental. Many
bedrooms have superb views; two have
balconies. The restaurant and lounge overlook
the harbour; the food is above-average. Sauna
and gym.

County Kerry

Butler Arms Hotel ($$)
*Waterville, Kerry tel: 066 947 4144
fax: 066 947 4520 www.butlerarms.com*
This famous owner-run hotel on the Ring of Kerry
was once a favourite haunt of Charlie Chaplin and
still offers the same high standards of comfort and
service. Most bedrooms have sea views; public
areas include sun lounges and a billiards room.
Championship golf opposite. Tennis court, private
fishing available.

Cleevaun Country Guest House ($)
*Lady's Cross, Milltown, Dingle tel: 066 915
1108 fax: 066 915 2228 www.cleevaun.com*
A simple but welcoming B&B in modern bungalow.
Rural setting overlooking Dingle Bay.

Dingle Skellig Hotel ($–$$)
*Dingle tel: 066 915 0200 fax: 066 915 1501
www.dingleskellig.com*
Well-located modern hotel with good facilities,
including massage, aromatherapy, and reflexology.
You will find this hotel on the sea side of the road
entering Dingle.

Greenmount House ($–$$)
*Dingle tel: 066 915 1414 fax: 066 915 1974
www.greenmounthouse.com*
This exceptionally well-appointed, comfortable
and hospitable B&B, just a five minute walk
from the town centre. An extension contains
six mini-suites, all overlooking Dingle harbour.
The breakfasts are outstanding.

Kathleen's Country House ($–$$)
*Madam's Height, Tralee Road, Killarney
tel: 064 32810 fax: 064 32340
www.kathleens.net*
An exclusive, modern, purpose-built guesthouse,
set in its own lovely gardens. Pleasantly furnished.
Kathleen's brand of hospitality engulfs you as
soon as you step inside.

Killarney Park Hotel $$$
*Kenmare Place Killarney tel: 064 35555
fax: 064 35266 www.killarneyparkhotel.ie*
If you have to stay in the centre of Killarney, this
attractive, well-run contemporary hotel is a safe
choice and has good facilities, including indoor
swimming pool and gym.

Park Hotel ($$$)
*Kenmare tel: 064 41200 fax: 064 41402
www.parkkenmare*
All the trimmings of this fine hotel, in lovely
grounds overlooking the Kenmare River estuary,
make it expensive, but its particular brand of
luxury is more than merely professional. It is also
remarkably friendly. Excellent food (see also
restaurants section, page 281).

Sallyport House ($$)
*Glengarriff Road Kenmare tel: 064 42066
fax: 064 42067 www.sallyporthouse.com*

This well-run, comfortable guesthouse lies on the edge of town within walking distance of restaurants and shops. One room has a four-poster bed.

Sheen Falls Lodge ($$$)
Kenmare tel: 064 41600 fax: 064 41386
www.sheenfallslodge.ie
Sheen Falls, a very expensive but extremely luxurious and friendly place, has views over the waterfalls. Excellent food and service. Indoor heated swimming pool.

Tahilla Cove ($$)
Tahilla, near Sneem tel: 064 45204
fax: 064 45104
This charming, relaxed waterside guesthouse, set in 5ha (13 acres) and overlooking Kenmare Bay, has pretty gardens and an exceptionally quiet location. Delicious home cooking. Dogs allowed.

County Limerick
Castle Oaks House Hotel ($$)
Castleconnell, Limerick tel: 061 377666
fax: 061 377717 www.castle-oaks.com
Castle Oaks, a fine old Georgian house with grounds reaching down to the River Shannon, is set in a tiny village. Features include river walks, fishing, and free use of a health centre.

Castletroy Park Hotel ($$$)
Dublin Road, Limerick tel: 061 335566
fax: 061 331117 www.castletroy-park.ie
Limerick city's leading hotel is just a short distance from the centre. Rooms are spacious, and leisure and business facilities good.

Dunraven Arms ($$$)
Adare tel: 061 396633 fax: 061 396541
www.dunravenhotel.com
This well-known village inn remains unspoiled despite the hordes from bus tours. Tasteful decor, some antiques, and comfortable public rooms. Refurbished bedrooms, some with four-poster beds. Good food, formal and informal (see also restaurant section, page 281). Beauty salon, gym, and sauna.

WESTERN COUNTIES

County Clare
Dromoland Castle ($$$)
Newmarket-on-Fergus tel: 061 368144
fax: 061 363355 www.dromoland.ie
A luxuriously appointed castle hotel in large estate, favoured by the wealthy. The hotel has a private golf course and heated indoor swimming pool.

Fergus View ($)
Kilnaboy, Corofin tel: 065 683 7606
fax: 065 683 7192
Expect exceptionally wholesome cooking and pleasant, simple decor at this reasonably priced guesthouse quietly set above the lakes.

Fitzpatrick Bunratty Hotel ($$$)
Bunratty, Clare tel: 061 361177
fax: 061 471252 www.fitzpatrickhotels.com
In a picturesque village famous for its medieval castle, this modern, ranch-style building is surrounded by lawns and flower beds. Bedrooms and public rooms are timbered, and there is a helipad in the grounds. Indoor heated swimming pool, gym, sauna, and solarium.

Halpin's Hotel ($–$$)
Erin Street, Kilkee tel: 065 905 6032
fax: 065 905 6317
www.halpinsprivatehotels.com
Personal service at a family-run hotel with a commanding view of the town. Attractive, comfortable bedrooms.

Rusheen Lodge ($)
Knocknagroum, Ballyvaughan
tel: 065 707 7092 fax: 065 707 7152
www.rusheenlodge.com
This highly thought-of guesthouse in a bungalow on the edge of the village, nestling in the valley of the Burren Mountains, makes an inexpensive, comfortable base for exploring the north of the Burren.

Sheedy's Hotel ($$)
Lisdoonvarna tel: 065 707 4026
fax: 065 707 4555
www.sheedyscountryhouse.com
Close to Lahinch Golf Course and the Cliffs of Moher. A friendly, family-run hotel, Sheedy's offers unexceptional accommodation but is renowned for its food (see also restaurant section, page 282).

County Galway
Abbeyglen Castle Hotel ($$–$$$)
Sky Road, Clifden tel: 095 21201
fax: 095 21797 www.abbeyglen.ie
Set in its own grounds with views over Clifden Bay, this friendly, family-run hotel gives high priority to hospitality and good food. Regular musical evenings in the bar, with log fires. Heated outdoor swimming pool and sauna. Golf tours can be arranged.

Ardagh Hotel ($$$)
Ballyconneely Road, Clifden, Connemara
tel: 095 21384 fax: 095 21314
www.commerce.ie/ardaghhotel
A modern hotel, overlooking a splendid chunk of Connemara's coastal scenery, the Ardagh has pleasing decor (lots of plants) and extensive public rooms. Spacious, comfortable bedrooms, many with sea views.

Ardilaun Conference & Leisure Centre ($$$)
Taylors Hill, Galway tel: 091 521433
fax: 091 521546 www.ardilaunhousehotel.ie
A tastefully furnished hotel with good facilities in a pleasant suburb near the resort of Salthill. Facilities include a gym and heated indoor swimming pool.

Ballynahinch Castle ($$$)
Recess, Connemara tel: 095 31006
fax: 095 31085 www.ballynahinch-castle.com
On the bus tour circuit, but set in beautiful scenery, this large estate house is very comfortable. Tennis courts, and private fishing available in salmon river. (See restaurant section, page 282.)

The Boat Inn ($)
The Square, Oughterard, Connemara
tel: 091 552196 fax: 091 552694
www.theboatinn.com
This is a popular guesthouse, bar, and bistro in the centre of the village near Loch Corrib. Excellent fishing and a choice of golf courses in the area. In summer, live Irish music is provided most evenings.

Hotels and Restaurants

Cashel House ($$$)
Cashel Bay, Connemara tel: 095 31001
fax: 095 31077 www.cashel-house-hotel.com
Cashel House, a peaceful, luxuriously furnished small hotel in a white-painted Victorian house by the coast, has lush, sheltered subtropical gardens. Many antiques and excellent food and wines.

Galway Ryan Hotel ($$–$$$)
Dublin Road, Galway tel: 091 753181
fax: 091 753187 www.ryan-hotels.com
A modern comfortable hotel with refurbished public areas, including a spacious, well-decorated lounge and health club.

Killary Lodge ($–$$)
Leenane tel: 095 42276 fax: 095 42314
www.killary.com
In common ownership with a nearby adventure centre, this guesthouse provides informal comfort and good food in a spectacular lake setting. Adventure sports such as mountain biking, rock climbing, and kayaking are available.

Lochlurgain Hotel ($–$$)
22 Monksfield, Upper Salthill, Galway
tel: 019 529595 fax: 091 522399
www.lochlurgain.com
A family-run hotel near the promenade and beach.

Rock Glen Country House Hotel ($$$)
Clifden, Connemara tel: 095 21035 or 095 21393 fax: 095 21737
This traditional hotel occupies a lovely setting above the bay. Inside it is solidly comfortable and has a relaxing and friendly air—and good food.

Ross Lake House Hotel ($$)
Rosscahill, Oughterard, Connemara
tel: 091 550109 fax: 091 550184
www.rosslakehotel.com
This modern, Georgian-style house is at the end of a winding country road in a panoramic garden setting. Family-run, with well-furnished rooms, and a comfortable, relaxed atmosphere. Four-poster bed available. Golf, lake fishing, and boating can all be enjoyed in the area.

Waterfall Lodge ($)
Oughterard, Connemara tel: 091 552168
An elegant period residence beside a river and waterfall, with private fishing. Antique furnishings, wooden floors, log fires. Nearby activities include pony trekking, mountain-climbing, golf, and fishing.

Zetland Country House Hotel ($$$)
Cashel Bay tel: 095 31111 fax: 095 31117
www.zetland.com
Sophisticated, comfortable country house hotel, with spacious public rooms and large bedrooms furnished with antiques. Wonderful views and good food served in the restaurant.

County Mayo
Gray's Guest House ($)
Dugort Achill Island tel: 098 43244 or 098 43315
Family-run guesthouse with numerous sitting rooms and sun lounges for quiet relaxation; open fires, genuine hospitality and garden. No-smoking dining room. Self-contained family villa also available.

Hotel Westport ($$).
Newport Road, Westport, Mayo
tel: 098 25122 fax: 098 26739
www.hotelwestport.ie
Set in parkland next to Westport House. Spacious restaurant and comfortable rooms, including six suites and one room with a four-poster bed. Swimming pool, sauna, and gym.

Olde Railway Hotel ($$)
The Mall, Westport tel: 098 25166
fax: 098 25090 www.anu.ie/railwayhotel
Characterful old coaching inn with open turf fires, set on a tree-lined mall overlooking the river. Comfortably refurbished in traditional style. En-suite bedrooms in varying sizes, some with four-poster beds.

Welcome Inn Hotel ($–$$)
Castlebar, Mayo tel: 094 22288 or 094 22054 fax: 094 21766
www.mayo-ireland.ie/mayo/tonns/casbar/welcinn/welcinn.htm
This central hotel with a Tudor facade has modern facilities. Rooms are well equipped; disco on some evenings, also traditional Irish music in summer.

NORTHWESTERN COUNTIES

County Donegal
Abbey Hotel ($$)
The Diamond, Donegal tel: 073 21014
fax: 073 21014 www.whites-hotelsireland.com
An owner-managed hotel in the centre of the town. Four-poster beds. Heated indoor pool. Golf nearby.

Castle Grove Country House & Restaurant ($–$$)
Castlegrove, Ballymaleel tel: 074 51118
fax: 074 51384 www.castlegrove.com
Elegant country house just outside Letterkenny, set in well-maintained gardens and parkland and furnished with antiques. Spacious, comfortable bedrooms; good food—restaurant open to non-residents.

Fort Royal Hotel ($$$)
Rathmullan tel: 074 58100 fax: 074 58103
www.fortroyalhotel.com
Period house overlooking Lough Swilly. Comfortable and restful, with attractively decorated bedrooms and pleasant public areas. Croquet, tennis, and golf are all available.

Harvey's Point Country Hotel ($$–$$$)
Lough Eske, Donegal tel: 073 22208
fax: 073 22352 www.harveyspoint.com
Swiss-owned modern hotel with alpine atmosphere, scenically located on the shores of the lough. Eighteen rooms have four-poster beds. Good facilities and fine food (see also *restaurants* section, page 282).

Rossaor House ($)
Ballyliffin tel: 077 76498 fax: 077 76498
www.ballyliffin.com/rossaor
Hospitable and very comfortable modern house which has spectacular views. The hotel stands among mature gardens in a peaceful setting on the Inishowen peninsula.

Sand House ($$–$$$)
Rossnowlagh tel: 072 51777
fax: 072 52100 www.sandhouse-hotel.ie

ng-established, family-run, castellated resort
tel on one of Donegal's best beaches. Many of
e rooms have sea views. Inside it is lively but
axing, with open fires and traditional furnishings.
nuggler's Creek ($)
ossnowlagh tel: 072 52366 fax: 072 22000
eerful and popular bistro-style bar overlooking
e bay. Bedrooms are fresh and clean with floral
allpapers and modern pine. Breakfast served in
nservatory extension with lovely views (see also
staurants section, page 283).

ounty Sligo
uckawn House ($)
allymote/Boyle Road Tobercurry
/fax: 071 85188
ww.sligotourism.com/cruckawn
is attractively decorated guesthouse is family-
n and offers comfortable accommodation. It has
od facilities, including a gym, and golf and
lmon and coarse fishing are available nearby.
ver Swan Hotel ($$)
igo tel: 071 43231 fax: 071 42232
mily-owned hotel on the banks of the
aravogue River in the heart of Sligo. Well-
rnished bedrooms and good bathrooms,
me with aero-spa baths. The Horseshoe Bar is
popular spot for snacks.
igo Park Hotel ($$–$$$)
earse Road, Sligo tel: 071 60291
x: 071 69556 www.leehotels.ie
t in parkland on the southern edge of Sligo,
is hotel is an ideal touring base for the
tractions of Yeats Country, and is also near
sses Point Golf Club. All rooms have modern
cilities, in particular the excellent "executive"
oms. Health centre with heated indoor pool;
od beaches nearby.

ORTHERN IRELAND

ounty Antrim
obbins Inn ($$)
–8 High Street, Carrickfergus BT38 7AP
l: 028 9335 1905 fax: 028 9335 1905
ww.dobbinsinnhotel.co.uk
storic family-run inn in town centre, offering
ain accommodation with private baths. Popular,
ely bar; good snacks and morning coffee.
ndonderry Arms ($$)
O Harbour Road, Carnlough BT44 0EU
l: 028 2888 5255 fax: 028 2888 5263
ww.glensofantrim.com
eeper-covered coaching inn with seaside
arden. Some rooms are furnished with antiques,
hile others are modern and functional. Hearty
sh food is served in the dining room, accompa-
ed by traditional music in summer. Private
hing. Golf available by arrangement.

ounty Down
he Narrows ($–$$)
 Shore Road, Portaferry BT22 1JY
l: 028 4272 8148 fax: 028 4272 8105
ww.narrows.co.uk
uilt around an 18th-century courtyard, the Narrows
as spacious guestrooms, and a restaurant with a
putation for imaginative, skilfully prepared food.

Portaferry ($$)
10 The Strand, Portaferry BT22 1PE
tel: 028 4272 8231 fax: 028 4272 8999
www.portaferryhotel.com
Traditional inn overlooking Strangford Lough, a
stone's throw from the ferry. Well-kept modern
rooms. Serves predictable, but enjoyable, seafood.
Slieve Donard Hotel ($$–$$$)
Downs Road Newcastle BT33 0AH
tel: 028 4372 3681 fax: 028 4372 4830
www.hastingshotels.com
This large Victorian redbrick hotel adjoining the
Royal County Down Golf Links and the beach is at
the foot of the Mountains of Mourne, in 2ha (6
acres) of gardens. Comfortable, well-furnished
bedrooms, spacious public areas, and excellent
facilities, including a heated indoor pool.

County Fermanagh
Dromard House ($)
Tamlaght, Enniskillen BT74 4HR
tel: 028 6638 7250 www.discoverni.com
Stately, 19th-century Dromard House is set on a
conservation farm with its own woodland trail
down to the shores of Lough Erne. Modern
accommodation in a converted stable block;
breakfast in the Victorian-style dining room in the
main house. Private fishing available.
Mahons Hotel ($$)
Mill Street, Irvinestown BT74 1GS
tel: 028 6862 1656 or 028 6862 8344
For over 100 years the Mahon family have been
welcoming guests to this popular hotel, which
combines the original character of the building
with modern comforts and amenities. Some rooms
have four-poster beds. Bar, lounges, coffee shop,
restaurant. Horseback-riding and golf available.

County Londonderry
Beech Hill Country House Hotel ($$–$$$)
32 Ardmore Road, Londonderry BT47 3QP
tel: 028 7134 9279 fax: 028 7134 5366
www.beech-hill.com
Comfortable country house with antiques, set in
13ha (32 acres) of woodlands and gardens, close to
the city. Public areas include a bar and airy restaurant overlooking the garden. Genuine hospitality and
good food. Facilities include a gym and sauna.
Everglades Hotel ($$)
Prehen Road, Londonderry BT47 2NH
tel: 028 7134 6722 fax: 028 7134 9200
www.hastingshotels.com
Modern hotel alongside the A5 and the River
Foyle. Cheerfully decorated bedrooms, including
one with a four-poster bed. Enthusiastic staff.
Greenhill House ($)
24 Greenhill Road, Aghadowey, Coleraine
BT51 4EU tel: 028 7086 8241
fax: 028 7086 8365
Georgian farmhouse in secluded countryside.
Relaxed and welcoming atmosphere with
substantial country cooking.
Radisson Roe Park Hotel and Golf Resort ($$$)
Roe Park, Limavady, Derry BT49 9LB
tel: 028 7772 2222 fax: 028 7772 2313
www.radissonroepark.com
Relaxation and elegance are on offer at this hotel,
with a golf course, health club, and beauty salon.

277

LAKELAND COUNTIES

County Laois
O'Sullivan Guesthouse ($)
8 Kelly Villa Park, Portlaoise tel: 0502 22774
Welcoming, family-run guesthouse with a friendly atmosphere, offering pleasant rooms and good value.

County Monaghan
Nuremore Hotel ($$$)
Carrickmacross tel: 042 966 1438
fax: 042 966 1853 www.nuremore-hotel.ie
With impressive grounds, well-maintained gardens and its own golf course, this is the leading hotel in a wide area and offers spacious accommodation, and excellent facilities, including indoor heated pool, tennis, and fishing.

County Roscommon
Abbey Hotel ($$)
Galway Road, Roscommon tel: 0903 26240
fax: 0903 26021
Fine, carefully restored 19th-century manor house. Rooms decorated in traditional period style, with modern facilities. Some four-poster beds. Comfortable foyer, lounge, bar, restaurant, and gardens. Indoor heated pool; golf available by arrangement.

County Westmeath
Hodson Bay Hotel ($$$)
Hodson Bay Athlone tel: 0902 80500
fax: 0902 80520 www.hodsonbayhotel.com
A lovely lakeside position, high standards of accommodation and excellent facilities make this the leading hotel in the area. Good food, golf, and water activities. Indoor heated pool.

Royal Hoey Hotel ($)
Mardyke Street, Athlone tel: 0902 72924
fax: 0902 75194
Family-run hotel in the centre of town, proud of its tradition of warm hospitality. Rooms are carefully maintained and well appointed, with an elevator to all floors; snacks are available all day in the coffee shop.

Woodlands Farmhouse ($)
Horseleap, Streamstown tel: 044 26414
Large, attractive house in 48ha (120 acres) of sylvan woodland off the Mullingar–Athlone road.

RESTAURANTS

The following restaurants have also been divided into three price categories: budget ($), moderate ($$), and expensive (more than $$$).

DUBLIN

(the code for Dublin is 01)

Bad Ass Café ($)
9–11 Crown Alley, Temple Bar, 2
tel: 671 2596
Lively pizza place in converted warehouse where Sinéad O'Connor (Irish songstress) was once a waitress. Popular with all age groups.

Bewley's Oriental Café ($)
Four central locations: Jervis Street, Mary Street, Westmoreland Street, and the main one in Grafton Street tel: 677 6761
Coffee shop *par excellence*, embellished with mahogany and stained glass. Sticky buns or full meals. Upstairs (in Grafton Street) it's less crowded, with a museum.

Burdock's ($)
2 Werburgh Street, 2 tel: 454 0306
A legend in fish and chips. Closed Sunday.

Chapter One ($$)
The Dublin Writers' Museum, 18–19 Parnell Square, 1 tel: 873 2266
Cellar restaurant below the Writers' Museum; great atmosphere and reliably good food.

The Commons ($$$)
Newman House, 85–86 St. Stephen's Green, tel: 475 2597
Urbane, classic French cooking served amid a fine collection of specially commissioned modern art. Terrace at the back, lovely in sunny weather. Closed Saturday and Sunday.

Cookes Café ($$$)
14 South William Street, 2 tel: 679 0536
Fashionable café-style restaurant. Cool, airy room and an appetizing mixture of modern and classical dishes are served.

Diep Le Shaker ($$–$$$)
55 Pembroke Lane off Pembroke Street, 2 tel: 661 1829
Chic, contemporary restaurant on two floors in a laneway near Fitzwilliam Square, featuring Chinese dishes (marked in blue on the menu) and Thai (marked in red). Hospitable service.

L'Écrivain ($$$)
109a Lower Baggot Street, 2 tel: 661 1919
One of the best restaurants in town. You will find delicious contemporary food served in a smart yet informal setting.

Elephant and Castle ($$)
18 Temple Bar, 2 tel: 679 3121
Bustling, youthful venue for drinks or dinner. Eclectic, Californian-style cuisine—burgers, guacamole and tortilla chips, pasta, omelets.

Fitzers, National Gallery Restaurant ($)
Merrion Square, 2 tel: 661 4496
Good self-service restaurant to stave off hunger brought on by cultural overdose. Reasonably priced wine. Open daytime only. Fitzers also has outlets in Temple Bar (tel: 679 0440) and Dawson Street (tel: 667 1155), all open evenings.

Les Frères Jacques ($$–$$$)
74 Dame Street, 2 tel: 679 4555
Very popular, very French restaurant. Delicious, if pricey, food and good atmosphere.

Gallagher's Boxty House ($–$$)
20 Temple Bar, 2 tel: 677 2762
A formula based on griddled Irish potato cakes (boxties) wrapping up all kinds of savory fillings. Bacon and cabbage, champ, smoked fish, and other Irish fare. Always popular. Modern country decor of pine and pottery.

Imperial ($$)
12a Wicklow Street, 2 tel: 677 2580
Superior Chinese, specializing in dim sum. Popular at Sunday lunchtime. Good value if you stick to tea rather than wine.

cob's Ladder ($$$)
Nassau Street, 2 tel: 670 3865
nimalist, upstairs restaurant overlooking the
aying fields of Trinity College. Owner-chef Adrian
che cooks in the new Irish style with international
luences.

lkenny Restaurant & Café ($)
assau Street, 2 tel: 677 7066
the Kilkenny shop. Excellent self-service coffee
op and restaurant, capitalizing on the success of
e original in Kilkenny. Always busy at lunchtime.

ermaid Café ($$)
9–70 Dame Street, 2 tel: 670 8236
aginative American-inspired cooking and
teresting decor in a small restaurant on the
lge of Temple Bar.

. 10 ($$$)
ngfield's Hotel, Fitzwilliam Street, 2
l: 676 1367
is intimate restaurant, in the basement of a city
ntre hotel, serves a successful blend of French
d Irish cooking. (See also restaurants section,
ge 270.)

he Pico ($$–$$$)
–6 Molesworth Place, 2 tel: 676 0300
is elegant restaurant seems traditional, but the
oking is contemporary. Ranks among Dublin's
st restaurants.

1 Talbot ($$)
01 Talbot Street, 1 tel: 874 5011
laxed and informal restaurant on the upper
or, on a popular shopping street north of the
er. Healthy mixture of European and Eastern
shes. Near the Abbey Theatre.

sta Fresca ($)
–4 Chatham Street, 2 tel: 679 2402
ylish Italian cuisine, including good versions of
ll-known favourites and more unusual things.
e pasta, of course, is fresca (fresh).

trick Guilbaud ($$$)
1 Upper Merrion Street, 2 tel: 676 4192
jacent to the Merrion Hotel, the hushed, reveren-
l atmosphere has modified somewhat but this
mains cuisine sérieuse: mostly classic French,
th an occasional pig's trotter thrown in for regional
terest. Business clients dine in discretion here.

ajdoot Tandoori ($$)
5–28 Clarendon Street, Westbury Centre, 2
l: 679 4274
gh-quality Moghul dishes are on the menu here,
rved in an elegant, discreetly formal setting.

oly's Bistro ($$)
Ballsbridge Terrace, 4 tel: 668 2611
ne of the most popular restaurants in town. A
eat atmosphere with delicious, reasonably priced
shes and excellent service.

alimar ($$–$$$)
7 South Great George's Street, 2
l: 671 0738
t another of Dublin's surprising ethnic winners.
rth Indian and Pakistani cooking.

e Side Door ($$)
Meridien Shelbourne, St. Stephen's Green,
 tel: 676 6471
 unexpected contrast to the ultratraditional
tel—this new minimalist restaurant on the side
the hotel is cool and trendy. (See also hotels
ction, page 271.)

La Stampa ($$–$$$)
35 Dawson Street, 2 tel: 677 8611
Elegant, mirrored surroundings reflect a serious
but unstuffy interest in food. Despite the name,
the style is French.

The Tea Rooms ($$$)
The Clarence, 6–8 Wellington Quay, 2
tel: 670 9000
A stunning room sets off a varied menu of modern
European dishes. Excellent service.

Thornton's ($$$)
1 Portobello Road, 8 tel: 454 9067
In an off-the-beaten-track, canalside location
Kevin Thornton—widely regarded as Ireland's
finest chef—runs this small but perfectly
formed two-story restaurant with his wife,
Muriel, and a very professional, mostly
French, staff. Seriously good cooking and
excellent service.

EASTERN COUNTIES

County Dublin
Abbey Tavern ($$–$$$)
Abbey Street, Howth tel: 01 839 0307
Old-world tavern (parts of the building can
be dated back to the 13th century) specializing
in fish. Traditional Irish music most nights
(separate annex). Bar meals available at
lunchtime.

Blue Orchid ($$)
*Newpark Centre, Newtownpark Avenue,
Blackrock tel: 01 283 1767*
Acclaimed traditional Thai menu with extensive
wine list.

Brasserie Na Mara ($$)
*Railway Station, Harbour Road, Dun Laoghaire
tel: 01 280 0509*
Contemporary style and cooking in one of Ireland's
earliest railroad stations. Fresh seafood dishes
are a house special.

Guinea Pig ($$)
*17 Railway Road, Dalkey
tel: 01 285 9055*
Seafood dishes are served up by a former local
mayor. There is also a good-value early bird dinner
menu.

King Sitric ($$$)
East Pier, Howth tel: 01 832 5235
Celebrated seafood in delightful harbourside
setting. Completely rebuilt in 1999—the
restaurant is now on the upper floor and there
are eight guest bedrooms.

Red Bank ($$)
*7 Church Street, Skerries
tel: 01 849 1005*
Relaxing family-run seafood restaurant in
converted bank. Lunch Sundays only.

County Kildare
Barberstown Castle ($$$)
Straffan tel: 01 628 8157
Imaginative dishes served in the impressive
16th-century stone banqueting hall.

Lawlor's Restaurant ($$)
Poplar Square, Naas tel: 045 897332
Hearty steaks and fish for the racing crowd. Lighter
meals served in the bar.

Hotels and Restaurants

Moyglare Manor ($$$)
Moyglare, Maynooth tel: 01 628 6351
Elaborate French menu complements the sumptuous decor (see also *hotels* section, page 271). Outstanding wine list.

County Louth
Black Bull Inn ($–$$)
Dublin Road, Drogheda
tel: 041 983 7139
Interesting, friendly roadside pub/restaurant and delicatessen. Good value all-day food.
Forge Gallery ($$)
Church Street, Collon tel: 041 982 6272
Well-established restaurant, decorated with the work of local artists. Generous portions of French provincial and traditional Irish cooking.
Jordans ($$)
Carlingford tel: 042 937 3223
Village centre restaurant with rooms. Good fish and baking, with some surprises.

County Meath
Station House ($$)
Kilmessan tel: 046 25239
Local fresh produce served in calm, unflashy setting.

County Wicklow
Avoca Handweavers ($)
Kilmacanogue tel: 01 286 7466
Stylish home cooking that's as healthy as it is delicious. There is also delicatessen.
The Hungry Monk ($$)
Southview Church Road, Greystones
tel: 01 287 5759
This unusual restaurant situated on an upper floor is run with style and flair. Particularly good for Sunday lunch. There is also a great wine list.
Rathsallagh House ($$$)
Dunlavin tel: 045 403112
This classy dining room serves interesting country cooking, and the menu also includes some more sophisticated fare.
Tinakilly ($$$)
Rathnew tel: 0404 69274
Elegant Irish/French cooking in formal surroundings (see also *hotels* section, page 271).
Tree of Idleness ($$)
Seafront, Bray tel: 01 286 3498
Unusually excellent Greek-Cypriot cooking in a restaurant situated in a Victorian house. Open for dinner only.

SOUTHEASTERN COUNTIES

County Carlow
Lord Bagenal Inn ($$–$$$)
Leighlinbridge tel: 0503 21668
Famous old riverside inn serving a good range of undemanding food in the bar, with more sophisticated French cuisine served up in the restaurant. Open fires and rustic decor. Guest accommodation available.

County Kilkenny
Café Sol ($–$$)
William Street, Kilkenny tel: 056 64987
Fun café-restaurant serving inexpensive home-sty daytime fare changing to more ambitious menus for evening diners.
Kilkenny Design Centre ($)
Castle Yard, Kilkenny tel: 056 22118
This sparkling self-service restaurant can be found in attractive upper floors of the castle stable building. It houses a fine selection of Irish craft products.

County Tipperary
Angela's Wholefood Restaurant ($)
14 Abbey Street, Clonmel
tel: 052 26899
A good organic café which serves healthy daytime snacks.
Chez Hans ($$)
Rockside, Cashel tel: 062 61177
Parisian bistro style in the setting of an old Bapti church. Generous portions. Local Cashel blue cheese figures on the menu.
Spearman Restaurant ($$)
97 Main Street, Cashel tel: 062 61143
Down-to-earth, family-run restaurant offering efficiently served, good value lunches, and more adventurous evening meals.

County Waterford
Dwyers ($$–$$$)
8 Mary Street, Waterford
tel: 051 877478
Pleasantly intimate restaurant a block or two bac from the waterside. Small, interesting menu. Ope evenings only.
Ship Inn ($$$)
Dock Road, Dunmore East tel: 051 383144
Nautically decorated bar/restaurant serving interesting fish dishes.
Waterford Castle ($$$)
The Island, Ballinakill, Waterford
tel: 051 878203
The restaurant serves classily presented gourmet food (lobster, asparagus, poached salmon) and home-style classics like bread-and-butter pudding.

County Wexford
Cellar Restaurant ($$)
Horetown House, Foulksmills tel: 051 56577
Country cooking in the characterful basement of a 300-year-old Georgian country house.
Dunbrody Country House ($$)
Arthurstown, New Ross tel: 051 389 600
The oak-floored dining room in this historic country house overlooks a sunken garden. Continental cuisine.
La Marine ($$)
Kelly's Resort Hotel, Rosslare
tel: 053 32114
This contemporary bistro/restaurant can be foun at Kelly's Resort Hotel. It serves Irish produce in Mediterranean style.
Marlfield House ($$$)
Courtown Road, Gorey tel: 055 21124
The style of the food, served in a luscious conservatory dining room, matches the rest of the house—rich, opulent, complicated. (See also *hotels* section, page 273.)

SOUTHWESTERN COUNTIES

County Cork
Aherne's ($$)
*3 North Main Street, Youghal
024 92424*
Excellent range of seafood produced in various
levels of elaboration in this thriving enterprise.

Ballymaloe House ($$$)
Shanagarry tel: 021 465 2531
An Irish legend that now dispenses the talent
and experience of the Allen dynasty through its
cookery school. Superbly accomplished and
reasonably priced food, using local produce to
best advantage (see also *hotels* section,
page 273).

Bosun ($-$$)
The Pier Monkstown, Cork tel: 021 484 2172
Thriving pub and restaurant (with rooms) beside
the Cobh car ferry.

Chez Youen ($$-$$$)
Baltimore tel: 028 20136
This popular Breton seafood restaurant
overlooks the harbour. The informal (and less
expensive) Jolie Brise, nearby on the square, is a
sister restaurant.

Crackpots ($-$$)
3 Cork Street, Kinsale tel: 021 477 2847
Unusual, stylish little restaurant, wine bar, and
pottery in the town centre.

Crawford Gallery Café ($-$$)
Emmet Place, Cork tel: 021 427 4415
A scion of the Allen family of Ballymaloe House
(see above) masterminds this attractive gallery
restaurant. Whether you call in for a cake or a full
meal, excellence is assured.

Eugene's ($$$)
Crus tel: 027 61127
Buffet-style seafood appetizers, local fish and meat,
and splendid desserts served on the grand piano. A
lovely Georgian house overlooking the sea.

Finins ($$)
Main Street, Midleton tel: 021 463 1878
Simple meat and seafood dishes, and soups are
served in this traditional pub and restaurant.

Isaacs ($-$$)
*MacCurtain Street, Cork
tel: 021 450 3805*
Good-value and stylish contemporary cooking
— the secrets of this city centre restaurant's
enduring popularity.

Larchwood House ($$)
Pearsons Bridge, Bantry tel: 027 66181
Imaginative and satisfying Irish country cooking in a
modest guesthouse (see *hotels* section).

Longueville House ($$$)
Mallow tel: 022 47156
Home produced and local ingredients prepared by
a talented young chef for serious eaters. (See also
hotels section, page274.)

O'Callaghan-Walshe ($-$$)
The Square Rosscarbery tel: 023 48125
Skilfully cooked local seafood is among the
specials at this simple restaurant.

Quay Coop ($)
Sullivans Quay, Cork tel: 021 431 7026
A selection of thoroughly imaginative wholefood
and vegetarian dishes.

Shiro ($$$)
Ahakista, near Bantry tel: 027 67030
Remarkably located restaurant serving exquisitely
presented authentic Japanese food. Attentive
service. Advance booking always essential.

County Kerry
Gaby's ($$$)
*27 High Street, Killarney
tel: 064 32519*
A long-established, good seafood restaurant.
Lime Tree ($$)
*Shelbourne Street, Kenmare
tel: 064 41225*
Intimate setting for contemporary fish and
meat dishes.
Nick's ($$$)
Killorglin tel: 066 946 1219
Relaxed, beamed dining room where excellent fish
dishes are prepared.
Park ($$$)
Kenmare tel: 064 41200
Gourmet food in serene surroundings. Outstanding
service (see *hotels* section, page 274).

County Limerick
Dunraven Arms ($$$)
Adare tel: 061 396633
Reliable Irish cooking, whether a sandwich in the
bar or a full meal in the restaurant (see also *hotels*
section, page 275).
Mustard Seed at Echo Lodge ($$$)
Ballingarry tel: 069 68508
Inventive food in charming country-house
restaurant. Organic produce from their garden
is served.

WESTERN COUNTIES

County Clare
Bunratty Castle ($$)
Bunratty tel: 061 360788
Classic medieval banquets and entertainment in
this well-known genuine 15th-century castle. There
are two sittings; book at any tourist office.
The Cloister ($$)
Abbey Street, Ennis tel: 065 682 9521
Simple seafood and snacks are available in
the bar from lunchtime onwards. For more com-
plex fish dishes, try the dining room. Delicious
treacle bread and Inagh goat's cheese salad are
specials at this restaurant.
Knappogue Castle ($$$)
near Quin tel: 061 360788
Medieval feasting in well-restored castle,
accompanied by entertainers recounting stories
of Celtic Ireland; book at any tourist office.
Manuel's Seafood ($$)
Corbally, Kilkee tel: 065 905 6211
If you find yourself exploring the South Clare
coast you might try this place at dinnertime for
local seafood dishes in a small, modern hilltop
restaurant.
Sheedy's ($$)
Lisdoonvarna tel: 065 707 4026
French and Irish cuisine is prepared by the
proprietor in this friendly hotel restaurant (see
hotels section, page 275).

Hotels and Restaurants

County Galway

Ballynahinch Castle ($$$)
Recess, Connemara tel: 095 31006
Formal food is served in a wonderful dining room overlooking the river. If you want something simpler, there is an excellent range of bar food available in the Fisherman's pub. (See also *hotels* section, page 275.)

Dunguaire Castle ($$)
Kinvara tel: 091 637108
Banquet fare accompanied by literary gleanings from Synge, Shaw, and O'Casey; book at any tourist office.

Erriseask House ($$)
Ballyconneely tel: 095 23553
Exquisite contemporary food in a magnificent setting on Mannin Bay. Cool, modern restaurant with rooms.

Fat Freddy's ($)
Quay Street, Galway tel: 091 567279
One of the best places for pizza; a cheerful, youthful, and informal atmosphere.

Hotel Inisheer ($)
Lurgan Village, Inisheer, Aran Islands tel: 099 75020
Simple Irish fare at a good price.

McDonagh's Seafood Bar ($–$$)
22 Quay Street, Galway tel: 091 565001
A great place for seafood, relaxed and informal, with long opening hours.

Moran's Oyster Cottage ($$)
Kilcolgan, Clarinbridge tel: 091 796113
Oysters are what they do best here, brought in from their own beds just outside. But you can get a great chowder, and lots of other seafood besides, accompanied by delicious soda bread and chilled white wine—or the customary Guinness.

Moycullen House ($$)
Moycullen tel: 091 555621
Surprisingly contemporary restaurant with accommodation in an unusual (and otherwise traditional) arts and crafts style sporting lodge in the hills above Moycullen.

O'Dowds ($–$$)
Roundstone tel: 095 35809
This popular pub and restaurant specializes in seafood: The O'Dowds' seafood chowder is renowned countrywide.

O'Grady's Seafood ($$)
Clifden tel: 095 21450
It was all change at this traditional seafood restaurant when the next generation of O'Gradys took over a while back—now it's a cool and contemporary space offering international cuisine.

Paddy Burke's ($$)
Clarinbridge tel: 091 796226
This is a great place for oyster-sampling, but you can find plenty of other seafood and hearty Irish cooking here. The place is always popular and bustling.

Rosleague Manor ($$)
Letterfrack, Connemara tel: 095 41101
Country-house restaurant serving seafood and home-grown vegetables.

County Mayo

Beehive ($)
Keel, Achill Island tel: 098 43134
Craft shop and informal daytime restaurant serv local produce, simply and pleasingly cooked. Baking is a specialty.

Durkans Weir House & Restaurant ($$)
Louisburgh tel: 098 66140
Traditional pub, with open fire and home-cooked bar food, and adjacent restaurant for more formal dining.

Lemon Peel ($$)
The Octagon, Westport tel: 098 26929
Popular, buzzy restaurant offering a pleasing mixture of style and good home-style cooking.

Quay Cottage ($$)
The Quay, Westport (near entrance to Westp House) tel: 098 26412
Atmospheric high-ceilinged wine bar and shellfish restaurant converted from a waterside cottage. Wood fires and nautical knickknacks o the rafters.

NORTHWESTERN COUNTIES

County Donegal

Le Châteaubrienne ($$)
Sligo Road, Bundoran tel: 072 42160
This professional but welcoming family-run place has had a dynamic impact on Donegal's food scene. The emphasis is on quality without pomposity. Imaginative use is made of fresh local ingredients.

Harvey's Point ($$)
Lough Eske, Donegal tel: 073 22208
Good French/Swiss cuisine served here in nouvelle style. The atmosphere is fairly formal. (See *hotels* section, page 276.)

Rathmullan House ($$$)
Rathmullan tel: 074 58188
Country-house restaurant with lovely views of the gardens; fixed price menus available to resident in the evenings. Local seafood and farmhouse cheeses offered.

St. Ernan's House ($$$)
St. Ernan's Island, Donegal tel: 073 21065
Attractively presented five-course dinners served true Irish country-house style.

St. John's ($$)
Fahan tel: 077 60289
Well-cooked local produce is accompanied by well-priced wine and great hospitality on the shores of Lough Swilly.

Smuggler's Creek ($$)
Rossnowlagh tel: 072 52366
Imaginative range of bistro fare is on offer at this simple stone-built inn. Ingredients used include fresh seafood and organically grown vegetables. (See *hotels* section, page 277).

County Sligo

Cromleach Lodge ($$$)
Castlebaldwin, near Boyle tel: 071 65155
Accomplished food is served in this renowned restaurant with rooms, in a scenic location overlooking Lough Arrow.

ebe House ($$)
llooney tel: 071 67787
is is a respected family-run restaurant which
so has some accommodation, and is located just
tside Collooney village.

arkree Castle ($$)
llooney tel: 071 67800
e food is assured at Knockmuldowney
staurant, in the medieval-looking setting of this
stle. (See *hotels* section, page 276.)

e Moorings ($$–$$$)
sses Point tel: 071 77112
ere is a relaxed atmosphere at this seafood
staurant serving fresh-cooked, popular dishes at
asonable prices. Close to the waterfront. Good
Sunday lunch.

ORTHERN IRELAND

ounty Antrim
dens ($$–$$$)
29 Upper Newtownards Road, Belfast
l: 028 9065 0079
armth, elegance, and good contemporary
oking, can all be found at this restaurant in
unlikely area of the city.

ayenne ($$–$$$)
haftesbury Square, Belfast
l: 028 9033 1532
sic, vibrant, informal re-invention of Roscoff, TV
efs Paul and Jeanne Rankins' original ground-
eaking Belfast restaurant.

own Liquor Saloon ($)
5 Great Victoria Street, Belfast
l: 028 9024 9476
e National Trust's superbly restored Victorian
ub is a must for any visitor; good lunchtime food,
cluding oysters throughout the year. Irish dishes
so available.

uropa Hotel ($$)
reat Victoria Street, Belfast
l: 028 9033 3366
plethora of eating options on offer in this
ty-centre hotel, from Irish stew in the stylish
bby Bar to the more elaborate cuisine of the
allery Restaurant.

iant's Causeway ($)
4a Causeway Road, Bushmills
l: 028 2073 1159
ter visiting the Causeway, the National Trust tea-
om is an ideal place for lunch or afternoon tea.

ick's Warehouse ($$)
5–39 Hill Street, Belfast
l: 028 9043 9690
orning coffee, lunchtime or evening snacks, or
ll meals are all available here either in wine bar
in the more formal restaurant setting.

amore ($$$)
e Harbour, Portrush tel: 028 7082 4313
assy contemporary waterside restaurant
erlooking the harbour, with informal sister
stablishments nearby—wine bar below and
aditional pub along the quay. Cooking was
ay ahead of its time and there is a good-value
ine list.

ayanne Country House and Restaurant ($$)
0 Desmesne Road, Belfast
l: 028 9042 5859

A range of varied and interesting fresh dishes
offered in the dining room of this elegant Victorian
house, set well back from the road and overlooking
its own lawns.

County Down
Castle Ward ($)
Strangford, Downpatrick
tel: 028 4488 1204
The tearoom at this National Trust property is a
good place for light lunches or afternoon teas.

Shanks ($$$)
150 Crawfordsburn Road, Clandeboye, Bangor
tel: 028 9185 3313
Classic, deceptively simple dishes with imaginative
variations. Excellent service.

County Fermanagh
Blake's of the Hollow ($)
Enniskillen tel: 028 6632 2143
Good sandwiches in characterful Victorian pub.

Florence Court ($)
Enniskillen tel: 028 6634 8249
National Trust tea-rooms; wholesome lunches
and snacks.

The Sheelin ($$)
Bellanaleck tel: 028 6634 8232
Thatched-cottage bakery serving teas, snacks, and
gourmet dinner.

County Londonderry
Ardtara House ($$$)
8 Gorteade Road, Upperlands
tel: 028 7964 4490
Elegantly prepared local produce served in classy
decorated setting.

Beech Hill Country House ($$$)
32 Ardmore Road, Derry tel: 028 7134 9279
Carefully prepared food using mostly organic
produce.

Brown's ($–$$)
Bonds Hill, Derry tel: 028 7134 5180
Popular long-established restaurant, valued for
its reliability.

The Lime Tree ($$$)
60 Catherine Street, Limavady
tel: 028 7776 4300
Creative Mediteranean cuisine, served in a relaxed
setting. Advance booking recommended.

LAKELAND COUNTIES

County Laois
Roundwood House ($$)
Mountrath tel: 0502 32120
Accomplished cooking by a natural hostess in
gently time-worn Palladian surroundings.

The Stables ($$)
6 Oxmantown Mall tel: 0509 20263
Simple but comfortable surroundings of plain white
walls and oakwood chairs make a perfect foil for
competently prepared local produce.

County Westmeath
Crookedwood House ($$)
Crookedwood, Mullingar tel: 044 72165
Copious and good, interesting food served in a
relaxing setting of a whitewashed cellar restaurant.

Index

285

Index

Index and Acknowledgments

Picture credits

The Automobile Association would like to thank the following photographers, libraries, and associations for their assistance in the preparation of this book.

BORD FÁILTE 22a horse-racing, 22b hurling, 23 football, 30a Muiredach's Cross, 102–103 Punchestown races, 105 Malahide Castle, 112b Slane Abbey, 122 Ardmore Round Tower, 127b Rock of Cashel Museum, 141 canno Rosslare, 142 Georges St., Waterford, 164b Ashford Castle Hotel, 165 Adare Manor Hotel, 175 banquet, Knappogue Castle, 179a flora, 190a Thoor Ballylee, 202a Glebe House, 202b Glencolumbkille standing stone, St. Eunan's, 249 Old Gaol. H. CHEVALLIER 177b Aran Island gate. G. GOSSIP 164a Bantry House, 242a Hilton Hotel, 242b, 243b Tullanisk. CHRISTOPHER HILL PHOTOGRAPHIC 7a lobster fishing, 10b Dunluce Castle, 15 Iris dancing, 16a W. B. Yeats, 18a Irish fry, 18–19 seafood, 20b farming, 24b Roundstone Bog, 32a Boa Island Figu 79a seafood, 155b Rowallane Gardens, 182–183 Clifden, 186 Oyster Festival, 190b Westport, 199 Donegal, 200–201 Atlantic Drive, 206 Grianán of Aileach, 208 Parke's Castle, 209a Lough Gill, 210a Sligo Abbey, 210b W. B. Yeats, 212 Crown Liquor Saloon, 214 Relief of Derry, 217a Belfast, 217b Larry's Bar, 218, 219a Cit Hall, 219b Palm House, 220 Opera House, 221a Queen's University, 222a Belfast Castle, 222b Belfast Zoo, 22 Navan Fort, 224 Derry, 225b St. Patrick's window, 226a Stone, 230b Wellbrook Mill, 232 Mourne Mountains, 2 Transport Museum, 238 Lough Key, 247b Lough Key, 251 Giant's Causeway, 256 cycles. KOBAL COLLECTION 204a The Quiet Man, 204b The Field, 205 Ryan's Daughter. MARY EVANS PICTURE LIBRARY 17a Samuel Becke 17b G. B. Shaw, 26a creatures, 27 Cuchulainn, 36b William III, 37 James II, 39 Lord Kilwarden, 40a de Valera a Lloyd George, 42b Sir Edward Carson, 63a G. B. Shaw, 63b W. B. Yeats, 114 St. Columba, 138 James Joyce. NATIONAL MUSEUM OF IRELAND 66 Tara Brooch. NATURE PHOTOGRAPHERS LTD 180a mountain avens (R. Bus 180b fly orchid (P. Sterry), 181a pine marten (W. S. Paton), 181b corncrake (P. Sterry). NORTHERN IRELAND TOURIST BOARD 227b Marble Arch Caves. OFFICE OF PUBLIC WORKS, DUBLIN 34a Silken Thomas. REX FEATUR 12b Mary Robinson. ROYAL GEOGRAPHICAL SOCIETY 28a map. STROKESTOWN PARK 250 Strokestown Park. TH SLIDE FILE 4 cottages near Moate, 10a children, 24–25 turf cutting, 126 Cashel Rock, 179b Burren, 194 currac 198 weaving, 239 Lough Oughter Castle, 245 Clonmacnois, 247a Killykeen Forest Park. THE MANSELL COLLEC-TION 34b Richard II campaign, 35 Oliver Cromwell, 36–37 Siege of Londonderry, 38b Emmett, 40a Sackville St., signing treaty, 43a Parnell, 43b Liberation of O'Connell, 54a Easter Rising, 54b GPO 1916, 55a Easter Rising, 6 Oscar Wilde. WATERFORD CRYSTAL 143a Copper Wheel Engraver, 143b Master Cutter. ZEFA PICTURE LIBRARY (U.K.) LTD 12a U.K. flag, 13a Irish flag.

All remaining pictures are held in the Association's own library (A.A. PHOTO LIBRARY) with contributions from:
L. BLAKE 11, 110, 115a, 145, 184, 185, 187, 188, 191, 226b, 240a, 241, 244, 246a, 260. J. BLANDFORD 9 21, 25, 121, 136, 146, 148, 149b, 152, 154, 155a, 155b, 159, 161, 163a, 163b. S. DAY 144. M. DIGGIN 9b, 87b, 195, 237. S. Day 5, 6, 243; D. FORSS 33, 51, 149a, 152–153, 162. C. HILL 3. S. HILL 14b, 30b, 123a, 147b, 150a, 150b, 151, 156, 157, 158, 167a, 167b, 168, 169, 170, 171, 172, 173, 174, 176, 177a, 189, 192a, 193a, 251b, 266, 268. J. JENNINGS 19b, 38a, 192b, 193b, 196, 213, 225a, 235a, 246b. T. KING 29b, 46, 55 83a, 98. G. MUNDAY 6, 26b, 29, 49a, 52, 53, 57a, 57b, 61a, 68a, 68b, 69a, 69b,70a, 70b, 72b, 76, 96, 104 112a, 116, 213, 215, 216, 219b, 221b, 227a, 228, 230a, 231, 233, 234, 269. M. SHORT 7b, 8a, 9a, 13b, 1 20a, 28b, 32b, 44–45, 45b, 47, 48a, 48b, 49b, 50, 56, 58b, 59, 60, 64, 65b, 67, 71, 72a, 74a, 74b, 75, 78, 79b, 80, 81a, 81b, 82, 83b, 84a, 84b, 85, 87, 88, 89a, 89b, 91b, 92, 94, 95, 97a, 97b, 99a, 99b, 100b, 101 102a, 103, 106a, 109, 111, 113, 115b, 117, 119, 124a, 124b, 128, 130a, 130b, 131, 132, 133, 135, 137, 139a, 140, 236, 248, 253, 258, 259, 262, 263, 264, 265, 269b. W. VOYSEY 42a, 58a, 61b, 65a, 77a, 77b. S. WHITEHORN 44a. P. ZOELLER 91a, 107, 108a, 108b, 118, 120, 123b,125, 127a, 129, 166, 267.

Acknowledgments

The author would like to thank the following for their help in the production of this book: Bord Fáilte; Aer Lingus; Avis/Johnson & Perrott; and British Midland Airways Ltd.

Contributors

Original copy editor: Hugh Chevallier
Revision verifier: Anto Howard